The Evolution of Financial Institutions and Markets in Twentieth-century Europe

edited by

YOUSSEF CASSIS, GERALD D. FELDMAN AND ULF OLSSON

SCOLAR PRESS

Published by
SCOLAR PRESS
Gower House
Croft Road
Aldershot
Hants GU11 3HR
England

Ashgate Publishing Company
Old Post Road
Brookfield
Vermont 05036
USA

British Library Cataloguing in Publication Data
Evolution of Financial Institutions and
Markets in Twentieth-century Europe
   I. Cassis, Youssef
   332.1094

   ISBN 1–85928–127–3

Library of Congress Cataloging-in-Publication Data
The evolution of financial institutions and market in twentieth-century
   Europe / edited by Youssef Cassis, Gerald Feldman, and Ulf Olsson.
      p.   cm.
    "Papers presented at the second academic colloquium of the
European Association for banking history held in Zurich,
Switzerland, on the 27th and 28th May 1993" — Pref.
   Includes bibliographical references.
   ISBN 1–85928–127–3
   1. Banks and banking—Europe—History—Congresses. 2. Financial
institutions—Europe—History—Congresses. I. Cassis, Youssef.
II. Feldman, Gerald D. III. Olsson, Ulf, 1939–
HG2974.D48 1995   94–15195
332.1'094'0904—dc20   CIP

ISBN 1 85928 127 3

Typeset in 10pt Sabon by Bournemouth Colour Graphics, Parkstone, Dorset and printed in Great Britain by Biddles Ltd., Guildford.

The Evolution of Financial Institutions and Markets in Twentieth-century Europe

Contents

Part II   Banks, Markets and Industry

Preface

This book contains some of the papers presented at the second academic colloquim of the European Association for Banking History held in Zurich, Switzerland, on 27 and 28 May 1993. We would like to take this opportunity to thank the Union Bank of Switzerland for generously hosting the conference, and the Association for Banking History (Switzerland and principality of Liechtenstein) and the European Association for Banking History, in particular their respective chief executives Dr Hugo Bänziger and Prof. Dr Manfred Pohl, for funding the event.

We should also like to thank Ms Andrea Voellmin, who dealt most efficiently with all the administrative side of the organization, as well as Dr J. C. Whitehouse of the University of Bradford, Department of Modern Languages, who translated quickly and skilfully Chapters 1, 3 and 14 from the French and Chapter 7 from the German.

The conference would not have been successful without the participation of several leading financial historians who chaired and commented the various sessions and enriched the discussions. We are particularly grateful, in addition to the contributors to this volume, to Michael Bordo, Forest Capie, Michael Collins, Philip Cottrell, Margarita Dritsas, Carl-Ludwig Holtfrerich, Valery Janssens, Eve Lange, Maurice Lévy-Leboyer, Pablo Martin-Aceña, Monika Pohle, Hansjörg Siegenthaler, Richard Sylla, Gyorgy Tallos, Richard Tilly, Gabriel Tortella and Eugene White.

Youssef Cassis
Gerald D. Feldman
Ulf Olsson

Introduction

Y. Cassis, G. D. Feldman, U. Olsson

The last decade has witnessed widespread deregulation in major international financial centres and increased globalization of financial activities. This phenomenon, which has been concomitant with increased deindustrialization in most developed countries, has raised a number of questions about the future role of financial services and their relationship with the 'real' economy. These questions have been abundantly discussed, in the first place, quite naturally, by financial analysts, but also by economists, social scientists, politicians, journalists and others.

Although historians have not been entirely left out, they have not directly contributed to the debate. The main effect of those mutations of the 1980s has been a considerable renewal of interest in financial history, especially in comparative financial history. This is witnessed by the number of conferences and ensuing books, which have been more particularly concerned with three themes: international banking, the relationships between finance and industry and banking in the interwar years,[1] all obviously related to today's interrogations.

This intense activity has paved the way for setting up major international research on the evolution of financial institutions and markets in 20th-century Europe and North America. The general results of this investigation have been presented at the Eleventh International Economic History Congress held in September 1994 in Milan.[2] This book is part of this collective effort and includes a number of original essays dealing more specifically with Western Europe.[3]

Whether as general surveys or as case studies, these essays are all concerned with the major questions related to the development of financial institutions and the interactions between banks, markets and industry in the 20th century. Some of them are excellent examples of the application of recent theories and empirical methods from the financial literature, in particular the theories of asymmetrical information and portfolio management. The geographical scope of the volume, which covers ten European countries – Belgium, Denmark, France, Germany, Great Britain, Holland, Norway, Portugal, Sweden and Switzerland – also offers ample scope for international comparisons.

Banking institutions

The chapters in the first part of this volume provide an excellent opportunity to study the process of institutional change in the 20th century. The main question raised here is that of *stability*. In particular, to what extent have state regulation and market forces stabilized or destabilized institutional structures?

It is often assumed that regulation increases stability. However, there is also clear evidence that financial institutions are more exposed to political intervention than many other economic institutions. Because of their central position in the economic process, and also because of their symbolic image in the capitalist system, banks are natural targets for political ambitions in the realm of economic policy. In time of major political upheavals, this tends to be a factor of instability.

From the overview of the banking systems of countries such as Belgium and Switzerland (Chapters 3 and 4), there can be little doubt that the bank reforms of the interwar years were not solely motivated by the need to make the system work, but also reflected ideological preferences. Thus the more or less simultaneous changes in rules and regulations leading away from market solutions towards more state intervention in the 1930s, cannot be fully explained by such factors as the similarity of the problems encountered in all European countries, or the interconnections between the various national financial markets. They also have their roots in a common '*Zeitgeist*', sometimes hard to nail down but no doubt existing.

On the other hand, there are also limits to what political ambition can achieve. Consider for example how governments employed different, already existing financial institutions in order to achieve a similar objective of stimulating economic growth through an interventionist credit policy. In Germany, the National Socialists integrated the rich and traditionally autonomous regional savings banks into their planning, while in Portugal the nationalist Salazar government mobilized the National Savings Bank, which was not only the largest savings bank but the largest financial institution in the country, for its programme of 'economic transformation'. Only in Norway, where the commercial banks were in a state of complete disarray and the savings bank system extremely fragmented, was the Social Democratic government forced to form a new, state-dominated 'manufacturing' bank. Sverre Knutsen, Paul Thomes and Jaime Reis's contributions (Chapters 5,7 and 8) thus illustrate how, despite the similarity of the policies pursued in three distanced European countries, the existing institutional set-up was used and institutional stability maintained as far as possible.

A similar lesson of this difference between function and form can be found in the activities of the French and Danish central banks analysed by Alain Plessis and Per Hansen (Chapters 1 and 2). The harsh realities of the interwar crisis forced both banks to take responsibility for the functioning of the financial system, while the formal emergence of a system of modern central banking was slow. A closer look at the development of the institutions of central banking thus reveals that they have also been more flexible than is evident from their formal structure.

The other main factor, besides regulation, affecting institutional stability are the market forces. Private actors have also tended to favour already existing formal institutions and tried to incorporate new lines of business into the old structure. This 'path dependence' is probably stronger in the banking sector than elsewhere, mainly because tradition and confidence have always been among the bankers' most important assets, making them somewhat conservative and long-lived. Radical changes have not been very common in the world of finance, and they certainly have not been very welcome.

The capacity of the actors to adapt to new situations, balancing the rules and regulations against the power of the market, is well illustrated in Mats Larsson's analysis of Swedish banking (Chapter 6). The lasting impression from this and other chapters in the first part of this volume is that, in the longer perspective, market forces have had an irresistibly destabilizing effect on financial institutions in Western Europe. The actors seem to have found ways of circumventing existing obstacles and, sooner or later, to have forced institutions, both state and private, to change not only in function but also in form. This tendency becomes very clear during the period of rapid internationalization of the financial markets towards the end of the 20th century.

Banks, markets and industry

The second part of this volume deals with the relationships between finance and industry. The main question here is that of *efficiency*. How to measure adequately banks' support to industry? Have bank-oriented systems been more efficient than market-oriented ones in channelling funds to industry? Have small and medium-sized enterprises been properly served by their respective banking system? These are old 'classical' questions in financial historiography. They are, however, being renewed, as can be seen from the chapters gathered in this section.

The main yardstick, used in all the chapters, in order to measure the efficiency of the financial sector, is the ability of the institutions and market to reduce the asymmetry of information existing between lenders and borrowers. The respective merits of the universal banks and the capital markets as the cornerstone of a given financial system have aroused much controversy. In the frenzy of the 1980s, capital markets have been critcized, in particular in Britain and America, for favouring short-term gains over longer-term expectations, thus being ultimately responsible for industrial decline. Similar arguments have been used to explain Britain's slower economic growth in the decades preceding the First World War.

Although the debate remains open, Katherine Watson's essay on the brewing and iron and steel industries (Chapter 10) takes it a step further by emphasizing the flexibility of the market and the adaptability of industry within which it is essential to differentiate between sectors. There was no scarcity of capital in either the brewing or the iron and steel industries because each industry adopted a capital structure appropriate to its specific conditions – high gearing ratio in the brewing industry, low in the iron and steel industry. The same conclusion that the market did not fail industry emerges from the essay on Holland between 1900 and 1940, although in a different context (Chapter 9). The Dutch capital market was glutted with funds and investment opportunities. This might have diverted banks from taking an active role in financial management, but most companies succeeded in finding finance.

These doubts about the alleged inefficiency of the market are reinforced by those which are being increasingly raised about the 'power' of the universal banks. This emerges clearly in the contribution of Dieter Ziegler and Harald Wixforth (Chapter 11). At a macroeconomic level, the superiority of the universal banks over the market in the collection and distribution of information remains as much a controversial issue in economic historians' empirical studies as in economists' theoretical efforts. At a microeconomic level, however, there is mounting evidence that the alleged power of the German big banks over industrial companies has been greatly exaggerated. In the same way, British banks, according to Duncan Ross's analysis (Chapter 12), performed their role efficiently if judged by their capacity of reducing information asymmetry.

There remains the problem of the small and medium-sized companies, which have on the whole suffered from both being neglected by the big banks and facing difficulties in appealing to the market. Recent research suggests that local and regional banks have been more able to respond to their needs. As is made clear in Michel Lescure's analysis of the French case (Chapter 14), they were particularly well placed to reduce the high degree of information asymmetry associated with small and medium-sized firms, mainly as a result of the physical proximity between bankers and customers.

The decline of local and regional banks could therefore have serious effects on the financing of small and medium-sized enterprises. This was the case in France in the interwar years, as parapublic financial intermediaries were slow, and often ill-prepared, to take over their role. This might also have been the case in Britain, where the level of banking concentration was higher than anywhere else in Europe, although there is no evidence of a systematic neglect of the small and medium-sized industrial companies on the part of the big London-based banks; the role of local, sometimes informal capital markets should also not be underestimated. The world of the big banks, however, is too often considered as a monolith. Francesca Carnivali (Chapter 13) shows, for example, that the decentralized structure of Barclays Bank allowed a large degree of autonomy to the regional boards who were closer to local industrialists and therefore better placed to reduce information asymmetries than the local managers in a centralized bank such as the Midland Bank.

Notes

1. See in particular Jones (1990, 1991), James *et al.* (1991), Cameron and Bovykin (1991), Cassis (1992) and Cottrell *et al.* (1992).
2. These results consist of reports covering six geographical areas: North America, the British Isles, Western Europe (France, Belgium, Holland and Switzerland), Central Europe (Germany and Austria), Scandinavia, and the Mediterranean area (Italy, Greece, Spain and Portugal). They are published as a B-volume as part of the Eleventh International Economic History Congress: B12, 'The evolution of modern financial institutions in the 20th century'.
3. Several regional groups have contributed to the debate. Studies dealing with North America are published in a separate volume edited by M. Bordo and R. Sylla, while more detailed questions related to France, Switzerland, Belgium and the Netherlands can be found in Levy-Leboyer (1994).

References

Cameron, R. and Bovykin, V. I. (eds) (1991), *International Banking 1870–1914*, Oxford.

Cassis, Y. (ed.) (1992), *Finance and Financiers in European History 1880–1960*, Cambridge.

Cottrell, P. L., Lindgren, H. and Teichova, A. (eds) (1992), *European Industry and Banking between the Wars*, Leicester.

James, H., Lindgren, H. and Teichova, A. (eds) (1991), *The Role of Banks in the Interwar Economy*, Cambridge.

Jones, G. (ed.) (1990), *Banks as Multinationals*, London.

Jones, G. (ed.) (1991), *Banks and Money: International and*

Comparative Finance in History, London.

Lévy-Leboyer, M. (ed.) (1994), *Les banques en Europe de l'Ouest de 1920 à nos jours*, Paris, Comité pour L'histoire économique et financière de la France.

PART ONE
Banking Institutions

CHAPTER ONE

The Bank of France from the early 20th Century to the 1950s

Alain Plessis

The combination of political, social and economic upheavals and monetary turbulence marking the first half of the present century had a profound effect on the position of the Bank of France. Its role changed significantly, and in order to assess the scope of that change, we need to take three levels of analysis into consideration.

The first is the functions proper to the Bank. These are apparent from the legal texts and statutes defining them, the thinking of its directors and the leaders of public authorities, and also from the reactions of public opinion. As those functions gradually changed, the vocabulary used to refer to the Bank became more diverse. Its initial role was essentially that of an 'issuing body' whose task was to provide a supply of sound fiduciary currency, and it has kept that designation right up to the present day. At the same time, it was also the 'reserve bank', as it held the reserves of gold (and later of gold and currency) considered to be the nation's supreme resource. Other terms, often of Anglo-Saxon origin and at first rather vaguely understood, were subsequently used as other functions emerged. It was also the 'banks' bank', claiming supremacy over second-order institutions by virtue of its support for them, the 'bank for times of crisis', since it intervened whenever there was a general shortage of liquid assets, or the 'lender of last resort'. The latter concept remained very broad for a long time, and was simply used to indicate its obligation to come to the aid of establishments experiencing problems but deserving its help.

The term 'central bank' appears to be of later origin, at least in its current sense. In the Bank of France's archives and publications it indicated, until the Second World War, its main establishment in Paris (rue de la Vrillière) as distinct from its provincial branches. Not until later was it used in a precise sense to refer to the concept of a two-fold responsibility for stable money and a secure credit system.

Second, the role of the Bank of France also depended on the extent of its autonomy or independence with regard to the state. This problem, which is currently important, has been a constant feature of its history since a law of 1806 specified that it should be headed by a governor and two assistant governors appointed by the head of state. The governor, who held 'executive authority', also had the right to veto on all the deliberations of the *Conseil de Régence* (Regents' Council). In addition, three of the fifteen elected *régents* (regents) had to be chosen from among the *receveurs généraux des finances* (or later the *trésoriers-payeurs généraux*) and were thus civil servants.

The law reflected Napoleon's determination to exert control over the Bank and his desire, as he said, to see it sufficiently but not excessively in government hands, He added, more bluntly, that he wanted to be master in everything that concerned him, particularly with regard to the Bank which, since it minted money, belonged more to the emperor than to the shareholders. The ensuing state supervision was essentially the consequence of the precarious nature of the governorship, which had no fixed term of office and from which the incumbent could therefore be dismissed by the government at will, a situation which meant that formidable pressure could be brought to bear. The regents certainly tried to use the fall of the empire to remove that provision, but it was promptly reintroduced on the restoration and has been retained in essence until the present day.

A removable governor was not the only limit on the independence of the Bank. There were various pressures that could be brought to bear to hamper its freedom of operation and prevent it from using the weapons it had. The problem is indeed a complex one, since we need to distinguish between the Bank's *de jure* independence resulting from the laws governing its working and its *de facto* autonomy, which could be restricted in many ways. The constraints imposed on the Bank of France by other central banks must also be be taken into consideration.

Third, the Bank's importance depends on the influence it can exert. The relations established between it and the state are not a one-way process. It can help to shape public policy, either directly or through public opinion, and also has varying degrees of major influence over other banks.

This means that in order to assess the Bank's real autonomy we have to go beyond the official texts and speeches and spend more time examining archive material, which is still far from abundant.

At the close of the *Belle Epoque*, the Bank was still primarily a body responsible for issuing notes always redeemable in silver or gold by the bearer on demand, and was governed by a single 'categorical imperative', that of ensuring the convertibility of its notes into precious metals. For the purposes of preserving or replenishing its reserves of the latter, it had at its disposal an essential weapon, adjusting its discount rate, supported by secondary means such as premiums on gold. It was therefore able to build up a considerable stock of gold which, between 1909 and 1913, was always worth more than four billion francs and covered 75 per cent of the notes in circulation, a sign of a very cautious issue policy.

It already had other functions which it managed to reconcile with and strictly subordinate to its principal responsibility. In times of crisis it was willing 'to help Trade and the Treasury' by making capital available to them – in so far as it could. On an *ad hoc* basis, it helped banks with temporary difficulties (such as the Société Générale in early 1914), but had no intention of fully taking on the role of a lender of last resort.

It sometimes happened that the government used the means at its disposal to influence the Bank's decisions (in order, for instance, to persuade it to delay raising its discount rate). On the whole, however, state supervision was not too heavy-handed and was only sporadically operated. Governor Pallain had no difficulty about staying in office from 1897 to 1920. The thinking of the Bank's leading officials on monetary matters was largely accepted by French society at the time and suited the public authorities. Indeed, the existence of large gold reserves seemed to provide a source of finances for war. The Regents' Council, moreover, tried to respond to the wishes of trade by moderating as far as possible the frequency and size of variations in the discount rate, which it generally kept below that of other central banks. Its large reserves also enabled it to act as a world cash reserve within the framework of the gold standard, and between 1906 and 1910 it came to the help of the Bank of England on several occasions. Although such aid did in fact coincide with the development of the 'entente cordiale' between the two countries, it need not be seen as the effect of real government pressure on the Bank.

The chief threat to the Bank came from the growth of large deposit banks. Credit establishments, as they were called, monopolized an increasing share of the bills of exchange in circulation and, as they had managed to siphon off a large proportion of French savings, kept them in their portfolios until they became due without needing to rediscount them with the central bank. The latter's commercial portfolio, which was largely fed by the rediscounts of local banks, declined in relative importance: in the late 1880s, it was comparable to the total combined portfolios of the three major credit establishments (the Crédit Lyonnais, the Société Générale and the Comptoir d'Escompte), but amounted to less than half of them by 1913. The decline, which in due course could have meant a minor role on the discount market for the Bank of France, represented a threat to its profits and cast doubt on its ability to influence the price of money in the short term, since adjusting the discount rate was only really effective when commercial banks needed to make use of the Bank of France at some time. The latter's reaction – increasing its direct discounts to industrialists – was the right one, but by behaving like a commercial bank it found itself competing with credit establishments and making them more determined not to ask for its help. It therefore had great difficulty in achieving recognition as a central bank.

In the period beginning with the outbreak of the First World War and ending with the close of the Second, the Bank of France was faced with quite new problems in the form of upsurges in inflation, wild swings in exchange rates, international movements on a hitherto unprecedented scale, and a major economic slump. Management thinking had scarcely changed, and the monetary responsibilities of the issuing body were still its major concern. In 1927, for example, when assistant governor Quesnay put forward the idea that in future the role of issuing banks would be to prevent variations in prices by reducing or increasing the volume of credits, governor Emile Moreau retorted:

> In my view, there are several objectives to be achieved in monetary policy. The most important is making sure that the national currency keeps a fixed relationship with those of other countries. To achieve that, we need only make gold the common basis for both. . . . With regard to stabilizing prices, the problem seems to me to be insoluble (Moreau, 1954: 384).

The same governor, questioned a year earlier about his views as to what the role of an issuing bank should be, had given the following very traditional reply:

> Fulfilling its monetary duty, namely ensuring that banknotes can be converted into gold at any time, as this is the common basis of all credit. Anything else is of secondary importance, to my mind. (Moreau, 1954: 170)

It was indeed to achieve these objectives that since 1926 the Bank has intervened on the gold and later on the foreign currency markets.

Such essentially monetary concerns on the part of the Bank had an effect on its behaviour at the time of the 1930 and 1931 banking crises, which were manifested in waves of withdrawals seriously affecting the whole structure of French banking (Hautcoeur, 1990). The Bank of France has been accused of showing excessive severity at the time and of thus systematically crippling local and regional banks. Indeed, it had savagely increased its rediscounts, to the benefit of major banks such as the Banque Nationale de Credit (BNC) (which was nevertheless later forced to liquidate), the Société Générale and the Credit Commercial de France (CCF) and a certain number of medium-sized provincial banks. There were many bank failures, however, with some 600 disappearing. What the Bank of France did not at first realize was that it was its responsibility to intervene massively to prevent the first failures from becoming contagious and thus endangering the whole credit system. In general, it operated on an *ad hoc* basis, helping only those concerns it saw as being healthy. In particular, it was hampered by its obsession with sound money, which induced it to adopt a restrictive policy and see deflation as the best remedy for the crisis. Its fear of feeding an excessive supply of credit largely explains its hesitant and clumsy approach, even if ultimately, under the pressure of circumstances, it gradually began to play its part as a lender of last resort.

Nevertheless, this did not make it a real central bank, and its relations with banks were rarely better than non-existent or unsatisfactory. They always looked upon it as a disloyal competitor, since it increased its direct discounts and intermittently practised an agressive policy of wooing new customers. Their directors therefore made it a point of honour not to make use of Bank of France rediscounts, which prevented it from being the money market leader, a state of affairs which led assistant governor Quesnay to envy 'the undisputed power of the Bank of England in the British money market, which is greater than anything we can imagine in France'. For his part, Moreau noted on 18 October 1926, after a long conversation with the chairman of the Comptoir d'Escompte on the situation on the money market: 'The major credit establishments affect to be on an equal with the Bank of France. This is still a state of affairs that needs reforming. It is the case everywhere but in France' (Moreau, 1954: 134).

As the discount rate turned out to be a fairly ineffective tool, the governing body of the Bank of France reflected in 1928 on 'the means the Bank of France needs to be given to enable it to meet its commitments in the monetary field and as the regulator of the credit market' (Moreau, 1954: 585). For the ministry, it composed 'a note showing the inadequacy of the means placed at its disposal in the prewar era for meeting this two-fold commitment' (ibid.). Ultimately, a decree-law of 17 June 1938 authorized the Bank to buy on the open market and resell without endorsement short-term public and private non-rediscountable private bills or, in other words, to operate on the open market. This new tool was, however, never put to great use for fear of a slide towards a policy of directed money perhaps leading to a sacrifice of money.

The debates leading up to the credit organization laws of 13–14 June 1941 disturbed both the directors of credit establishments, led by H. Ardant of the Société Générale, who wanted to promote a corporative credit organization, and the representative of the issuing body, who favoured a state system in which the Bank would play a dominant part (Andrieu, 1990).

Throughout this whole period, Bank–state relationships were difficult and often marked by conflict, as illustrated by the frequent change of governors, who mostly resigned as a result of disagreements with their ministers. With the suspension of banknote convertibility in 1914, the Bank was deprived of both a norm which had offered it protection and an argument it could invoke when resisting Treasury demands. Thus, during the First World War, when it had acted in accordance with the terms of a secret agreement made in 1911 obliging it to put 2.9 billion francs at the disposal of the government in the case of a general mobilization, it had subsequently had to finance the continuation of the conflict by creating money. Subsequently, from 1924 to 1926, its directors clashed with left-wing governments. The Bank's demands (which contributed to the downfall of more than one minister), its power and its part in the '*mur d'argent*' are usually stressed, but the fact that it drew up false balance sheets to hide the size of its issues of notes and its help to the state were the factors seen by Moreau and financial circles as indications of its serious weakness and the vigorous attacks on its independence.

Even when the '*Cartel des Gauches*' had been overthrown, relations with the new government were still tense. Poincaré, for example, was irritated on 27 July by Moreau's criticisms, and rebuffed him with the observation that he was a government-appointed civil servant who no longer had the right to speak. When the governor was finally given the opportunity to have his say, he was determined to explain his understanding of his role: 'I was appointed governor of the Bank of France to see that the law is observed and that the statutes, which it is my task to defend against the encroachments of both the regents and the government, are observed' (Moreau, 1954: 46).

These small gestures of independence on the part of the governor were inspired by the suggestions made by Benjamin Strong and Montagu Norman, the governors of the Federal Bank and the Bank of England respectively. A week before the Poincaré-Moreau altercation, Strong had insisted to the latter that it was absolutely necessary that the Bank should be independent of the state, and Norman had gone further, expressing his wish that the independence of the Bank be made clear not only in its policy, but also perhaps by changes in its statutes and even its constitution.

Moreau, not content with simply defending himself 'against overt or covert attempts on the part of the state to restrict the Bank's rights and prerogatives' (Moreau, 1954: 81), wanted to be virtually irremovable from office for a specified number of years. Poincaré made one or two promises, but said that he did not think it possible to get a law guaranteeing this through Parliament. In 1930, Moreau was finally to sum up his experience as the head of the Bank in the following way: 'I have often told ministers that they have only one right, that of dismissing me from office. . . . In my view, the governor of the Bank of France must be independent' (Moreau, 1954: 610). He had also been an influential governor, since he had helped pave the way for stabilizing rather than seeking to revalue the franc.

During the 1930s the Left's attacks on the Bank led to the reforms of the Popular Front government in July 1936, which enabled the state to assume exclusive control of it (Bouvier, 1989). Once the regents, the representative of the great business circles, had been eliminated from the Regents' Council and that body had been transformed into the General Council, the state was 'apparently in sole charge of the management of the issuing body'.

After the end of the war, the Bank tried to escape complete nationalization by proposing that it should be changed into a semi-public body under the control of a governor and assistant governors who could no longer be dismissed at the will of the government, but would have a five-year term of office. Once again, it was trying to rid itself of the most symbolic aspect of the dependence established in 1806.

It *was* finally nationalized, however, along with the other four major banks. The fact that its capital was now entirely state property was scarcely of any consequence, as it merely meant that the positions of the two *conseillers généraux*, and that of the *censeurs* elected by the shareholders, no longer existed.

In the climate of those times, marked by a wave of state control and anti-capitalism, the influence of the Bank seemed, however, to be on the point of disappearing completely. The bill drawn up by the socialist minister André Phillip was aimed at 'strengthening the spirit in which nationalization was decided upon and preventing the Bank of France from being tempted in the future to adopt a policy independent of that of the government' (archive of the Bank of France). The press wanted the governors 'who have furthered to too great an extent the interests of the establishments they have headed to become more amenable civil servants', and it was even envisaged that the government should be responsible for fixing the discount rate. A Bank memorandum dated 23 October 1945 and preserved in its archives expresses the fear that the issuing bank might well 'become no more than an institution merely carrying out the will of the state and an agency transmitting decisions taken by ministers'. Bills of that kind did not only emanate from the left-wing parties dominant in the National Assembly at the time. The economist François Perroux had his own justification for state control of a modern issuing bank:

> The move to subject it ever more rigorously to state control is not a
> sequence of intermittent reactions but an in-depth modification of
> structures . . . . Clemenceau said of war that it is too serious a
> business to entrust to soldiers alone. It could be said that issuing
> money and investment are matters too serious to be totally entrusted
> to bankers, even semi-public ones. (Perroux, 1944: 498)

Hence, perhaps, the lapidary phrase, later attributed to Milton
Friedman, to the effect that money is too serious a business to be
entrusted to central banks.

In 1945–46, the Bank seemed on the point of becoming no more than
an appendage of the state, a mere instrument of executive power. Yet by
early 1947 Lhomme was writing of the likely shape of things to come:

> Written law is not everything, and we need to reckon, and perhaps
> chiefly reckon, with the spirit in which it is applied. . . . The Bank of
> France has not always had need of it to guide its policy in the past.
> . . . . The character of the Governor will be in the future, as it has
> been in the past, a deciding factor. (Lhomme, 1947: 123)

From that point, when it seemed to be in a very serious situation, the
Bank was to enjoy a new lease of life and reimpose its authority. Its two
successive governors Emmanuel Monick (1944–49) and Wilfrid
Baumgartner (to 1959) remained in office longer than the ministers of
the time. Both were men of character and influence with a wide network
of contacts in the upper civil service and the business world, as well as
abroad. They were able to put their position as vice-chairman of the
Conseil National du Crédit to good use and to count frequently on
conseillers généraux who, although they were senior civil servants, were
able to demonstrate independence of mind when the need arose. With a
justified confidence in their own know-how and that of the directors of
the Bank's main departments, and skilfully playing such trump cards,
they managed at once to widen the role of the Bank considerably, to
assert its authority over second-level banks, and to regain a certain
influence with representatives of the state. The trauma of the war years,
an acquaintance with new ideas and the needs of the period of
reconstruction all helped to destroy the strength of traditions and bring
in new ways of thinking. Even though the Bank continued to engage in
direct discounts (a practice which lasted until the early 1970s), it now
saw itself as a true central bank. In its own 1946 draft revision of its
statutes, it assumed its obligation to 'ensure, in the general interest, that
the necessary financial means be put at the disposal of public and private
undertakings, taking into account the priorities established by the public
authorities' (archive of the Bank of France). Although there was no
official text sanctioning this extension of its functions, it now saw itself
as the guardian of money in the wider sense, and not only as far as notes

were concerned. From 1943 onwards it had produced a large number of studies on the instruments of monetary policy capable of completing the effects of changes in the discount rate and the practice of the open market, which it began to implement immediately after the liberation. The main point is that its policy was no longer determined by essentially monetary concerns. By allowing the growth of medium-term credit in an order of the General Council of 11 May 1944 and playing a moving part in the growing distribution of bank credits, it first encouraged economic growth at the expense of price stabilization, and then to some extent attempted to slow down price rises. Above all, it became the keystone of the whole credit system and soon managed to assert its authority over the French banking world.

There were two reasons for this. The first was that French banks could see their deposits rapidly melting away and were forced to become its clients and thus to accept its conditions. The second was that in 1944–45 the directors of the Bank, although they tried in vain to escape nationalization, made full use of the wave of support for state control to the benefit of their institution. A Bank of France memorandum on credit policy of 1945 and preserved in the archives explains, no doubt for the benefit of the minister, that:

> nationalizing credit means, if it is to be effective, increasing and asserting the authority of the central bank over other banks by incorporating into the wording of an act its right to advise and remonstrate and, whenever necessary, to direct. . . . To that effect, the Bank would have the right to request information and engage in intermittent or permanent surveillance, by means of investigations in the first case or of commissioners to the main credit establishments in the latter.

Another memorandum specifies that 'banks must accept the discipline the issuing Bank is expected to impose on them' (archive of the Bank of France). Not all these wishes were fully granted in the short term, since no law formally establishing its power over other establishments was passed and credit management was entrusted to the Conseil National du Crédit (CNC), and not to it. Nevertheless the Bank, by taking advantage of the governor's role within the CNC (he normally chaired its meetings) and the fact that the CNC had no adequate departments of its own, it became in fact the executive and informational arm of that body, which was reduced to merely rubber-stamping its decisions (as Andrieu [1990] notes). Thus the Bank was able to overcome the resistance of the directors of the credit establishments, who initially saw themselves as the governor's peers and were reluctant to forward their balance sheets to him. Ultimately, it became the institution to which they were to pass on information and which sent information to them by way of the central risk department. In addition the governor, as vice-chairman of the CNC, would send them his recommendations, instructions and occasional threats of sanctions, usually in the form of letters to the chairman of the professional association of banks. From 1948, the Bank also set them upper limits for discounts. All this led to increased control by the central bank.

Its continuing close relationship with the state often gave rise to sharp debates. Confrontation was initially related to credit policy, once the Bank wished both to introduce discrimination with regard to beneficiaries and to raise the still modest discount rate enough to make it an instrument of monetary policy. On the other hand the Bank, which since 1936 had no longer had the right to refuse to discount 90-day public bills for its customers, was also bombarded by the Treasury with incessant demands for direct advances.

Given the nature of the times, it was obviously impossible for the Bank to refuse all help to the Treasury or to practise a credit policy not approved of by an energetic finance ministry. As a rule, it merely expressed its reluctance to comply, or even its 'gravest reservations'. This can normally be seen as an obligatory but rather meaningless ritual and an expression of pointless criticism, since in the end, it usually gave way. (For greater detail, see Koch [1983], Prate [1987] and Bouvier [1989].) If we look more closely, however, we can see that although the Bank was unable to refuse, it did regain a certain power to influence the will of the government and even to inform interested circles, by constantly making its protests clear, stipulating conditions for its acceptance, and specifying given ways and means of implementation.

What is particularly revealing in this connection is governor Baumgartner's letter of 29 February 1952 to Prime Minister Edgar Faure, stressing 'France's urgent need for both a government and a programme for recovery [since] the state as well as private citizens is living beyond its means'. The letter was not a piece of minor and insignificant improvization. A recent archive-based study has shown that it was the result of a carefully thought-out decision of the Conseil Général, since it was preceded by long debates and the sending of two memoranda. It was part of a strategy the Bank had carefully prepared, aimed at exerting pressure in order to obtain a profound change in economic policy. It had some success, as Faure's successor, A. Pinay, took the Bank's suggestion into account to some extent (Feiertag, 1993).

References

Andrieu, C. (1990), *La Banque sous l'occupation*, Paris.
Bouvier, J. (1989), 'La Banque de France et l'Etat des années 1850 à nos jours', Paris, *L'Historien sur son metier*, pp. 369–98.
Feiertag, O. (1993), 'Entre le défense du franc et les impératifs de l'économie nationale: les pouvoirs de la Banque de France et du gouverneur sous la IVe République', in Comité pair l'histoire économique et financière, *Du franc Poincaré à l'écu*, Paris.
Hautcoeur, P. C. (1990), 'La Banque de France et la crise bancaire de 1930–1932', *Etudes et Documents*, II, pp. 295–316.
Koch, H. (1983), Histoire de la Banque de France et de la monnaie sous la IVe République, Paris.
Lhomme, J. (1947), 'La Nationalisation de la Banque de France et le controle du crédit', *Annales des Sciences économiques appliquées*, April.
Moreau, E. (1954), Souvenirs d'un gouverneur de la Banque de France, Paris.
Perroux, F. (1944), 'Les Banques d'émission et l'État', *Revue d'Economie politique*, December.
Prate, A. (1987), *La France et sa monnaie*, Paris.

CHAPTER TWO

Banking Crises and Lenders of Last Resort: Denmark in the 1920s and the 1990s

Per H. Hansen

Introduction

The purpose of this chapter is to discuss certain aspects of crises in Danish banking, and the evolution of the micro-function of the Danish central bank, the National Bank.[1] The Chapter will compare two periods when the financial system was distressed: the 1920s, when a breakdown of the banking system was close, and the present, the 1990s, when the financial industry has faced severe losses which have, in a few spectacular cases, led to bankruptcy.

The second section presents the macroeconomic background for the banking crisis of the 1920s, and analyses the crisis and the National Bank's role as a 'lender of last resort'. The financial distress of the 1990s is considered in the third section, and the chapter is concluded in a fourth section.

The interwar period[2]

The causes of financial crises are still subject to much disagreement among economists and economic historians. The main topics of disagreement are whether financial crises are caused by endogenous or exogenous factors, and what role should be assigned to the money supply. There is no disagreement about the fact that some sort of correlation exists between the money supply and financial crises, but the direction of causality is disputed.

This section does not pretend to resolve the dispute. What it does, however, is analyse the development of certain real and financial economic variables before and during the banking crisis of the 1920s and the 1930s and to throw light on the background of the severe banking troubles and the role of the central bank during these years.

The macroeconomic development

As in many other countries, prices in Denmark exploded during the First World War, while at the same time real economic growth was ambiguous. Imports of raw materials for agriculture were hampered by the war, resulting in a decline in output, especially following the blockade exercised from January 1917. However, due to soaring prices caused by a booming domestic economy and price increases in the major trading partner countries, the rise in agricultural nominal incomes more than counterbalanced the decline in output. Until the end of 1917, industrial output increased, but in 1918 production declined about 15 per cent. Still, as with agriculture, rising prices more than compensated for this.

Most spectacular, however, was the situation in the shipping trade. With Denmark a neutral nation, the shipping industry prospered, earning so much that the index of share prices in the shipping business increased from 100 in 1914 to 425 in 1918.

The strong inflationary movement during the First World War which lasted until 1920, the subsequent postwar deflationary crisis, and the

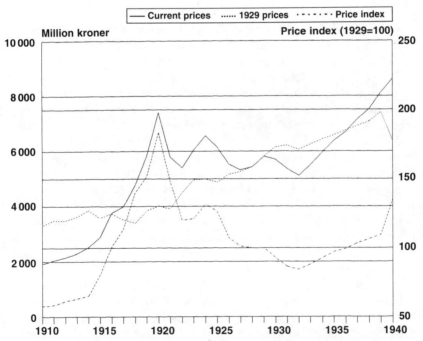

Figure 2.1   GDP at factor costs, 1910–40. *Source:* Hansen (1984). *Note:* From 1922, Southern Jutland is included.

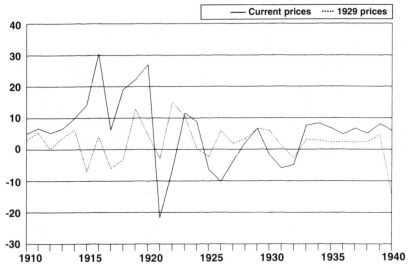

Figure 2.2   GDP at factor costs, percentage annual change, 1910–40.
Source: Hansen (1984).
Note: From 1922, Southern Jutland is included.

downturn in the price trend until 1932, are evident from Figure 2.1. In real terms, however, the trend in production increased from around 1918 until the beginning of the Second World War.

The crisis of the 1920s was primarily a deflationary crisis as opposed to a real crisis, which indicates that debt burdens which increase in real terms during deflation, must have been a major problem for the economy (Fisher, 1933; Bernanke and James, 1991).

As suggested by Figure 2.1 and emphasized in Figure 2.2, there were, however, three years during the deflationary crisis in which real output declined, namely 1921, 1925 and 1932. It is interesting that an upswing in prices as well as production took place during 1922 and 1923. Except for Norway (Petersen, 1982: 16), this short upswing was, to my knowledge, unique to Denmark and should be seen in connection with a massive 'lender of last resort' operation performed by the National Bank and the state in 1922, when the Landmandsbanken, Scandinavia's largest bank, was bailed out by the state.

In 1924–25, the National Bank initiated a deflationary policy of credit-reduction in order to bring Denmark back to gold. This policy brought the temporary increase in prices and production to an end, and even though the causal relationship remains unclear, production in real terms declined in 1925 for the second time in five years, and the GDP in current prices declined from 1925 to 1927.

Again at the beginning of the 1930s, the great depression in combination with the breakdown of the international gold standard hit the Danish economy, leading to a decline in production in 1932. Given this background it is reasonable to expect, that the troubles in the banking sector fell into three subperiods, namely 1921 to 1922, 1925 to 1927, and the beginning of the 1930s.

During the First World War, Denmark had become a creditor nation due to its large earnings in foreign exchange. Large gold holdings led to an increased liquidity in society, which, combined with a shortage of spending opportunities, meant that idle money accumulated in the balance sheets of the commercial banks, where it formed the basis for a credit expansion (Johansen, 1988).

The monetary policy of the National Bank and the increasing liquidity of the commercial banks contributed to the inflation of the war years. Since the fiscal policy of the government was largely neutral, except for 1918, it did not compensate for this development.

The considerable increase in note issue during and after the war is seen in Figure 2.3. A very large part of this was due to the Bank's buying of gold and lending to foreign countries in order to finance their imports of Danish products. This policy was to a large extent politically and not economically inspired, as the Danish government tried to maintain normal relations with both sets of belligerents. Furthermore, in 1918, the state accumulated a large debt to the Bank and, after the war, the Bank

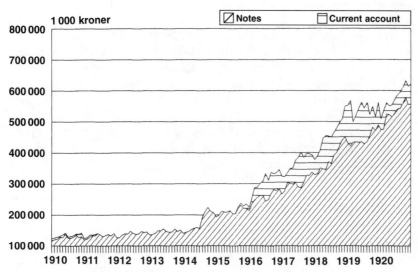

Figure 2.3 Note issue and deposits on current account at the National Bank, 1910–20. *Source:* Yearly accounts of the National Bank.

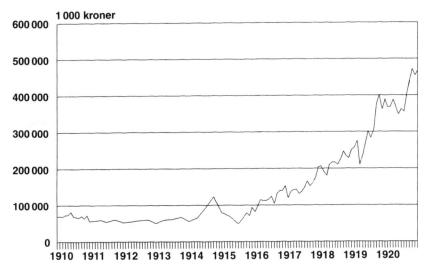

Figure 2.4   Advances and rediscounts of the National Bank, 1910–20.
Source: Yearly accounts of the National Bank.
Note: Advances with real estate as collateral are not included.

did not embark upon a deflationary policy for fear that an increase in unemployment would spark social unrest. In other words, production was given priority over currency stabilization. As indicated in Figure 2.4, no real attempt was made in the postwar period to reduce lending by the Bank.

The money supply remained at a high level, and GDP, in current as well as real terms, continued to rise in both 1919 and 1920. There were certain indications, however, that the business outlook was becoming more pessimistic: the share prices of industrial and banking companies declined from late 1918, and this decline continued until 1922 (see Figures 2.5 and 2.6).

Unemployment increased from 5.1 per cent in 1916 to 9.7 per cent in 1917 and to 18.1 per cent in 1918 – while the number of work stoppages increased from 66 in 1916, to 215 in 1917, to 253 in 1918, and to a record high of 472 in 1919 (Johansen, 1985: 286, 289). It would seem that the fear of the National Bank that social unrest would intensify was well founded.

The banking crisis of the 1920s

The scanty literature on Danish banking in the 1920s is in agreement that the Danish banking system was very much hit by a crisis during

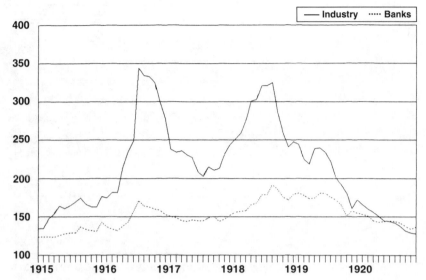

Figure 2.5 Index of share prices, 1915–20 (1914 = 100). *Source:* Cohn (1928).

these years. But can this recognition of a banking crisis stand up to the stringent (and narrow) definition of a real financial crisis introduced by Anna Schwartz?[3]

Without going into further detail on this subject, Table 2.1 offers evidence on the money supply during the 1920s. According to the definition offered by Schwartz the money supply should have been declining for the banking troubles to qualify as a real financial crisis.

The data in Table 2.1 indicate that there was a threat of a real financial crisis in 1922, when bank deposits were reduced by 20 per cent and high-powered money increased by 10.5 per cent. The crisis was prevented by the 'lender of last resort' action by the National Bank. For the remaining 1920s and the beginning of the 1930s, there is considerable evidence that there was a so-called pseudo financial crisis in the form of a period of deflation, that was long drawn out, reduced nominal wealth and increased real debts. However, the figures are only annual, and, according to Schwartz's definition, a real financial crisis is short-lived. Thus, more research into the subject is needed.

If we take a more detailed look at the period from 1920 onwards, the impact of the decline in the international price level in 1920–21 and of the deflationary policy of credit-reduction from 1924 is clearly seen in Figures 2.7 and 2.8. While the reduction in note circulation was partly due to a general decline in the transaction demand for money, because of

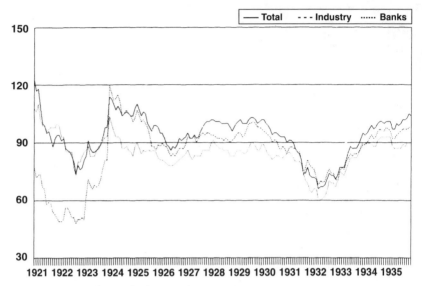

Figure 2.6 Index of share prices, 1921–35 (1914 = 100). *Source: Statistiske Efterretninger*, 1921–36.
Note: Landmandsbanken is excluded from the bank index from September 1922; The large increase in the bank index from 1924 was in part due to a change in the method of computing the index.

falling prices, it is evident from Figure 2.8 that the advances and rediscounts of the National Bank were strongly correlated with the periods of deflation.

Figures 2.7 and 2.8 indicate that the Bank acted as a 'lender of last resort'. Thus, the Bank's lending was dramatically increased several times in the subperiod before credit rationing began in early 1924 and again in late 1931, when the gold standard broke down.

During the sub-period of credit rationing, two major banks, the Andelsbanken and the Diskonto- and Revisionsbank were under siege and both eventually failed. Thus, the currency stabilization policy won priority, and for the rest of the decade lending stabilized in consequence, as the note circulation and current account deposits at the Bank remained at a much more moderate level. An interesting point concerning the liabilities of the Bank is that the current account made up an increasing part of high-powered money (cf. Figure 2.7). This was probably because the support for distressed banks was placed at their disposal in their accounts at the National Bank.

Table 2.2 presents the gross number of banks that were either reconstructed, liquidated or taken over by other banks. Tables 2.3 and

Table 2.1   Money supply, 1914–35, end of year data, million kroner

Year	Sight deposits and notes	Bank deposits	Savings bank deposits	M2 money supply	% change Deposits/ currency ratio	GDP/ M2 ratio
1914	221	957	909	2.087	—	1.21
1915	236	1.077	995	2.308	4.03	1.25
1916	341	1.372	1.123	2.836	−16.63	1.33
1917	386	2.175	1.267	3.828	21.86	1.01
1918	545	2.669	1.472	4.686	−14.80	1.02
1919	535	3.550	1.480	5.565	23.68	1.05
1920	608	4.037	1.459	6.104	− 3.83	1.21
1921	560	4.168	1.517	6.245	12.28	0.93
1922	619	3.326	1.620	5.565	−21.28	0.97
1923	531	3.179	1.785	5.495	17.02	1.10
1924	513	2.639	1.823	4.975	6.95	1.32
1925	504	2.357	1.872	4.733	− 3.56	1.30
1926	421	2.196	1.913	4.530	16.33	1.22
1927	396	2.270	1.949	4.615	9.12	1.15
1928	407	2.172	1.970	4.549	− 4.41	1.20
1929	420	2.248	2.018	4.686	− 0.20	1.24
1930	424	2.344	2.097	4.865	3.05	1.17
1931	406	2.245	2.179	4.830	4.11	1.11
1932	458	2.108	2.169	4.735	−14.31	1.08
1933	446	2.228	2.162	4.836	5.35	1.14
1934	496	2.330	2.185	5.011	− 7.52	1.19
1935	471	2.197	2.190	4.858	2.31	1.31

Source: Johansen (1985).
Notes: Sight deposits in column 1 are deposits on current account at the National Bank. They are considered high-powered money because they could instantly be converted into cash by the banks holding accounts at the National Bank. From 1924 deposits of savings banks in Southern Jutland are included. The GDP is in current prices and, from 1921, Southern Jutland is included.

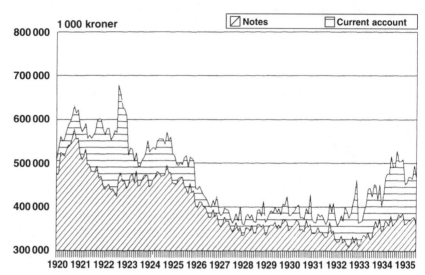

Figure 2.7 The National Bank note issue and current account, 1920–35, million kroner. *Source:* Yearly accounts of the National Bank.

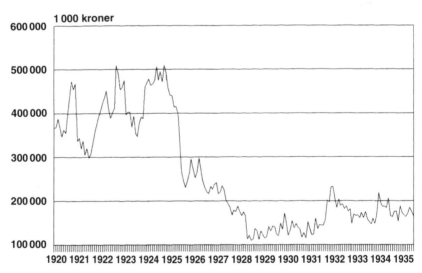

Figure 2.8 Advances and rediscounts of the National Bank, 1920–35, million kroner. *Source:* Yearly accounts of the National Bank.

Table 2.2   The banking crisis of the 1920s and 1930s

Year	Banks taken over	Reconstructed banks	Liquidated banks	Total
1920	0	0	2	2
1921	5	1	5	11
1922	6	13	4	23
1923	0	3	4	7
1924	1	2	5	8
1925	0	3	2	5
1926	1	1	6	8
1927	2	1	2	5
1928	1	3	5	9
1929	2	1	0	3
1930	0	2	0	2
1931	0	0	1	1
1932	3	0	2	5
1933	0	4	1	5
1934	0	0	0	0
Total	21	34	39	94

Source: Hansen (1994b).
Note: Banks that only received loans are not included. Fourteen banks are included twice. Of these nine were reconstructed but failed later, three were reconstructed twice, one was reconstructed and taken over later and one liquidated and then taken over. One bank, the Landmandsbanken, was reconstructed three times.

2.4 present data on the losses and earnings of the banks during the crisis from 1920 to 1932, when, finally, bank earnings began to increase again. In 1932 bank equity had been reduced by one-third from its maximum of 631 million kroner in 1921, and the number of banks was reduced from 208 in January 1921 to 174 in 1933. The reduction in the number of banks continued during the rest of the 1930s when 12 more banks were taken over. Thus, the financial instability during the interwar period gave impetus to the concentration of Danish banking, nevertheless the banking system remained rather decentralized.

Among the other consequences of the banking crisis was a more restrictive bank act, passed through parliament in 1930, and also that the banks became more conservative in their lending to business during the 1930s. While this was not exactly a credit crunch, it meant that

Table 2.3 Depreciations and provisions in the Danish banks, 1921–33, million kroner

Year	Total Assets	Depreciations and provisions on loans	Depreciations on securities	Total depreciations and provisions on losses	As % of assets
1921	4 921	64.2	3.9	69.6	1.41
1922	4 423	240.1	24.2	265.3	6.00
1923	4 213	62.6	5.5	68.7	1.63
1924	3 859	19.0	29.3	49.0	1.27
1925	3 398	141.8	55.5	202.9	5.97
1926	3 085	14.5	5.7	21.1	0.68
1927	2 956	29.3	0.4	31.5	1.07
1928	2 887	75.1	1.3	77.5	2.68
1929	2 969	12.4	0.2	13.5	0.45
1930	3 059	16.2	0.2	17.4	0.57
1931	2 874	11.2	40.7	52.7	1.83
1932	2 777	15.5	1.5	18.7	0.67
1933	2 919	14.1	2.1	16.2	0.55

Sources: Banktilsynet (1945) and Hansen (1991: 37).

Danish companies had to rely more on self-financing than before the 1920s.

It has been argued that the worst excesses of the banking system could have been avoided if the first Danish Bank Act had been passed before the First World War instead of in 1919. This is not a testable hypothesis, but there may be some truth to it in the sense that an earlier establishment of a bank supervisory authority might have prevented the worst excesses of the banks. Also, a tighter monetary policy on behalf of the National Bank might have given sound banking practices pre-eminence in the banking system during and after the war. However, the managers of the Bank considered the maintenance of employment and production more important than the currency problems. Finally, there are indications, that 'moral hazard' problems were present in the sense that the banks expected to be able to borrow liquidity at the National Bank when needed.[4]

The reasons for the banking crisis were the unfortunate combination of overindebted companies and the change from an inflationary to a

Table 2.4   Net earnings in the Danish banks, 1921–33, million kroner

Year	Equity beginning of year	Net earnings before adjusting for securities	Net earnings	Net earnings as % of equity
1921	587	N/A	23.3	3.9
1922	631	N/A	−199.9	−31.7
1923	546	2.8	−2.7	−0.6
1924	545	55.8	26.5	5.0
1925	510	−93.5	−146.8	−28.8
1926	374	21.5	20.2	5.3
1927	378	2.3	16.4	4.2
1928	379	N/A	−33.1	−8.7
1929	430	N/A	25.9	6.1
1930	434	N/A	25.0	5.8
1931	437	N/A	−9.6	−2.3
1932	416	21.7	31.8	7.7
1933	423	20.8	43.1	10.2

Source: Banktilsynet (1945).

deflationary economy, causing prices to decline and demand to be brought to a halt.

The fact that some banks managed to get along with reasonable profits, and losses less than average suggests, however, that even though deflation was an important reason for the crisis of the 1920s it was not the only one. The asset composition of individual banks mattered too, of course, and depended, among other things, on the size and location of the individual bank. Thus, the likelihood of failure was not the same for a large bank, financing major industrial and trading companies and a little provincial bank, financing small artisans and shopkeepers. Finally, the lending practices of the banks were of some importance. Business practices and speculative activity were partly responsible for the large losses of the banks in the years following the First World War.

Research into the American banking system has stressed that a decentralized unit-banking structure may leave the banking system more crisis prone than a centralized branch-banking system (Bordo, 1990). As in the United States the Danish banking system was decentralized, with many small local banks spread over the country. Branch banking was not prohibited, but a lot of small banks were unit banks servicing only local urban or rural communities.

There is ambiguous Danish evidence, however, that small banks were more crisis prone than large banks or that unit banks had a higher probability of failure. The six largest Danish banks all experienced serious problems during the 1920s and the beginning of the 1930s and two of them were liquidated, while the Landmandsbanken only survived because the state covered a considerable deficit.

Bank failures and reconstructions were not restricted to certain areas of the country. But there was some concentration of bank liquidations, takeovers and reconstructions in Copenhagen in the sense that 62 per cent of banks located in the capital in 1920 failed during the next 13 years. In the remaining six regions outside the capital the percentages varied from 19 to 52 per cent.

There is also evidence that younger banks had a higher probability of failure than older banks. Thus 46 per cent of all banks established after 1914 failed between 1920 and 1933. The corresponding figure for banks established before 1900 was 28 per cent and for banks established from 1900 to 1909 and 1910 to 1914 were 35 and 31 per cent respectively. This may suggest that free entry into banking, which was a distinct feature of the unregulated banking system until 1920, did not contribute to the stability of the Danish banks. On the contrary it seems to have contributed to the instability of the banking system (Hansen, 1994b).[5]

Thus the reasons for the severe banking troubles during the interwar years were primarily a combination of deflation with internal conditions in the banks. There is no evidence that banking structure mattered much, but competition seems to have contributed in a number of cases to bad banking practices resulting in the deterioration of loan portfolios.[6] A somewhat larger rate of failure in areas with many banks than in areas with fewer banks supports this hypothesis. This may also be the reason why larger provincial banks came through the deflation with much less pain than the small, medium-sized and very large banks. Large provincial banks were old and well established in their areas, and competition from smaller, younger banks could not threaten these banks or force them into more risky lending practices. Competition between the main banks and between smaller banks on the other hand seems to have been considerable, and this may be partly to blame for the fact that these banks failed more often than the large provincial banks (Hansen, 1994b).

The 'lenders of last resort'

Only fragmentary evidence exists for the National Bank's advances and discounts towards individual banks in crisis, but Figures 2.7 and 2.8 give an impression of the aggregate 'lender of last resort' activities of the Bank.

In all the Bank paid new capital into 21 banks to a total of 62 million kroner and, thus, went beyond the Bagehot rule of supplying liquidity to troubled banks. In some cases it even bailed out insolvent banks. This was in consideration for depositors and the region in which the bank was located (Hansen, 1994a, 1994b).

In addition, the National Bank was an ordinary 'lender of last resort' to some distressed banks in the interwar period until 1933, supplying liquidity to illiquid banks. As indicated above, however, the 'lender of last resort' policy did not go unchanged between 1920 and 1933. The willingness of the National Bank to support banks in crisis diminished from 1924, when the return to the gold standard at prewar parity became the primary target for monetary policy. In 1931, when the gold standard broke down the National Bank decided, after some hesitation and political pressure, to devalue the krone and to once again place consideration for production and employment above consideration for the currency (Hansen, 1994a, 1994b). This stripping off of the golden fetters of the international gold standard, may be said to have been the most important factor in Denmark avoiding another serious banking crisis.[7] The National Bank felt that it was absolutely necessary to support the banking system, and especially large banks like the Landmandsbanken in 1922 and the Privatbanken in 1928. Both were considered too big to fail.

Considerable assistance to the main banks was perceived as necessary to avoid any harmful consequences to the real economy, which might be caused by a major bank failure. One of the considerations of the National Bank and the Government was the anxiety that the failure of a major bank would harm Denmark's financial standing and reputation abroad. When the country's fourth and fifth largest banks failed in 1924 and 1925 respectively, there were no disastrous consequences to the economy, however. This suggests, at the very least, that the 'too big to fail' doctrine should only apply to a few banks with a dominating market share.

As already mentioned it was not only large banks that were reconstructed with the Bank's assistance. Small provincial banks were supported too, and in this case there seems to be no doubt that the National Bank did not only take the well-being of the economy in general into consideration. Political and social goals were considered as well, meaning that depositors' losses were in some cases covered by the Bank, and that a local bank was rescued if it was the only bank in the area. In a few cases, in 1922, the Bank even went so far as to agree that the shares of a failed bank should be written up by a certain percentage some years after the reconstruction of the bank. This can only be seen as a bribe to shareholders in order to secure their agreement at shareholders' meetings.

Besides the National Bank the main commercial banks paid 19.5 million kroner of new capital in to troubled banks while others, including private companies, provincial banks and boards of the failed banks, paid in 57.4 million kroner. Taxpayers, however, were the main contributors, since the state paid 260 million kroner in to the Landmandsbanken, before the hole was plugged. Most of this money was paid in in 1928, when the current expenditure for the fiscal year 1927–28 was 332 million kroner. Some of this money was later paid back, when the Landmandsbanken was reprivatized. All in all, the Landmandsbanken was reconstructed three times and the lion's share of new capital paid into troubled banks went to the Landmandsbanken.

The main money centre banks in Copenhagen, even the Landmandsbanken in spite of its own *de facto* insolvency, also participated in rescue operations towards each other and towards troubled provincial banks. In the case of provincial banks, the supporting bank was typically the correspondent bank to the one in crisis, which meant that there was a direct economic motive for support.

To sum up, in supporting banks the National Bank went far beyond the Bagehot rule of 'lender of last resort', paying in new capital in cooperation with one or more of the main banks. It did not restrict itself to the supply of liquidity to banks with their capital intact (Hansen, 1994a, 1994b).

It is most likely that the Danish banking system would have collapsed in 1922 if the National Bank, and, in the case of Landmandsbanken, the state, had not acted as a 'lender of last resort' to the commercial banks in that crisis year. While some 'lender of last resort' operations had social and political motives, it is doubtful if they were all necessary to protect either the banking system from collapse or the real economy from spillover effects. The failure of two large banks in 1924 and 1925 demonstrates that large banks could indeed fail without disastrous consequences to the real economy.

The 1990s

In this section some evidence is presented to allow a brief comparison between the financial distress of the 1990s and the banking crisis of the 1920s.

Macroeconomic development, 1980–93[8]

In recent years the Danish economy has entered a period of disinflation, when the annual increase in the price level has declined from more than 10 per cent at the beginning of the 1980s to about 1 per cent in 1993. This development has contributed to a high real interest rate, which combined with a tax reform has made it considerably more expensive to borrow. Tax reform was introduced in the autumn of 1986 in order to curb debt-financed consumption, which was ruinous to the balance of payments position.

Economic policy during the last seven years has aimed at turning the deficit in the balance of payments into a surplus, and this has been achieved by a relatively tight fiscal policy and a curbing of the public's propensity to debt-finance consumption. One cost of this economic policy has, in combination with the international recession, been a significant increase in unemployment, falling prices in the real estate market and a decline in real economic growth.

At the same time, the foreign exchange and credit markets as well as the financial sector have been deregulated during the 1980s. This has given rise to new types of business and a more intense competition in banking, which in turn has increased the risk exposure of many banks.

The foreign exchange turmoil within the exchange rate mechanism (ERM) in the autumn of 1992 and early 1993 and the resulting pressure on the Danish krone contributed further to this development. The protective raising of the bank rate to a very high level made it harder for many firms to serve their debts. However, following the restructuring of the ERM in August 1993, which meant a *de facto* devaluation of the krone, it seems that the National Bank gained more liberty of action in monetary policy. A series of interest rate reductions have followed in the wake of the ERM change, and they have not resulted in a deterioration of the value of the krone. This development, which in general should increase economic activity, may pose problems to the banking system however, since the banks are trapped in an interest rate mismatch. This mismatch comes about because the interest rate on deposits cannot be lowered further and means that the continuing reduction of the discount rate by the National Bank squeezes bank profits (*Ugebrevet*, no. 38, 1993). Indeed, the problem is growing because bank lending is declining as a result of falling demand from the public for loans, and at the same time, deposits are increasing.[9]

To sum up, a combination of disinflation, high real interest rates and low economic growth, especially domestically, forms the background to current problems in the financial sector. Furthermore, the 'get rich quick' culture of the 1980s has also influenced the risk exposure of some banks, and thus bears part of the blame. Danish banks have competed on volume rather than earning power with the consequence that costs have grown out of control. The net earnings of the banks before price adjustments on securities have been and still are too small. Increases in security prices, especially bonds, have been the single most important contribution to profits in years when these have been high. Since increases in bond prices of such magnitude do not seem likely in the future it is necessary for the banks to provide a more adequate relation between basic earnings and costs (Jørgensen, 1993; Tønnesen, 1992). This painful restructuring has been started. Employment in the financial sector is being reduced and branches are closing. This is only one of the consequences of the crisis in the financial sector.

Is there a banking crisis in the 1990s?

The data in Tables 2.5 and 2.6 show a considerable difference between depreciations and provisions against loans in the 1920s and in the 1990s. In addition, even though Danish banks have lost very large amounts in recent years, there is still a long way to go before the distress of the 1990s compares with that of the 1920s. While the data indicate that the banking crisis of the 1920s was much more severe than the present one, Figure 2.9 presents an index of share prices from 1987 to November 1993, that shows a decline in the price of bank shares of the same magnitude as in the 1920s.[10] However, even though the current problems of the financial industry are less severe than in the 1920s, one should be cautious in concluding that the outlook for the financial system is bright.

It is true that share and bond prices have increased in 1993, and this has given the banks a result before taxes of 6.1 billion kroner against a deficit of 11.7 billion kroner in 1992. The surplus, however, comes almost exclusively from the significant increase in price adjustments for securities, while ordinary earnings have only increased about 10 per cent and depreciations and provisions on loans were 15.1 billion kroner against 15.8 billion kroner for 1992 (Pressemeddelelse [press release from the Financial Supervision Authority], 25 February 1994).

There are currently no signs of a general banking crisis, but individual market participants have experienced serious hardship. The largest insurance company in Denmark went bankrupt in 1992, and was taken over by a smaller competitor. The troubles were mainly due to unsuccessful attempts at hostile takeovers of two other large insurance companies. The second largest Danish insurance company was rescued

Table 2.5   Depreciations and provisions against loans in Danish banks, 1980–93, billion kroner

Year	Total assets	Depreciations and provisions on loans	Net price adjustments on securities	Total losses	As % of assets
1980	288.1	2.05	2.34	2.05	0.71
1981	326.4	3.25	3.11	3.25	1.00
1982	362.8	4.65	4.76	4.65	1.28
1983	483.0	4.41	21.40	4.41	0.91
1984	586.6	3.06	−1.50	4.56	0.78
1985	765.6	3.98	22.35	3.98	0.52
1986	824.8	2.03	−10.88	12.91	1.57
1987	873.7	4.35	−1.46	5.81	0.66
1988	972.9	8.04	8.82	8.04	0.83
1989	1 060.1	7.39	−0.59	7.98	0.75
1990	1 121.6	11.41	−2.12	13.53	1.21
1991	1 009.8	13.59	4.58	13.59	1.35
1992	935.8	15.55	−3.00	18.55	1.98
1993	1 041.8	15.11	9.17	15.11	1.45

Sources: Banker og sparekasser 1979–87; Finanstilsynets beretning 1988–92; Pressemeddelelse af 25 februar 1994 fra Finanstilsynet vedr. pengeinstitutternes regnskabsresultater for 1993 (press release from the Financial Supervision Authority).
Note: Price adjustments on securities are only included in the total losses column when negative.

from a liquidity squeeze by Den Danske Bank (Bøggild, 1993).

The three market-dominating building societies have lost several billions of kroner because of an unfortunate combination of excessive and over optimistic lending, and falling prices in the real estate market for private as well as business real estate. One consequence of the large losses in the building societies has been that the conditions for obtaining new real estate loans have tightened. The worst problems seem to be over, but the prospects of even further falls in prices in the real estate market cannot be ruled out because of considerable uncertainty about the future of the tax rebates of interest paid on loans.

In the banking sector, too, many banks have made substantial losses in the 1990s. In 1992 the second largest bank, Unibank, which was formed in a merger between two banks and a savings bank in 1990, lost 4.5

Table 2.6 Net earnings before taxes of Danish banks and savings banks, 1980–92, billion kroner

	Equity at the beginning of year	Net earnings before taxes and price adjustments on securities	Net earnings before taxes	Net earnings before taxes as % of equity at the beginning of year
1980	19.2	1.0	3.4	17.7
1981	21.3	–0.3	2.8	13.2
1982	22.9	–0.7	4.1	17.7
1983	25.7	–1.4	20.0	77.7
1984	37.6	2.0	0.5	1.3
1985	38.0	0.3	22.7	59.8
1986	52.3	8.0	–2.9	–5.5
1987	54.2	4.3	2.8	5.2
1988	57.2	–0.5	8.3	14.5
1989	65.0	3.4	2.8	4.3
1990	70.1	–0.8	–3.0	–4.2
1991	66.7	–4.5	0.1	0.1
1992	67.6	–8.3	–11.3	–16.7
1993	55.4	–3.1	6.1	11.0

Sources: See Table 2.5.

billion kroner before taxes, due to depreciations, and losses of 6.3 billion kroner and another half billion kroner due to price adjustments on securities. In 1991 the corresponding figures were a loss of 1.7 billion kroner before taxes, depreciations and provisions of 5.4 billion kroner and a gain in price adjustments on securities of 1.2 billion kroner. Due to the increase in securities prices and a reduction in depreciation and provisions, Unibank has earned a surplus of 0.9 billion kroner in 1993. The bank has appointed a new chief executive, who seems to have put the bank back on the track, but critics maintain that the distressed situation is not over yet.

Denmark's largest bank, Den Danske Bank, which is also the result of a large merger in 1990, seems to have a less risky loan portfolio than Unibank. However, it too reported a loss for 1992 of 1.6 billion kroner before taxes, due to depreciations and provisions of 2.9 billion kroner and a loss on price adjustments on securities of 1 billion kroner. For 1993 the bank has reported a surplus of 2.4 billion kroner. In general the bank is considered healthy due to its conservative lending practices

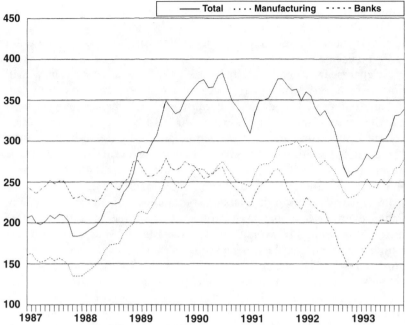

Figure 2.9   Index of share prices, 1987–93 (1983 = 100). *Source:* Den Danske Bank: Teleservice.

during the 1980s, and has even been able to support the aforementioned troubled insurance companies, in order to avoid considerable losses.

The outlook seems to be worst for the medium-sized banks. These banks were most involved in the intense competition of the 1980s, and as a result their current problems are more significant than for the largest banks and the smaller provincial banks. Some of them may experience more problems if the current situation makes it harder to get new capital from share or bond issues. It is precisely this that seems to be one of the unfortunate consequences of the current distress in Danish banking. The banking problems have entered into a new phase where a general lack of confidence among depositors as well as investors may threaten even sound banks (*Ugebrevet*, no. 32, 1993; *Børsen*, 4 October 1993).

The National Bank as a 'lender of last resort' in the 1990s

In the 1920s, as discussed above, several banks, small as well as large, had to close their doors due to insolvency. In recent years, however, most bank failures have been resolved by a takeover of the troubled bank by a larger one, and only a few very small banks have been liquidated (Industriministeriet, 1992: 164–5, 191). From 1975 to 1985, about 35 banks went out of business either due to failure, mismanagement or fraud, while in the period from 1987 to the first quarter of 1992, 70 banks have been in distress. These figures indicate, that banking troubles have intensified in recent years.

Arrangements whereby a large bank takes over a troubled bank will not be seen very often in the future, partly because competition on volume has ceased, and partly because some of these takeovers have clearly demonstrated that the asset portfolio of the failed bank may contain unpleasant surprises. The attitude of the National Bank and the Financial Supervision Authority is that an insolvent bank should be allowed to fail, if it proves impossible to arrange a takeover (Industriministeriet, 1992; *Politiken*, 7 November 1993).

Prominent persons in the banking community have advocated that the banks themselves should take care of their problems, and that state intervention should be avoided at all costs. The undisputed leader of the banking community, the chief executive of Den Danske Bank, Knud Sørensen, who is also chairman of the Financial Council, an association of banking and credit companies, has been a vigorous advocate of this view. Den Danske Bank itself has supported the two largest insurance companies in Denmark with capital, and together with the Nationalbanken, and six other banks, it guaranteed the liquidity of a medium-sized bank, the Varde Bank, when it came under pressure in late 1992 (Danmarks Nationalbank, 1992: 73). Another example took place in February 1993. When a provincial bank needed new capital in order to observe the capital adequacy ratio of the Danish Bank Act, member banks of the Association of Danish Provincial Banks came to its rescue by guaranteeing an issue of new capital, buying some of the troubled bank's branches and supplying liquidity.

The reason for these attempts of the banks to take care of their own troubles is that they hope to avoid a new wave of financial regulation, which could be the consequence if the state and the National Bank were to supply new capital in support of failed banks, as is currently happening in Norway and Sweden.

In the autumn of 1993, however, new developments made the question of free riders among the banks and of a 'lender of last resort' topical. Intensified banking troubles in the autumn of 1993 inspired Knud Sørensen and the Chief executive of the Jyske Bank, another large Danish bank, to demand that sound banking practices must be enforced in the banking industry. Among the means to achieve this goal, more information about the standing of individual banks, and risk-priced payments to the Deposit Insurance Fund have been mentioned (*Ugebrevet*, no. 38, 1993; *Jyllands Posten*, 24 August 1993).

The 'lender of last resort' issue has come into prominence, because the state has become involved in bank rescues for the first time since the 1920s. First, when a small bank failed in August 1993, a larger bank agreed, after considerable pressure from the government, to take over the sound assets and the liabilities of the bank. Apparently the government was instrumental in the conclusion of the agreement and agreed to allow a very large tax deduction for the rescuing bank. Later this agreement was the source of much political turmoil, and it contributed to a decline in the public's confidence in the banking system (*Jyllands Posten*, 15 November 1993).

More important, the aforementioned Varde Bank has had new difficulties in spite of the guarantee from the National Bank and some commercial banks. This time, however, the National Bank proved unwilling to go further. Following intense negotiations, the sound assets and liabilities of Varde Bank were taken over by another bank, while the state has guaranteed depositions against losses on the bad assets.

Thus, in spite of declarations that the state will not enter into rescue operations for failed banks, as in Sweden and Norway, there has been a slide towards government intervention. In addition to 'free rider' problems, where aggressive banks enjoy the reputation of more conservative banks, this poses problems of 'moral hazard'.

The reason for the Danish state's unwillingness to allow banks to fail is, as in the 1920s, the fear that a bank failure may have destructive effects on the economy, especially in the local areas where the failing bank is sited. There has been no anxiety over a contagion of bank failures and a resulting banking panic in general. This should be of no concern since bank deposits are protected by a deposit insurance scheme, financed by the banks and guaranteed by the state. In the aforementioned case, when the state assisted a takeover of the sound assets and deposits of a failed bank, the reason for government intervention was clearly concern about the regional economy, not the payment system or contagion (*Jyllands Posten*, 8 October 1993; *Berlingske Tidende*, 24 August 1993; *Børsen*, 24 August 1993). It is a paradox that the government, in assisting the takeover, indirectly supported the deposit insurance fund and depositors with claims larger than the maximum of 250 000 kroner, covered by the deposit insurance. By making the takeover possible, the bank-financed deposit insurance fund (that is, the banks) saved money, and all deposits were saved, not only those below the limit of 250 000 kroner.

In doing so the state may have created expectations among banks as well as depositors, that future bank crises will be solved in the same way (*Berlingske Tidende*, 27 October 1993). Such expectations may contribute to future 'moral hazard' problems in the banking sector. Thus, while the government claims that distressed banks will not be bailed out by the state, it seems that practice has drifted in precisely that direction. It is generally accepted that a few banks are too big to fail. If one of the two largest banks were to fail, the odds are that the state would take action in order to avoid a breakdown of the payment system and the credit market.

In the summer of 1992 when there were rumours in the market that Unibank was to suspend its payments, the Financial Supervision Authority publicly declared that there was no substance in the rumours, while the National Bank in a press release informed the public that it was ready to supply the necessary liquidity to the Unibank if needed (Danmarks Nationalbank, 1992: 69). The rumours faded away and the Unibank survived, but later in the year, the chief executive of the bank was removed following a loss of confidence in the bank.

The National Bank still has the will to support the banking system when needed, but it seems that a change has occurred, especially as a consequence of the latest developments. Thus, in November 1993, the chief executive of the National Bank stated that it is not the task of the National Bank 'to grant loans or guarantee the supply of unlimited liquidity, if the solidity of a bank can be called into question' (*Politiken*, 7 November 1993). The National Bank is more reserved in supporting small provincial banks in the 1990s than it was in the 1920s and 1930s. The 'too big to fail' doctrine is still in existence, however, and there is no doubt that the willingness of the National Bank as well as the government to support troubled banks is still intact, particularly when the consequences of a failure are considered to be of national significance and there is the possibility of international repercussions.

Conclusion

In the preceding pages, the banking crises of the 1920s and 1990s and their macroeconomic background have been analysed. The purpose of this paper was to compare the two crises and the policy of the National Bank as a 'lender of last resort'.

Three main results are indicated by the discussion. First, there are parallels in the macroeconomic backgrounds of the two crises. Both are connected to the international economic situation. Most important are: the shift from high inflation to deflation or disinflation resulting in an increased real debt burden for companies; low or negative real economic growth making it even more difficult for firms to service their debts; and overoptimistic lending practices on behalf of the banks. Intense competition between unregulated banks in the 1920s, and competition brought about by deregulation and internationalization in the 1980s, are certainly partly to blame for the bad banking that the crises have brought to light.

Second, the paper has shown that even though there is some resemblance between the two, the crisis during the 1920s was of a larger magnitude than the present one. It should be remembered, however, that we have probably not yet seen the end of the banking crisis of the 1990s. Very much depends on the business outlook for 1994. If real economic growth stays low or becomes negative and real interest rates remain at a high level, the situation for the business community as well as private households may become even worse, and this may have devastating effects on bank balance sheets. More banks in distress may further damage the reputation of the banking system, making it difficult for some vulnerable medium-sized banks to survive.

Third, the National Bank has demonstrated that it is willing to support the banks when needed, but there currently seems to be a more reserved attitude than in the 1920s. This is paralleled by the banks themselves and by the Financial Supervision Authority. Thus it has been emphasized several times that the banks should take care of their own problems, or they should be allowed to fail. There may be a number of reasons for this attitude. The banks may see an opportunity to avoid, and also to get rid of, 'free rider' problems. The Financial Supervision Authority and the National Bank on the other hand recognize that very few banks are too big to fail, but that the rest of the banks should be able to take care of their own problems. This attitude may be part of a strategy to reduce 'moral hazard' in the banks, but it is also possible that these signals were especially emphasized by the conservative–liberal government which was replaced in January 1993 by a social democratic–centre coalition.

In the autumn of 1993 the state again entered the scene, guaranteeing a troubled medium-sized bank and supporting the takeover of a smaller provincial bank. This may be the beginning of more active state intervention in the banking sector, and may increase 'moral hazard' in the future. With that background it cannot be ruled out that, if banking troubles continue in the next few years, the state may yet support the banking system with capital, as has been the case in other Scandinavian countries.

Notes

1. The terms micro- and macrofunctions are from Goodhart (1988), and refer to the function of the central bank as a banker to the commercial banks and as the monetary authority respectively.

2. For an introduction to the development of the Danish banking system before the period treated here, cf. Hansen (1991, 1994a).

3. The concept of a real financial crisis is from Schwartz (1986), who defines a real financial crisis, as opposed to a pseudo financial crisis, as a short-lived scramble for high-powered money, ending with a slackening of the public's demand for additional currency. The conversion of financial assets into high-powered money is precipitated by the public's fear that means of payment will be unobtainable at any price. According to Anna Schwartz, a real financial crisis should be distinguished from a deflation or a disinflation, which may be long drawn out, reduce nominal wealth and increase real debts. As indicators of a real financial crisis Schwartz uses the deposit/currency and the deposit/reserve ratios (pp. 11–12, 28).

4. Certainly, the managers of the National Bank were aware of the imminent moral hazard problems related to the lender of last resort function. Nevertheless, it seems that at least some banks expected to be able to borrow liquidity in the National Bank if necessary, and this must have contributed to moral hazard problems. These expectations which were also present in the public and the press, were created during the banking crisis of 1907–8, when the state, the National Bank and the main banks guaranteed all claims on insolvent banks (Hansen, 1994a, 1994b).

5. In Norway, with no bank regulation either, younger banks had a higher failure rate too. (Nordwik, 1992).

6. These findings are consistent with the hypotheses of Barclay (1978) and Revell (1986).

7. Following the argument in Fisher (1933), Eichengreen (1992) and Bernanke and James (1991).

8. The account of macroeconomic development is primarily based on Nielsen (1992 and 1993) and Finansrådet (1993).

9. It has been debated whether the reduction in bank lending is due to supply or demand factors. There is, however, no sign of a general credit crunch, and there is no doubt that the savings quota is increasing. For a discussion, see Nielsen (1993).

10. It should be noted, however, that less than ten banks were quoted on the stock exchange during the 1920s, and that the shares of the Landmands-banken are excluded from the index from October 1922.

Sources

Banker og Sparekasser, 1979–87 (Financial Supervision Authority report)

Berlingske Tidende

Børsen

Danmarks Nationalbank, beretning og regnskab (annual report, Danish central bank)

Finanstilsynets beretning, 1988–93 (Financial Supervision Authority report)

Jyllands Posten

Politiken
Pressemeddelelser fra Finanstilsynet (press releases, Financial
    Supervision Authority)
Statistiske Efterretninger (Danish Statistical Bureau)
Ugebrevet Mandag Morgen

References

Banktilsynet (1945), *Banktilsynet, 1920–1945*, Copenhagen.
Barclay, C. (1978), 'Competition and Financial Crises – Past and
    Present', in J. Revell (ed.), *Competition and the Regulation of Banks*,
    Bangor Occasional Papers in Economics, no. 14, pp. 1–23.
Bernanke, Ben and James, Harold (1991), 'The Gold Standard, Deflation
    and Financial Crisis in the Great Depression: An International
    Comparison', in R. Glen Hubbard (ed.), *Financial Markets and
    Financial Crises*, Chicago, pp. 33–68.
Bordo, Michael D. (1992), 'The Lender of Last Resort: Alternative Views
    and Historical Experience', *Federal Reserve Bank of Richmond
    Economic Review*, 76 (1), January/February, pp. 18–29.
Bøggild, Peter Andreas (1993), 'Situationsrapport fra den store nordiske
    forsikringskrig', *Fagskrift for Finansvæsen*, 2.
Cohn, Einar (1928), *Danmark under den Store Krig*, Copenhagen.
Eichengreen, Barry (1992), *Golden Fetters: The Gold Standard and the
    Great Depression, 1919–1939*, Oxford.
Finansrådet (1993), *Danske Pengeinstitutter midt i en Omstilling: En
    International Sammenligning*, Finansanalyse nr. 1, Copenhagen.
Fisher, Irving (1933), 'The Debt Deflation Theory of Great Depressions',
    Econometrica, 1 (4), pp. 337–57.
Goodhart, Charles (1988), *The Evolution of Central Banks*, Cambridge,
    MA.
Hansen, Per H. (1991), 'From Growth to Crisis. The Danish Banking
    System from 1850 to the Interwar Years', *Scandinavian Economic
    History Review*, 39 (3), pp. 20–40.
Hansen, Per H. (1994a), 'Production versus Currency: The Lender of
    Last Resort Policy of the Danish Central Bank in the Banking Crisis of
    the 1920s', in Alice Teichova, Terry Gourvish and Agnes Pogány
    (eds.), *Universal Banking in Twentieth Century Europe*, London.
Hansen, Per H. (1994b), *På Glidebanen til den Bitre Ende: Dansk
    Bankvæsen i Krise, 1920–1933*, dissertation.
Hansen, Svend Aage (1984), *Økonomisk Vækst i Danmark: Bind II:
    1914–1983*, Copenhagen.
Industriministeriet (1992), *Fremtidens Finansielle Sektor: Finans-*

verdenens nye Spilleregler. Rapport afgivet af Industriministeriets arbejdsgruppe om finansielle institutters virksomhedsområde og anbringelse. Betænkning nr. 1232.

Johansen, Hans Chr. (1985), *Dansk økonomisk statistik*, 1800–1980, Copenhagen.

Johansen: Hans Chr. (1988), 'De private banker under den første verdenskrig' in *Om Danmarks historie 1900–1920, Festskrift til Tage Kaarsted*, Odense, pp. 165–79.

Jørgensen, Jørgen S. (1993), 'Indtjeningen i bankerne og sparekasserne i 1992', *Fagskrift for Finansvæsen*, 1.

Nielsen, Peter Erling (1992), 'Finanssektorens problemer', *Beretning fra Finanstilsynet*, 1991, pp. 9-23.

Nielsen, Peter Erling (1993), 'Finansiel skrøbelighed – i lyset af de danske pengeinstitutters situation, *Nationaløkonomisk Tidsskrift*, 131 (1), pp. 94–107.

Nordwik, Helge W. (1992), 'Bankkrise, bankstruktur og bankpolitikk i Norge i mellomkrigstiden', *Historisk Tidsskrift*, no. 2, pp. 170–92.

Petersen, Kaare (1982), *Bankkriser og Valutauro. Forretningsbankenes Krise i Mellomkrigsårene*, Oslo.

Revell, J. (1986), 'The Complementary Nature of Competition and Regulation in the Financial Sector', in E.P.M. Gardener (ed.), *UK Banking Supervision: Evolution, Practice and Issues*, London, pp. 161–81.

Schwartz, Anna J. (1986), 'Real and Pseudo-financial Crises' in Forrest Capie and Geoffrey E. Wood (eds.), *Financial Crises and the World Banking System*, London, pp. 11–31.

Tønnesen, Lars (1992), 'Krise i de danske pengeinstitutter', *Fagskrift for Bankvæsen*', 1.

CHAPTER THREE

Commercial Banks in Belgium, 1935–90

G. Kurgan-van Hentenryk

Although Belgium is well known for its early development of mixed banks, historians have still scarcely tackled the question of the way the banking system has evolved since the reform of 1934–35.

It is worth recalling briefly that after a period of great international expansion, the First World War brought banking activity back into the sphere of the national economy, concentrated banking and industrial undertakings within the framework of powerful financial groups, and replaced capital exports with colonial ventures. It was the need to ensure financing for industry that encouraged banks to develop their networks systematically both by opening new branches and by taking over or absorbing other banks. In 1930, this concentration of banking interests led to fierce competition between a few groups dominated by the Société Générale, whose network controlled 55 per cent of resources.

Belgium was affected by the world slump and threatened with the collapse of its banking system, which it subjected to a thorough reform. By a royal decree of 22 August 1934, mixed banks were obliged to split into deposit banks and holding companies. The royal decree of 9 July 1935 confirmed this division by allowing only deposit banks operating within a two-year term to call themselves banks. Henceforth, banks were subject to a series of regulations and tight controls aimed almost exclusively at protecting savings. However, although the reform was seen at the time as a victory for the proponents of state intervention, the fact of the matter is that it was largely the brainchild of private banks anxious both to restore public confidence and protect their own interests.

Within a few years the banking system had been completely transformed. As banks were forbidden to acquire stock in industrial companies and there was little demand by firms for short-term credit, they were obliged to use their funds to provide credit for the public authorities (Vanthemsche, 1991; Kurgan-van Hentenryk, 1992). The result of the Second World War was to strengthen the system introduced in 1935.[1]

The so-called 'operation Gutt' of October 1944, an attempt to rehabilitate the currency by freezing bank assets and the conversion of notes issued by the Banque Nationale, created a psychological shock but did not quite manage to curb inflation. It was followed in 1946 by a ruling of the Banking Commission, a body set up in 1935 to control banks, imposing banking ratios which, when applied, amounted to ensuring a cheap supply of finance for the public authorities at the expense of the private sector. In addition to cash and solvency ratios, banks were required to provide adequate cover for deposits in the form of treasury bonds, which might amount to 65 per cent of their commitments. For ten years or so, interest on this short-term debt was at the reduced rate of 1.15 per cent, which hampered their ability to reward deposits. The war also changed the relationship between banks and the monetary authorities, with the prewar *de facto* supremacy of private concerns giving way to close cooperation between banks and the monetary authorities.

The structural development of the banking system was not unaffected by this new climate, as is shown by Table 3.1, which clearly illustrates the preponderance of public credit institutions until the end of the 1960s.

The late 1960s marked a turning point in the postwar development of commercial banks, which took place in two stages. The main features of the first were the constraints imposed by the public authorities and their effect on banking activity, the concentration of the system and the early stages of internationalization. The second, which started around 1970, was characterized by the revolution in technology, the intense competition sparked off by deregulation, and the impact on a small open economy of operations on a world-wide scale.

Table 3.1   Structural development, 1950–90: relative importance of the three main groups of financial institutions over the whole balance sheet, percentages

Year	Banks	Savings banks	Publicly-owned banking institutions
1950	45	5	50
1960	40	9	51
1970	52	10	38
1980	63	9	28
1990	67	11	22

Source: Association Belge des Banques, *Vade-Mecum statistique du secteur bancaire. Aspects et documents.*

Although banks enjoyed a stable environment protected by regulations principally aimed at security, they nevertheless sought to engage in wider activities than financing the public authorities by acquiring current deposits.

It may have been a slow process, but the renewal of operations in the private sector (see Tables 3.2 and 3.3) was encouraged by the Banque Nationale, which encouraged the reappearance of bills of exchange by creating the visa system and offering rediscount rates that stimulated discount and acceptance credits while maintaining the ability to intervene rapidly on the market and control inflation. In 1960, the commercial banks granted 43 per cent of their credits to the public authorities, with discounts representing 62 per cent of those provided to the private sector Alongside this, they were engaged in a policy of systematically collecting the disposable savings of households by widening their networks through an increase in both the number of their branches and the degree of concentration. Between 1945 and 1949, 22 new counters were opened every year; between 1950 and 1962, the number increased to 70, and reached 94 between 1962 and 1965. At the end of 1967, there were 2 546 , or one for every 3 700 inhabitants.

After the 1934 reform there were 125 banks in Belgium, 27 of them operating in tandem with a holding company. Even then, there were three dominant banks controlling 66 per cent of deposits and 74 per cent of counters in 1939. These were led by the Banque de la Société Générale with 45 per cent of deposits and 31 per cent of counters, followed by the Banque de Bruxelles (18 per cent and 23 per cent) and in third place the

Table 3.2 Distribution of credits by beneficiaries

	Belgian private sector and abroad (%)			Belgian public	Total	
Year	Residents	Non-residents	Total	authorities (%)	BF (bns)	Index 1951= 100
1951	56.5	0.5	57.0	43.0	90.6	100
1960	54.0	2.5	56.5	43.5	161.7	178
1970	48.7	12.8	61.5	38.5	523.8	578
1980	43.6	23.3	67.9	33.1	758.1	838
1990	42.9	18.4	61.3	38.7	2 194.6	2 422
1991	46.5	17.4	63.9	36.1	2 056.1	2 269

Source: Association Belge des Banques, *Vade-Mecum statistique du secteur bancaire. Aspects et documents.*

Table 3.3   Credits to Belgian and foreign private sectors by type (%)

Year	Total	Cash Credits			
		Fixed-term advances	Discount credits	Acceptance credits	Documentary and guarantee credits
1960	26		62	12	*pro memoria*
1970	40		32	9	19
1980	61	17	20	3	17
1990	75	24	7	1	17
1991	74	24	6	2	18

Source: Association Belge des Banques, *Vade-Mecum statistique du secteur bancaire. Aspects et documents.*

recently-created Kredietbank (5 per cent and 20 per cent).

After the Second World War, the number of banks fell considerably, to around 80. For 20 years, the activities of the Banking Commission tended to prevent the three major banks absorbing others, but it was not opposed to the smaller banks merging to strengthen their market position. In 1965, under the pressure of both the new wider European market and competition from the United States, the trend was reversed with the merger of the Banque de la Société Générale, with its subsidiary the Banque d'Anvers and the Société Belge de Banque founded by the Solvay group in 1931. The number of working branches rose from 350 to 738 and the number of employees went up to 11 000. The outcome was that in 1966 the three big banks controlled 84 per cent of deposits and 80 per cent of counters. There was a further spectacular increase in the level of concentration when the Banque de Bruxelles and the Banque Lambert, respectively the second and fourth largest in the country, merged in 1975. This also clearly illustrates the influence of financial groups, in so far as it was a consequence of the earlier merger of the Brufina and Lambert holding companies in 1972.

This rapid increase in the number of new branches meant that there were three or four banks at many street corners in towns and that the proportion of the public making use of banking services was increasing rapidly in the 1950s and 1960s. Between 1953 and 1967, the number of bank accounts almost trebled (from 1 803 000 to 3 052 000) and the number of inter-account transfers increased five-fold, from 17 to 87 millions (Timmermans, 1969: 22–4, 123–5).[2]

In order to attract customers, banks tried to diversify their takings in savings accounts by encouraging term deposits and using the methods employed by their competitors, savings banks and public credit institutions, through introducing pass books and issuing bonds and cash vouchers. It is nevertheless true that current and term deposits were still their main sources of funds (see Table 3.4).

Although the choice of location of new branches and the offer of new customer services is a clear indication of competition, fixing interest rates on current account and fixed-term deposits had been a matter for joint agreement between banks since 1941. With regard to creditor interest rates, therefore, there was a cartel aimed at avoiding price wars and further ensuring the security of the system (Minguet, 1990: 81).

The 1935 legislation certainly introduced the principle of bank autonomy by preventing the banks from holding portfolios of the stocks of industrial and commercial undertakings, but there was no legal provision to stop an industrial or financial company holding major interests in the capital of a bank, which explains why the biggest banks were a part of industrial and financial groups.

From the late 1950s the Belgian banking system, like its European counterparts, was moving towards an international role as the direct result of a number of factors. The return to external convertibility, the increase in international trade and the inflow of American investments into Europe were decisive influences in this development, which was evident at both the operational and structural levels of the system.

Brussels played an early part in the development of Eurocurrency markets, and the Kredietbank was a pioneer in issuing and placing Eurobonds (van der Wee and Verbeyt, 1985: 285–6).

Foreign banks had been established in Belgium for many years, a

Table 3.4 Make-up of deposits and share of banks in the whole banking system (bs)

Year	Current account deposits		Term deposits		Bankbooks		Bonds/cash vouchers	
	%	% bs	%	% bs	%	% bs	%	% bs
1950	71.1	54.3	17.6	57.0	10.8	13.4	0.5	0.8
1960	56.3	56.7	24.2	63.1	12.7	12.4	6.8	7.7
1970	36.6	53.7	38.2	60.7	19.2	26.7	6.0	7.3
1980	24.4	46.9	37.7	68.3	24.8	34.2	13.1	15.7
1990	18.1	54.5	47.5	71.8	18.4	36.9	16.0	24.4

Source: Association Belge des Banques, Vade-Mecum statistique du secteur bancaire. Aspects et documents.

phenomenon amply indicated by the considerable influence of the Banque de Paris et des Pays-Bas on the Brussels market since the end of the 19th century and the installation of American Express and the Morgan Guaranty Trust as early as 1919. From the 1960s onwards, however, the number of foreign banks grew, and after 1970 the pace increased at the expense of banks controlled by a majority of Belgian shareholders (Smets, 1973; Bussière, 1992; *Internationalisation*, 1972).

Table 3.5 illustrates this development, which was produced in two ways. Either foreign banks were established directly in Belgium by opening subsidiaries or branches to provide their customers with a wider geographical network, as was the case with the six American banks setting up in Europe between 1962 and 1971 in the wake of American investments, or certain foreign banks acquired shares in Belgian banks in order to have direct access to Belgian customers, as happened when Chase Manhattan subscribed to an increase in the capital of the Banque de Commerce (controlled by the Banque de Bruxelles, with whom it created an equal-share joint venture). Three years later, the Royal Bank of Canada acquired 25 per cent of the shares of the Banque Belge pour l'Industrie, linked to the Empain group.

For their part, the Belgian banks extended their foreign networks, with all the major ones acquiring subsidiaries in Luxembourg and Switzerland, attracted by the legal and fiscal advantages the two countries offered. They also joined international 'bankers' clubs',

Table 3.5   Number of banks by nationality of owners

Year	Belgian law, Belgian majority	Foreign banks			Grand total
		Belgian-law subsidiaries	Branches	Total	
1960	67	9	7	16	83
1970	51	16	11	27	78
1980	27	31	25	56	83
1991	21	34	35	69	90

Source: Association Belge des Banques, *Vade-Mecum statistique du secteur bancaire. Aspects et documents.*

informal international networks set up in Europe after the Treaty of Rome was signed.

Although the effect of postwar economic growth and greater international trade was to some extent to loosen the straitjacket the banking system had to work in and to introduce a series of changes, the monetary troubles and the economic crisis of the early 1970s marked the beginning of a period of major upheavals.[3]

At first, the financial markets were not affected by the slow-down in industrial growth and continued to expand, at a time when the technological revolution was calling the activities of banks and their way of functioning into question.[4]

As was the case elsewhere in Europe, that revolution took place in Belgium in the wake of events in the United States. After the introduction of computers to reduce the cost price of repetitive administrative tasks by automation, the volume of investments made it necessary to make the best possible use of electronic facilities. Rapid developments in office practice and telecommunications stimulated the creation of new products and services, changed relations with customers profoundly, and once again raised the question of staff management.

The high level of electronic transfers brought about two major innovations, electronic inter-bank links and ATMs. Distance inter-bank collaboration began with the adoption of a uniform structure of account numbers and major banks' membership of the Swift network, the first international system of electronic links between banks, whose headquarters has been located in Brussels since 1973.

In order to attract private customers, banks offered new products and services to facilitate and speed up cash and information flow. The introduction of bank cards, permanent standing orders, cash dispensers and ATMs stimulated the circulation of bank deposits in a country where they were not popular with the population as a whole, and between 1970 and 1990, their share of the monetary stock rose from 52 per cent to 70 per cent. The adoption of monthly salary payments as the norm, making accounts available to young people and the sharp rise in consumer credit spread the habit of banking among the mass of the population, with a consequent shift to a more passive attitude and a different relationship with money.

The development of new kinds of services profoundly changed the make-up of accounts and the share of banks in the banking system. As Table 3.4 shows, that of deposits on current account fell spectacularly, accounting for under 20 per cent of resources as against over 70 per cent in 1950. This was accompanied by a decline in the share of commercial banks in the acquisition of deposits on current account in the 1980s, with a recovery over the last few years. The diversification of resources was dominated by increased fixed-term deposits, with the banks consolidating their leading position in this area.

Although other explanatory factors should not be neglected, the technological revolution radically changed the activity of banks in Belgium with the large-scale erruption of inter-bank operations onto the scene, a phenomenon strikingly demonstrated by the data in Table 3.6. This new development, which started in the early 1970s, moved at a faster pace from 1980, when the volume of operations had almost doubled over ten years, with net resources from the inter-bank market accounting for over 30 per cent of the total. Since 1990, the volume and relative importance of such operations have been falling as a result of the recession.

The 20 years of stability and security were followed in Belgium by a period of ever-increasing competition for commercial banks. As in other countries' postwar economic growth, the new opportunities for expansion and the pressure brought to bear by the banks and the body speaking for them, the Association Belge des Banques, founded in 1936, convinced the public authorities of the need to make the rules they were subject to, more flexible. In addition, the coexistence of banks, private savings banks and public credit institutions had led to a trend towards despecialization, with each institution trying to reach new groups of clients by offering an increasingly wide range of products and services.

Table 3.6 Growth in resources from bankers

Year	I Bankers' deposits*		II Reinvestment with bankers*		I–II Net resources	
	Total (bns)	% total liabilities	Total (bns)	% total liabilities	Total (bns)	% total deposits
1950	6	7.7	5	6.2	1	2.5
1960	17	10.7	11	7.0	6	5.2
1970	260	33.6	177	22.9	83	17.6
1980	2 232	54.4	1 594	38.8	638	30.2
1990	6 617	53.0	5 061	40.5	1 556	26.5
1991	5 920	47.4	4 941	39.5	979	17.1

Source: Association Belge des Banques, *Vade-Mecum statistique du secteur bancaire. Aspects et documents.*
*Excluding day-to-day operations.

The result was a process of deregulating the banking system, taking into account both despecialization and internationalization and at the same time developing new rules to face up to the changes in the machinery of credit.

There were three main stages. The first had its origins in a series of measures taken in 1967 to bring the financial system up to date. The law of 3 May 1967 abolishing all restrictions on bond holdings made the conditions governing shareholding by banks more flexible and reduced the constraints of cover ratios.

The second began in October 1969 as a result of parliamentary questions about a foreign bank, the Algemene Bank Nederland, receiving from the Brufina holding company a considerable number of its shares in the Banque de Bruxelles, the second largest in the country. Subsequently, a reform commission presented its proposals in November 1970. They were to give rise to the 'Mammoth' law of 1975, which revised the legal status of banks and private savings banks, the latter receiving the right of carrying out banking activities and being made subject to banking legislation. At the technical level, structural ratios were drastically modified. Paradoxically, the incident bringing about the reform did not fall within the purview of the law, but was the result of the signature in February 1974 of new protocols between the Banking Commission and the country's three biggest banks. Banking autonomy was strengthened by setting up two distinct bodies within banks, the board of directors, which was responsible for determining general policy and supervising the management committee, charged with running the bank, whose membership was governed by strict requirements of incompatible interests. In order to ensure shareholder stability, the Banking Commission was empowered to intervene if there were any significant changes.

The stock exchange reforms introduced by the law of 4 December 1990 marked the third stage in the move towards despecialization insofar as it abolished the monopoly of stockbrokers and authorized banks to participate in stock exchange companies. With a view to bringing the Belgian banking system into line with European directives, new rules governing solvency were introduced by establishing three new ratios in that area, the most important of which was the risk/assets ratio, the ratio of equity to the weighted volume of risks, with a target of 8 per cent by 1993(Internationalisation, 1972, Bruyneel, 1975, 1991; Commission Bancaize et Financière, 1991).

The accelerated switch to a world-wide banking system brought about by the technological revolution taking place over the last 20 years has not been without its consequences for Belgium. The first of these was a major transformation of the industry, which became dominated by foreign concerns (See Table 3.5). In 1991 only 21 banks out of 90 were controlled by a majority of Belgian shareholders. In 1990, the three big banks accounted for 46.1 per cent of the balance sheet, the corresponding figures being 6 per cent for the remaining 18 Belgian banks and 48 per cent for foreign-controlled ones (Commission Bancaize et Financière, 1990/91).

Although most foreign banks worked chiefly on the inter-bank market with a small number of important clients, some of them had become involved in acquiring deposits of funds. This was the case with the Banque de Paris et des Pays-Bas, which in 1968 brought its branch into line with Belgian legal requirements by setting up a corresponding holding company, COBEPA. Similarly, the Crédit Lyonnais has recently become involved in an aggressive campaign to acquire deposits by acting on its own initiative outside the *de facto* inter-bank agreement on creditor interest rates.[5]

These two French banks and the Morgan bank are among the 14 primary dealers dominating the treasury bonds market, which is quite an important one, given the major part played by the banking sector in financing public authorities as a result of increasing budget deficits since 1984. It should be noted that among these primary dealers there are four Luxembourg banks, all of which are subsidiaries of Belgian banks (Association Belge des Banques, 1991: 100). This highlights the fact that although Belgium offers advantages with regard to location and openings, there are tax drawbacks which have until recently led to a flight of savings abroad, a phenomenon which has been called the 'Belgian dentist syndrome'. That is why Dutch and Luxembourg banks attract the deposits of Belgian residents, which they then invest very remuneratively on the Belgian money market (Abraham, 1988).[6]

The combined effect of a less specialized and more international approach has brought about major changes in banking activity. Although there have been few innovations in acquiring funds, the changes in the structure of resources noted in 1970 (Table 3.4) have continued, with a slackening-off in deposits on current account and a rise in fixed-term deposits, cash vouchers and bonds. To combat competition from insurance companies, whose increasingly sophisticated products are attracting a growing volume of savings, Belgian banks have, since 1988, been providing bank insurance services, either by acquiring shares in insurance companies or by setting up their own subsidiaries in the field (Lierman, 1991: 3).

The most striking changes have been in the provision of credit facilities after the collapse of traditional forms such as discount and acceptance credits (Table 3.3), and the modifications which have taken place in the nature of cash credits. Since the mid-1970s, straight loans have appeared on the scene due to the influence of Anglo-Saxon banks, with a fixed term not exceeding a year and a fixed rate of interest. On the other hand, cash credits are now arranged for longer periods, as they include investment credits, granted for from three to twelve years with rates revised every five years, and rotating credits with variable rates, usually for five years. Since 1974, a semi-official committee within the Association Belge des Banques has been issuing directives on debtor rates, fixing the base rate for cash and acceptance credits with an upper and lower limit, which is applied by the big banks. The effect of such changes has been to reduce the influence of the Banque Nationale in fixing interest rates. The former supremacy of rediscount and advances rates of the central bank has been replaced by a consideration of short-term public bill rates, the borrowing rate on the inter-bank market, the rate for fixed-term advances influenced by the inter-bank market and the rate for large fixed-term deposits (Minguet, 1990: 75ff.).

While credits to non-residents grew until 1984, so did the share of the banks in consumer loans, and they also engaged in mortgage loans.

With the increasing indebtedness of public authorities, there has been an upturn in credit offered to the public sector since 1980. Since in Belgium the public bills market has long been the monopoly of financial intermediaries and regulated by a semi-official body, the Consortium des Banques, which is dominated by the Générale de Banque, banks have been all the keener to help finance public authorities as the inversion of interest rates would give them greater profits than those from traditional credits. The result was that the Banque Nationale fixed the discount and advances rate by reference to that for three-month cash certificates in order to avoid banks exceeding their upper limit for rediscount so as to buy treasury bonds (Minguet, 1990: 162ff.).

The changes in the type of credit were accompanied by a decline in the credit function to the benefit of an extension of financial operations linked to the decline of the part played by intermediaries. They also occurred alongside a movement towards greater security, with portfolios containing fewer less readily mobilizable credits and more negotiable debt securities (Minguet, 1990: 52).

The traditional occupation of commercial banks has been selling securities and organizing secondary markets. During the last few years they have developed their corporate finance activities, and the three big commercial banks have set up specialized departments with operations akin to those of merchant banks. These various factors have given rise to the growth of the share of commissions in their income, to the detriment of profits from their credit operations, yet in 1990 their share of interest earnings rose to 72 per cent, compared with between 55 per cent and 70 per cent in the other EC countries.[7]

Despite modernization and the increasingly international nature of the banking system, it has to be said that, contrary to developments in other countries, Belgian banks are still not of a size to play a significant part at the international level. As Table 3.7 shows Belgium's biggest establishment, the Générale de Banque, was next to the last in the league-table of the first 100 world banks, whereas Switzerland and Holland both had three banks in the group.

Following the failure of the bankers' clubs, the two main credit establishments tried unsuccessfully to solve the problem of size by means of alliances with Dutch institutions. The projected association of the Générale de Banque and Amro Bank came to nothing (Vincent, 1990: 74ff). The proposed merger of BBL and the Dutch ING group also caused a serious internal crisis in the bank in 1992 and led to its withdrawal from the national market.[8] It should be noted that in both cases the proposed merger failed because of a change of management patterns in one of the two institutions involved.

The pressure of the recession and the prospects of a more open European market have brought new trends in the banking system to the surface in recent years. Some of them are the result of state measures at the fiscal level and its relationship with credit establishments. In this connection, the lowering of the rate of deduction from transferable income from 25 per cent to 10 per cent has led to a massive return of saving since 1990. The close link between the Belgian franc and the German mark and the modernization of markets has accentuated the trend. Furthermore, the fact that since 1989 public authorities have no longer been financed through the intermediary of the Consortium des Banques but directly by the market on the one hand and the opening up of the treasury bonds market on the other, have led to a decrease in the use of intermediaries. This has been made more marked by the attraction for savers of large, high-yielding fixed-term deposits and treasury SICAVs (Société d' Investissement à Capital Variable), and a decline in investments in stocks and shares.

The vulnerability of Belgian banks has less to do with their small size than with their low level of profitability. Since the 1970s the net profit margin has narrowed as a result of the pressure of competition, in particular their growing dependence with regard to the inter-bank market, but also as a result of high running costs. Because of the *de facto* cartel-like nature of the banking system, competition between the various types of establishment has affected the proximity and provision of services rather than prices. The network of branches is so dense that in 1990 there was one for a little over 1 000 inhabitants. Of the 9 000 branches in the whole of the system, the banks own 3 600, the savings banks 2 000 and the public credit institutions 3 300, excluding the

Table 3.7 Ranking of banks in small European countries in the 100 leading world banks, 1990

Country	No. of banks ranked			Main bank	Capital (bns)	Ranking	Assets (bns)	Ranking
	1–50	50–100	Total					
Austria	0	1	1	Credit–Anstalt Bank–Verein	2.6	85	53.1	110
Belgium	0	1	1	Générale de Banque	2.4	99	75.3	71
Denmark	0	2	2	Den Danse Bank	3.5	61	63.0	90
Finland	0	1	1	Kasalis–Osake–Pankki	2.9	80	45.1	124
Netherlands	2	1	3	ABN–AMRO Bank	8.9	16	232.6	16
Sweden	1	1	2	Skandinavia Enskila Banken	4.5	44	79.5	66
Switzerland	3	0	3	Union de Banques Suisses	13.2	5	180.6	23

Source: After The Banker, 74, July 1991.

considerable network of authorized agents the latter two types of establishment have. From a total number of staff of 22 592 in 1960, a peak of 52 917 was reached in 1989. The outcome was, in the words of the governor of the Banque Nationale, banking over-capacity. The density of the network might well have been a heavy financial burden, but it did offer a real advantage against competitors tempted to set up in business in Belgium as a result of the opening-up of the European market (Quaden, 1992).

Over the last three or four years the major private and public banking establishments have been calling in outside consultants to redefine strategy and plan restructuring, a process which has speeded up the spread of new ideas about both banking activity and the banking profession.[9] The increasing volume of technological investment and scale of costs have clearly shown how ill-adapted staff are to new working conditions and the inappropriateness of traditional management styles. Automating administrative tasks has meant a shift towards commercial functions and the rise of a new kind of workforce made up of information technicians. Operating costs have been cut back by reducing staff, particularly in those large, underqualified categories it is difficult to retrain. In order to make investments more profitable, there has been a much greater use of electronic facilities, certain networks in the process of being introduced have been rationalized, and staff training schemes have been inaugurated. All this has led to major changes in the structure of employment, with the proportion of managerial and executive staff rising from 19 per cent to 35 per cent between 1960 and 1991 and that of operatives falling from 81 per cent to 65 per cent.

In order to encourage customers to make greater use of electronic payments, banks have drawn up price lists for their services, and there is a trend towards moving away from despecialization and towards concentrating on those basic tasks in which the banks have built up a tradition of excellence. Although there has been a return to the model of the mixed bank in France and Holland, Belgium has not been keen to take the same road, even though credit establishments are in favour of more flexible legislation to enable them to face up to foreign competition in investment banking activities.

In conclusion, it can be said that although it is not a major financial centre, Belgium has the highest level of international activity in its banking after Luxembourg and the United Kingdom. With its small-scale open economy, the country has been fairly quick to follow the changes that have occurred in the banking sector since the 1970s. As distinct from what has happened in other countries, such as Luxembourg or Switzerland, no Belgian bank has grown big enough to act as a 'global player'. One of the reasons for this is the fact that the way Belgian firms have developed has produced hardly any multinationals and that over recent years foreign control of industry has become much more marked, increasing economic dependence on other countries. In addition, taxation on transferable incomes has until recently had the effect of siphoning off a considerable proportion of savings to Luxembourg, Holland and Switzerland, thus depriving Belgian banks of the chance of acquiring resources locally.

At the present time, strategies aimed at achieving 'global player' status have failed, and the international ambitions of several establishments have been radically reassessed. It remains to be seen whether the strategy of carving out a safe niche based on the density of the banking network and an alliance with the insurance companies will enable Belgian banks to play an important regional part within the European market. When, in 1988, the French Suez group acquired control of the Société Générale de Belgique, the main shareholders in the Générale de la Banque which is still seen as the leading Belgian bank, the move represented a shift towards such a regional strategy with a relocation of its international branches in the border areas of the country where its main trading partners are concentrated.

Notes

1. For the history of banks after the Second World War, the main sources used are the *Rapports annuels de la Commission Bancaire* (Commission Bancaire et Financière since 1991) and numerous publications of the Association Belge des Banques, especially the *Vade-Mecum statistique du système bancaire: Aspects et Documents*, published annually. There are two major basic works by practising and academic jurists: Timmermans (1969) and Minguet (1990). For the period before 1973 see also Smets (1973). There is also an excellent monograph by van der Wee and Verbeyt (1985).
2. On mergers of major banks in Belgium in 1965 and 1975, see Vincent,(1990: 73–4, 202–4).
3. On the growth and regulation of banking margins, see Timmermans (1969: 51ff).
4. On the technological revolution, see de Carmoy (1988).
5. The Crédit Lyonnais has long been established in Belgium, but discreetly until a very bold and dynamic international strategy was put into operation by the present management (Maerschalk, 1989).
6. The author is a member of the management committee of Paribas Belgium.
7. On recent developments see Commission Bancaire et Financière (1990–91), Association Belge des Banques (1991), Lierman (1991) and Quaden (1992).
8. On the BBL case see the daily press and in particular *La Libre Entreprise*, 29 February and 21 November 1992 and 20 February 1993.
9. On the Générale de la Banque, see Vincent (1990: 78–80).

References

Abraham, J.-P. (1988), *The Process of Change in Belgian Banking*, Institute of European Finance, Bangor (Research Papers in Banking and Finance).

Association Belge des Banques (1991), *La Banque*, dossier 37, Brussels.

Association Belge des Banques, *Vade-Mecum statistique du secteur bancaire. Aspects et documents*, various years.

Bruyneel, A. (1975), 'La loi du 30 juin 1975: Mammouth, souris ou pot-pourri?', *Journal des Tribunaux*, 22 November: 649–60.

Bruyneel, A. (1991), 'La réforme financière de 1990', Journal des Tribunaux, 21 December: 549–63.

Bussière, E. (1992), *Paribas 1872–1992: L'Europe et Le Monde*, Antwerp.

de Carmoy, H. (1988), *Stratégie Bancaire: Le refus de la dérive*, Paris.

Commission Bancaire et Financière, *Rapports annuels*, various years (Commission Bancaire before 1991).

'L'Internationalisation du système bancaire belge', (1972) *Courrier hebdomadaire du C.R.I.S.P.*, 4 February.

Kurgan-van Hentenryk, G. (1992), 'Finance and financiers in Belgium 1880–1960', in Y. Cassis (ed.), *Finance and Financiers in European History*, Cambridge and Paris, pp. 317–35.

Lierman, F. (1991), 'La métamorphose des institutions financières belges', *Paribas-Belgique: Notes économiques*, special edition no. 55.

Maerschalk, R. L. (1989), *1889–1989: Un siècle, une banque*, Crédit Lyonais-Belgique.

Minguet, A. (1990), *Les Marchés financiers belges*, Brussels and Louvain-la-Neuve.

Quaden, G. (1992), *Les Banques belges à la veille de 1993*, Centre International de Recherches et d'Information sur l'économie publique Working Paper 92/03, Liège.

Smets, P. F. (1973), 'La Banque et les structures bancaires en Belgique de 1830 à nos jours: Un essai de vulgarisation', *Revue de la Banque*, 37(3): 195–235.

Timmermans, A. P. (1969), *Les Banques en Belgique 1946–1968*, Courtrai.

Van der Wee, H. and Verbeyt, M. (1985), *Mensen maken Geschiedenis: De Kredietbank en de Economische Opgang van Vlaanderen, 1935–1985*, Brussels. (Abridged French version without bibliography: *Les Hommes font l'histoire: La Kredietbank et l'essor économique de la Flandre, 1935–1985*.)

Vanthemsche, G. (1991), 'State, Banks and Industry in Belgium and Netherlands, 1919–1939', in H. James, H. Lindgren and A. Teichova (eds), *The Role of Banks in the Interwar Economy*, Cambridge and Paris, pp. 104–21.

Vincent, A. (1990), *Les groupes d'entreprises en Belgique*, Brussels.

CHAPTER FOUR

Commercial Banks in 20th-century Switzerland[1]

Youssef Cassis

Switzerland and banking have almost come to be synonymous, with one of the most remarkable aspects of 20th century Swiss banking being the very marked shift from domestic to international business, particularly on the part of the country's 'big' banks. As a result of this transformation, in 1990 Switzerland's three major institutions (Union Bank of Switzerland, Swiss Bank Corporation and Crédit Suisse) were among the 50 largest banks in the world, possibly a unique achievement for a country of such a relatively small size.

However, it is important to recognize at the outset of any consideration that this rise to being of global importance is a comparatively recent development. Although its origins can be traced back to the different effects and subsequent consequences of the First World War, Switzerland's financial markets only clearly gained global status in the wake of the Second World War. Furthermore, the related international ascendency of the major Swiss banks during the first half of the 20th century has not been uninterrupted, with the 1930s depression having caused a major check.

When coming to analyse this transformation, the importance of some of the unique characteristics of Swiss banking have to be clearly recognized. There has been, until the 1960s, a relatively low degree of concentration, arising from the persistence of a multiplicity of institutions within the system. The most important domestic components of the system are the 'big' banks and the cantonal banks, the former being corporate 'universal' banks, the latter public institutions controlled by the various Swiss cantons.[2] The creation of new, although largely foreign-owned, banks has been a feature of Swiss financial development during the third quarter of the 20th century. Moreover, Swiss banking and more generally Swiss financial markets remain untypical of either a small country, or a major economic power, despite the fact that, as a financial centre, Switzerland has been capable from the 1960s of competing succesfully with, and even overtaking, such centres as Frankfurt or Paris.[3]

This chapter will highlight the most dominant aspects of the 20th

Table 4.1 The Swiss 'big' banks in the 20th century, total assets in million Swiss francs

	1908	1918	1928	1935	1945	1955	1965	1975	1985	1992
Crédit Suisse	375.9	809.1	1 349.1	1 009.5	1 606.0	3 043.1	9 375.4	36 798.8	88 661.6	143 426.8
Swiss Bank Corporation	385.3	1 001.5	1 407.8	1 044.1	1 826.4	3 148.4	10 137.6	49 838.3	127 932.9	171 753.5
Union Bank of Switzerland	—	387.7	808.7	441.4	1 156.7	2 386.7	9 574.1	47 294.1	139 453.1	206 087.2
Swiss Volksbank[2]	316.1	779.0	1 439.6	837.3	792.6	1 599.5	3 938.3	10 581.0	25 625.7	46 013.6
Leu & Co.[3]	174.1	341.0	324.5	299.2	161.5	316.0	841.6	2 484.6	12 953.7	—
Federal Bank[4]	176.8	343.8	735.8	307.9	—	—	—	—	—	—
Commercial Bank of Basel[5]	83.8	334.7	666.6	286.8	—	—	—	—	—	—
Banque d'Escompte Suisse[6]	—	154.2	429.6	—	—	—	—	—	—	—

Sources: Ritzmann (1973); Swiss National Bank (various years).

1 Formed in 1912 by the amalgamation of the Bank in Winterthur and the Toggenburger Bank.
2 Taken over by Crédit Suisse in 1993.
3 Taken over by Crédit Suisse in 1989.
4 Taken over by Union Bank of Switzerland in 1945.
5 Taken over by Swiss Bank Corporation in 1945.
6 Considered as a local bank until 1914. Known as the Comptoir d'Escompte de Genève until 1931. Collapsed in 1934.

century development of the Swiss 'big' banks, these being the most important constituents of commercial banking within the country. Given the space available, it will only be possible to outline a broad picture of their long-term development. Their modern evolution, however, will be discussed with reference to the most critical feature of their environment – Switzerland's developing international financial role.

International finance and domestic banking before 1914

Prior to the First World War, Switzerland was a capital exporting economy of some significance; Bairoch's estimates indicate that in 1913 Swiss overseas holdings amounted to some $2.7 billion, equivalent to $700 per head. Even when errors of estimation are taken into account, such data place Switzerland ahead of Britain in international league tables compiled on the basis of the amount of capital exported per head.[4] In terms of institutions, 18 per cent of all Swiss banks' assets consisted of foreign securities, ranging from 32 per cent in the case of the 'big' banks down to 6 per cent for the cantonal banks (Banque nationale suisse, 1906–13). However, before 1914 Switzerland was only of secondary importance in global financial terms since very few international loans were floated on Swiss financial markets at the turn of the century and, furthermore, Swiss banks then had few overseas branches.

Prior to 1914 the physical international presence of the Swiss banks was both puny and very recent. It consisted of the Swiss Bank Corporation's two London branches (one in the City opened in 1898, followed by a 'West End' office in 1912), and the two South American subsidiaries of the Crédit Suisse. These were the Schweizerisch-Argentinisch Hypothekenbank, established in 1910 to facilitate Swiss investment in Argentina, and the Schweizerisch-Südamerikanische Bank of 1912, which had the objective of both fostering Swiss commerce with Argentina and, more generally, developing banking links between the Old World and the New (Cassis, 1990). Even allowing for the small size of the country, this was minuscule compared with either the 1 387 branches of British banks in 1913, or a possible total of 500 foreign branches for the French and German banks.[5]

However, a foreign branch, or agency, was not the only way of establishing an international network. Often a representative was sufficient and the Crédit Suisse had had such a presence in Paris since 1890. An interest in a foreign bank constituted a further alternative and the Swiss Bank Corporation had participated in the foundation of the Banque Internationale de Bruxelles in 1898, followed by the acquisition in 1906 of a significant interest in the Banque Suisse et Française (Paris) and in 1907 of shares of the Amsterdam bank of Labouchère & Oyens and Co (Bauer, 1972: 152–3). Yet, all in all, this was hardly substantial and it was directly mirrored by few foreign banks establishing branches in Switzerland: the major exceptions were the Geneva offices of the Banque de Paris et des Pays-Bas, opened in 1872, and of the Crédit Lyonnais dating from 1876 (Bouvier, 1961; Bussière, 1992).

It is also significant that the size of even the biggest Swiss banks was modest in comparison with that of their major European counterparts. In 1914, the total assets of the Swiss Bank Corporation, the then largest Swiss institution, amounted to less than £25 million, whereas those of the biggest British (Lloyds Bank, London City and Midland Bank, London County and Westminster Bank), French (Crédit Lyonnais) and German (Deutsche Bank) banks exceeded £100 million (*Banking Almanac*, 1913). Swiss 'big' banks, as a group, were hardly dominant even within their own domestic environment; their share of the Swiss total banking assets amounted to only 27 per cent as opposed to 38 per cent for the cantonal banks and 35 per cent for all banks (a heterogeneous group comprised of local and regional banks, savings banks and mortgage banks).

The impulse of World War I

Changes started to occur from 1914. As with the economies of the other European neutrals, especially the Dutch, Switzerland's international financial position was augmented as a consequence of the demands arising from the conduct of the First World War. The Central Powers and the Entente approached Switzerland for credits, mainly through official, or semi-official, negotiations although some were obtained privately or consisted of security issues (Ruggia, 1993). The subsequent monetary disorders which followed in the wake of the hostilities, especially the Austrian and German hyperinflations, caused a few Swiss banks, most notably Leu & Co. among the 'big' banks, to suffer heavy losses. However, the postwar strength of the Swiss franc, like the Dutch guilder, attracted inflows of foreign funds, fleeing from the financial chaos in Central and East-central Europe.

It still remains difficult to establish with any precision the extent of foreign funds then deposited in Switzerland. At the end of 1929, G. Bachmann, the head of the Swiss National bank, estimated their volume at 1–1.3 billion Swiss francs (Worner, 1931: 101), equivalent to between 5 and 7 per cent of the total deposits of the country, but between 13 and 17 per cent of the deposits of the 'big banks', the main recipients of foreign capital.[6] These funds were mobile, a component of the 'hot money' of the 1920s, and a significant proportion was re-exported, primarily as short-term capital. During the 1920s Switzerland as a financial centre gained other new international roles, particularly through floating new overseas issues. Between 1924 and 1931 foreign loans on Swiss markets totalled 1.11 billion francs, of which 31 per cent was raised on behalf of German borrowers and 26 per cent for French (Worner, 1931: 111).

Largely as a consequence of their developing international business, the eight Swiss 'big' banks grew substantially between 1914 and 1930, with their total assets increasing at current prices by a multiple of 3.45 – from 2.5 to 8.6 billion francs. As a result the two largest banks, the Swiss Bank Corporation and the Crédit Suisse came to approach in size the stature of the major French and, to a lesser extent, German banks: in 1928 total assets of the Swiss Bank Corporation stood at £57.6 billion in 1928 to be compared with £86.5 billion for the Société Générale, £146.9 billion for the Deutsche Bank and £431 billion for Lloyds Bank (*Banking Almanac*, 1928).

During this period the assets of the cantonal banks increased at a lesser rate, slightly more than doubling from 3.6 to 7.4 billion francs. Consequently, the 'big' banks replaced the cantonal banks as the largest component of the system and by 1930, their share of the total Swiss banking assets reached 41 per cent as against 36 per cent for the cantonal banks and 23 per cent for all 'other' banks. A further development of the 1920s was the growth of financial companies, often founded by the banks: their number rose from 20 in 1913, to 25 in 1920 and 46 in 1930 (Banque national suisse, various years).

In spite of the significant changes which had set in from 1914, Switzerland's international financial influence remained limited. Until 1939 Swiss banks continued to favour their prewar methods of foreign expansion: namely relying on mere representation in overseas centres, or acquiring interests in foreign banks. The most favoured approach was investment in Dutch companies: in 1922, to strengthen links between Zurich and Amsterdam, Crédit Suisse established a subsidiary – Effekten-Maatschappij 'Amsterdam' – while in 1924, the Swiss Bank Corporation was one of the founders of the Internationale Credit Companie in Amsterdam. (Jöhr, 1956: 298; Bauer, 1972: 234–5). It was only in 1939 that both Crédit Suisse and the Swiss Bank Corporation opened branches in New York, a reflection of the growth of financial relations between Switzerland and the United States.

On the other hand, there was a growth in the number of foreign banks opening for business in Switzerland. Among the more significant entrants were Lloyds Bank International, which had a branch in Geneva from 1919,[7] American Express Bank, which opened in Zurich in 1921, and Barclays Bank, which established a branch office in Geneva in 1934. Switzerland's prestige as an international financial centre was undoubtedly enhanced by the decision to locate the Bank for International Settlements at Basle. Yet this was not positively related to the emergence of Swiss institutions within global finance, but rather was a direct consequence of the major powers' failure to agree over siting this bank's offices in a financial centre of the first order such as London, Paris or even Amsterdam (Dulles, 1932).

Swiss banking in the world crisis

The rapid growth of the Swiss 'big' banks was halted by the 1930s depression, especially the Austrian and German banking crises of 1931 and the subsequent moratoria and Stillstands. Precise data regarding the 'big' banks' involvement with Germany remain lacking, but Germany's indebtedness to Switzerland in 1932 has been estimated at 2.7 billion Reichsmark, including 1.11 billion short-term bank credits and 296 million long-term bank investments. During the early 1930s Switzerland was Germany's fourth largest creditor (Ehrsam, 1985: 87).

The 'big' banks were the most affected by the 'Great Slump' because of the magnitude of their foreign transactions. This became very evident during the first half of the 1930s, when their total assets fell from 8.6 billion francs in 1930 to 4.1 billion by 1935 and, over the same period, their net profits declined from 74 to 2.1 million francs. Only the two largest – Swiss Bank Corporation and Crédit Suisse – were able to avoid large reductions of capital. The Banque d'Escompte Suisse, Geneva, collapsed in 1934 and the Swiss Volksbank, Berne, which had overextended during the 1920s, was only saved by the intervention of the Federal government. The total losses incurred by the shareholders and creditors of the six troubled big banks have been estimated at some 1.4 billion francs (Ehrsam, 1985: 89–90).

The cantonal banks fared better, mainly because, as a rule, they were protected by the state's guarantee, although some faced difficulties as a result of adverse local economic conditions, as, for example, the cantonal banks of Neuchâtel, Berne and the Grisons.[8] Overall, their total assets slightly increased between 1930 and 1935 – from 7.4 to 7.8 billion francs – leading them to regain their dominant position within the system. In the mid-1930s the cantonal banks accounted for 40 per cent of banking assets, the 'big' banks 21 per cent and 'other' banks 39 per cent. A further pointer to this somewhat contrasting experience is that the largest Swiss bank was now the Cantonal Bank of Zurich, which in 1935, had assets of 1.35 billion francs, as against 1.01 held by the Crédit

Suisse and 1.04 in the case of the Swiss Bank Corporation.

As in most other European countries, the banking crisis of the early 1930s in Switzerland led to tighter state regulations. The Banking Act of 1934 had deep roots, going back to the late 19th century, but for nearly half a century bankers had successfully opposed any attempts to introduce regulation by legislation. In part this had been due to the operation of a 'gentlemen's agreement' under which, especially during the 1920s, the banks had accepted several directives from the National Bank. These had aimed at staunching the inflow of foreign funds, through measures which included not paying interests on such deposits. However, with the deepening impact of the economic crisis during the early 1930s, political pressure could no longer be parried (Bänziger, 1986).

The Banking Act only led to moderate state interference, arising from the establishment of a Federal Banking Commission to supervise the system. The first objective of the legislation was the protection of creditors, on a collective basis, through attempting to avoid bank insolvencies (Hirsch, 1985: 271-2). Unlike in Belgium and the United States, the ability to pursue 'universal' banking was not opposed; instead a general framework was established for banking practice, running from obtaining a necessary operating licence, a requirement with which foreign banks also had to comply, to measures regarding bank management, in which a special emphasis was placed on the personal responsibility of managers. The Act also established liquidity ratios, while a further control on banking business was introduced by requiring the independent auditing of accounts. Banks facing difficulties were allowed to seek a moratorium. Finally, the 1934 Banking Act introduced what were to become the notorious 'banking secrecy' provisions.

With the Second World War, Switzerland moved into the top rank of international financial centres. Yet Switzerland's role during the hostilities war, especially with regard to its relationship with Germany, has generated considerable controversy (Rings, 1985; Marguerat, 1991). Since Switzerland was, from 1941, the location of virtually the only free market for gold and foreign exchange, approaches came from all the belligerants. Furthermore, this led to the Swiss franc gaining a double function – as a 'refugee' currency and as an international medium for payments. There are no precise data available regarding the amount of funds deposited in Switzerland during the war, but it is evident that their volume exceeded 3 billion francs (Perrenoud, 1987–88: 51). During the Second World War the banks' main activity was financing the state and the war economy. As a result, up to half of their assets came to comprise Federal bonds while Treasury bonds of two to four years' maturity dominated their short-term investments (Bauer, 1972: 274–6). Whereas the 'big' banks grew more rapidly than the cantonal banks over the course of the hostilities, this had no major effect upon their respective position within the Swiss banking system, which was to remain little changed until the 1950s. However, the number of 'big' banks continued to decline; in 1945 the Commercial Bank of Basle was acquired by the Swiss Bank Corporation, and the Federal Bank was taken over by the Union Bank of Switzerland.

With the peace, the banks' business rapidly returned to its normal course and, from 1946, loans to private customers became once again the main item within their assets. In 1947 the first foreign loan was floated since 1939 – undertaken by the Swiss Bank Corporation on behalf of the Régie des Télégraphe et Téléphone de Bruxelles.

The golden age of Switzerland as an international financial centre

The period from the 1950s to the 1980s has come to be regarded as the 'golden age' of Switzerland as an international financial centre. By the 1960s, Switzerland ranked third in global importance behind London and New York and was only recently displaced from that position by the emergence of Tokyo. In 1965, Switzerland's share of international banking activity, as indicated by banks' foreign assets, was 8.3 per cent, only surpassed by the United States with 23.7 per cent and the United Kingdom with 17.1 per cent. A decade later the respective positions were Switzerland 8.4 per cent, the United Kingdom 22.2 per cent and the United States 9.7 per cent (International Monetary Fund, 1981).

Swiss markets have never attempted to compete with other major international financial centres with regard to the overall volume of transactions. Rather its competitive advantage has lain in the specialist development of a certain number of 'niche markets', such as those for the international bonds, foreign exchange, private portfolio management and trade in bullion, all of which experienced considerable growth during the 'long boom' of the third quarter of the 20th century.[9]

Between 1947 and 1971, Swiss banks' total assets increased six-fold, when measured at current prices. This expansion arose from a fundamental change in the structure of the Swiss banking system. The 'big' banks began to grow rapidly once more, after a decade and a half of relative stagnation, with their total assets expanding eight-fold between 1945 and 1965. This was largely due to their substantial involvement in international business, on both sides of their balance sheets, to a much greater degree than other Swiss banks, as became even more clearly evident during the 1960s. Whereas the foreign assets of all

Swiss banks rose from 9.4 billion francs in 1962 (15.8 per cent of total assets) to 86.5 billion by 1972 (38.6 per cent), those of the 'big' banks increased from 7.1 billion francs (29.1 per cent) to 49.6 billion (41.3 per cent). With respect to foreign liabilities, these increased for all Swiss banks from 9.7 billion francs in 1962 (17.2 per cent of total liabilities) to 71.7 billion francs in 1972 (32 per cent), but in the case of the 'big' banks from 6.04 billion (24.9 per cent) to 60.5 billion (59.4 per cent) (Speck, 1974: 35, 42).

Further evidence of the international nature of the Swiss 'big' banks is provided by their opening branches in all major international financial centres. This occurred not only in London and New York, but also in Paris, Frankfurt, Amsterdam, Luxembourg, Tokyo, Hong Kong, Singapore, etc. From a mere 11 foreign branches of Swiss banks in 1965, the figure rose to 41 in 1975 and 79 in 1985, and would be 167 in that year if the representative offices were to be added (Banque nationale suisse, 1965, 1975, 1985).

The greater involvement of the Swiss 'big' banks in overseas transactions went hand in hand with the development of branch network spanning the whole Confederation. Whereas the number of branches of the cantonal banks increased from 1 031 to 1 252 between 1946 and 1975, those of the 'big' banks rose markedly from 184 to 688. In this process, the Union Bank of Switzerland quadrupled the number of its local branches, whereas both the Crédit Suisse and the Swiss Bank Corporation doubled the size of their respective networks. These new branches were a reflection of the 'big' banks' renewed interest after the war in developing private customer business, which brought them into competition with the cantonal banks, the savings banks and the local and regional banks. The domestic strategy of the 'big' banks proved to be successful as their share of retail banking rose from little more than 20 per cent in 1946 to nearly 40 per cent by 1970 (Banque nationale suisse, various years).

The other postwar change in the structure of the Swiss banking system was the rapid development of banks occupying new functional categories. Under the classification system of the Swiss National Bank, these newcomers come under the amorphous heading of 'other banks', but in practice consist of two main types – domestic Swiss institutions and foreign banks. The new home banks were mainly specialized concerns, being largely involved in operations on the stock exchange, other forms of share dealing, private portfolio management, private loans, hire purchase and consumer credit provision. The international importance of Swiss financial markets during the third quarter of the 20th century was reflected in the growing importance of foreign banks operating within Switzerland. Their total numbers have continued to increase, rising from 88 in 1970 to 120 in 1985, by when they accounted for 11.9 per cent of total Swiss banking assets. This particular growth has occurred in two ways – the opening of Swiss branches by foreign banks and the establishment of foreign-owned banks registered under Swiss law.

The process of concentration within the Swiss financial sector, which had been halted during the 1930s depression, regained momentum after the war and especially during the 1960s. The 'big' banks' share of the total Swiss banking assets increased from 31 per cent in 1955 to 40 per cent in 1965, and to 45 per cent in 1970. Conversely, that of the cantonal banks fell from 40 per cent to 36 per cent between 1955 and 1965 and then down to 23 per cent during the five ensuing years. The rising proportion held by all banks outside of these two types, from 29 to 33 per cent by 1970, was due to the growing importance of institutions classified as 'other banks', and above all the foreign concerns. Local and regional banks, together with savings banks, experienced a decline comparable with that of the cantonal banks, with their share falling from 30 per cent in 1947 to 19.5 per cent in 1968 (Banque nationale suisse, various years).

Recent developments

The 1980s in Switzerland, as in other industrialized countries, have been marked financially by deregulation and increasing foreign competition. A series of liberalizing measures, beginning in the late 1970s, lifted the restrictions on capital inflows, by which the authorities had attempted during the two previous decades, albeit with little success, to prevent the appreciation of the Swiss franc. In August 1980, the ban on payment of interest on deposit in Swiss francs held by non-residents, and the levying of negative interest on increases in such deposits, were abolished. Competition on the Swiss capital market, with respect to international operations, has intensified as a result of foreign banks and finance companies forming *ad hoc* syndicates, of which one outcome was that the share of the 'big' banks syndicate fell from 75 per cent in 1982 to 66 per cent by 1985 (Braillard *et al.*, 1987: 32–9).

Since 1970 concentration has proceeded little further, with the big banks' share of total Swiss banking assets falling only slightly from 49 per cent to 48 per cent during the 1980s, and the cantonal banks' from 21 to 20 per cent. Domestic banking is still characterized by the prevalence of many restrictive practices arising from the application of numerous conventions particularly those covering interest rates. Market imperfections have constituted one factor responsible for the still increasing number of banking institutions – from 557 in 1980 to 625 in

1990. Although most of this rise has been due to the continuing growth of foreign banks and finance companies, none the less in 1990 there were still 204 local banks. Yet, the degree of concentration within the Swiss banking system should not be downplayed. In 1980, 82.17 per cent of total Swiss banking assets were controlled by 10 per cent of all banking establishments and by 1989, their share had increased to 83.35 per cent (Bossard *et al.*, 1992: 82).

The big banks and the foreign banks have continued to reinforce their positions, especially through off-balance sheet operations. Particularly important have been payment transactions, foreign exchange operations, dealing in bullion, fiduciary accounts, stock exchange dealing, bond issues, portfolio management, and business consultancy. These have constituted areas of expansion which since the 1970s have experienced growth at rates outstripping those for all other banking activities and among which the most spectacular has been fiduciary accounts, rising from less than 1 billion francs in 1962, to 34 billion in 1972, 183 billion in 1983 and to reach 299 billion in 1989. The share of foreign banks in off-balance sheet operations has grown significantly over the 1980s from 39.8 to 43.3 per cent, whereas that of the big banks has declined, with their share falling from 39.3 to 34.7 per cent; the share of the cantonal banks has remained almost insignificant, increasing from 1.6 to 2 per cent (de Saussure, 1985; Bossard *et al.*, 1992: 82). These changes are reflected in shifts in the sources of profits. In the case of the 'big' banks, the share of income arising from interest differential fell from an average of 30 per cent, 1972-75, to just over 15 per cent during the period 1980-85, whereas it has continued to contribute around 50 per cent for the cantonal banks (Braillard *et al.*, 1987: 211, 215).

The 1980s proved to be an exceptional decade for the Swiss banks, with assets, incomes and profits attaining new levels in 1989. During that decade banking became more important as a constituent of the Swiss economy, its share of national income increasing from 6.5 per cent in 1980 to 8.8 per cent in 1989. Growth rates of added value, and of employment, were higher in banking than in any other sector of the economy. This expansion stimulated other sectors, ranging from building to computers and telecommunications (Bossard *et al.*, 1992). None the less, since the early 1990s, there has been a growing unease regarding Switzerland's long-term future as an international financial centre. Some long-standing competitive advantages, as with social and political stability, are now shared by most other European countries, whereas the legendary strength of the Swiss franc has of late been somewhat diminished, a possible reflection of the rate of inflation being higher than that experienced in several other Western European countries. Furthermore, the refusal by the Swiss people in 1992 to join the

European Economic Area may incur the risk of further isolating the Confederation. Finally, the winds of international financial competition are now stronger, arising not only from the three global financial centres – London, New York and Tokyo – but also from a host of others located in Europe and also in Asia. In the end, it may prove the case that the long-term future of Switzerland as an international financial centre, and that of its three big banks as major international global players will no longer necessarily go hand in hand. These banks now seem even better placed to confront international competition, even though it has been suggested that only two will be in existence by 2005. They may still be based in Switzerland or, should that be more advantageous, may have migrated to other major financial centres where they are already firmly established.

Notes

1. I am grateful to Philip Cottrell for his suggestions and corrections on an earlier draft of this paper.
2. On the evolution of the Swiss banking system, see Ritzmann (1973); see also Cassis and Tanner (1992).
3. The notion of Switzerland as a financial centre is commonly used to describe the international role of the Swiss financial markets, particularly since the 1960s. This is reflected in the title of such books as M. Iklé, *Die Schweiz als internationaler Bank-und Finanzplatz* (1970), Benedicte V. Christensen, *Switzerland's role as an International Financial Centre* (1986), P. Braillard *et al.*, *La place financière suisse: Politique gouvernmentale et compétitivité internationale* (1987). Strictly speaking, a financial centre consists of an array of financial markets located in one urban area, and one should therefore distinguish between Zurich – the most important – Geneva or Basle as financial centres.
4. See Bairoch (1984: 134). Other estimates, however, put Britain in first place with 1 981 francs capital exported per head in 1913 as against 1 575 for Switzerland; Stauffacher (1929).
5. For the British banks, see Jones (1993: 396–7); see also Aliber (1984).
6. Percentages calculated from the data provided by the Swiss National Bank, *Les banques suisses en 1929*. The private banks, which did not publish their balance-sheet, are not included in these statisitics.
7. This was not, however, very successful; see Jones (1982).
8. A good example is provided by the Cantonal Bank of Neuchâtel; see Perrenoud (1993).
9. On Switzerland as an international financial centre, see Iklé (1970) and Christensen (1986).

References

Aliber, R. Z. (1984), 'International Banking: a Survey', *Journal of Money, Banking and Credit*, 16: 661–78.

Bairoch, P. (1984), 'L'économie suisse dans le contexte européen: 1913–1939', *Revue Suisse d'historie*, 34: 468–97.

Banking Almanac, Yearbook and Directory, various years.

Banque nationale suisse, *Les banques suisses*, various years.

Bänzinger, H. (1986), *Die Entwicklung der Bankaufsicht in der Schweiz seit dem 19. Jahrhundert*, Basle.

Bauer, H. (1972), *Société de Banque Suisse, 1872–1972*, Basle.

Bossard, A., Wirth, M. and Blattner, N. (1992), 'The Swiss Banking Sector: Development and Outlook', in N. Blattner, H. Genberg and A. Swoboda (eds), *Competitiveness in Banking*, Heidelberg.

Bouvier, J. (1961), *Le Crédit Lyonnais de 1863 à 1882: Les années de formation d'une banque de dépôts*, 2 vols, Paris.

Braillard, P. *et al.* (1987), *La place financière suisse: Politique gouvernmentale et competitivitè internationale*, Geneva.

Bussière, E. (1992), *Paribas, 1872–1892: L'Europe et le monde*, Antwerp.

Cassis, Y. (1990), 'Swiss International Banking, 1890–1950', in G. Jones (ed.), *Banks as Multinationals*, London.

Cassis, Y. and Tanner, J. (1992), 'Finance and Financiers in Switzerland, 1880–1960', in Y. Cassis (ed.), *Finance and Financiers in European History, 1880–1960*, Cambridge.

Christensen, B. V. (1986), *Switzerland's Role as an International Financial Centre*, IMF Occasional Paper no. 45.

de Saussure, C. (1985), 'Les opérations "hors bilan" des banques', in Eidgenossische Bankenkommission, *50 Jahre eidgenossische Bankenaufsicht*, Zurich.

Dulles, E. L. (1932), *The Bank for International Settlements at Work*, New York.

Ehrsam, P. (1985), 'Die Bankenkrise der 30er Jahre in der Schweiz', in Eidgenossische Bankenkommission, *50 Jahre eidgenossische Bankenaufsicht*, Zurich.

Hirsch, A. (1985), 'Les objectifs de la loi sur les banques', in Eidgenossische Bankenkommission, *50 Jahre eidgenossische Bankenaufsicht*, Zurich.

Iklé, M. (1970), *Die Schweiz als internationaler Bank-und Finanzplatz*, Zurich.

International Monetary Fund (1981), *International Financial Statistics Yearbook*.

Jöhr, W. A. (1956), *Schweizerische Kreditanstalt 1856–1956: Hundert*

Jahre im Dienst der schweizerischen Volkwirtschaft, Zurich.

Jones, G. (1982), 'Lombard Street on the Riviera: the British Clearing Banks and Europe, 1900–1960', *Business History*, 24: 186–210.

Jones, G. (1993), *British Multinational Banking, 1830–1990*, Oxford.

Marguerat, P. (1991), *La Suisse face au IIIe Reich*, Lausanne.

Perrenoud, M. (1987–88), 'Banque et diplomatie Suisse à la fin de la deuxième guerre mondiale: Politique de neutralité et relations financières internationales', *Etudes et Sources*, 13–14: 7–128.

Perrenoud, M. (1993), 'Crises horlogères et interventions étatiques: Le cas de la Banque cantonale neuchâteloise pendant l'entre-deux-guerres', in Y. Cassis and J. Tanner (eds), *Banques, et Crédit en Suisse, 1850–1930*, Zurich, pp. 209–40.

Rings, W. (1985), *L'or des Nazis*, Lausanne.

Ritzmann, F. (1973), *Die Schweizer Banken: Geschichte, Theorie, Statistik*, Bern.

Ruggia, L. (1993), 'Les relations financières de la Suisse pendant le première guerre mondiale', in Y. Cassis and J. Tanner (eds), *Banques et Crédit en Suisse, 1850–1930*, Zurich, pp. 77–95.

Speck, K. (1974), *Strukturwandlungen und Entwicklungstendenzen im Auslandgeschäft der Schweizerbanken*, Zurich.

Stauffacher, W. (1929), *Der schweizerische Kapitalexport*, Glaris.

Worner, B. (1931), *La Suisse, centre financier européen*, Argenton.

CHAPTER FIVE

Phases in the Development of the Norwegian Banking System, 1880–1980

Sverre Knutsen

Introduction

As indicated in the title, the purpose of this essay is to describe and analyse some of the main features of the development of the Norwegian system of financial institutions and markets in a historical perspective, but with an emphasis on the banking system. The relations of the banking system to industry will also be discussed to a certain extent. The analysis on this point will, however, concentrate upon *how* industry was financed during the period from 1910 to 1980, chiefly to answer the following question: What type of banking system or, more generally, what kind of financial system was prevailing in Norway during this period? The approach of this essay is dual and basically institutional: we examine how state policy and regulatory measures have affected the shaping and transformation of the Norwegian system of financial institutions, and we focus on how the organizational and institutional form of the financial system has influenced the allocation of financial resources to industry.

This study is in six sections. The second section gives a general view of the system of Norwegian financial institutions on the eve of the First World War. The third section outlines the tremendous expansion of the banking system during the war and postwar boom and the subsequent banking crisis of the 1920s. The fourth section outlines the changes in the financial system taking place from the early 1930s until 1950. In particular, attention will be paid to the substantial changes in the credit and capital market structure during the 1930s and the movement away from market mechanisms, a development which was reinforced by wartime controls and regulations during the German occupation. The fifth section presents the development of the banking system under a new regulatory regime 1950–80, while the sixth section will summarize the essay with some concluding remarks.

The Norwegian system of financial institutions on the eve of the First World War

At the turn of the century, the organized Norwegian credit system included the following institutions: commercial banks, savings banks, insurance companies, private and public pension funds and state owned banks. From 1907 there are also private credit unions, funding themselves by issuing bearer bonds. I shall give a brief survey of the role and function of these institutions until 1914.

The structure of the banking system and its role in the economy.

The Norwegian banking system on the eve of the First World War was decentralized and fragmented, consisting of a large number of small, independent commercial banks and even smaller savings banks. As Table 5.1 shows, this unit-banking system was made up of 111 commercial banks and 487 local savings banks in 1910. Through most of the 19th century, the total assets of the savings banks exceeded those of the commercial banks, but this situation had altered by the turn of the century.

With few exceptions there was no branch-banking in Norway before the First World War. The commercial banks did not operate on a national level and none of them had been able to develop an extensive network of local branches until 1913. Earlier attempts to build branches had failed, mainly because of resistance from local political and business communities. On several occasions this resistance had even been confirmed at a national political level, when bank matters were discussed

Table 5.1 Number of banks and total assets, commercial banks and savings banks, 1890–1913 (Assets in current million NOK)

	Commercial banks		Savings banks	
	Total assets	Number of banks	Total assets	Number of banks
1890	172	44	221	350
1895	220	48	257	373
1900	427	83	344	413
1905	477	89	422	446
1910	669	111	570	487
1913	718	116	684	519

Sources: (Matre Imset, 1992a) and Historical Statistics 1978.

in the Parliament (Storting). The decentralized institutional structure of the banking system corresponded largely with the pre-1900 industrial structure of the country. The decentralized Norwegian unit-banking system was first and foremost a credit-system for locally based trade and agriculture. By the end of the 19th century, it had also begun to provide local, small-scale industrial firms with credit.

Norwegian business had, to a considerable extent, been self-financed through most of the 19th century. The funds needed to set up a new textile factory, a sawmill or a pulp factory came from the entrepreneurs' own savings, from family or partners or through retained earnings. Recent research on the financing of firms in manufacturing industry shows that credit provided by commercial banks was almost absent, or at least uncommon, before 1890. It is not until the late 1890s that commercial bank loans became customary in the balance-sheets of the sample-firms (Knutsen, 1992). But from the turn of the century the Norwegian commercial banks increasingly directed their operations towards industrial companies. However, their lending was limited to short-term loans. Despite this trend the banks remained too small and fragmented to provide the expanding manufacturing industry with sufficient and adequate credit during the period 1890–1914. New projects and new companies in particular had difficulties in obtaining credit from the commercial banks.

Numerous waterfalls and new electrotechnical innovations gave Norway a unique opportunity to produce cheap hydroelectric energy. From the turn of the century this huge energy resource served as a base for the development of an electrotechnical, electrometallurgical and electrochemical industry. These new industrial enterprises were large-scale and capital intensive. The limited ability of the Norwegian banking system to finance industrial expansion in the pre-1914 period was particularly demonstrated during the start-up and expansion of this new, large-scale industry. In expectation of high profits, foreign investment capital was pulled into the new enterprises such as mining, hydroelectric power stations and energy-intensive industries such as aluminium, carbide and nitrogen-based fertilizers after 1900. It was mainly Swedish, French and German capital behind these foreign investments, taking the form of owner capital or direct foreign investment. The Norwegian banking system hardly took any part in capital mobilization for these evolving industries. In addition to the direct investments in share capital, foreign banks also provided the new energy-intensive enterprises with short-term credits for current operations. Although some of the largest Norwegian commercial banks were minor participants in syndicating such loans, in the main, they stayed away from involvement in financing the hydro-power based new, large enterprises.

Table 5.2 Growth in total institutional lending (current NOK), 5-year periods, 1890–1915

1890–1895	1895–1900	1900–05	1905–10	1910–15
27 %	53 %	14 %	35 %	59 %

Source: Matre Imset (1992b).

From 1895 commercial banking expanded considerably. As shown in Table 5.1 the number of banks increased by 63 during the period 1895–1910, while total assets more than tripled. From Table 5.2. we see that the whole credit market expanded substantially after 1895. But the market share of the commercial banks increased more relative to other credit-institutions (see Appendix, Table 5.A.1). The commercial banks' share of total institutional lending actually grew from 30 per cent in 1890 to 47 per cent in 1915.

The rapidly increasing need for investment capital between 1890 and the First World War was an underlying factor in the general expansion of the credit-market as well as in the increasing role of the commercial banks in the economy during this period. It should be emphasized, though, that the 19th-century credit-system in Norway was characterized by strong public sector involvement. In 1850 almost 70 per cent of all known lending was provided by public sector institutions. In 1890 this share had dropped substantially, but was still as high as 30 per cent.

The observed increase in relative importance of the commercial banks on the credit market was partly a consequence of the inability of the public sector institutions to meet the growing need for investment capital as noted above. This increasing inability of the financial system to meet the challenges put forward by economic and technological development was intensified by the savings banks' growing difficulties in substituting commercial bank functions. The savings banks were not suited to the task of providing an adequate finance for modern manufacturing industries or modern trade. In addition, the role of the public sector banks in the economy was primarily designed to meet the needs for credit in agriculture. These conditions set the scene for the rapid expansion of commercial banking during the period from 1895 to 1915.

The lending policies of the commercial banks before the First World War were short-term and current drawing accounts increased its share of total lending substantially between 1900 and 1913. At the same time loans against bills and 'bond bills' as a share of total lending decreased considerably. Originally the operations of the commercial banks had been almost completely directed against commerce. But a shift from loans against accommodation bills and bills of exchange to current drawing accounts indicates that the commercial banks' relations with manufacturing industry were strengthened during these years. The current drawing account is a type of loan that was more suitable than the bill in providing short-term working capital to manufacturing enterprises.

Originally, the Norwegian savings banks had been established with a philanthropic purpose, but they gradually changed and philanthropy gave way to business. From the 1840s the savings banks primarily operated as credit-institutions. As has already been pointed out, the savings banks occupied a central position in the Norwegian financial system at the turn of the century. As Table 5.1 shows, there were 350 savings banks in Norway by 1890, of which 65 were located in towns and 283 in the countryside. By 1913 the figures were respectively 65 and 454. Thus the development of the savings banks system during the period under consideration mainly took place in rural areas. By the turn of the century, the savings banks' principal borrowers were agriculture, municipalities and municipal institutions (Knutsen, 1993).

In 1895, almost 75 per cent of the savings banks' total lending were loans secured by personal collateral, while approximately 25 per cent were mortgages. In 1910 the corresponding figures were 60 per cent and 35 per cent. One major factor behind these changes in the types of loans provided by the savings banks was an alteration in the Norwegian legislation on interest-rates in 1888, when regulations stipulating an interest-rate ceiling on mortgages were abandoned and the banks were free to let the market determine the interest rate on both loans and deposits. Until this change in legislation, the interest rate on mortgages and all other types of loans exceeding a six-month term had, since 1857, been fixed by law to a 5 per cent p.a. maximum. The discount rate on bills, however, had been free since 1799.[1] Loans against 'bond bills' were short-term from a formal point of view, but every six months a minor instalment could be paid, and the loan renewed. Through continuous renewal, the legislation on usury was circumvented, and such loans could serve as a substitute for long-term loans. This practice had a substantial impact upon the mix of different types of loans provided by the savings banks until, at least, the First World War.

Although the setting of the mortgage interest rate to a legal maximum affected the credit policies of the savings banks, the liquidity problem was a more decisive factor underlying their large share of loans secured by personal collateral. The banks could legally withdraw loans against 'bond bills' in a situation when for instance a depositor run threatened their liquidity. Since mortgages were long-term loans, the banks could not legally withdraw them at short notice. Hence, they regarded an overly large share of mortgages as a threat against their liquidity. Consequently they stuck by the so called 'bond bill' loans.

The savings banks of course could in principle have solved this dilemma by investing a larger share of their assets in easily negotiable securities. But the Norwegian savings banks portfolio of such securities indeed constituted a very low share of total assets. The Storting passed new legislation on savings banks in 1887. According to Section 8 in the new law, it became compulsory for the savings banks to invest a minimum of 10 per cent of their assets in negotiable securities such as government bonds, municipal bonds or bonds issued by the state-owned Royal Norwegian Mortgage Bank. This clause met with considerable resistance from the parliamentary spokesmen of the savings banks. In response it was amended, so that the clause could only be implemented after a five-year transition period. During this period the 10 per cent liquidity clause was reduced, and finally abolished in 1903 (Egge, 1972: 134 ff.). A major reason for this resistance in the Storting was strong, local opposition against savings banks' investments in securities, since this allegedly 'drained resources' from local communities to other parts of the country. Since the start-up of the savings banks, their activities had been interwoven with the leadership of the local municipalities. The influence of the local authorities on the savings banks actually turned them into some kind of semi-public institutions on local level. Even today, remnants of this municipal influence on savings banks still remain.

Some remarks on capital market and non-bank institutions before the First World War

The bond market   This study broadly defines the capital market as the market for financial instruments and securities with more than one year to maturity. In this context, the major financial instruments and securities traded in the capital market are government and corporate bonds and corporate stocks. Thus the capital market is separate from the credit market, which is a loan market. This distinction emphasizes that the capital market and the credit market are alternative financial sources for the firm. The following sections briefly surveys some main trends in the development of the capital market until the outbreak of the First World War.

During most of the 19th century the issue of bearer bonds was subject to a state monopoly and thus prohibited for private firms and institutions. In 1897, banks and private companies with limited liability were permitted a limited right to issue bearer bonds, but only after obtaining permission from the government. The rules were strict, however, and the changes had limited practical impact until the law was further liberalized in 1913.[2] Violation of the prohibition of private issue of bearer bonds was even considered a criminal offence until 1902, when this clause was finally abolished through a thorough revision of the criminal law. Despite these changes in legislation, the government continued to enact separate laws permitting particular institutions to issue bonds. During the interwar period, however, several bond issues were carried through by private companies without any licence from the Ministry of Finance. The authorities did not interfere with these issues, and from this juncture, there existed a free entry into the bond market. This situation prevailed until the German occupation during the Second World War, when the bond market was strictly regulated again. Table 5.3 gives a general view of the bond market from the turn of the century until 1920.

The capital markets were rather undeveloped through most of the 19th century. A domestic bond market did evolve, however, during the second part of the century. Almost all the loans on the bond market were floated by public institutions such as the Royal Norwegian Mortgage Bank, the municipalities and the Treasury. The buyers of negotiable

Table 5.3 Bearer bonds by debtor and credit sectors, 1899–1920 (Million current NOK)

	1899	1914	1920
Issued by:			
Commercial banks, credit unions, etc.	9	21	34
State banks	119	214	271
The Treasury	199	361	922
Municipalities	58	167	501
Private enterprises	4	63	148
Total bearer bonds loans:	389	826	1876
Owned by:			
Central government	3	18	48
Banks and credit unions, etc.	56	125	484
Insurance	4	22	155
The public	11	43	433
Foreign countries	315	618	756

Source: Skånland (1967).

bonds were mainly financial institutions. But Table 5.3 reveals some important changes in this pattern between the turn of the century and 1920. More than 80 per cent of the total bearer bond loans were floated on foreign capital markets in 1899, while this share was reduced to 40 per cent in 1920. During the same period the bond market expanded substantially, which demonstrates the breakthrough of a domestic market during the First World War. In 1899, only 1 per cent of total loans were issued by private enterprises, while their share was increased to 8 per cent in 1920. This growth shows that financing through the bond market gradually increased in importance for private enterprises. It should be emphasized, however, that private companies still occupied a modest role on this market in 1920. On the other hand the table shows that private persons and firms were almost absent on the investor side of the bond market in 1899. Table 5.3. reveals that this situation changed substantially during the next 20 years and in 1920, private persons and private enterprises owned 57 per cent of total outstanding bearer bonds this year, against only 3.5 per cent in 1899.

The stock market   An organized stock market did not exist in Norway until 1881, when a stock exchange was established at Kristiania Bourse. Until then this bourse was primarily a currency exchange and a market place for the trade in bills of exchange as well as accommodation bills. The first breakthrough for a modern stock market in Norway took place during the boom of the late 1890s, when the trade in shares on The Kristiania Stock Exchange expanded tremendously. The boom ended in the so-called 'Kristiania crash' in 1899, when the stock market collapsed and depression ensued. Activity remained rather low until 1907–8, when a new upswing began.[3]

The equity market and supply of share capital became increasingly important for the financing of Norwegian business from the turn of the century. For business enterprises, issues of shares became one of the most important sources of supply of investment capital (Skånland, 1967: 133). During the period 1900 to 1920, investments in shares became almost as important as bank deposits as a form of saving by the public. The First World War is characterized by an immense expansion of the stock market, and a considerable financial bubble developed (Knutsen, 1991: 52f.). The major object of speculation during the war time boom was financial assets, in particular corporate stocks in shipping as well as industrial shares. The vigorous trading in financial assets dropped a little immediately after the end of the war in November 1918. But the speculative bubble was inflated during the postwar boom until it reached its peak in the summer of 1920. So many insiders left the sinking ship during the early autumn, that a panic became unavoidable. This was soon followed by a stock market crash. The collapse of the stock market was exacerbated by the international postwar slump of 1920–21 and entailed a substantial drop in the market value of the stocks quoted at the Kristiania Bourse Stock Exchange during the period 1920 to 1923.

Credit unions and insurance   In 1907 the Storting passed legislation, permitting credit unions to fund themselves by issuing bearer bonds. At first, the credit unions were engaged in financing real estate, particularly housing. But very soon they expanded their activities to include the financing of shipbuilding, manufacturing plants, etc. The credit unions' growth in assets was rather slow to begin with, hence their lending operations also developed rather slowly. It was not until the late 1930s that they got significant market shares on the credit market. A major obstacle to their development was the lack of adequate funding. For instance, the life-insurance companies were not allowed to buy bonds issued by credit unions, since the public 'Insurance Commission'[4] did not accept them as objects of investment for life-insurance premium reserves. This situation was not changed until 1922, when such bonds were quoted on the Kristiania Stock Exchange. From this juncture, the Insurance Commission accepted credit union bonds.

Ten Norwegian and 12 foreign life-insurance companies were operating in Norway at the eve of the First World War (1912). At the same time 152 non-life insurance companies were in business, of which 73 were Norwegian. A structural change took place in Norwegian insurance from approximately 1910, when the largest companies expanded their operations from one into several fields of insurance. In 1911 legislation was passed, regulating the activities of insurance companies. Premiums on direct insurance rose from 48 million NOK (current prices) in 1912 to 176 million NOK in 1939. The total assets of life-insurance companies increased substantially from 91 million to 936 million NOK during the same period.

Before the First World War almost all the funds accumulated by the insurance companies were invested in mortgages. In 1913, 72 per cent of life-insurance companies' assets were in this form of investment. During the 1920s this share decreased to approximately 50 per cent of the investments. The insurance companies' share of the credit market fluctuated between 3 and 5 per cent of total outstanding loans during the period 1900–14. After a decrease during the war, their credit market share stabilized on the prewar level soon after. But during the last part of the 1930s the life-insurance companies became a lender of consequence on the Norwegian credit market, providing 9–12 per cent of total loans (see Appendix, Table 5.A.1).

Central banking and state banks in Norway on the eve of the First World War

Important changes concerning the function, role and organization of the Bank of Norway were put into effect during the 1890s. The aim was to modernize and centralize the operations and the functions of the Bank. During most of the 19th century the Bank had competed with the savings banks as well as the commercial banks on the credit market. The Bank lent money directly to business clients, and most of the loans were, paradoxically, mortgages. It was not until the 1870s that the mortgages as a share of the bank's total lending sank below 50 per cent.

All earlier legislation referring to the national bank was codified in a new Act on the Bank of Norway, which was passed in 1892. This law was in force for more than 90 years until new legislation was passed in 1985. From 1893 the discount rate was fixed by the central board of directors of the Bank. Until then, it had been set separately by the local branches. From 1897 the central administration of the Bank was moved from Trondheim to the capital, Kristiania. At the same time a more flexible system of reserve requirements for the Bank's note issue was introduced, replacing an older and very inflexible one. During a banking crisis in the 1880s, the Bank had not considered it a task for the national bank to supply the distressed banks with liquidity (Sejersted, 1968). In times of crisis, the Bank considered its main task to protect the currency against depreciation, but during the 'Kristiania Crash' in 1899, when another banking crisis occurred, the Bank for the first time acted as a lender of last resort.

Formally, the Bank of Norway was organized as a joint-stock company, mutually owned by the state and private stockholders. But in reality – by legislation – the national bank was completely controlled by the Storting. In addition to the Bank, there were two state-owned, public banks of significance in operation in Norway on the eve of the First World War. One was The Agricultural Properties Bank of Norway, which had been established in 1903 with a clear, social purpose: to finance housing and outbuildings for smallholders in rural areas. However, the operations of The Royal Norwegian Mortgage Bank was far more important. This bank, established in 1851, was run as an ordinary banking business. The purpose of the bank was to provide the agriculture sector with mortgages. The bank, owned by the state and controlled by the Storting, was given the right to issue bonds. Primarily, the Royal Norwegian Mortgage Bank funded its operation on foreign capital markets. As a lender on the Norwegian credit market, its market share varied between 15 and 20 per cent of total institutional lending before the First World War. This position made the bank a very prominent part of the Norwegian system of credit institutions.

From expansion to crisis: 1914 to the early 1930s

Banking and credit expansion, 1914–20

A severe bout of inflation developed in Norway during the First World War and the subsequent postwar boom. This inflation became particularly strong in Norway, even in comparison with some of the belligerent Powers. As has already been pointed out, rapidly increasing speculation in shares developed during the spring of 1915. The speculation surge was fuelled by easy credit provided by the commercial banks. To a large extent, the driving force underlying this process was a formidable supply of liquidity from the Treasury and the Bank of Norway, caused by the extensive wartime controls and the rather desultory public purchase of supplies. The so-called 'political loans' in Norwegian currency, with the purpose of financing trade agreements with Britain and Germany during the war, intensified inflation substantially. The damage to the Norwegian economy, caused by inflation, wartime controls and fiscal policy, became very serious in the long run.[5]

The commercial banks were more affected by wartime inflation and boom, than any other sector of the economy. For the commercial banks, the massive monetary expansion led to a steep rise in deposits, which in turn entailed an extensive increase in their liquidity. The steep growth in assets made increasing demands on the commercial banks for good investments and yields. On the other hand, the war and the ongoing blockade limited the opportunities for profitable investment projects. But the scarcity of commodities, as well as inflation, increased demand and nominal profits. This put an increasing pressure on the commercial banks to grant loans to finance all kinds of obscure projects and investments. This increased push for lending and demand for loans led to a frivolous financing of a large number of risky projects in shipping, fish export, import trade and manufacturing industry and, in particular, all sorts of surrogate production.

Table 5.A.4 in the appendix presents data showing the expansion in commercial banking during the period 1914–20. According to these data, the growth was considerable. Lending increased substantially, while current drawing accounts at the same time showed an ample growth relative to other types of loans. In 1900 the share of current drawing accounts was 30 per cent of the total lending provided by the commercial banks. In 1914 this share reached 46 per cent of total lending and as much as 73 per cent in 1918. To an increasing extent, the commercial banks engaged in lending on securities. Actually, the banks provided their customers with this type of credit in order to finance speculation on the stock market, especially in the new issues by all the companies which were mushrooming during the war.

The data presented in Table 5.A.4 in the appendix also show a substantial increase in the number of commercial banks during the war. The growth was particularly extensive from 1916. After 1918 the establishment of new banks came to a stop, not least because of the provisional Commercial Bank Act passed by the Storting in March 1918. Norway had no separate legislation on commercial banking until 1918. Everybody had been free to establish a commercial bank. This freedom of trade in commercial banking had even comprised the right to establish joint-stock banks.

The provisional Act on commercial banking now made it compulsory to have a licence from the Treasury in order to establish and operate a new bank or even a new local branch, if this was located outside the municipality where the bank had its headquarters. The original aim of the liberal government in proposing this provisional legislation was to curtail the unchecked growth in number of new commercial banks, which occurred during the war. The parliamentary debate on the proposal, however, was primarily concentrated upon whether or not a concession should be compulsory in order to establish a branch office. A clause implying this was proposed and the motion was carried unanimously on this point. The mover, representing the conservative party, argued that the establishment of local branches of large banks based in the capital represented a major threat to local business interests.[6] This clearly reflected the strong local patriotism that characterized Norwegian political life, even on a national level in the Storting. It was an expression of the strong local opposition to the development of major banks with a nationwide network of local branches.

In contrast to the amalgamation movement in commercial banking in several other European countries during this period, the decentralized structure of the banking system was maintained and even reinforced in Norway during the First World War and the following years. Every small town and local competing business groups within these towns were striving for their own bank, causing a substantial growth in the number of small local banks. This development was made possible by attitudes and ideologies deeply rooted in Norwegian culture. These attitudes and values favoured small units and local business, and the power of concentrated financial institutions was distrusted. Policy choices based on popular ideologies and values like this contributed to the fragmentation of the Norwegian banking system.

Although the new legislation entailed an end to the establishment of new banks and the credit expansion stagnated, the commercial banks' lending still increased by 10 per cent each year during the years 1918–20. This reflected the postwar boom, which developed until the crash occurred during the autumn of 1920.

The postwar slump and the banking crisis of the 1920s

The commercial banks' risk exposure increased heavily during the wartime and postwar boom. When the exceptional underlying conditions for the development in commercial banking during the First World War disappeared and the postwar slump occurred, both the real economy and the banking system were dramatically affected. For more than a decade following 1920, the Norwegian economy was characterized by protracted cyclical and financial crises.

Nicolay Rygg was appointed the Bank of Norway's new governor from 1 November, 1920. The main task from the beginning – as Mr Rygg understood it – was to curb inflation. In tune with the prevalent contemporary monetary theory, governor Rygg considered a contractive monetary policy to be necessary to reach that goal. The supply of money and credit had to be reduced (Rygg, 1950: 21). Based on a strong wish to 'return to normality', it was a major objective to Mr Rygg to re-establish the gold standard, which had been suspended since the early days of the war, and fix Norwegian currency to its prewar gold parity. This deflationary policy was approved by the political authorities (Rygg, 1950: 19 ff, 77 ff; Hanisch, 1979: 241 f.). The postwar slump and the Bank of Norway's change to a deflationary monetary policy occurred simultaneously, and triggered a financial crisis in Norway. During 1921 it gradually became obvious that a serious banking crisis was developing, and this banking crisis became very extensive and protracted.[7]

The banking crisis of the 1920s developed through several distinctive phases (Knutsen, 1991; Nordvik, 1991). The first phase was the period from 1915 until autumn 1920, characterized by boom, credit expansion and the establishment of a large number of new commercial banks. The second phase lasted from autumn 1920 to 1921. This phase represents the 'turning point', since it was then that the first sign of an emerging banking crisis occurred. The first indication of a financial crisis is very often a collapsing bank (Kindleberger, 1989). Already during 1920, the Bank of Norway had to engage in support actions for six distressed banks. In particular, serious problems occurred for a commercial bank by the name of Søndenfjeldske privatbank in Kristiansand. This bank had provided the Kristiansand Nickel Refinery and the British American

Nickel Corporation with large business loans, but as a result of the collapse of the international nickel market during the autumn of 1920, these enterprises were unable to fulfil their obligations to the bank. All six faltering banks were exposed to depositor-runs and they all met with severe liquidity problems. Later on, most of the faltering banks turned out to be, not only illiquid but even insolvent.

Most of the banks getting into trouble in this initial phase of the banking crisis were banks located along the coastal line, mainly occupied with loans to shipping and fish export. Some had also provided local manufacturing firms with loans. These maritime-related businesses were very soon affected by the international postwar slump, which in turn led to bank failures. Bad loans were a major reason for the banks' trouble. But the deflation and the deflationary policy were also of vital importance in developing insolvency. In addition, the structure of the banking system contributed decisively in aggravating the banking crisis. All the banks that got into trouble during 1920–21 were small provincial banks, which had overburdened themselves with loans to faltering industrial clients.

The banking crisis became worse during 1921. This year, the Bank of Norway had to organize rescue operations for 38 troubled commercial banks and 10 savings banks. Even the Storting was soon involved in supporting action for distressed banks, and granted 15 million NOK in order to prop up faltering banks. In 1922 the Storting granted another 25 million NOK.

The third phase comprises the years from 1922 to 1928, and is characterized by a partial breakdown of the banking system. Several of the largest banks in the capital now began to falter. The banking crisis reached such an extent that the stability of the financial system was threatened, and foreign trust in Norwegian financial institutions was jeopardized. During this phase, three of the six largest banks in Norway experienced problems so great that they later had to close down. These banks were Centralbanken for Norge, Andresens Bank-Bergens Kreditbank and Den Norske Handelsbank. The authorities' bank-support policy was changed during the spring of 1923. Until then, assistance to distressed banks was carried out in the form of *ad hoc* rescue actions. The main feature of these policies was the supply of support loans from the Bank of Norway and the Treasury, combined with loan guarantees issued by the Storting in order to raise loans to banks in trouble. As already mentioned, the Storting also granted money to be put into the faltering banks as deposits in order to strengthen their liquidity. The ultimate aim was to reconstruct the banks., however, the bank-support policy became too expensive to the authorities and largely unsuccessful. The bank-support policy reflected a wish by the authorities to protect jobs and production. But governor Rygg became increasingly reluctant to let the central bank provide the massive rescue loans that were needed. Being the main executor of the deflationary policies in Norway, he probably viewed the extensive and growing supply of liquidity to the faltering banks as contradictory to the goal returning to gold at the prewar parity. The net supply of liquidity from the central bank to the banking system during the period 1921–23 was almost 200 million NOK. This certainly does not look like a deflationary policy, but this increase in emergency loans to the banks was at the same time compensated by a corresponding reduction of loans to other borrowers, primarily municipalities and private enterprises. Evidence for this is presented in the Appendix (Table 5.A.5), surveying the Bank of Norway's lending to the banks. The figures show an extensive increase in loans to the banks, reaching a maximum of 476 million NOK in July 1923. At the same time, as the data show, the banks took an increasingly larger share of the central bank's total lending. By 31 January 1920, the banks' share of total loans provided by the Bank of Norway was only one-third. This share increased to as much as 87 per cent of total loans in November 1924.

As the banking crisis evolved, it became increasingly difficult for the Bank of Norway to decide whether a faltering bank should be supported or not. In most of the cases, it was very difficult to get a realistic judgement of the bank's position. But although the authorities wished to alter the bank-support policy, this could not mean leaving the banks to their own devices. Mr Rygg viewed an uncontrolled wave of bankruptcies as a disaster for the Norwegian banking system. The task of limiting the decreasing confidence in the Norwegian financial system among international financial circles was a major concern for him in this situation, as it was for the government.

The solution to this problem was searched for in legislation. On the initiative of the central bank and governor Rygg, the authorities passed the so-called 'Bank Administration Act' of 24 March 1923, in order to prevent an uncontrolled breakdown of the banking system. According to this law, troubled banks could seek protection from creditors and avoid bankruptcy by demanding to be subject to public administration. If this was accepted by the authorities, the bank was placed under the supervision of the central bank. A new board of directors was appointed by the Bank of Norway and former deposits as well as old debts were 'frozen'. The administered bank was now permitted to accept new deposits, which were given priority over earlier deposits. In the short run, the intention was to protect temporarily illiquid but solid banks against panics and depositor-runs. From a long-term perspective, the goal was to reconstruct sound banks or, in the worse case; liquidate them in an organized way.

This reconstruction policy turned out to be very unsuccessful. Most of the administered banks did not get on their feet again. In addition, they became a problem for the banks in free operation, because the administered banks attracted deposits away from them. The reason for this was the public guarantee given to new deposits in the banks under public administration. The depositors of course preferred to put their savings into banks, where deposits were guaranteed by the state! This created liquidity problems for the banks in free operation. Against this background the policy towards the commercial banks was changed again. Until the summer of 1925 the reconstruction line was followed by the authorities. From that juncture, however, the course was changed to a policy of liquidation of banks under public administration and establishment of new banks to replace those which had collapsed (Nordvik, 1992: 12). The banking crisis of the 1920s became severe and extensive and shocked the banking system in Norway to its very foundations. Altogether 129 commercial banks were dissolved during the interwar years, and their total losses for the period 1920–28 is estimated at 1 500 million NOK (Knutsen, 1991).

When the Storting passed the provisional Act on commercial banking in 1918, it also granted money in order to have a committee draw up a report on permanent commercial banking legislation. The local patriotic opposition to branch banking was incorporated in the work of the banking legislation preparatory commission, which presented a proposal to new legislation on commercial banks in March 1921. Based on this report, the Ministry of Finance presented its proposal in the spring of 1923[8] and on 4 April 1924 the first comprehensive legislation on joint-stock banking was passed. The law was not enacted in direct response to the ongoing banking crisis. The crisis had a considerable impact on the content of the law, however, and consequently the law emphasized the protection of depositor interests in particular. Legislation on savings banks was also thoroughly revised in 1924. Finally, legislation creating a new regulatory commission, which comprised both commercial and savings banks, was enacted. Thus a new regulatory system for the banking sector had emerged in Norway. With the exception of some minor revisions, the legislation on commercial and savings banks remained unchanged until 1961.

The banking system 1930–50: reconstruction, consolidation and the movement away from market mechanisms

Structural changes on the capital and credit markets in the interwar years

A major consequence of the banking crisis was the diminishing role of the commercial banks within the financial system. Their share of the credit market was reduced from 60 per cent of total lending in 1920 to 30 per cent in 1930. During the same period the savings banks increased their share of total lending from 26 per cent to 35 per cent (see Appendix, Tables 5.A.1–5.A.3). But these relative changes between commercial and savings banks must be related to the fact that the role of the entire banking system was diminishing relative to other financial institutions during the interwar years. Figure 5.1, which gives an overall picture of the changes in the credit market structure between 1910 and the Second World War, clearly reveals this trend. Insurance and pension funds grew considerably in importance as suppliers of credit after 1920. The most important change, however, is the remarkable increase in the market share of the state or public banks from 12 per cent of the loan market in 1920 to 26 per cent in 1940. By this year, there were nine Norwegian state-owned public banks in operation , of which five were established during the inter-war years.[9] The basis for the development of a public bank system was political efforts to secure the supply of credit to particular sectors of economic life according to regional, industrial or social criteria. A new semi-public bank was initiated and put into operation by the new Labour government in 1935–36.[10] The major task of this new bank, The Manufacturing Bank of Norway Ltd (Aktieselskapet Den Norske Industribank), was to provide manufacturing industry with credit.

The extensive changes in the structure of the capital and credit markets is clearly revealed when we focus the development on the bond market.

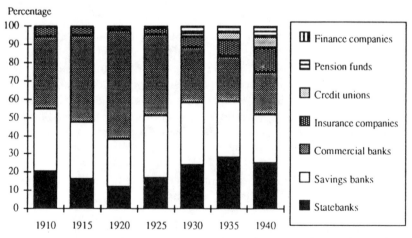

Figure 5.1 Financial institutions' markets shares on the credit market, 1910–40. (*Source:* Appendix, Table 5.A.1)

In 1920, the outstanding bearer bond debt was 20 per cent of total outstanding debt at the year-end. This share rose to 44.5 per cent in 1930. Issues of bearer bonds had increased by more than eight times between 1914 and 1921. After a substantial drop until 1923, the floating of new loans against bearer bonds stabilized at a rather low level for some years. From 1933, however, the issue of bonds rose rapidly again. Since the stock market nearly collapsed during the years following 1920, and actually dried up completely as a source for corporate finance during the interwar years, the importance of the bond market increased substantially as a capital source during this period.

The public banks owned by the state were still the major borrowers on the bond market during the interwar years. In 1939, the state was responsible for 70 per cent of total bond debt. The bond debt of the municipalities expanded heavily from 1914 to 1926. The main reason for this was the municipalities' extensive investments in hydroelectric power plants during this period. This strong public activity limited the possibilities for private enterprises to float loans on the bond market and the commercial banks were responsible for a tiny share of the bond debt during most of the period under consideration. The credit unions, however, increased their role on the bond market during the 1930s. Private enterprises never became a major issuer of bearer bonds. But on average they represented 7–8 per cent of the bond debt during the interwar period and the private sector as a whole, increased its role as a borrower in the bond marked.

From Table 5.3 we learned that as little as 1 per cent of bearer bonds were issued by private enterprises in 1899. If banks and credit unions are included, the share was approximately 3 per cent. In 1920, this share increased to 10 per cent and in 1939 to almost 18 per cent. Since the volume of bond issue increased continuously during the 1930s from 100 million NOK in 1932 to almost 800 million NOK in 1938, and since the supply of loans decreased both relatively and absolutely during these years, we must conclude that the bond market grew in importance as a source for industrial finance. So, to a certain extent, this development

Table 5.4 Bearer bonds in NOK, percentage of total bearer bond debt

	1899	1914	1920	1926	1930	1939	1945
Bearer bonds, NOK	12	22	64	71	70	66	82

Source: Skånland (1967).

compensated for the failure of the banking system, as well as the collapse of the stock market, during this period.

As pointed out already, Norwegian bonds were mainly sold on foreign capital markets until the First World War. Table 5.4, however, demonstrates that the domestic bearer bond debt had reached a share of approximately two-thirds of total bond debt in 1920, and this share was stabilized at a slightly higher level for the remainder of the interwar period.

Some additional remarks on the development of the banking system in the 1930s

It has been demonstrated already that the role of the banking system as suppliers of credit – taking both commercial and savings banks into consideration – was reduced substantially during the interwar period. The volume of credit provided by the commercial banks was halved. Also, the number of banks in operation was reduced by 46 per cent from 192 in 1920 to 104 in 1940. The number of savings banks, however, increased from 562 to 605 over the same period. This indicates primarily a weakening of the commercial banks' position in the financial system. Indeed, this trend is clearly demonstrated when we analyse the development in assets. It should also be noted that the value of Norwegian currency rose substantially during the period under consideration. In Table 5.5 total assets in commercial banks and savings banks are presented, both in current NOK as well as in constant 1938 prices.

These data confirm what we have already suggested: the reduction of

Table 5.5   Total assets in commercial and savings banks, figures in current and constant prices (1938=100) (1000 NOK)

Current NOK:	1920	1939	Change in per cent
Savings banks	2 253	2 267	+ 0.6
Commercial banks	5 461	1 855	– 66.0
total assets	7 714	4 122	– 46.6
Constant 1938 NOK:			
Savings banks	1 300	2 238	+ 72.2
Commercial banks	3 151	1 831	– 41.9
total assets	4 451	4 069	– 8.6

Source: Historical statistics (1978).

assets in the banking system as a whole during the interwar years was exclusively caused by a dramatic drop in commercial banks' assets. At the same time the data on asset values measured in constant prices reveal that the savings banks strengthened their position relative to the commercial banks. The decrease in the commercial banks' assets was caused by several factors. First of all, the banks deliberately reduced their assets in order to reduce their risk exposure. The large difference on interest rates between deposits in commercial banks relative to other parts of the monetary and capital markets, which developed during the interwar years, was also an important factor. A third major cause was the fact that savers lost confidence in the commercial banks because of the banking crisis of the 1920s, and hence preferred other alternatives for savings and personal investments.

A banking crisis of the same dimensions as that of the 1920s did not reoccur during the 1930s, even though two out of the three largest Norwegian commercial banks got into trouble during the years of severe depression, 1931–32. Both Bergens Privatbank and Den norske Creditbank encountered liquidity problems and depositor runs during the autumn of 1931, and had to ask the authorities to sanction a moratorium, which was accepted. The Bank of Norway and the political authorities declared full support for the two banks, and they were successfully refinanced during the moratorium period. In contrast to what happened during the 1920s, the support from the Bank of Norway and the authorities at this time was unambiguous and without hesitation (Nordvik, 1990).

Debate on the question of regulating the rate of interest during the 1930s

A representative of the Agrarian Party criticized the commercial banks (In the Storting in March 1928) asserting that they earned excessive interest rate margins.[11] The idea underlying this criticism was that the difference between the interest rate on deposits and the interest rate on loans was too great. The Agrarian Party also moved that the government should be responsible for having a report drawn up on the subject. Such a report was produced by the Banking Regulatory Agency on behalf of the government, and presented to the Storting in April 1929.[12] But the Liberal government repudiated any need for legislative action.

The Norwegian Farmers' Association (Norges Bondelag) put forward a proposal for a preliminary law in January 1933, aiming to give the government authority to administer the interest rate on several types of loans.[13] This proposition was discussed in the Storting during the spring of 1933. The most far-reaching of the initiatives to regulate interest rates by law was a proposal from the Labour Party, demanding a 4 per cent p.a. interest rate ceiling on loans.[14] For tactical reasons, the social-liberal government followed up the different initiatives and made a proposal to the Storting on a preliminary law, advocating a less extreme alternative.[15] This was to be an enabling law, giving the government the authority to regulate interest-rates whenever it felt this was necessary.

The Labour Party proposal did not obtain a majority vote in the Storting, which thus rejected it. The Conservative party was opposed to adopt any legislation at all in this matter, but several MPs across party boundaries argued in favour of interest rate reductions, and consequently a new preliminary law was passed. This law gave the government the authority to fix the interest rate on loans provided by commercial and savings banks.[16] However, this could only be done after consultation with, and statements from, the Norwegian Bankers' Association, the Central Association of Savings Banks, the Bank of Norway and the Banking Regulatory Agency. This preliminary law of 29 June 1934 was never used by the social-liberal Mowinckel government, nor by the succeeding Labour government. In 1936, another law was enacted which put a substantial tax on all deposits in banks! This law contributed to the drop in the commercial banks´assets.

The banks took their own measures to restrict competition and curtail political pressure during the inter war years. In the summer of 1921, the commercial banks in Kristiania made a confidential agreement in order to cut down the interest rate on deposits.[17] In the original proposal for the new joint-stock bank Act, which was presented in 1923, the government was given authority to fix the interest rate on both deposits and loans.[18] But the proposal was met with fierce opposition on this point from the Norwegian Bankers' Association. They argued that legal regulation of the interest rates was unnecessary, with reference to their own agreement and cooperation with the Bank of Norway to monitor the implementation of it. In 1924, new private agreements were established by the banks.

The interest rate on loans, however, was not regulated by private agreement until 1930. In November 1930 the 'Oslo-agreement on minimum interest rates on certain loans' was arranged by ten commercial banks in Oslo.[19] Loans on bills of exchange, 'bill bonds' and current drawing accounts were regulated by this agreement. This agreement among the Oslo banks, as well as the former agreements mentioned above, had an impact on the interest rates on a nationwide level.

Some main features of the Norwegian system of financial institutions, 1945–80

From credit rationing to deregulation: a survey of Norwegian monetary and credit policy, 1945 –80

Some important changes in the financial system occurred during the German occupation. The tendencies towards increased public control over financial institutions and financial markets, which developed in the 1930s, were actually reinforced during the war. In the beginning of the occupation, the so-called 'Administration Council'[20] (Kofoed, 1940: 184 f.) passed resolutions on 11 May and 28 May 1940, stipulating a maximum rate of interest on deposits as well as loans. In July, 1940, the price cartel agreement between the Oslo banks, already mentioned above, was revised and prolonged. The 'Reichskommisariat' and the Nazi-controlled Ministry of Finance also took action to have the stock market and the bond market regulated. These changes had a great impact on the development of the financial institutions and the capital markets during the postwar period. The reconstruction period of the 1940s was characterized by a comprehensive system of economic planning, based on strict and direct regulations. Investment was given priority over consumption, while resources were distributed to different sectors of industry in a planned way. Controls were imposed upon industry and investment. The system was managed by allotment of quotas and rationing of most types of goods, from bricks to consumer goods. The whole arrangement depended heavily on strict import controls.

However, most of the controls were gradually removed during the early 1950s and the dirigiste version of planning was abandoned. But the government did not give up its ambition to plan and manage economic development. The system of direct regulations had been giving scope for microlevel regulations, but when it was partly dismantled, a shift to the use of more indirect measures in economic policy was implemented.

The Labour party government regarded sustained economic growth as a necessity in order to achieve its goals of full employment and the building up of a welfare state. Modernization through industrialization was seen as a primary task to enable this. A comprehensive industrial drive was considered the main tool to build up the nation's productive capacity, particularly in sectors of expected comparative advantage like construction of hydroelectric power plants and development of the energy-intensive electrochemical and metallurgical industries. A precondition for the implementation of an industrial strategy was – according to the Labour party leadership – the power and ability to manage flows of capital and thus be able to control the allocation of credit to Norwegian industry in a planned way. The objective of the Government was both to play a preponderant role in the allocation of private investment as well as to secure the funding of the state banks.

Consequently, however, it became apparent that the financial system had to be changed in order to accomplish these tasks. Through changes in Norwegian monetary and credit policies, which were introduced during the early 1950s, a new financial regulatory regime was established. The Norwegian regulatory system gradually took on all the important features which characterized a system based on the ambition of extensively governing the economy. A cornerstone in the new system was the supply of low-priced credit to selected projects and firms who conformed to the government's economic strategy. This policy was based on price control through administratively fixed interest rates, which entailed a system of credit rationing. In 1953, a new preliminary law authorized the authorities to set the maximum interest rates on loans and deposits. Furthermore, Section 3 of the law provided for the regulation of the bond market, by giving the government the power to determine the total volume of bond issues and to decide their issue terms as well as their distribution among various borrowers. The implementation of this discretionary system of credit allocation was accompanied by additional regulatory efforts:

- Extensive currency regulation.
- Strong restrictions to entry through a system of concession, prohibition of foreign institutions entering financial markets ,etc.
- Introduction of a comprehensive investment control for banks and insurance companies.

These extensive regulations had a decisive impact on the operations of the banks and other financial institutions and markets during the postwar period.

Between 1951 and 1965, the governing of interest rates and credit and capital flows took place within a democratic, corporatistic framework. A Joint Consultation Council (or the Cooperation Committee) was established in January 1951, where representatives from the commercial and savings banks met with the authorities. Representatives from the life insurance industry were also coopted in 1955. During the first four years of its existence, the Joint Consultation Council passed resolutions, laying down general guidelines for the lending and investment policies of the banks. In principle the banks were free to follow these instructions, but the authorities both considered and referred to them as 'agreements'. From 1955, however, a system based upon one-year binding agreements was adopted. These annual agreements laid down the rules for the lending policies the banks were obliged to carry through the following year, and established a system of direct quotas on bank lending. These agreements also stipulated the amount of government securities the financial institutions were obliged to buy.

Why did the commercial banks, as well as the other financial institutions, allow such a strict regulatory regime to emerge during the 1950s without tangible resistance? The main reason seems to be the banks' preference for regulation through agreement in contrast to enforcement of credit policy by legal measures, which was an alternative option for the authorities if the financial institutions did not want to cooperate. As a 'return service' for the voluntary cooperation of the banks, the authorities desisted from the enactment of a new, extensive regulatory legislation (Eide and Holli, 1980). Actually, the Ministry of Finance had a primary preference for legal measures – in combination with agreements – in order to facilitate the enforcement of the decisions on credit policy, when agreement could not be reached. The decisive factor underlying the maintenance of the agreement system through almost 15 years, was the position of the Bank of Norway. The Bank of Norway played a major role in the work of the Joint Consultation Council and in the negotiations taking place there, hence the Central Bank's preferences for managing the monetary and credit policies by a system of agreements. In this context, the maintenance of the agreement system was seen as a key to secure the Bank of Norway's strong influence on the shaping of the monetary and credit policies (Graff Hagen, 1977: 112).

No significant disagreement stemming from the work of the Joint Consultation Council was exposed to the public until 1958–59. Discord and conflicts, however, were simmering beneath the surface. During the autumn of 1958, the Ministry of Finance prepared a bill imposing obligatory bond holding requirements on life insurance companies and put the matter before the Council. The representatives of the financial institutions responded to this initiative with a proposal to appoint a committee with the task of drafting a broad report on the use of monetary and credit instruments. A major motivation for this suggestion was probably to have legislation postponed. The Ministry of Finance asked the Joint Consultation Council to elaborate such a report:

> on policy instruments and their use in the monetary and credit policy, which – on the basis of Norwegian economic and institutional conditions – might be of current interest, including bond market transactions, liquidity reserve requirements and obligatory holdings of Norwegian Treasury Bills.[21]

The Joint Consultation Council set up a working committee immediately, and experts were attached to its work. A preliminary draft was discussed in the working committee during May 1959. This debate revealed strong differences of opinion on the major topics under consideration among the members of the committee as well as between the experts.[22] There were two major conflicting views. On the one hand there was a view emphasizing the establishment of an unregulated capital market, and to have interest rates determined by this market. This view also emphasized that liquidity management by open market operations carried out by the Bank of Norway should be introduced and that there was no need for bond investment regulation. On the other hand, there was the view stressing the necessity to regulate the volume of credit through direct liquidity management and the setting of maximum interest rates on loans. This view even contained a preference for bond investment regulations and regarded bond issue regulations as a necessity.[23] In 1950, the government set up a committee to prepare a comprehensive revision of the 1924 legislation on both commercial and savings banks, and the committee's draft was submitted in December 1958. One of the proposals for amendments created a great deal of discord among the members of the Joint Consultation Council. The bank legislation committee proposed publicly appointed members of the commercial banks' board of directors and of the savings banks councils. This proposition created turmoil among the representatives of the financial institutions in the Joint Consultation Council. The representatives of the Norwegian Bankers' Association passed severe censure on the proposition and stated that such an Act would harm the banks' relations to their depositors and clients, as well as their connections to international financial circles. The representatives of the commercial banks concluded that

> such a far-reaching encroachment in the commercial banks' independence would be irreconcilable with a continuation of the cooperation, which hitherto has been carried out in the Joint Consultation Council between the authorities and the credit institutions.[24]

The outcome of this conflict was a compromise. The government desisted from the proposition of publicly appointed members of the commercial banks' board of directors. The negotiations entailed a Framework Agreement for 1960–64 between the government and the credit institutions, hence the agreement system continued for another five-year period.

Finally, a new public committee was appointed in order to have the principles of monetary and credit policies further discussed. The committee's report was submitted in 1963. A growing dissatisfaction with the functioning of the regulations and the lending quota arrangements emerged among both the authorities and the financial institutions during the early 1960s. Consequently, the whole system of agreements was undermined and the financial institutions were regulated by comprehensive legislation in 1965, based on the report mentioned above. This new Monetary and Credit Policy Act was an enabling law, which gave extensive discretionary power to the government to impose monetary and credit controls on the financial institutions.

The former agreement system had attempted to govern the supply of credit by the regulation of quantity. The new law, on the contrary, attempted to regulate the ability of the banks to provide loans by governing their liquidity. Moreover, the plan was to govern more directly the remaining institutions such as the non-life insurance companies and finance companies. A clause in the new law made it obligatory for banks and insurance companies to hold a certain percentage of growth in assets each year in state or state guaranteed bonds. This made it possible for the authorities to canalize a substantial share of insurance and bank savings into the Treasury, hence the flows of credit and investment capital could be allocated according to the priorities of the government. These bond holding requirements were used for the first time in 1969 and remained in force until 1985. In addition, regulations stipulating the maximum rate of interest were included in The Monetary and Credit Policy Act as a policy tool. The Act provided several additional monetary and credit instruments such as liquidity reserve requirements, supplementary reserves, deposits in the central bank against increases in foreign liabilities, direct regulation of lending and the regulation of bond issue. Section 15 of the Act provided for the latter instrument.

From the formal introduction of the new Act early in 1966, the government attempted to implement a policy combining liquidity regulation with the maintenance of interest rates at a low level. The years 1965–69 were a period of transition, when different clauses of the new law were tested. In the autumn of 1965 a 'credit budget' coordinated with the annual national budget was made public for the first time. The purpose of this 'credit budget' was to establish a ceiling for the supply of credit to the public. Basically, the credit market was seen as divided in submarkets, which could be governed almost independently. It should be emphasized, however, that the Norwegian administration – building on the work of the Norwegian economist Frisch and his students – had delivered the first full-blown annual national budgets from 1947 onwards (Pekkarinen, 1989). By the mid-1950s, credit flows had been included in a comprehensive survey of the economic outlook and economic policy. Until 1965, however, the 'credit budget' was primarily used as an unofficial planning tool by the Ministry of Finance.

The maintenance of a 'low level interest rates' policy and a credit rationing system led to imbalance and unintentional structural changes in the credit market during the 1960s. The government launched some measures during the autumn of 1969, in order to curb a steep increase in the credit institutions' supply of loans. For the first time since 1955 the discount rate was raised from 3.5 per cent to 4.5 per cent. During the 1970s the interest rate level increased gradually, but did not keep up with inflation. Hence, an increasingly negative real interest rate developed during these years.

The post-war monetary and credit policy, hence the financial regulatory regime, affected the structure of the financial markets substantially. The credit rationing system gave impulses to institutions to evade and circumvent the interest rate and credit regulations. When new regulations were imposed on a group of institutions, this stimulated the establishment of new, unregulated financial institutions. In the same way, unregulated submarkets emerged, providing for credit outside the regulated markets. The main objective of the monetary and credit policies and regulations during the 1960s was to obtain a rigid governance of bank lending. But, while the authorities strived to gain control over the credit flow from banks, new problems emerged in unregulated areas. An illustrating example is the growth and expansion of non-bank financial institutions, which were not a subject of regulation.

One consequence of the prevailing credit rationing system was the expansion of unregulated or so-called 'grey market' loans. The loans in this market were mediated by brokers outside regulated institutions such as the banks. The public was both lender and borrower. This market had already started to expand during the early 1950s, when the lending of banks and insurance companies was limited by quotas. It was not, however, until the 1970s that this unregulated loan market expanded substantially. Loans backed with a guarantee issued by a bank or an insurance company, were doubled from 1 600 million NOK in 1974 to 3 200 million NOK in 1979. In 1979, 66 per cent of all loan guarantees were issued by life insurance companies. The authorities tried to stop the leakage in several ways. Among other things direct regulation was imposed on the financial companies lending in July 1970. This of course affected the insurance companies' operations on the credit market, since they were widely involved in such companies. In addition new forms of credit market instruments emerged.

Thus, the actions of the authorities during the period 1970–77 were increasingly consistent with an ambition to manage the whole ambit of financial institutions and markets, not only the banking sector and the bond market. When the authorities started to use the 'credit budget' as a major tool in governing the credit market, a substantial deviation between the planned and the real annual credit flow was revealed.

Actually, this happened every year. It appeared to be very difficult to reach the annual goal for total credit supply, when the interest rate mechanism was excluded.

In the autumn of 1977, the interest rate policy was altered and the fixing of interest rates on bank loans by the government was abolished. Also, the authorities announced that interest rates on the bond market gradually were to be determined by the market. But the government had no intention of giving up the ambition to manage the credit markets by the 'credit budget'. The adjustment of interest rate regulations led to a rise in the nominal interest rate level during 1977–78. But in order to curb heavy inflation a price and income freeze was launched in September 1978 and the interest rates on all types of loans were regulated by law. Neither was the bond market liberalized. In autumn 1978, however, the government decided to have a committee report drafted on the subject of interest rates. In November 1979 the report was submitted, proposing a radical break with the postwar 'low interest rate' policy. The report pointed out a range of different arguments on the necessity of letting the market mechanism determine interest rate levels in financial markets, and thus increase competition on the credit market.[25]

However, the prevalent regulatory regime was still basically unchanged. The authorities continued a monetary and credit policy, depending on strict regulation of financial markets and institutions. This policy was deeply rooted in a politically determined interest rate level based on the so-called 'interest rate declarations' issued by the Minister of Finance. But the leakages continued. Against this background the credit market and the financial institutions were particularly strictly regulated from 1981 until 1983. During these years, more regulations were put to use than in any year after 1965 (Bergo, 1989). But in spite of this sharpening of monetary and credit policies, the discrepancy between planned and real supply of credit increased dramatically during the 1980s.

During the 1950s and early 1960s, the aim of monetary and credit policies had been dual: on the one hand, the government wanted policy tools to carry out Keynesian demand management. On the other hand, the Labour party government viewed monetary and credit policy as a means to control the financial system, and thus as a major instrument to allocate economic resources. Even in the Joint Consultation Council the parties involved were unanimous on such an understanding. In the proposition to the Framework Agreement for 1960–4 between the government and the credit institutions, we find formulations supporting this interpretation:

purpose of the monetary and credit policy to provide for such a
distribution of credit on sectors, industries and regions, that – from
the point of view of the industrial policy – a balanced growth can be
maintained.[26]

In the historiography of the Norwegian monetary and credit policy, there
has been a clear trend to overemphasize the Keynesian demand
management aspect of Norwegian monetary and credit policy, and thus
regard it as a means of macroeconomic stabilization. Consequently, the
moulding of the financial system as a tool to achieve microeconomic
planning has been underplayed. I would stress, however, that the basic
purpose of the monetary and credit policy changed during the 1970s.
Macroeconomic stabilization, not microeconomic planning and resource
allocation, gradually became the sole reason to maintain the monetary
and credit policy, provided for by the 1965 Act. Unstable currency rates,
inflation problems and the recession following the OPEC crisis in 1973
were the driving forces underlying this process.

Despite the trend to even stricter regulation of the financial market
during the early 1980s, the changes in interest rate policies in 1977, and
the committee report on future interest rate policy in 1979, represented
a watershed in Norwegian monetary and credit policies. An ideological
and political process was initiated, resulting in a comprehensive
deregulation process taking place from 1984 to 1990. All price control
through administratively fixed interest rates, as well as every quantitative
regulation of the lending of the credit institutions, was abolished during
this period. Foreign banks were allowed to be established in Norway,
and a concession from the government was no longer needed for a bank
to establish new branches. The bond market was liberalized, and the
investment controls of banks and insurance companies were abolished.
In 1990, the currency regulation was abolished as well.

A survey of the financial institutions' market share in the credit market

Figure 5.2 demonstrates the development of the long-term trends on the
credit market, showing the market shares of the different financial
institutions. These data present a credit market undergoing considerable
change. The major trends may be summarized as follows.

First, we emphasize that both the commercial and the savings banks'
weight on the loan market was reduced during the 1960s and 1970s.
Actually, the market share of the private banking system decreased by
more than 10 per cent. Second, the insurance companies' market share
on the loan market increased to a 15 per cent peak in 1965. Then their
market share gradually decreased to a level around 9.5 per cent during
the 1980s. A major reason for this was the life insurance companies'

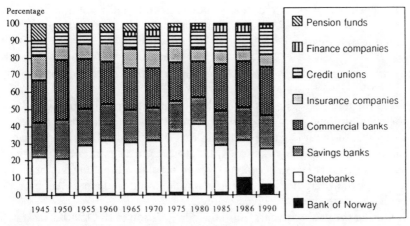

Figure 5.2   Financial institutions' market shares on the credit market, 1945–90. (*Source:* Appendix, Table 5.A.1)

market share gradually decreased to a level around 9.5 per cent during the 1980s. A major reason for this was the life insurance companies' obligation to invest their annual increase in assets in state and state-guaranteed bonds. This was as high as 60 per cent in 1978. Credit unions and finance companies (here considered collectively) also increased their shares substantially from 8.5 per cent in 1950 to 21.5 per cent in 1988. The growth was particularly steep after 1985 for this group of institutions and above all applies to the credit unions. Third, there is a marked trend that the state banks increased their market share substantially during the period 1945 to 1980. This development reflects the important position the government assigned to the state banks in the financial system. In conjunction with the deregulation process after 1980, however, the position of the state banks in the credit market was substantially weakened. In 1950, the state banks' share of total lending was 20 per cent, and this share increased to almost 40 per cent in 1980. In 1988, however, the share had decreased to 20 per cent. The state bank system's greatest expansion took place in the last part of the 1970s. This is related to an extensive and wide-ranging countercyclical economic policy, which was put into effect during these years.

After a long-lasting decline during the years from 1920 to 1945, the domestic supply of loans on the credit market increased continuously during the postwar period. The growth shows an almost exponential pattern. But there are also periods with marked trend breaks. We find such a turning point in 1984, when the supply of credit increased dramatically in comparison with previous years. The banks, and in the development occurred again, and the total credit volume sank by almost 42 per cent. With this dramatic drop, a deep and protracted banking and financial crisis started in Norway.

Some remarks on the postwar development of the capital markets

From the mid-1950s net issues on the bond market (both directly and by the credit unions) represented 10 per cent of total annual supply of credit to public and municipalities. During the 1960s and 1970s, the floating of loans on the bond market provided from 13 to 17 per cent of the total supply of credit. The government led and regulated bond market became an important credit source for manufacturing industry. Additional evidence on this point is given below.

During the postwar years, until the deregulation in the 1980s, the state was the dominating borrower on the bond market. Besides, the government decided which private enterprise, municipality, etc. should be permitted to float bond loans on the domestic bond market, as well as on foreign markets, according to the bond issue regulations. The Ministry of Finance made its final decision on the recommendation of the Bank of Norway. A cooperative body, comprising members appointed by the government together with central bank officers, it advised on the issue of bearer bond loans.[27] The sale of the low interest rate bonds was secured by the agreement system described above, and later on by the bond investment requirements imposed on the banks and the life insurance companies.

The stock market, playing such a dominant role during the period 1900–20, represented 9–10 per cent of annual supply of investment capital to public and municipalities. From the mid-1960s until the early 1980s, this share dropped to approximately 5 per cent. Actually, the issue of shares was of secondary importance as a source for investment capital during the post war period. However, both issues of shares and trade on the secondary market expanded substantially during the 1980s. The traded volume on the Oslo Stock Exchange rose from 7 000 million NOK in 1983 to 30 000 million NOK in 1985 (Synnestvedt, 1988). In spite of the stock market crash in October 1987, stock market trade continued on a high level.

A survey of the development of the commercial and savings banks during the postwar period

Structural changes in the banking system, 1945–90   Table 5.6 reveals a marked change in banking structure since 1945. The number of independent commercial banks was reduced by 76 during the period

Table 5.6   The banking structure, 1945–89: number of banks

	1945	–50	–55	–60	–65	–70	–75	–80	–85	–90
Commercial banks	99	89	76	68	50	40	28	24	27	23
Savings banks	606	606	603	597	567	493	390	322	198	142

Source: Statistical yearbooks.

1945–90. As has been pointed out already, this process of structural change can be traced back to the interwar years, caused by the severe banking crisis of the 1920s. The concentration movement after 1945, however, was not caused by crisis. The main feature of this structural change was the amalgamation of small provincial banks with the larger commercial banks located in the three largest cities in Norway. The savings banks show the same pattern of development. But as mentioned above the number of savings banks was not reduced during the interwar years. Their concentration did not start until the decade from 1965 to 1975, when mergers among savings banks increased substantially in numbers. Another important factor in the later concentration of savings banks must be related to the interlocking relationship between savings banks and local political and business interests, representing a strong opposition to mergers and concentration (Nordvik, 1989).

When analysing the causes of the concentration process in the banking system, factors relating to economic efficiency seem to be of minor importance. Recent research shows that large units do not show better profitability than smaller units in banking (Fon, 1991). This indicates that the moving forces behind the concentration in the banking sector may instead be found among factors such as market power, technology and organization.

It is important, however, to emphasize that concentration in Norwegian banking is no no way identical to centralization. On the contrary, the decentralized character of the Norwegian banking industry was maintained within the major banks through an extensive network of branches with a very high degree of independence. The deregulation of the financial institutions during the 1980s, caused the number of branches to be expanded substantially, creating an 'over-banking' problem in Norway. From 1981 to 1987, the number of branches of commercial and savings banks increased by almost 300 from 1887 in 1981 to 2 177 in 1987.

Banks and customers, 1927–89   Surveying the banks' distribution of

Banks and customers, 1927–89   Surveying the banks' distribution of lending according to industry and occupation, Tables 5.7 and 5.8 reveal the sectors which have been the major customers of the commercial and savings banks. The data demonstrate that bank–customer relations have undergone sweeping changes during the half century from the 1930s to the 1980s. Until 1920 almost all loans provided by the commercial banks were business loans. Most of the savings banks' borrowers were farmers, business firms or municipalities (Knutsch, 1992). From the 1930s, however, personal loans increased as a share of savings banks' total lending. In 1950 almost 40 per cent of total loans were personal loans. This development was particularly related to the financing of housing. This pattern of lending developed through the 1960s and 1970s.

Almost all credit provided by the commercial banks before the First World War, as well as during the interwar years, was in the form of loans to business clients. But during the period from 1950 to 1980, the customer profile changed substantially. From a circle of customers almost exclusively comprised of business firms, the balance of personal clients and industry became nearly even during these years. In 1970 approximately 20 per cent of total credit provided by the commercial banks was in the form of loans to personal clients. In 1980, this share was 40 per cent. This change of course reflects the credit financed expansion of consumer markets, but it also reflects the strict public regulation of financial markets and institution: 'The personal market became a tempting substitution for the lack of other possibilities' (Lange,

Table 5.7   Commercial banks' distribution of lending according to borrowers' type of business (percentages)

	1927	1950	1955	1960	1970	1980	1985
Public institutions	5.5	0.6	1.6	1.9	4.2	3.0	2.2
Primary industries	10.0	5.0	4.2	3.2	2.6	2.3	2.9
Manufacturing industry	42.3	32.9	28.4	32.8	20.3	12.5	11.6
Public and private services	34.9	40.0	44.6	34.2	31.6	27.5	35.2
Housing, real estate etc.[28]	0.5	16.4	17.6	23.8	39.0	47.6	37.4
Miscellaneous	6.8	5.0	3.5	4.1	2.1	7.1	10.7
Total lending	100	100	100	100	100	100	100

Source: Lange (1992).

Table 5.8 Savings banks' distribution of lending according to borrowers' type of business (percentages)

	1930	1950	1955	1960	1970	1980	1985
Public institutions	12.8	1.2	1.6	2.7	3.5	7.1	5.1
Primary industries	36.1	25.1	23.0	20.9	15.2	9.4	6.8
Manufacturing industry	8.0	15.9	13.5	11.5	12.9	9.6	6.6
Public and private services	10.6	12.2	14.0	15.1	14.9	18.9	16.8
Housing, real estate etc.[29]	23.1	42.7	47.4	48.9	53.1	53.0	59.8
Miscellaneous	9.4	2.9	0.5	0.8	0.4	1.9	4.9
Total lending	100	100	100	100	100	100	100

Source: Lange (1992).

1992: 13).

The development described here should be seen in a wider context. It has been emphasized that the stock market has been a minor source in corporate finance after the Second World War. But, also the role of the banks in financing manufacturing industry has decreased. Table 5.9 clearly demonstrates this.

A glance at Table 5.9 reveals that the floating of bond loans (credit unions and bearer bonds, directly) has been very important in the financing of manufacturing industry. This indicates that investments, to a substantial degree, have been allocated according to the goals of industrial policy. The data shown by the table demonstrate that the role of banks in industrial finance decreased substantially during the period under consideration. The steep rise in state bank lending to industry during the last part of the 1970s was primarily caused by the extensive countercyclical policy noted above.

Conclusions

The analysis has identified three main phases in the development of the financial system in Norway during the period 1900 to 1980.

From 1900 to the middle of the 1930s. This phase comprises what we may call the rise and fall of the classical, liberal and decentralized banking system operating within the framework of a market-based financial system. The banks' clients are typically business firms, but

Table 5.9 Outstanding loans to manufacturing industry provided by the regular domestic credit market, percentages

	1955	1960	1965	1970	1975	1980
Commercial banks	43.7	40.8	33.5	32.5	29.1	22.5
Savings banks	11.1	11.3	8.1	7.9	7.5	6.6
State (public) banks	6.3	5.8	7.1	7.1	9.6	18.5
Finance companies			3.4	3.7	3.4	2.9
Non-life insurance	0.9	1.2	1.2	1.9	3.3	2.6
Life insurance	6.4	11.4	10.9	9.7	9.9	7.8
Credit unions	6.8	7.6	13.9	19.7	23.4	28.1
Bearer bonds, directly	24.8	21.9	21.9	17.5	13.8	11.1
Total	100	100	100	100	100	100
Total, million current NOK	3 095	4 105	7 735	13 184	20 931	35 329

Source: Hunstad and Selte (1993).

Second, from the mid-1930s to 1950. The banking crisis of the 1920s and the depression in the early 1930s initiated a transition period towards essential changes in the financial system. The banks, in particular the commercial banks, lost influence as well as market share in the credit market during this phase.

Third, from 1950–51 to 1980. Influenced by the legacy of the interwar years, a new regulatory regime was established based on credit rationing, the main purpose which was to help achieve the Labour party's strategic goals in economic policy: modernization through industrialization, economic growth and redistribution. This entailed a comprehensive shift in the overall character of the financial system, which definitively changed to a state-led, credit-based system.

From the end of the 1970s, or early 1980s, a new break can be identified, related to the start of the overall deregulation of the financial markets during the 1980s.

Appendix

Appendix appears on the following five pages.

Table 5.A.1 Total institutional lending, 1890–1920 (million NOK), outstanding loans by 31 December

	1890	1895	1900	1905	1910	1915	1920
Total lending:	424	549	852	973	1312	2078	6724
Bank of Norway	34	37	52	44	53	87	506
State banks	83	111	131	161	210	240	310
Savings banks	173	210	278	340	449	656	1732
Commercial banks	130	167	349	376	524	985	4034
Life insurance companies		21	36	46	62	89	103
Non-life insurance companies	4	3	6	6	8	10	16
Credit unions					6	11	23
Finance companies							
Pension funds, etc.							
Percentage:	1890	1895	1900	1905	1910	1915	1920
Bank of Norway	8.02	6.74	6.10	4.52	4.04	4.19	7.53
State banks	19.58	20.22	15.38	16.55	16.01	11.55	4.61
Savings banks	40.80	38.25	32.63	34.94	34.22	31.57	25.76
Commercial banks	30.66	30.42	40.96	38.64	39.94	47.40	59.99
Life insurance companies	0.00	3.83	4.23	4.73	4.73	4.28	1.53
Non-life insurance companies	0.94	0.55	0.70	0.62	0.61	0.48	0.24
Credit unions	0.00	0.00	0.00	0.00	0.46	0.53	0.34
Finance companies	0.00	0.00	0.00	0.00	0.00	0.00	0.00
Pension funds, etc.	0.00	0.00	0.00	0.00	0.00	0.00	0.00
Sum	100.00	100.00	100.00	100.00	100.00	100.00	100.00

113

Table 5.A.2 Total institutional lending, 1925–55 (million NOK), outstanding loans by 31 December

	1925	1930	1935	1940	1945	1950	1955
Total lending:	5204	4293	4337	4764	3699	9538	17246
Bank of Norway	309	194	222	93	22	43	120
State banks	546	820	981	1104	787	1915	4772
Savings banks	1805	1491	1347	1258	754	2245	3760
Commercial banks	2299	1295	1069	1104	910	3287	5006
Life insurance companies	168	233	372	580	459	666	1259
Non-life insurance companies	18	21	31	57	54	94	255
Credit unions	46	79	158	290	334	808	1322
Finance companies							
Pension funds, etc.	13	160	157	278	379	480	752
Percentage:	1925	1930	1935	1940	1945	1950	1955
Bank of Norway	5.94	4.52	5.12	1.95	0.59	0.45	0.70
State banks	10.49	19.10	22.62	23.17	21.28	20.08	27.67
Savings banks	34.68	34.73	31.06	26.41	20.38	23.54	21.80
Commercial banks	44.18	30.17	24.65	23.17	24.60	34.46	29.03
Life insurance companies	3.23	5.43	8.58	12.17	12.41	6.98	7.30
Non-life insurance companies	0.35	0.49	0.71	1.20	1.46	0.99	1.48
Credit unions	0.88	1.84	3.64	6.09	9.03	8.47	7.67
Finance companies	0.00	0.00	0.00	0.00	0.00	0.00	0.00
Pension funds, etc.	0.25	3.73	3.62	5.84	10.25	5.03	4.36
Total	100.00	100.00	100.00	100.00 100.00	100.00	100.00	100.00

Source: Matre Imset, H. (1992b).

Table 5.A.3 Total institutional lending, 1960–90 (million NOK), outstanding loans by 31 December

	1960	1965	1970	1975	1980	1985	1988
Total lending:	25145	40051	67230	129439	263958	556260	960403
Bank of Norway	75	84	126	1266	814	4147	76380
State banks	7839	12012	21160	46067	107648	156088	186637
Savings banks	5381	7629	12620	22917	42093	111073	186689
Commercial banks	6231	9681	15762	29374	54551	152128	250544
Life insurance companies	2279	3970	6067	9503	14585	34465	61880
Non-life insurance companies	342	530	1039	2614	4504	7022	6996
Credit unions	1789	3031	5404	11273	29537	61815	139307
Finance companies		1023	2332	3372	6424	23303	43287
Pension funds, etc.	1209	2091	2720	3053	3802	6219	8683
	1960	1965	1970	1975	1980	1985	1988
Percentage:							
Bank of Norway	0.30	0.21	0.19	0.98	0.31	0.75	7.95
State banks	31.18	29.99	31.47	35.59	40.78	28.06	19.43
Savings banks	21.40	19.05	18.77	17.70	15.95	19.97	19.44
Commercial banks	24.78	24.17	23.44	22.69	20.67	27.35	26.09
Life insurance companies	9.06	9.91	9.02	7.34	5.53	6.20	6.44
Non-life insurance companies	1.36	1.32	1.55	2.02	1.71	1.26	0.73
Credit unions	7.11	7.57	8.04	8.71	11.19	11.11	14.51
Finance companies	0.00	2.55	3.47	2.61	2.43	4.19	4.51
Pension funds, etc.	4.81	5.22	4.05	2.36	1.44	1.12	0.90
Total	100.00	100.00	100.00	100.00	100.00	100.00	100.00

Source: Matre Imset, H. (1992b).

Table 5.A.4 Commercial banks: balance sheets (extracts), 1913–25 (million NOK)

	1913	1914	1915	1916	1917	1918	1919	1920	1921	1922	1923	1924	1925
Assets													
Cash	17	24	34	92	145	130	135	164	145	142	100	92	82
Deposits with banks	85	111	187	442	755	773	776	670	551	415	319	300	214
Stocks and bonds	62	70	94	152	270	307	278	324	512	638	596	563	547
Loans, total	720	752	985	1755	2640	3346	3755	4034	3668	3176	2609	2377	2299
Mortgages	62	69	70	70	75	71	51	57	52	51	60	90	88
Bills and 'bond bills'	327	329	397	573	759	834	950	996	952	810	650	599	743
Current drawing accounts	324	348	506	1096	1794	2437	2745	2973	2659	2311	1891	1682	1450
Foreign bills	17	6	12	16	12	4	9	8	5	4	8	6	18
Other claims	6	12	24	30	87	136	236	232	174	117	199	265	437
Fixed assets	10	10	10	12	20	28	31	37	39	44	45	47	56
Total assets	910	979	1334	2483	3917	4720	5211	5461	5089	4532	3868	3644	3635
Liabilities													
Deposits	592	630	856	1441	2200	2720	2973	3113	2982	2697	2261	2065	1993
Of which demand	27	49	103	227	413	224	208	206	162	137	139	115	142
Deposits from banks	85	92	151	349	567	512	614	618	605	474	520	643	630
Other debts	107	114	165	363	572	598	709	822	650	496	541	470	640
Equity	126	143	162	330	578	890	915	908	852	865	546	466	372
Total liabilities	910	979	1334	2483	3917	4720	5211	5461	5089	4532	3868	3644	3635
Number of banks	116	119	122	138	160	193	195	192	185	170	166	165	160

Sources: Statistical Survey 1948, Historical Statistics 1968.

Table 5.A.5 The Bank of Norway's lending, 1920–24 (million NOK)

Date	Total lending	To banks	To commercial banks	To savings banks
31 Jan. 1920	329.2	109.8	101.2	8.6
15 May 1920	399.4	168.6	155.6	13.0
15 Aug. 1920	440.3	162.1	150.8	11.3
15 Nov. 1920	434.9	192.0	179.0	13.0
28 Feb. 1921	440.7	237.7	224.4	13.3
31 May 1921	427.4	244.1	234.5	9.6
31 Aug. 1921	454.8	266.5	250.5	10.6
15 Dec. 1921	445.9	296.6	282.8	5.4
31 Mar. 1922	448.5	328.2	312.3	5.1
31 Jul. 1922	445.3	329.7	289.3	3.8
30 Nov. 1922	446.3	345.6	296.1	2.0
31 Mar. 1923	464.0	375.6	325.2	2.4
31 Jul. 1923	475.9	389.6	337.9	3.4
30 Nov. 1923	454.5	394.7	341.8	4.1
31 Mar. 1924	412.9	348.2	324.9	3.3
31 Jul. 1924	442.4	362.8	338.1	4.2
30 Nov. 1924	410.5	356.9	333.3	3.4

Source: Rygg (1950: 171).

117

Notes

1. Royal decree of 6 December 1799 (Kanseliplakat).
2. Some exceptions from the prohibition had earlier been given by separate Acts, permitting particular institutions to issue bearer bonds, for instance the state owned Royal Mortgage Bank in 1851, the municipalities in 1857 and private railroad companies in 1863.
3. Until 1910, when the Storting passed an Act on joint-stock companies, there had been no such legislation in Norway. At this time a proposal for a new law had been discussed since 1881.
4. Public inspection board, established in 1912.
5. A more detailed study on the relations between the government, banks and business during the First World War is in Knutsen (1990).
6. Parliamentary minutes from the discussion in the Odelsting, Stfh. no. 8, 1918, pp. 171 ff.
7. For a more thorough analysis on the banking crisis and its causes, see Knutsen (1991).
8. Ot. prp. nr. 13, 1923 (Bill No. 13, 1923), cfr. Parliamentary minutes, 1923.
9. Kongeriget Norges Hypothekbank (The Royal Mortgage Bank of Norway) (1852), Statens Fiskarbank (The Government Bank for Fishermen) was established in 1919, Den norske arbeiderbruk – og boligbank (Agricultural Properties Bank of Norway) (1903), Noregs småbruk – og bustadbank (The Agric. Small-Holding and Housing Bank of Norway) (1917), Norges Kommunalbank (The Norwegian Municipal Bank) (1926), Lånekassen for jordbrukere (Farmers' Loan Fund) (1935), Lånekassen for fiskere (Fishermen's Loan Fund), (1938), Driftskredittkassen for jordbruket (Operating Credit Agency for Agriculture) (1938) and finally A/S Den Norske Industribank (The Manufacturing Bank of Norway) (1936).
10. The first Labour party government was established in 1928, but lasted for only a couple of weeks, from 28 January to 15 February. In 1935, another Labour party government with J. Nygaardsvold as prime minister came to power, and stayed there as a minority government until the German occupation in 1940. During the years in exile in London, the government was extended to a coalition government. A new Labour party government came to power in the autumn of 1945, and kept this position for nearly 20 years.
11. Moseid/Agrarian Party, cfr. Parliamentary minutes, 1928, 7a.
12. Government report to Parliament No. 29, 1929; cfr. Parliamentary minutes, 1929.
13. The Bank of Norway's Archive (NBA), I-5-1, PM by A.E / G.E. on 'Norges Banks og visse andre seddelbankers diskonto'.
14. Bill No. 104 – 1934, cfr. Parliamentary minutes, 1934.
15. Ot.prp. nr. 61 – 1934 (Bill), cfr. Parliamentary minutes, 1934.
16. Preliminary Act of 29 June 1934 giving the government authority to fix the interest rates of commercial and savings banks.
17. NBA, ibid.
18. Ot. prp. nr. 13, 1923 (Bill), p. 12.
19. NBA, ibid. The capital changed name to its old name Oslo in 1923.
20. Established 14 April 1940 in order to administer the occupied parts of Norway in 'cooperation' with the German occupation authorities. The German 'Reichskommisar' dissolved the 'Administration Council' on 25

September 1940.
21. NBA/Joint Consultation Council Archive: Letter from the Ministry of Finance to the Joint Consultation Council, 27 December 1958. Here quoted from letter from the Joint Consultation Council to the Ministry of Finance, 5 September 1960. (My translation from Norwegian/S.K.)
22. NBA/Joint Consultation Council Archive: Letter from the Joint Consultation Council to the Ministry of Finance, 5 September 1960.
23. NBA/Joint Consultation Council Archive: Minutes from the meeting 27 August 1959.
24. NBA/Joint Consultation Council Archive: Letter from the Joint Consultation Council to the Ministry of Finance, 5 September 1960, p. 17. (My translation from Norwegian/S.K.)
25. Rentepolitikk, NOU 1980: 4 (On Interest Rate Policies; Norwegian Public Committee Report 1980: 4).
26. NBA/Joint Consultation Council Archive: Letter from the Joint Consultation Council to the Ministry of Finance, 5 September 1960, p. 14. (My translation from Norwegian/S.K.)
27. Until 1965, this body was called the section 3 committee, referring to the § 3 of 1953 Act on interest rates. From 1965, the name became the section 15 committee, according to the corresponding section in the Monetary and Credit Policy Act.
28. Including personal loans.
29. Including personal loans.

References

Bergo, J. (1985). *Det norske penge – og kredittsystem*. Oslo: Norges Bank.

Egge, Å. (1972). 'Trekk ved sparebankvesenet og sparebanklovgivningen i slutten av forrige århundre', in A. Jensen *et al.* (eds), *Studier i Sparing og Sparebankvesen i Norge 1822–1972*, Oslo: Gyldendal Norsk Forlag. pp. 101–53.

Eide, L. and Holli, K. (1980). *Det norske penge- og kredittsystem*. Oslo: Norges Bank.

Fon, A. M. (1992). *Konsentrasjon og fusjon blant norske forretningsbanker 1945–1990*. Report No: SNF-rapport 9/92, Bergen.

Graff Hagen, M. (1977). *Samarbeidsnemda. En studie av samarbeidet mellom staten og de private kredittinstitusjonen 1951-1965*, Master Thesis, University of Oslo.

Hanisch, T. J. (1979). 'Virkninger av paripolitikken. Et essay om norsk økonomi i 1920–årene.', *Historisk tidsskrift* (3).

Hunstad, T. and Selte, N. K. (1993). *Statsbankenes rolle i industrifinansieringen, 1955–80*, Diploma thesis, Norwegian School of Management.

Kindleberger, C. P. (1989). *Manias, Panics, and Crashes. A History of Financial Crises*, N.Y. and London: Macmillan.

Knutsen, S. (1990). 'Noen merknader til relasjonene stat, bank og bedrift under jobbetiden 1914-20', Noras: Det nye pengesamfunnet/Research on Banking, Capital, Society. Report No. 13.

Knutsen, S. (1991). 'From Expansion to Panic and Crash. The Norwegian Banking System and its Customers 1913–1924', *Scandinavian Economic History Review*, Vol. XXXIX (3): pp. 41–71.

Knutsen, S. (1992). 'Banker og Næringslivskunder under ekspansjonsfaser. 1890–1913' in E. Lange *et al.* (eds), *Bankstruktur og kundeforhold i langtidsperspektiv*, Noras: Det nye pengesamfunnet/Research on Banking, Capital, Society. Report No. 31.

Knutsen, S. (1993). *Det norske system av finansinstitusjoner og kapitalmarkeder.* Working paper: 1993/5, Norwegian School of Management.

Kofoed, H. (1940). *Den Norske Bankforening 1915–1940. Trekk av Norsk Bankhistorie.*, Skrifter utgitt av den Norske Bankforening NR. 64, Oslo: Den Norske Bankforening.

Lange, E. (1992). 'Bankstruktur og kundeforhold. Et historisk overblikk' in E. Lange *et al.* (eds), *Bankstruktur og kundeforhold i langtidsperspektiv*, Noras: Det nye pengesamfunnet / Research on Banking, Capital, Society. Report No. 31.

Matre Imset, H. (1992a). *Norske Forretningsbanker 1848–1990. En tilbakeføring av forretningsbankstatistikken.*, Noras: Det nye pengesamfunnet / Research on Banking, Capital, Society. Report No. 41.

Matre Imset, H. (1992b). *Norske Kredittinstitusjoner 1850–1990. En statistisk oversikt.*, Noras: Det nye pengesamfunnet / Research on Banking, Capital, Society. Report No. 42.

Nordvik, H. W. (1989). 'Struktur og Sanering. Sparebanker i strid og samling 1960–1989' in H. W. Nordvik *et al.* (eds), *Penger spart, penger tjent. Sparebanker og økonomisk utvikling på Sør-Vestlandet fra 1839 til 1989*, Stavanger: SR-Bank.

Nordvik, H. W. (1990). 'Penge- og valutapolitikk, Bank og Kredittvesen og Krisen i Norsk Økonomi på 1930-tallet' in E. Hovland, E. Lange and S. Rysstad (eds), *Det som svarte seg best. Studier i økonomisk historie og politikk*, Oslo: Ad Notam Forlag.

Nordvik, H. W. (1991). 'Banks and their customers in times of crisis: Norwegian experiences in the 1920s', paper presented at the conference: *Banks and customers. Institutional theory and banking practices: Banking and client relations in interwar Central Europe and Scandinavia*, BHU, London School of Economics and Political Science, 11–14 Sept. 1991.

Nordvik, H. W. (1992). 'Den norske bankkrisen i mellomkrigstiden – En sammenligning med dagens bankkrise.', *SNF-Bulletin* (No. 1).

Pekkarinen, J. (1989). 'Keynesianism and the Scandinavian Models of Economic Policy' in P. A. Hall (ed.), *The Political Power of Economic Ideas: Keynesianism across Nations.*, Princeton: Princeton University Press.

Rygg, N. (1950). *Norges Bank i mellomkrigstiden*, Oslo: Gyldendal Norsk Forlag.

Sejersted, F. (1968). 'Bokanmeldelse av: G. Jahn *et al.*, "Norges Bank gjennom 150 år".', *Historisk Tidsskrift* (47).

Skånland, H. (1967). *Det Norske kredittmarked siden 1900.*, Samfunnsøkonomiske Studier, Oslo: Statistisk Sentralbyrå.

Synnestvedt, T. (1988). *Aksjemarkedet*, Working paper No. 21, Finansdepartementet Økonomiavdelingen.

CHAPTER SIX

Overcoming Institutional Barriers: Financial Networks in Sweden, 1910–90

Mats Larsson

This chapter will focus upon the development of Sweden's financial system and its institutions in the 20th century. During this period Sweden developed from a country dominated by agriculture, with industrialization being in its initial stage, to a high technology society with a large public sector. During different periods there were special demands made on the credit market. For example, at the beginning of the century there developed a need for capital in the industrialization process, while the expansion of the public sector after the Second World War brought about other requirements on the financial system.

Thus, changes in demand had a large impact on the financial market, but the development was also shaped by the institutional regulations. In fact for some periods public guidelines and control were very important for the financial system. Therefore, agents in the financial market were compelled to draw a balance between market demands and institutional regulations. What role did norms, traditions and legislation play in the shaping of the financial system? This question is intimately connected with institutional theory.

In a broad sense the function of a financial system is to be the transmitting link between those supplying and those demanding capital. The structure of a financial system is often determined by social traditions, but governmental regulations also have a strong impact on the system. It is common to define the financial system as being either bank or market-oriented. The market-oriented system includes extensive financing through share and bond issuing, while banks play a vital role in financing in a bank-oriented system. This division of the financial system can also be supplemented by the role of governments. The ultimate governmental financial system would thus be in a planned economy; however in economies dominated by private enterprise, governmental measures can also be of the utmost importance. This could mean, for example, that a financial system could be bank or market-oriented within limits set by government (Zysman, 1983; Neave, 1991).

This chapter will also examine these broader structures in terms of the Swedish financial system.

Institutional and market traditions

Modern credit market started to develop in Sweden when the savings banks movement was introduced in the 1820s. These banks concentrated primarily on local depositing and lending to the agricultural sector. But in some regions savings banks also started to play a more important role for other financing, thus competing with business houses and private financiers.

Together with mortgage institutes and the Swedish central bank (Riksbanken), savings banks dominated the credit market until the second half of the 19th century. Institutional borrowing was thus far dominated by the agricultural sector, while industry in this early phase of industrialization mostly depended on private capital. When industrial growth accelerated in the 1850s, especially due to the expansion of the sawmill industry, the need for external capital increased. Commercial banks came to play a major role in this process.

Commercial banks had been established in Sweden as early as the 1830s, organized as joint-stock banks with unlimited liability, with the owners being liable one for all, all for one for the bank's obligations. These banks were primarily engaged in issuing banknotes, and initially they showed little interest in increasing customers' deposits. With industrial development, however, deposits became increasingly important. More capital was accumulated in society and, at the same time, the need for capital to invest in industrial development increased. With the establishment of the first Swedish joint-stock banks with limited liability in the 1860s and 1870s deposits became the prime capital base for the business of all commercial banks. In the 1870s commercial banks began to dominate the whole Swedish credit market. This development was also boosted by the industrial boom in the 1890s (Larsson and Lindgren, 1992: 337 ff.).

The development of industry resulted in the increased importance of the markets for bonds and shares. Bonds were primarily used for the construction and development of infrastructure, especially Sweden's railway system. Although the construction of railways was undertaken by both private companies and public interests, the acquisition of capital for these investments was organized and administered mainly by the state through the National Debt Office (Schön, 1989: 13 ff.). Bonds were also used for the financing of larger industrial investments. In the issuing of these bonds as well as in the trade of other bonds, commercial banks played an important role, thus confirming the strong connections between industry and commercial banks.

However, for the financing of industry the introduction of joint-stock companies was of far greater importance than bond issuing. With the industrial growth in the 1870s joint-stock companies became a common means of organizing large-scale industrial production, as well as medium-sized companies. In order to stimulate the trade in shares a stock exchange had to be developed. However, a more general breakthrough for trade in shares did not come about until around the turn of the century.

Industrial development also resulted in the alteration of the traditional banking system that had been organized in the 1820s and 1830s. In this early period British deposit banking was used as a model for Sweden's banking system. To begin with, short-term lending dominated commercial banking, but with the growing need for long-term credits in industry, these loans were gradually prolonged. Several of the largest commercial banks – such as Skandinaviska Kredit AB and the Wallenberg-owned Stockholms Enskilda Bank – were also involved in the restructuring of industrial companies (Larsson and Lindgren, 1990: 140 ff.).

Using the example of German universal banking, Sweden's banking system gradually changed, to become a deposit banking system performing elements of universal banking. An important difference compared with Germany was that Swedish commercial banks were not allowed to acquire shares in industrial companies. However, towards the end of the 19th century this question was being scrutinized by bankers as well as politicians.

With the expansion of both savings and commercial banking advances from the central bank (Riksbanken) became of minor importance. Towards the end of the 19th century the Riksbank's activities were concentrated on central banking, being a lender of last resort and the maker of monetary policy. The private banknote issuing rights were also abolished in 1886, but it was not until 1904 that the last private notes were taken out of circulation (SOU 1955: 43, pp. 11 f.).

Around the turn of the century Sweden had a financial system mostly based on traditions, with savings banks and mortgage institutes mainly concerned with lending to the agricultural sector, while commercial banks concentrated on industrial advances. So far this system had functioned without any extensive legislation but in the beginning of the 20th century, laws and public control became more important in forming the financial system.

In spite of a growing market for bonds and shares, Sweden's financial system by the turn of the century was basically bank-oriented.

Commercial banks not only dominated institutional lending but also played a major role in the trade of shares and bonds. Towards the end of the 19th century banks also had strong direct connections with industrial companies through interlocking directorates and private shareholdings.

Crises in an expanding market, 1910–39

The demand for financial services: an overview

The demand for financial services increased at the beginning of the 20th century. In the first two decades the financial market was characterized by a boom, while the following 20 years were notable for economic and financial crises. Although these two periods differ substantially in structure, a common feature for agents on the financial market was the search for an institutional identity. The basis for this development was the change in demand for capital on the financial market. While the first 20 years of the 20th century were distinguished by an increased demand for capital in industry and trade, the following period is best characterized as one of transition. Internal financing gradually became more important for private enterprises and the financial market gradually stabilized. Both the bond and share markets exhibited a low level of activity and the expansion of the banking sector was halted.

The 1920s and 1930s was also a transitional period in terms of the demand for credits. Up to the 1920s industrial need for capital constituted the basis for banking, with commercial banks expanding rapidly. Low incomes hampered lending to private persons, but with increased real wages during the interwar period, and due to the cheap money policy in the 1930s, private lending became more important. Thus, it is possible to look at the interwar period as a transitionary state between a financial market dominated by industrial expansion and one based on private demand for credits. However, the real breakthrough for the consumption society and lending to private persons instead of enterprises did not come about until after the Second World War.

Activities on the stock market also changed dramatically around 1920. During the First World War trade with shares expanded fast, resulting in rising prices. During this boom speculation increased heavily, involving banks as well as other financial institutes. With the deflation crisis in 1920 the strong development of the stock market was halted. Prices fell, with consequent large losses for shareholders as well as for financiers. Compared with the heavy fluctuations in the 1910s and beginning of the 1920s, the rest of the interwar period saw a stable development of the stock market. The issuing of new shares on the open market decreased in importance and internal financing became more widespread.

The bond market was also influenced by economic development during the First World War. Due to large exports and falling imports, Sweden's balance of payments improved rapidly and bonds, issued to finance new infrastructure in the 19th century, could be repurchased. Thus, foreign debt became a governmental debt to Swedish capital owners, especially banks and insurance companies. During the war the issuing of new bonds was more or less reserved for the government. This development continued also after the financial crisis in the 1920s, and in the 1930s private bond issuing became rare, thus increasing the tendency towards the bank orientation of the Swedish financial system (Kock, 1961: 101 ff.; Franzén, 1989: 275 ff.). This was primarily an effect of the cheap money policy that had been conducted, which made borrowing from banks and insurance companies as cheap as bond issuing.[1]

Governmental control

Due to the expansion of the financial market the need for governmental involvement and control increased. Thus, at the beginning of the century several new laws regulating financial activities were enacted.

Insurance activities were to a large extent free during the 19th century. This resulted in cooperation between companies, in the form of pools or cartels, to avoid 'destructive' competition. In the 19th century several companies were already in favour of a common regulation for all insurance companies. But it was not until 1903 that the first joint insurance legislation for life as well as property insurance companies was adopted. However, this new law did not regulate the establishment of new companies to any greater extent; instead it focused on economic stability. For life insurance companies this meant an extensive control of capital investments in order to secure the capital of policy holders. Only a minor part of life insurance capital could be placed in securities other than bonds and certificates (Larsson, 1991: 16 ff.). The effect of this regulation is obvious. An internal market was created involving, primarily, the central government and mortgage institutes as issuers of bonds, and insurance companies and to some extent savings banks as buyers.

The protection of the customers' capital also influenced the commercial banking laws adopted in 1903 and 1911. Through a regulation of cash reserves and other reserve requirements, the depositors' capital could to some extent be guaranteed. With increased requirements on the size of equity in banking companies, financially weaker banks were also often forced to liquidate or merge with larger banks. From 1912 onwards this resulted in a structural change for commercial banks (Söderlund, 1978).

The establishment of a commercial bank was thus made more difficult by the Banking Law of 1911, compared with the insurance legislation. But with regard to the activities of the banks, the new legislation was more open. With a limited right to acquire shares, Swedish commercial banking took a further step towards German universal banking and a more bank-oriented financial system.

Another development which came with the new laws was an increased role for the Swedish Bank Inspection Board as well as the National Swedish Private Insurance Inspectorate. Both these organizations had been created in the 19th century, but with the new regulation their financial independence was guaranteed; at the same time their authority increased.

The Bank Inspection as well as the Insurance Inspectorate, focused their central supervision primarily on four principles:

1. Ascertaining that banks' and insurance companies' business activities were in accordance with legislation.
2. Official control over the establishment of banks and insurance companies.
3. Supervision of the obligations of banks and insurance companies to publish annual economic reports.
4. Developing standards for good insurance and banking practice.

Thus, besides having control functions, the inspectorates played a major role in creating sound business practice and good accounting principles. By the 1910s a certain unity had been imposed on banking as well as on insurance activities. This probably helped to weed out financially weaker companies in both lines of business even before the crises in the interwar period.

In spite of an extensive legislation, economic problems could not be avoided by the commercial banks in the 1920s and 1930s. A high rate of inflation and lending on bad collateral during the expanding 1910s resulted in large losses for the banks at the beginning of the 1920s. For a time commercial banks could absorb these losses but when deflation hit the Swedish economy several banks had to be liquidated. To save the Swedish financial system the government, through a special organization – AB Kreditkassan – transferred capital to banks in crisis. Governmental support was also of great importance for the banking system after the Kreuger crash in 1932 (Söderlund, 1978; Lindgren, 1988).

The interwar period as a whole was characterized by the increasing role of public guidance in the financial system. This involved legislation as well as public control and direct financial and institutional involvement. Thus the bank-oriented financial system, which developed at the beginning of the 20th century, came increasingly under public control and guidelines.

Financial networks circumvent legislation

The Swedish financial market was, by the 1910s characterized by extensive fluctuations, especially concerning the interest in, for example, the bond and stock markets. Agents on the financial market often attempted to adapt to these changes in demand in order to increase profits. Through the cooperation with agents in other parts of the financial market, financial networks were created to look after the interests of the customers as well as the financial institutions.

The establishment of these networks was probably stimulated by early segmentations within the financial market, and by legislation preserving market divisions, with for example commercial banks concentrating on industrial lending and mortgage institutes on agricultural credits. The construction of financial networks at the beginning of the 20th century was an attempt to adjust to this situation. The commercial banks were central to these early networks. With their dominance over institutional lending they held a strong position in relation to other agents on the market. This resulted in a concentration of power in the financial market towards commercial banks, and in spite of structural changes and fluctuations during the following decades, the largest banks especially managed to preserve their strong position.

Through financial networks commercial banks could undertake short as well as long-term lending – and not only to industry. With affiliated special credit institutions, mortgage institutes, for example, banks could take an active part in the growing housing industry.

Commercial banks also developed extensive cooperative links with insurance companies. The four largest banks – Skandinaviska Kredit AB, Svenska Handelsbanken, Göteborgs Bank and Stockholms Enskilda Bank – organized a system of cooperating insurance companies covering different insurance fields. However, the decentralized structure of the insurance market at this time made it difficult to establish more than regional contacts. Since cooperation made it possible to jointly recruit customers, this could be advantageous for both banks and insurance companies.[2]

However, the best examples of financial networks during the 1910s and interwar period were the close contacts between banks and investment companies. The basis for this cooperation was the bank legislation adopted in 1911, which made it possible for banks to own and trade in shares. The right to acquire shares was limited by the size of the banks' equity, but with the establishment of affiliated investment companies (so called 'Emissionsbolag') it became possible to increase the involvement of commercial banks in industry.[3]

These affiliated investment companies were often founded with low equity. However, with good banking contacts it was easy to borrow capital for investments in shares. The collateral used for such advances was nearly always the shares which the investment company had acquired. These close contacts between commercial banks and investment companies added extra fuel both to bank lending and to the stock market. These affiliated investment companies also participated in the introduction of new companies to the stock market as well as the issue of new shares. This gave both investment companies and banks (as shareholders and suppliers of capital) a dominant position on the expanding stock market. Commercial banks also held a strong position in connection with other – not directly affiliated – investment companies (see Figure 6.1). This helped to increase the role of commercial banks on the financial market.

Commercial banks could also be included in these financial networks through a shared ownership in affiliated investment companies. The best example was the creation of Centralgruppens Emission AB, an affiliated investment company in 1920 jointly owned by ten commercial banks. Thus, affiliated investment companies became bridges between dominating centres in the financial system. These close connections probably helped to create a joint responsibility for the financial system when the crisis in the 1920s hit Swedish banking. This shared ownership also enabled larger financial obligations to be undertaken than otherwise would have been possible.

During the 1920s connections between commercial banks and investment companies changed. A new law in 1924 prohibited banks from owning shares in companies whose main activity consisted of administering or trading shares. This legislation was primarily caused by the high risk to which commercial banks were exposed to in their share-trading through investment companies. However, the affiliated investment companies had already been liquidated during the crisis and the banks had taken over their shareholdings to protect their claims, so the legislation did not affect the close connections between banks and industry. After the Kreuger crash in 1932 the banks' rights to acquire shares was totally abolished, and shareholdings had to be sold within five years, provided this could be done without losses. This was a serious threat to the close bank–industry relations that had been established. But this legislation could also be circumvented by the financial networks. Through the establishment of other affiliated investment companies

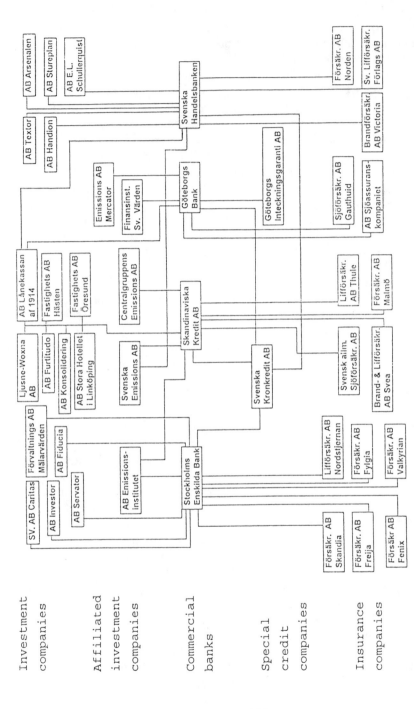

Figure 6.1 Financial networks of the four largest commercial banks in Sweden 1920. (*Note:* These networks are based on the existence of interlocking directorates, where bank directors were represented on the board of directors in other financial companies. *Source:* Research based on Key-Åberg (1921))

where the control was based on personal connections and not ownership, the banks could preserve their interests in industry.

Thus, in the period up to 1940 financial networks basically achieved three practical results:

1. They enabled the participants in financial networks to jointly recruit customers, thus increasing the companies' market share.
2. They increased the cooperation between agents in the financial system, both horizontally and vertically, thus creating a joint responsibility for the survival of the financial system, especially during the crisis in the 1920s. This cooperation also made it easier to mobilize the capital assets needed for undertaking large-scale financing.
3. Financial networks also gave commercial banks – being the centre of the financial system – the opportunity to perform activities which were not intended in the banking legislation.[4]

Control of a financial system, 1940–79

Increasing governmental activities

Governmental control and guidelines had, even prior to the Second World War, increased their role in the Swedish financial system. However, as the social democrats gained more power and Keynesian theories were adopted, interest in the financial market grew. Monetary and credit policy became a vital part in the restructuring of Sweden's economy, especially after 1950.

The large public interest in the financial system can be explained by the desire to avoid a postwar depression and to make a gradual adjustment from a wartime to a peacetime economy. One of the major reasons for regulating the financial market was also that the government wanted to adopt a cheap-money policy and still keep inflation low. On an unregulated market this would lead to a credit boom and rising prices. Low interest rates were regarded as important to ensure cheap capital for the structural rationalization of Sweden's agriculture, for investments in housing and for the development of a national electricity system (SOU 1949: 13, pp. 35 ff.).

New policy was not based on extensive legislation but on an increased control of lending and investments as well as of the pricing of credits. General economic policy became the basis on which the guidance of the financial system was founded. This development not only increased the role of the central bank (Riksbanken), but also of the Bank Inspection

Board and the Private Insurance Inspectorate.

During the 1950s and 1960s an arsenal of governmental guiding measures was developed which gave the different financial agents very little freedom (see list below). To begin with these measures were organized as 'voluntary' agreements between the Riksbanken and the financial agents, but gradually the authority of the central bank increased. During the period 1950–85 these regulating measures were used to a varying extent, but sometimes resulted in severe control over the financial market. In 1969 for example the Riksbank used all available measures in order to restrain the economy.

Special monetary and credit measures for financial institutions:
- Regulation of interest rates.
- Introduction of penalty rates on the central bank's lending to commercial and savings banks.
- Rationing of credits.
- Special quotas for liquidity and cash reserves.
- Control of bond issuing.
- General investment control.
- Foreign exchange control.

As a result of this financial regulation, competition between traditional financial agents decreased and the market became more oligopolic. It was not until the late 1960s that the governmental policy promoted competition between different credit institutions. For example, new legislation made it possible for savings banks and special agriculture banks to increase lending to industrial companies. Another effect of the strict financial policy was the establishment of a large 'grey' credit market and, of special importance, the creation of finance companies.

On the whole, Sweden's financial system changed considerably between the Second World War and the 1980s. However, the bank-oriented system that had developed, particularly in the 1910s and 1920s, was not changed into a market-oriented system. Instead governmental regulation and control were imposed on the existing system, resulting in a mixture which left little room for the market. However, later in this chapter I will show that it was possible to alter even this system with the development of financial networks.

A changed financial market

The regulation of the financial market also had effects on the structure of lending. Private issuing of bonds was more or less reserved for mortgage institutions and investments in hydroelectric power, and not for ordinary industrial investments. For industrial companies, internal financing became of prime importance instead, while lending from commercial as well as savings banks was dominated by demands from households – an effect of rising wages and increased levels of consumption.

The increased significance of private credits in the financial system was also seen in a shift of the relative importance of different institutions in the financial market. For example the significance of mortgage institutions engaged in lending for housing construction grew steadily from the 1950s. Restrictions on banks' lending helped promote this structural change.

However, on the whole the distribution of institutional lending remained stable until the late 1960s, when legislation made it possible to compete in areas other than the traditional ones.

Structural changes on the lending market also reflect a shift in private savings. The development of a social welfare system, and especially the introduction of a general supplementary pension, made long-term saving in the form of life insurance less attractive. With lower savings in the 1960s and 1970s, the level of lending by insurance companies also decreased. Only when inflation and favourable tax regulation made long-term saving in life and personal insurance favourable, did these types of savings start to increase again.

Financial networks on a regulated credit market

Financial networks established in the 1910s and during the interwar period had often been built up to make it possible for commercial banks to perform activities prohibited by legislation. Governmental regulation of the financial market in the 1950s and 1960s was to some extent also circumvented by the establishment of financial networks with commercial banks in the centre (see Figure 6.2).

Thus, the introduction of bank affiliated special credit companies started as early as the middle of the 1950s. These institutes primarily handled credits connected with building activities, and can be characterized as mortgage institutes. But there were also special credit companies handling large and long-term lending to, for example, shipbuilding. Through cooperation with these special credit companies it was possible for banks to expand their interest in areas of the economy that would otherwise have been impossible because of strict regulation of the banks' activities. The same explanation can be used when banks in the late 1950s began to establish finance companies. Banks were not allowed to perform factoring and leasing, and to be able to give the customers these services affiliated finance houses had to be founded.

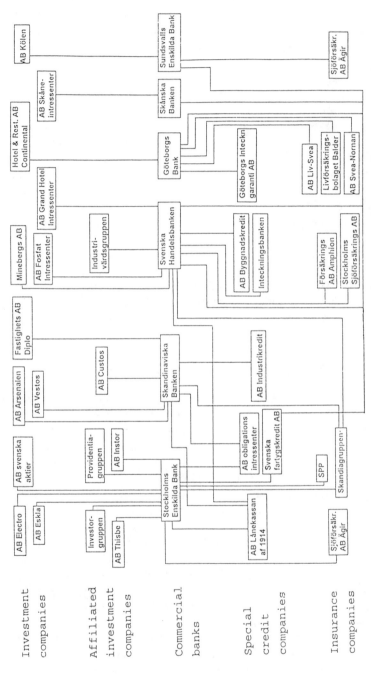

Figure 6.2 Financial networks of the largest commercial banks in Sweden 1955. (*Note:* These financial networks are based on the existence of interlocking directorates, where bank directors were represented on the board of directors in other financial companies. *Source:* Research based on Svenska aktiebolag (1955–56))

Cooperation between banks and insurance companies also developed after the Second World War. Banks sometimes acted as insurance agents, while insurance companies recommended their customers – especially industrial and trading companies – to establish contacts with certain banks.

The banks' interests in Swedish industry had been built up in the 1910s and 1920s and had managed to survive the withdrawal of the commercial banks' right to acquire shares. When the banks' shareholdings were transferred to affiliated investment companies, their interest in industry could be maintained. The investments of these bank groups continued to increase during the 1950s and 1960s. By the end of the Second World War about 30 per cent of all industrial workers were employed in companies within these bank groups' holdings, but by the end of the 1970s this share had increased to over 40 per cent. Two banks in particular, the Wallenberg-dominated Stockholms Enskilda Bank and Svenska Handelsbanken, held strong positions in Swedish industry through their investment companies (Lindgren, 1990).

Compared with the interwar period the financial networks of 1955 were very concentrated. The over-establishment of banks, insurance companies and investment companies had diminished, partly through legislation promoting larger financial institutions. Three larger commercial banks had extensive connections with other financial agents and thus had come to dominate the market. Besides these banks, there were a couple of regional banks working together with insurance companies, but without affiliated investment companies.[5]

The concentration of the financial networks underlines the oligopolic structure of Sweden's financial market especially in the 1950s, 1960s and 1970s. This concentration was a foreboding of the close connection which was to develop between, for example, banks and insurance companies in the 1980s and 1990s. With the concentration of Sweden's financial capital the need for connections between banks and bank groups were diminished, and there were only a few examples of these jointly controlled financial companies in 1955 compared with 1920.

The internationalization of the financial market also resulted in a further development of financial networks. Up to the 1960s and 1970s financial networks had primarily been national, but in order to compete on the international market, cooperation with international agents became more important. With the establishment of bank syndicates in Geneva and London both Svenska Handelsbanken and S-E-Banken cooperated with other Nordic banks. However, it looks as if these joint Nordic efforts had their greatest importance at the beginning of internationalization. In the 1980s there was a tendency instead to establish foreign subsidiary companies, while syndicated banks were often taken over by one of the participating bank partners (Marquardt, 1992: 63 ff.).

Deregulation and boom, 1980–90

The fall of a regulated system and its consequences

During the economic recession in the 1970s the need for capital in the public sector increased. To begin with this demand could be satisfied through the use of the central bank's ordinary regulation measures. But already towards the end of the 1970s and at the beginning of the 1980s the need for new financial instruments became obvious. In order to finance the national debt the National Debt Office began to issue bills on the money market in 1982. This successful move made the use of compulsory investments for banks unnecessary, and in September 1983 a deregulation of Sweden's credit market began. But it must be noted that the banks had already developed methods to circumvent regulatory legislation. With the issue of bank certificates the banks could increase their capital without expanding deposits, which in turn made it possible to meet obligations to increase investments in bonds. In fact the development of the money market made it possible to overcome nearly all regulatory measures. The internationalization of the financial market also made it impossible to retain the regulation.

The deregulation of Sweden's financial market was carried out with great speed and by 1986 all regulatory measures, which had been introduced in the 1950s and 1960s, had been abolished. This development also made a change in monetary policy necessary. The stability of the rate of exchange became the primary aim for the central bank, and transactions on the open market replaced regulatory measures as the basis for the policy.

Deregulation totally changed the rules of the financial market. While deposits were still fairly stable, competition for good borrowing customers increased. Not only banks but also mortgage institutions, finance companies and insurance companies accepted higher risks in their lending, without really compensating for this with higher interest rates.[6] An increased market share became more important than long-run economic stability. This development was promoted by an overheated national economy, high inflation rates and increased consumption. In the market for real estate, prices rose especially rapidly.

High expectations on the real estate market were also one important factor behind the financial crisis which hit Sweden's economy in 1990. Finance companies had often taken the largest risks in their lending and were therefore the first to experience losses, but in addition some banks were hit by financial problems in the early phase of the crisis. Those banks that had been most aggressive in the 1980s in trying to expand their market share faced severe economic problems. In the second phase of the crisis the more cautious banks also began to make losses on outstanding credits. It was primarily falling prices on the real estate market that caused problems for the banks. Mortgage institutions and insurance companies were similarly influenced by this development. When, in 1991–92, the economy was hit by the general depression, losses within the financial system increased even further and the banks were compelled to seek public support to avoid liquidation.

In many respects the 1990s financial crisis exhibits great similarities with the banking crisis in the 1920s. In both cases the years before the crisis were distinguished by an economic boom, speculation and high inflation rates. Prices on real estate and on the stock market rose rapidly, which made the economy vulnerable to general and sectoral deflation. The risks connected with the banking business were also heightened by the financial networks – with an excess lending to affiliated investment companies in the 1910s and to bank affiliated finance companies in the 1980s.

During the 1910s as well as the 1990s the crises were preceded by extensive amendments in the banking legislation. The liberalization of the credit market in the 1990s contributed to the granting of large credits with insufficient or no collateral. Thus, developments resembled those of the 1910s when commercial banks were also given a larger degree of freedom to develop their business with the right to acquire shares.

Financial networks on a deregulated credit market

A major reason for the development of financial networks in the 1950s and 1960s was to circumvent regulations on the financial market. One might then assume that the deregulation of the financial market would result in a dissolution of established financial networks. But this has not been the case. The networks have instead been tightened, forming consolidated groups of financial institutions with banks and insurance companies at the centre (see Figure 6.3). This development has been made possible by a change in legislation allowing banks to acquire shares and thus to form consolidated groups centred on joint ownership.

The development of close connections between banks and insurance companies developed further in the 1980s than during previous decades. The liberalization of the credit market reduced the differences between financial institutes with respect to their business, and new financial products developed. This was also reflected in the merger between the Bank Inspection and the Insurance Inspectorate to form the Financial

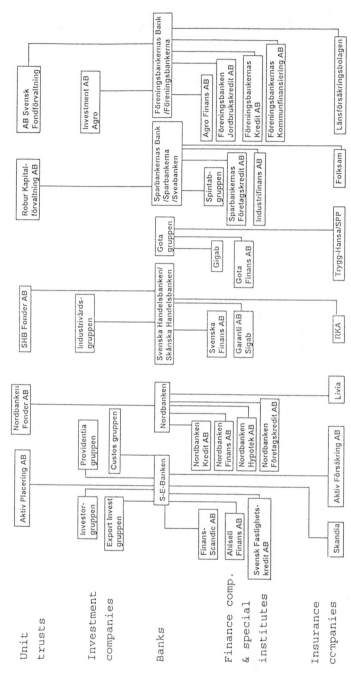

Figure 6.3 Financial networks of the largest banks in Sweden 1990. (*Note:* These networks are based on the structures of the spheres of interest as presented in the banks' annual reports.)

138

Inspectorate.

In 1991 all larger banks were closely connected with at least one insurance company. This meant that the capital of life insurance companies affiliated with banks included over 80 per cent of the total capital administrated by life insurance companies.

As a result of the regulated economy, the importance of mortgage institutions and finance companies increased in the 1960s and 1970s. The affiliation of these agents to banks also increased the role of banking groups in the economy. However, after deregulation, with increased competition on the market, the significance of finance companies was reduced.

The financial networks in 1955 as well as in 1990 comprised extensive shareholdings. With rising prices on the stock market in the 1980s, public interest in shares as investments increased. This promoted the establishment of new forms of investment companies connected to banks. However, since these companies are administrating their clients' investments, they cannot be regarded as directly affiliated to the banking business.

Compared with 1920 and 1955, financial networks in 1990 were well connected groups, only a step away from financial 'department stores'. The concentration of capital and the large size of these groups has diminished the role of connecting agents in the financial system. National cooperation between groups is no longer of current interest. However, the financial crisis might change these patterns of cooperation, resulting in new partnerships and new structures.

Conclusion

The development of Sweden's financial system in the 20th century can be divided into three separate periods, each characterized by distinctive patterns of development.

During the first phase – 1910–39 – Sweden's financial system became increasingly bank oriented. Commercial banks not only promoted industrial development, but they were also the centres in financial networks connecting different types of agents on the financial market. During this early period of the 20th century these networks served mainly three purposes:

1. Enabling the participants in financial networks jointly to recruit customers, thus increasing the companies' market shares.
2. Increasing the cooperation between agents both horizontally and vertically in the financial system, thus creating a joint responsibility for the persistence of the financial system and also creating the

capital for undertaking large-scale financing.

3. Financial networks also gave commercial banks – being the centres of the financial system – the opportunity to perform activities which were not intended in the banking legislation.

With the Second World War Sweden's financial system changed. Particulary in the 1950s and 1960s the financial system was subordinated to general financial and monetary policy. This meant an extensive regulation of the business of traditional financial agents such as banks and insurance companies. Thus, up to the 1980s, Sweden's bank-oriented financial system was strictly limited by governmental policy. During this period – 1940–80 – financial networks played a particulary important role in the circumvention of the regulated economy.

When deregulation started during the first half of the 1980s, Sweden's financial system underwent a gradual shift towards market orientation. Competition between financial agents increased and the stock market became more important for raising capital. However, this did not result in the dissolving of financial networks. Instead the networks were solidified, thus forming consolidated groups of financial institutions with banks and insurance companies in the centre. Financial networks had become instruments to counteract the increased market orientation of the financial system.

The establishment and early development of financial institutions was based primarily on traditions and norms within society. Special legislative measures for the financial market were not of great importance until the beginning of the 20th century, when for example the business of insurance companies as well as that of banks was more closely regulated. This early legislation was to a large extent based on practices and traditions that had developed within the financial system. With laws regulating the market the development towards a bank-oriented system was strengthened. Another effect of the legislation was that agents in the financial market were given different roles that tended to become rigid over time and that counteracted competition.

It is clear that governmental regulation and economic considerations have played a major role in the development of Sweden's financial system in the 20th century. The structural stability of the financial market has partly been shaped by governmental guidelines. Also of special importance is the early establishment of the bank and insurance inspectorates, which, particularly at the beginning of the century, through their central supervision, helped companies to develop standards for good insurance and banking practices.

This might leave us with a view of the Swedish financial system as being undynamic and rigid, but the functioning of the system is primarily an effect of how regulatory measures were actually adopted. The most dynamic force in Sweden's financial system has been the commercial banks, which due to traditions – path dependence – have performed new activities and taken larger risks than other agents. The creation of financial networks is one example of how commercial banks have acted to adjust to new market conditions.

Notes

1. The cheap money policy also resulted in economic problems for life insurance companies. After 1933 and for the rest of the 1930s the official discount rate was around 3 per cent and lending rates from banks around 4 per cent. This made it difficult to maintain a yield of 4 per cent that life insurance companies were obliged to give on private insurances. This problem was to some degree counteracted by legislation allowing a 3.5 per cent yield on insurances.
2. An example of the close cooperation between banks and insurance companies is given in Lindgren (1988: 279 f.). Stockholms Enskilda Bank and the insurance company Skandia not only jointly recruited customers, they also worked together on the bond market and in long-term lending, in Sweden as well as on the international market.
3. The limitation of the right to acquire shares was mainly in order to protect the customers' capital. To avoid high risk exposure, shareholdings had to be restricted, but with the establishment of affiliated investment companies this restriction was circumvented. See Östlind (1945).
4. Through tradition and legislation it was impossible to pull different types of financial institutions together in the same group of companies. The use of affiliated companies based on personal relationships was thus the basis for institutional cooperation.
5. After the legislation in 1933 prohibiting the acquisition of shares, Göteborgs Bank was the only larger commercial bank to sell its holdings in industry. The three other larger banks retained their interests through affiliated investment companies.
6. The expansion of credits could not be covered by increased deposits. To be able to compete, banks therefore had to borrow money on the international market. Also, finance companies were dependent on the banks' ability to raise international capital.

References

Föreningsbankernas Bank, årsredovisning (1990), *Annual Report*.
Franzén, Christer (1989). 'När utländsk statsskuld blev inhemsk', in Dahmén Erik (ed.), *Upplåning och utveckling, Riksgäldskontoret*

1789–1989, Stockholm.

Gota-gruppen, årsredovisning (1990), *Annual Report.*

Key-Åberg, Karl (1921), *Svenska aktiebolag och enskilda banker*, Stockholm.

Kock, Karin (1961), *Kreditmarknad och räntepolitik, första delen*, Stockholm.

Larsson, Mats (1991), *Den reglerade marknaden: svenskt försäkringsväsende 1850–1980*, Stockholm.

Larsson. Mats and Lindgren, Håkan (1990), 'Risktagandets gränser' in C. G. Thunman and Kent Eriksson (eds), *Bankmarknader i förvandling*, Lund.

Larsson, Mats and Lindgren, Håkan (1992), 'The political economy of banking: retail banking and corporate finance in Sweden 1850–1939', in Youssef Cassis (ed.), *Finance and Financiers in European History 1880–1960*, Cambridge.

Lindgren, Håkan (1988), *Bank, investmentbolag, bankirfirma. Stockholms Enskilda Bank 1934–1945*, Stockholm.

Lindgren, Håkan (1990), 'Affärsbankerna – näringslivets herrar eller tjänare' in *Pecunia n. 1*, skrifter utgivna av Kungl. Myntkabinettet, Stockholm.

Marquardt, Rolf (1992), *Svenska bankers internationaliseringsprocess*, Uppsala.

Neave, Edwin. H. (1991), *The Economic Organization of a Financial System*, London and New York.

Nordbanken, årsredovisning (1990), *Annual Report.*

Östlind, Anders (1945), *Svensk samhällsekonomi 1914–1922*, Stockholm.

Schön, Lennart (1989), 'Svensk statsskuldspolitik genom tvåhundra år', in Dahmén Erik (ed.), *Upplåning och utveckling, Riksgäldskontoret 1789–1989*, Stockholm.

S-E-Banken, årsredovisning (1990), *Annual Report.*

Söderlund, Ernst (1978), *Skandinaviska Banken i det svenska bankväsendets historia 1914–1939*, Stockholm.

SOU (Statens Offentliga Utredningar) 1949:13, *Förslag om inrättandet av statlig affärsbank*, Stockholm.

SOU (Statens Offentliga Utredningar) 1955:43, *Om riksbankens sedelutgivningsrätt*, Stockholm: Allmänna förlaget.

Sparbankernas Bank, årsredovisning (1990), *Annual Report.*

Svenska aktiebolag 1955–1956 (1956), Stockholm: P.A. Norstedt & Söner.

Svenska Handelsbanken, årsredovisning (1990), *Annual Report.*

Zysman, John (1983), *Governments, Markets, and Growth. Financial Systems and The Politics of Industrial Change*, Ithaca and London.

CHAPTER SEVEN

German Savings Banks as Instruments of Regional Development up to the Second World War

Paul Thomes

In the first half of the century, German savings banks played a more outstanding part in the field under discussion here than all other types of credit institutions. Starting from this thesis, I shall first describe how they gradually assumed that role and then proceed to a concrete analysis of their various levels of competence in the context of a political and economic background marked by multiple changes. They centre around the three sectors of business activity involving assets, liabilities and – last but by no means least – surpluses. For a better understanding of the process, a preliminary consideration of the way savings banks came into being and developed is advisable.

Institutional factors

Despite the local and regional contrasts so typical of the history of German savings banks, the following general points are relevant.[1]

It is quite certain that the original founders were not primarily concerned with the role specified in the title of this chapter. Nor could they be aware until late in the 19th century that they had created an instrument that would help to hasten the collapse of the archaic structures of the credit sector that had developed over hundreds of years and open up totally new directions.

Indeed, the intentions of the savings bank movement were motivated by exclusively social concerns with no commercial background and were at first primarily concerned with what was later to be called liabilities. The dominant foreground business feature was the acceptance of relatively small savings hitherto virtually valueless as investments, a forward-looking innovation destined to give them a monopoly in that field for a long time to come.

The target group was those sections of the 'poor', but certainly not destitute, population that had increased in number as a result of demographic growth in the 18th century, for whom the interest on deposits, even if the return was low, would provide an additional incentive to save. The implicit intention was to provide, as far as possible, a greater degree of stability in what we should now see as the more than impoverished circumstances of those concerned (seeing, in short, institutionalized saving as an instrument of self-help), thus helping, of course, to ease the burden on local authority provision for the poor.

Research all too often ignores the fact that in acting thus, savings banks were innovative in two respects. In this connection, therefore, a specific observation is appropriate: they were not only the first credit institutions to concern themselves with the needs of the broad mass of the population, but also – and this is of prime importance in connection with our theme – they assumed from the very beginning responsibility for the large area of non-urbanized regions so far untapped from a credit point of view.[2]

They thus deserve recognition for offering a new kind of financial service and being the first to open up to the capital market a considerable financial potential with what at the time were scarcely foreseeable development prospects, which until then had consisted of people who often kept their savings under the mattress and had found no place in economic circles. In this field, the savings banks were undoubtedly pioneering institutions.

The observation is all the more important as on the one hand the future of both non-cash transactions and paper money was to a large extent in the lap of the gods. On the other hand, however, the amount of disposable money was continually growing as a result of industrialization, since increasing sections of the population found themselves for the very first time in a position to save as a result of the constant opportunities for earning provided by industry (Wysocki, 1980: 45 ff.; Thomes, 1991: 240–52). The speed of the savings-bank diffusion process speaks for itself (Thomes, 1992: 187 ff.) and *post factum* it is scarcely surprising that in a situation of rapid expansion they were administering, by 1900, accounts to the value of around 9 billion marks in some 15 million savings accounts (Born, 1977: 207).

The holders – mostly local authorities at district level, less frequently at that of provinces or Länder – found themselves confronted, as a result of such unexpected success, with the important and difficult problem of how to put the influx of capital to the best possible use. By that time, they had already abandoned the more or less naive and inappropriate notion of paying interest out of local authority budgets.[3]

As a result, savings banks were more or less forced to build up what in the circumstances was a highly diversified assets operation almost equal to that of the banking sector.[4] In the second half of the 19th century, they were subsequently to perform a further important function, which was also fully in accordance with their sociopolitical mandate, in channelling combined 'small' savings directly into the economic circuit in the form of credits.

What was initially a charitable institution had become a provider of financial services with a charitable background, particularly since it was authorized to act as a drawee in 1908. This opened up the forward-looking field of giro business to savings banks and hence very usefully made them of even greater interest, especially to regionally-operating medium-sized companies (Trende, 1957: 440 ff.,446 ff.).[5]

Since their geographical sphere of interest usually coincided with their guarantors' administrative units, they were virtually predestined to assume a significant role in regional economic development. In addition, gradually taking on this task was more or less written into their regionally-based articles of foundation, a phenomenon pithily and appositely summarized in the title of Bodo Spiethoff's book *Ungewollt zur Größe (Greatness Thrust Upon Them)* (Spiethoff, 1958). What has been said so far represents the basis of a specific structural consideration of savings banks.

The place of savings banks in credit business

Without a comparative dimension, the information provided by data is always in a sense incomplete. If we are to picture the significance of savings banks within the credit field – and also their relative share of business and their financial potential – we need to cast a brief evaluative glance beyond the boundaries of our immediate concern and out into the general field of banking.

In 1913, there were 3 133 savings banks with some 7 000 branches administering deposits of around 20 billion marks, with corresponding assets,[6] an increase of over 120 per cent on the 1900 figure.

Cooperative credit banks, which operated on the same local basis as savings banks, but of which there were 19 300, nevertheless held in the same year between 5 and 6 billion marks. The corresponding figure for 1900 was probably around 2 billion marks.[7]

The 160 joint-stock credit banks in Germany had a relatively modest 9.6 billion marks in deposits and credits[8] before the First World War, while mortgage banks had issued 11.5 billion marks in debentures,[9] and (to provide an outside comparison) the frequently-mentioned German foreign capital investments accounted for between 25 and 30 billion marks.[10]

These details confirm that up to the outbreak of the First World War savings banks made a continuous and considerable contribution to financing the rapidly-growing need for economic investment, a fact long overlooked by researchers in economic history, dazzled by the fascinating performance of the major credit banks (Hoffmann,1969: 592 ff.; Wysocki, 1980: 119 f.).[11]

If we exclude purely industrial financing as being the particular field of the credit banks, we can even talk of the dominant position of savings banks. In the case of hitherto largely rural regions, where the only serious competitors were the cooperative credit banks and perhaps one or two private banks (Wysocki, 1980: 174 ff.), this was very much the case.

Twenty-five years later,[12] when Germany had lost a world war, after hyperinflation, monetary reform and the 'savings miracle', the devastating effects of the world economic crisis and the forcing into line of the German economy by the National Socialists, 2 517 savings banks with 11 335 branches and deposit counters[13] were again administering 18 billion reichsmarks in savings deposits and some 2.9 billion in at sight and fixed-term deposits.[14] Their total balance was 22.5 million reichsmarks,[15] corresponding to a share of 28.6 per cent in terms of all German credit institutions.[16] These figures are all the more noteworthy as competitors had recognized the advantages of small savings and were making increasingly aggressive attempts to gain a foothold in a field which had always been the particular province of the savings banks.

Nevertheless their bitterest rivals, the cooperative credit banks, showed a balance of just 6 billion reichsmarks. The five remaining major banks in Berlin showed a balance of 9 billion reichsmarks, of which 10 per cent were in savings accounts. Thirty-seven provincial banks showed a balance of 1.4 billion reichsmarks, with 17 per cent in savings accounts, whereas ten years previously the figure had been under 4 per cent. Finally, as regards the mortgage banks, they had lost a great deal of their importance since the monetary reform, with the balances of 30 institutions reaching 8.6 billion reichsmarks,[17] of which savings accounts amounted to 2 per cent (Hoffmann, 1969: 576 ff.).

A word also needs to be said about the density of the savings bank network. Despite the success of the idea, which is reflected in the overall data, it would lead to error if a regular nationwide distribution were to be assumed. Here too there is evidence of the almost proverbial variation in extent between the Länder states and also down to the level of provinces and regions.

Although there was a savings bank for every 1 197 inhabitants or 10 square kilometres in Württemberg in 1905, the corresponding figure for Hessen was 25 191 for 160. In Prussia, which had by far the largest area, there was one savings bank for every 7 518 inhabitants or 77.2 square kilometres. For Bavaria, the statistics show one for every 6 535 inhabitants or 77.2 square kilometres (Trende, 1957: 336). Even if the differences became smaller over time, they were still quite clear up to the beginning of the Second World War as a result of the markedly decentralized nature of the savings bank movement. The very varying intensity of the involvement of the competent supervisory or administrative authorities proved to be the deciding factor in maintaining this level of heterogeneity, apart from such particular organizational features as the relatively strong position of district savings banks in Prussia, Baden and Württemberg (Sommer, 1934: 75 ff; Trende, 1957).

The few basic data quoted should, however, indicate that savings banks maintained their strong position within the credit economy over the whole period under consideration (Hoffman, 1969: 592 ff; Thomes, 1992),[18] even though in the debit sphere, which had once been their monopoly, they now had to face up to competition from almost all sides, be it cooperative credit banks, private bankers or a branch of one of the large banks. The latter had increasingly branched out, at least in regional large and medium-sized centres, in order, as had been their practice since the last quarter of the 19th century, to penetrate those areas which had previously been the exclusive province of the savings bank movement.[19]

Savings banks and liabilities in a regional perspective

At first glance one is strongly inclined to limit enquiries to assets, on the one hand because it is there that results provide the most striking documentary evidence, and on the other hand because they can also be concretely quantified or classified. However, it would be quite wrong to ignore liabilities as an important factor in regional economic development.

That is because from the point of view of business management, liabilities created for savings banks, which initially operated without any capital, more than for their competitors in the credit sector, the prerequisites for the assets side. They therefore refinanced themselves overwhelmingly by means of deposits, that is, from local savings, the safety of which was guaranteed by local authority guarantors. Their effectiveness as an instrument of regional development was, and still is, consequently closely tied up with their local acceptance.

From an economic point of view, too, capital created by institutionalized saving is to be evaluated as a positive step towards financing consumption or investment which is in one way or another of great benefit to the local economy. Such findings were all the more valid as the original socially-motivated barriers to access gradually fell.[20] In practice, savings banks in the 20th century were open to anyone, irrespective of financial means or social standing. Only the notion of common benefit was reminiscent of their originally predominantly social aspirations.[21]

Nevertheless, customers were overwhelmingly recruited from the lower classes and the middle class. In 1936, three-quarters of all savings books were for accounts standing at below 300 reichmarks, a fact which says a lot, even though their total amounted to only 8.4 per cent of deposits.[22]

If we see savings as a means of providing for future contingencies or creating liquid reserves, then savings banks may also be said to have made a certain contribution to improving the continuity of demand in their catchment areas. For it was not only individuals in difficulties who were helped by their meagre savings as the need arose. The same was just as true for times of general economic stagnation. In addition, savings in times of prosperity helped reduce purchasing power and could thus reduce a short-term overheating of the economy. All these were compensatory functions with levelling effects beneficial to both individuals and the economy. To that extent, they could be seen as having had a positive effect on regional economic development.[23]

What has been said above about the density of the savings bank network can also be applied to the intensity of saving. There was some not insignificant variation – although the trend was always upwards – as can be seen from the relative number of accounts and the level of credit as statistical indicators of the degree of regional penetration.

To give just one significant snapshot: in 1920 in Prussia, which alone held over 60 per cent of all deposits in German savings banks, 57 out of every 100 inhabitants had a savings book, which in fact matched the average for the whole country. This was an impressive figure, as at the turn of the century only one in four Prussians had had a savings account. It simply means that almost every Prussian family had made use of the savings bank movement.

Bavaria lagged behind, with 30 out of every 100, almost half the national average in the 1920s, and came ahead only of Mecklenburg-Schwerin, where the figure was 28. In Saxony, on the other hand, an almost inconceivable 93 per cent of the inhabitants were depositing money in savings banks. The rate was also very high in the city-states of Hamburg and Bremen (91 per cent) and in Thuringia (84 per cent)

(Höpker, 1924: 82).

An examination of deposits per inhabitant shows that at the same time Prussia, with 799 marks, was exceeding the national average of 744 (Cremer, 1925: 433 ff.). Bavaria was limping along here too, far behind the rest at only 359 marks while Baden, with a statistical savings account of 1013 marks per head of population, was the undisputed leader (Höpker, 1924: 82).

Despite such discrepancies, the trend was for deviations to decrease. In line with the national average, the figures came closer together, from state to state and region to region. Bavaria was the only significant exception (Hoffmann, 1969: 572 ff.).

These findings provide documentary evidence of an important fact. Although a close connection between saving and income or the level of industrialization can hardly be disputed, saving is not necessarily an exact indicator of the prosperity of an area. This is also supported by the fact that the effects of a general interruption of growth, such as the world economic crisis, always affected the *Länder* in more or less the same way (Hoffmann, 1969: 574 ff.).[24] As decisive criteria for the development prospects of liabilities, the form of organization and the local competitive situation, along with the aforementioned involvement of the relevant authorities or holders' guarantors, showed themselves to be rather more important.

As regards the form of organization, it is clear that district savings banks with subsidiaries reached a wider circle of people than municipal ones operating from the central town of a district or area without a network of branches. This was all the more so as a visit to the head office for people living in the surrounding areas always involved a considerable expenditure of time, despite the rapidly improving transport situation after the First World War (Thomes: 1988a,1988b). Considered from this point of view, it was not statutory requirements but the relative efficiency of the infrastructure that decisively limited the catchment and business area of savings banks. If a Prussian savings bank administered 13470 accounts in 1920 and its Bavarian counterpart only 5505, the discrepancy in Prussia's favour was to no small extent the result of a more effective regional organizational structure of the kind that the Prussian authorities had developed since the middle of the 19th century and vigorously encouraged.[25]

With regard to competition, the saying 'first come, first served' should be seen as valid up to a point. That is to say, if a degree of saturation was reached, it was very hard for new savings banks, or their branches, to reconquer occupied territory from competitors, especially in the shape of credit unions, even if the means used were better conditions or aggressive marketing.[26]

The growth of deposits in savings banks was hesitant because of their decentralized structure in certain special and highly localized economic situations,[27] an important drawback in the regional principle, at least theoretically. In practice, however, this was of no consequence in the period in question. The savings banks' own internal balancing systems (Thomes, 1985b: 48 ff.), like the regional banks and Giro offices[28] solved such liquidity problems as there were very efficiently.[29]

We can sum up the liabilities side by saying that the regional basis of the savings bank movement, with its decentralized organization that was quite consciously used and defended as a counterweight to the trend towards increased concentration so marked in the credit field at the time, should be seen in a positive light, especially as the long-visible and deep-seated reluctance of potential customers towards a municipally-controlled institution had changed into a relationship of confidence in a comprehensible and reliable one.

Indeed, this quasi-psychological relationship, together with the charitable status and persistent pressures from local authorities, created the conditions for developing hitherto idle capital for a regional demand rising in step with industrialization, which the major banks could not and still cannot fully achieve (Henze and Schmidt, 1955: 46ff.).

The assets side of savings banks in a regional perspective

Investing savings as far as possible within the business area was indivisibly linked to both the concept of decentralization and the sociopolitical mandate of savings banks.[30] As a result of the competitive situation sketched in above, savings banks *per se* took on a decisive importance for regional development with regard to the assets side too.[31] The question of how beneficial debit capital was at the local level (as well as all the assertions to the contrary) had already been comprehensively addressed well before the 20th century began. Moreover, providing credit soon emerged as a function of equal importance to that of accepting savings.[32] The one-sided view of savings banks as nothing but savings institutions is thus 'historically false' (Henze and Schmidt, 1955: 12).

The decisive factor apart from economic need[33] was the latent need for credit over a broad range of social classes, combined with the struggle against the hated usurers, which was totally in accordance with the savings banks' sociopolitical mandate. By the time of the 1838 Prussian regulations governing savings banks, there was provision for investment in first mortgages, local authority credit, and the financing of possible local community loan institutions, as well as more generally in domestic state securities and bonds or 'in other fully secure areas' (see Hahn, 1920: 7 ff.; Trende, 1957: 103 ff., 474 ff.; Spiethoff, 1958: 58 ff.; Hoffmann, 1969: 584 ff.).

If the language used in the rules of some local commitment was far from explicit,[34] we should not be surprised to find that many of the constitutions of savings banks, like that of the Teltow district savings bank in Prussia, which we can take as an example, contained such limitations (Hahn, 1920: 38 ff.)[35] without completely closing the channels for diverting surplus liquidity onto the national capital market.[36]

The propagation of local investment was also to a considerable extent the result of the chief and most fundamental rule of business policy which postulated, with whatever nuances and variations, the totally uncompromising principle of 'investing funds securely'.[37] And what better place to reduce risk than in a known and readily-visible environment?[38]

With regard to credits, savings banks were obviously less innovative than in the field of liabilities, since they encountered a large number of already established[39] private and institutional competitors, such as foundations (Thomes, 1985a: 77 ff.; Hruschka, 1990: 175 ff.). Gaining a foothold was all the harder when on the one hand they were not always in a position to offer better conditions because of the constraints of having to pay interest on deposits.[40] On the other hand, the security aspect often made the approval proceedings administratively unrewarding and clearly acted as a deterrent. Thirdly, it would be wrong to exaggerate the demand. Outside the industrial centres, the need for capital was relatively modest. Fairly often, investment plans were limited to mere replacement. Their main emphasis was on acquiring buildings and land, renovation and the financial settlement of inheritances. Above and beyond this, the need for finance in a rural economy grew as arable land was realigned, improvements were carried out and livestock was increased.[41]

In this context, it should be noted that the fact that investment in bonds was so popular in many places is in itself hardly sufficient to indicate a lack of local investment opportunities. The time-consuming administration and associated risk of small-scale business was frequently alarming to honorary trustees, whereas state-guaranteed securities had the advantage of imposing only minor burdens in this respect (Thomes, 1985a: 284 ff.).

We should now look at how, at the turn of the century, German savings banks did in fact invest the money entrusted to them.[42] It was to a very large extent in loans connected with land,[43] which always accounted for well over 50 per cent of the assets side in individual states.

In Prussia, it was just under 60 per cent (Höpker, 1924: 82).[44] In Saxony and Hessen the share by volume of mortgage loans amounted to a good 80 per cent (Trende, 1957: 499 f., 508 ff.),[45] in Baden and Württemberg to a little over 70 per cent (Trende, 1957: 501 ff.), and in Bavaria to around 50.[46]

A little way behind on the popularity scale came securities with for the most part quotas above 10 per cent, although they were to a certain extent only to be acquired if there were no other possibilities.[47] They subsequently performed the important function of acting as a kind of reserve of liquidity. At the very top came the Bavarian savings banks, with a share of 46.3 per cent in 1900 (Spiethoff, 1958: 58ff.). In the same year, 26.1 per cent of deposits in the Prussian savings banks were invested in bearer bonds, and Saxony followed with around 15 per cent.[48]

Local authority credit[49] formed the third group of assets, with quota percentages oscillating between under 2 in Saxony and over 10 in Prussia and Württemberg.[50]

Finally, personal credit, once at the centre of savings bank activities but which since the 1870s had been abandoned to the cooperative credit banks virtually without a struggle, dragged a long way behind, with quotas still mostly below 5 per cent.[51] Before the First World War, exchange discounts, loans on security and current account credit were of no real significance.

This pattern remained more or less unchanged until 1914. Quantitatively, only investment in bearer bonds increased slightly, and this was much more the result of massive state interest than of the wishes of the savings banks.[52] Qualitatively, it is worth mentioning that urban mortgages became more significant, which reflected on the one hand the marked urban dynamics of the time and on the other the growing competition from the cooperative credit banks in the countryside.

Incidentally, the shape the assets business took in individual cases could vary quite strikingly from the average. To give just one or two examples, the municipal savings bank in Zweibrücken in the Bavarian Pfalz granted its very first mortgage loan in 1890, whereas its neighbouring counterpart in Primasens had put 90 per cent of its resources into mortgages at the beginning of the century. The average for the Bavarian Pfalz fluctuated around 60 per cent. Many of the savings banks in the area provided no municipal credit at all.[53] Much the same was true of Lower Bavaria, where in 1911 63.6 per cent of resources went in mortgages and 34 per cent on bearer bonds. In such cases, there was little room for other forms of investment (Hruschka, 1990: 224).

On the other hand, in 1900 over 60 per cent of the assets of the

Düsseldorf municipal savings bank consisted of securities. The figure for local authority credit was 18 per cent, with real credit barely reaching 23 per cent (Haas, 1976: 391). In 1914, some 10 per cent of Prussian savings banks were not involved in personal credit at all, and 57 per cent involved less than 5 per cent of their assets. Yet 27 per cent of institutions had invested over 30 per cent of their resources in this area (Henze and Schmidt, 1955: 37). The Schleswig-Holstein savings banks reached an average level of around 15 per cent here (Föh, 1988: 77).[54]

In spite of all the variations, this finding provides pertinent documentary evidence of the overwhelmingly regional orientation in the years leading up to the First World War. Mortgage, local authority and personal credit were invested to a very great extent within the guarantor's own locality. In addition, a certain proportion of money invested in securities must have flowed back to its place of origin.

The performance of savings banks in regional financing must remain an open question, as the volume of private financing cannot be precisely calculated. However, all the indications are that even if not absolutley dominant, the savings banks' quota was nevertheless far from insignificant.

A further observation concerning the qualitative use of resources indicated above needs to be made. As far as local authority credit is concerned, they were decisive in facilitating the financing of increasing obligations towards residents as standards rose. In addition, local administrations showed 'greater entrepreneurial spirit', particularly in the decade before the war, entailing a considerable further increase in the need for finance (Haas, 1976: 168).

The lion's share went to the infrastructure: providing and supplying electricity, gas, drinking water, building roads and bridges, creating local public transport services in the form of trams, acquiring land and earmarking it for building, industrial areas or railway tracks. This entailed an increase in the construction of such public buildings as town halls, schools, hospitals, churches and the like (Haas, 1976: 166 f.; Thomes, 1985a: 276 ff.). The effects of this involvement on regional economic development were subsequently to be seen on all sides.

The same is unreservedly true of real credit, as it would be erroneous to see this sector as identical with purely private investment. Firms made use of real credit as a tried and tested financial instrument to at least the same extent.

Hotels and department store buildings were also financed by savings banks, as were also workshops, business firms or the most varied plants, provided the necessary securities were available (Haas, 1976: 162 ff.; Thomes, 1985a: 260 ff.). Thus the most striking feature of mortgage operations was their distinctly commercial nature, since at least in characteristically urban regions they had been directly concerned with local undertakings.

The First World War had a major effect on what had hitherto been the real economic determinants, for like all wars it shifted the structures of financial requirements and hence the direction of the flow of capital. The local concerns of savings banks took a poor second place to those of the nation as a whole, from which, as public institutions, they neither could nor would distance themselves. This was expressed in a considerable reduction in mortgage business[55] to the benefit of investments in bonds, as the savings banks themselves played a decisive part in war loans.[56]

From the assets of the Prussian savings banks (24.3 billion marks at the end of 1918) 10.9 billion marks or 44.9 per cent were invested in bearer bonds, as against 20.4 per cent in local authority credit. Mortgages were stagnant around 8 billion marks, or 32.9 per cent.[57]

Two years later, in 1920, the statistics once again show a renewed shift in the centre of gravity. Of the assets totalling 30.4 billion marks, 24 per cent were allocated to mortgages, 30.8 per cent to bonds and 42 per cent to local authority credit. Within the space of six years what had seemed to be permanent statistical structures had broken down. Public credit had definitely stepped into the foreground for the first time.

In line with this, the share of commercially-invested resources had to decrease. Even from a qualitative point of view there was a new modification, as local authority credit, which was increasing rapidly as a result of the effects of the war, became more directed towards consumption. That is to say, money lent out largely served to finance social measures and less to provide direct support for investment projects.[58] In this way, not only did it make an important contribution to supporting the new democracy, but also to ensuring that basic local needs such as food, clothing and housing were met. There is no need to point out that credit became an extremely high-risk business during the period of hyperinflation. In its long-term form, it subsequently almost came to a halt.

The good five years between the stabilization of the Weimar economy in 1924 and the world economic crisis – a period of enormous and seemingly impossible transformation that we usually look back on as the golden 1920s – brought business back towards normal pre-war structures (Krafft, 1968:125; Haas, 1976: 211). With an accumulated 65 per cent share of mortgage, personal and local authority credit for 1929, it becomes clear that the prewar regional functions described above were once again unambiguously the main spurs of the activities of the savings bank movement.[59]

The negative experience in securities had no doubt been a not unimportant contributory factor. The commercial and industrial middle class was wooed ever more assiduously, and with the much higher levels of current account business that had been achieved in the meantime, the savings banks had an extra trump card that offered business customers the option of non-bureaucratic short-term company credits alongside spot settlements of payments.[60]

The local authorities' need for finance became increasingly the concern of the giro centres rather than that of the savings banks themselves (Zweig, 1986: 45 ff.). A further characteristic of interwar savings bank business with marked local connections was the intensive involvement in residential building as a result of constant and continued need for housing, together with a rapid rise in real credit.[61]

The National Socialists' takeover of power in 1933 again led to a turning point which was to strip the savings banks of their function as instruments of regional development more thoroughly than ever. The basis for this was the 1934 credit law, which both integrated them fully into the credit system and at the same time reduced them to the level of dependent instruments of a central economic control.[62] They were first enmeshed in the consolidation of Reich finances, and then very soon, as a matter of prime importance, required to help as unobtrusively as possible with financing the totalitarian regime's preparations for war (Spiethoff, 1958: 236 ff.; Krafft, 1968: 139 ff.; Haas, 1976: 272 ff.).

Against such a background the supervisory authorities gradually reduced the still major investment in mortgages, while the ban on local authority credit introduced by the savings bank reform[63] of 1931 was only insignificantly eased.[64] The result could only be a renewed and marked change in structure, away from the traditional regional principle. The break is readily comprehensible from the statistics, which indicate a fast-growing volume of Reich stocks and bank credits. In 1934, the three traditional pillars of the assets side were still amounting to 63 per cent of the rapidly increasing nominal balance figure, but by 1939 they had fallen to only 45 per cent. At the end of 1944 their share had melted away to a mere 10 per cent as a result of a war prosecuted with the utmost vigour.[65]

The Nazi regime had insisted on the priority of central needs for finance more radically than had ever been the case in the history of the savings banks. This did not apply solely to them, of course, but the fact that they were based on public law meant that they were immediately doomed to be subjected to state influence. The totalitarian way in which control was implemented was not tempered by deviations from legal constraints, as had happened often enough in the past. Consequently, direct provision for the local economy faded into the background, and their sociopolitical objective of meeting the need for credit of the 'weaker sections of the people' continued to exist only on paper.[66]

'Surpluses' and regional development

Although maximum profit was clearly not the overriding aim of the business policy of the savings banks, operating surpluses could hardly be avoided sooner or later. Even if not every institution was in the black,[67] profits at the beginning of the century totalled a good 24 million marks nationally. In 1909, they amounted to more than 41 million which, once a reasonable sum had been paid into the reserves, could be used for 'public purposes' or extraordinary municipal needs, with or without restrictions of aims.[68] Another way of saying this is that a good part of the profits were more or less at the disposition of the trustees, to be used as they saw fit, and so it is only too understandable that as profits grew, so did economic interest in their institutions.[69]

Nevertheless, funds diverted in this way did in certain circumstances considerably help to broaden the area of financial operations. Thus in Prussia alone a total of 4.1 million marks in 138 districts was disbursed. In the kingdom of Saxony resources provided for the local authorities[70] rose from 2.25 million marks in 1887 to 7.4 million in 1908. In over half of the Saxon municipalities, at least 10 per cent of all income came from this source, and the figures for the other Länder were similar (Haas, 1976: 173 ff., 229 ff.; Thomes, 1985a: 222 ff.).

In many places the local authority regularly depended on the savings bank 'to avoid unduly high local taxation' (Knebel Doeberitz, 1907: 127f.). The effects of a combination of a moderate tax burden and further public commitments on the local economic climate needs no special explanation, however.

Little needs to be said about the use of resources, which varied in terms of regional norms. They flowed into such varied areas as development of the infrastructure, social housing, improvements in baby care and 'school health', the provision of schools and scholarships, financing public gardens, parks and reading rooms, free subscriptions to advisory literature, the interest-free supply of seeds and fertilizers, promoting livestock-raising and growing fruit trees, setting up dung heaps and so on.

To some extent they were also used within the savings banks themselves to raise holdings or reduce interest on debits or to fund affiliated savings institutions in schools or for old people. The constant concern for their sociopolitical mandate is very impressively brought to mind by the way in which they used the proceeds of their cheque operations, originally heavily criticized as being too 'bank-like', to reward small savers (Trende, 1957: 527 ff.; Haas, 1976: 174 f.; Wysocki, 1980: 154 ff.; Thomes, 1985a: 223 ff.).

At the time of hyperinflation and the loss of almost all their reserves, these practices came temporarily to a sudden end. Once again, building up their safety reserves, which had to be brought into as reasonable a relationship as possible to the growing volume of deposits, took priority. The unavoidable 'donations' to the social institutions of the National Socialist apparatus only came back partly and indirectly to those areas in which they had been earned.

Savings banks and regions: an overview

Given both their sociopolitical mandate and their local roots, savings banks were almost automatically obliged to concentrate their operations within the regional field. This was all the more so as the development of an informed commercial opinion strongly based on local persons and institutions went hand in hand with the organizational principle of connection with a specific area. This means that right from their inception the importance of their role in regard to the function we are debating here cannot be overestimated.

In general, from a credit point of view, they played a decisive part in preventing large areas of a hitherto rural nature from being too scattered to benefit from credit for economic development. More specifically, their close ties with local government worked against a flight of capital from such areas to the major financial and industrial centres. They were thus regional levellers of capital, as is shown to some extent in the security market, but normally only in so far as the channelling of surpluses was concerned. What was important in this context was that they acquired the medium-sized industries as an important group of customers at a very early stage.

This investigation has shown that this combination remained fully effective until the First World War, with their great emphasis on their sociopolitical mandate also playing a considerable part in stabilizing the socioeconomic situation.

In the exceptional circumstances of the First World War, the national dimension came into the foreground for the first time. Savings banks became collection points for capital to finance national interests. Once things became normal again, however, the pendulum swung extraordinarily quickly in the other direction, indicating the relative strength of the regional connection described above, if we assume the free play of forces.

The lamentable period of Nazi dictatorship showed more clearly and more radically than ever that regional roots of the kind still very much in evidence today can be suppressed only by extremely severe legal sanctions.

As far as savings banks and regional economic development are concerned, it should be stressed that they are optimally complementary. Had the former not already been in existence in the early 20th century, we should have had to invent them.

Notes

1. See Knebel Doeberitz (1907); Trende (1957); Spiethoff (1958); Hoffmann (1969: 125); *Deutsche Bankengeschichte*, 2 and 3, Frankfurt/Main, 1982-83. For further reading, consult the works listed in References section. It should be noted that in general there are more gaps in research on the 20th century than for earlier periods.
2. This refers only to the overwhelmingly private nature of credit relationships.
3. See the appropriate chapters in the general literature.
4. Here too it is difficult to generalize. A great deal depended on those entrusted with running the business.
5. On the whole, savings banks were permitted to engage in all non-speculative business.
6. Including 1 765 savings banks in Prussia with deposits of 13.1 billion marks. Including branches and subsidiaries, there were 9 127 savings banks in 1905 (Trende, 1957: 366).
7. Estimated value.
8. The comparable figure for 1900 was 118 institutions with a balance of 7 billion marks. Their share capital also rose rather slowly from just 2 million to just 3 million marks in 1913.
9. 1900: 6.5 billion marks in deposits and credits amounted to 800 million marks in 1913, and the capital stock 890 million.
10. All the details given above are from *Deutsches Geld-und Bankwesen in Zahlen 1876-1975*, Frankfurt/Main, 1978; all values are rounded off.
11. Savings banks achieved the highest amount for all independent groups in the credit business
12. *Deutsches Geld-und Bankwesen in Zahlen*, 69 ff.; all values are rounded off.
13. There were just 57 000 employees. The information is partly contradictory. *Deutsche Bankengeschichte*, 3, pp. 297 ff.; *Sparkasse*, 1941, 10.
14. *Handwörterbuch der Sozialwissenschaften*, 9, Stuttgart, 1956, pp. 673 ff. Particularly after 1923, giro business quickly became significant, and in 1939 160 million transactions were carried out. See also Spiethoff (1958: 155 ff.).
15. Excluding Girozentralen and Landesbanken.
16. *Deutsches Geld-und Bankwesen in Zahlen*, pp. 74 f., 121.
17. Including mixed mortgage banks, with a balance of 1.95 billion reichsmarks.
18. For an inter-state comparison, see Thomes (1988a: 71 ff.).
19. In 1907, the 421 German joint-stock credit banks were operating 1 076 branches. Savings banks were particularly in demand in conurbations. See Krafft (1968: 94) and Thomes (1988b: 95 ff.).
20. See for instance the Prussian savings banks regulations of 1838, reprinted

in Hahn (1920: 5 ff.).

21. See Trende (1957: 511 ff. and Thomes (1985a). In Bavaria the 1874 ordinance removed certain restrictions; see Spiethoff (1958: 68 ff).

22. *Handwörterbuch der Sozialwissenschaften*, 9, 1956, p. 672; Wysocki, (1980: 84 ff.).

23. See Sommer (1934) and Hoffmann (1969: 579 ff.). The criteria for the 20th century are different from those for the 19th. Overall, different socioeconomic factors influenced the development of deposits.

24. For specific examples of the contrasts between industrial and agricultural areas, see Thomes, 1988.

25. On policy decisions in Prussia, see Thomes, (1985a: 15 ff, and the chapters on branches).

26. As a result of the regulations on reserve funds, the savings banks already found themselves at a disadvantage with regard to the cooperative credit banks. See Thomes (1988) and Hruschka (1990: 232 ff., 373 ff.).

27. Spiethoff (1958: 247 ff.) provides an example from 1936.

28. *Bankengeschichte*, 3, pp. 279 ff. The founding of the German savings banks and giro association took place in 1924; see Zweig (1986).

29. See Spiethoff (1958: 207 ff.); *Deutsche Bankengeschichte*, 3, pp. 284 ff.

30. Regional savings banks, such as those in Württemberg or Oldenburg, with a business area covering the whole state territory, were no exception in this respect.

31. C. A. Malchus (1838); quoted from Henze and Schmidt (1955: 19).

32. With regard to the close links between the two fields, see the introduction to this chapter.

33. In this connection too, see the introduction to this chapter.

34. With few exceptions, the same was true of the other German states.

35. Subsequently further limitations were imposed for the same reason (Thomes, 1985: 181 ff., 260 ff.).

36. In this connection, see for instance the provisions of the Prussian regulations. In Bavaria the state bank for discharging debts took over the saving banks' monies for a time (Spiethoff, 1958: 36 ff., 58 ff.).

37. Safety was followed by liquidity and profitability as further business aims, with the result that there was a different stress on investment policy from that prevailing in the credit banks.

38. The criteria for security were low limits on mortgage loans and usually double security for personal credit. Gilt-edged securities such as state guarantees were the prerequisite for purchasing bonds.

39. A large proportion of credit business was carried out on the basis of personal relationships. Proceeds from credit business provided security in old age for many rentiers. Wysocki (1980a) stresses a different emphasis.

40. Interest rates varied much less than they do nowadays. In the 19th century interest on credit remained around 5 per cent.

41. There is general agreement on this point in the literature.

42. Corresponding figures for the Reich are not available. In many statutes firmly established upper limits for individual investments were often ignored in practice.

43. Normally up to 58 per cent, later up to 75 per cent.

44. Including 50 per cent for municipal mortgages.

45. 1903 = 81 per cent.

46. *Handwörterbuch der Staatswissenschaft*, Jena, 1910, p. 650; Hruschka

(1990: 223 f.).

47. For purchasing, a guarantee from a public institution was required, particularly in the case of railways.

48. In Baden, 7.1 per cent was allotted to bearer bonds in 1903. In Hessen, the figure for 1900 was 8.8 per cent (Spiethoff, 1958: 58 ff.).

49. Credits to guarantors, local authorities and local public institutions.

50. Prussia, 10.3 per cent; Saxony (1903), 1.4 per cent; Baden, 7.5 per cent; Württemberg (1907), 18 per cent.

51. Selected rates: Prussia, 2.5 per cent; Saxony, 0.8 per cent; Baden (1903), 4.8 per cent. See Seidel and Pfitzner (1913a 1 ff.), Henze and Schmidt (1955: 36 ff.) and Föh (1988: 84 ff.).

52. As shown in the relevant laws. See in particular Seidel and Pfitzner (1913b), Hahn (1920: 244 ff.), Henze and Schmidt (1955: 28 ff., 56 ff.), Trende (1957: 505) and Föh (1988: 87 ff.).

53. Speyer, 150 Jahre *Sparkasse*, pp. 27 f.

54. For mortgage credit the rate was 75.

55. The inflation which set in as the war began and the general reluctance to invest at times of crisis played a certain part.

56. Investment in other securities was virtually impossible, as stock exchanges were closed when the war began.

57. *Geld- und Bankwesen in Zahlen*, p. 64.

58. Ibid.

59. As a result of deliberations on liquidity at the savings banks' conference in 1926, it was recommended that there should be a maximum proportion of 40 per cent for mortgages.

60. See *Geld- und Bankwesen in Zahlen*, pp. 102 ff.; Henze and Schmidt, (1955: 61); *Deutsche Bankengeschichte*, III, pp. 279 ff.; Will (1942: 117 ff.); *Der Personalkredit der Sparkassen*, in *Sparkasse*, 10, 1950; Haas (1976: 218 ff.).

61. See Neuss (132: 229 ff.), Krafft (1968: 139 ff.) and Haas (1976: 223 ff.). In 1929, the Düsseldorf savings bank financed one-third of all the new house building in the city.

62. See *Deutsche Bankengeschichte*, III, pp. 289 ff.; Henze and Schmidt (1955: 72).

63. See *Deutsche Bankengeschichte*, III, pp. 284 ff., 288 f.; Spiethoff (1958: 20 ff.).

64. *Deutsche Bankengeschichte*, III, pp. 291 ff.

65. See Henze and Schmidt (1955: 72 ff.); Krafft (1968: 169 ff.); *Deutsche Bankengeschichte*, III, pp. 293 ff.; *Geld- und Bankwesen*, pp. 102 f.; Zweig (1986: 61 ff.); Hoffmann (1969: 586 ff.); Born (1977: 538 ff.).

66. Demand nevertheless falls during a war, once the basic needs had to some extent been met.

67. Just half the Prussian savings banks in 1900.

68. On each occasion, with the approval of the supervisory authorities. See Knebel Doeberitz (1907: 127 f.); Reusch (1911, 1913); Trende (1957: 527 ff.); Wysocki (1980: 154 ff.).

69. Maximizing profit was not then a major aim of business policy.

70. In terms of savings banks working at a profit.

References

Born, K. E. (1977), *Geld und Bankem im 19. und 20. Jahrhundert*, Stuttgart.

Cremer, J. (1925), 'Geschichte des Sparkassenwesens in der Rheinprovinz', *Zeitschrift für Kommunalwirtschaft*, 15.

Föh, T. (1988), *Die Entwicklung des Sparkassenwesens in Schleswig-Holstein 1864–1914*, Neumünster.

Haas, E. J. (1976), *Stadt-Sparkasse Düsseldorf 1825–1972*, Berlin.

Hahn, M. (1920), *Handbuch der preußischen Sparkassengeset zgebung*, Berlin.

Henze, W. and Schmidt, H. (1955), *Grundriß für die Sparkassenarbeit*, 1, Stuttgart.

Hoffmann, W. G. (1969), 'Die Entwicklung der Sparkassen in Rahmen des Wachstums der deutschen Wirtschaft (1860–1967)', *Zeitschrift für die gesamte Staatswissenschaft*, 125.

Höpker, H. (1924), *Die deutschen Sparkassen, ihre Entwicklung und ihre Bedeutung*, Berlin.

Hruschka, M. (1990), *Die Entwicklung des Geld- und Kreditwesens unter besonder Berücksichtigung der Sparkasse im Raum Straubing-Bogen, 1830–1972*, Straubing.

Knebel Doeberitz, H. V. (1907), *Das Sparkassenwesen in Preußen*, Berlin.

Krafft, H. (1968), *Immer ging es ums Geld: 150 Jahre Sparkassen in Berlin*, Berlin.

Neuss, E. (1932), *Geschichte der Stadtsparkasse zu Halle*, Halle.

Reusch, H. (1911), *Die Überschüsse der preußischen Sparkassen, Verwaltung und Statistik*.

Reusch, H. (1913) 'Die Zinspolitik der Sparkassen', *Schriften des Vereins für Sozialpolitik*, 137.

Seidel, M. and Pfitzner, G. (1913a) 'Der Personalkredit der Sparkassen im Vergleich zu anderen Instituten', *Schriften des Vereins für Sozialpolitik*, 137 (I).

Seidel, M. and Pfitzner, G. (1913b) 'Die Sparkassengesetzgebung in den wichtigsten Staaten', *Schriften des Vereins für Sozialpolitik*, 137 (III).

Sommer, A. (1934), *Sparkassen und Konjunktur*, Berlin.

Spiethoff, B. (1958), *Ungewollt zur Größe: Die Geschichte der bayerischen Sparkassen*, Munich.

Thomes, P. (1985a), *Die Kreissparkasse Saarbrücken 1854–1914*, Frankfurt.

Thomes, P. (1985b), 'Kooperation statt Konkurrenz: Der Konferenzbezirk der Sparkassen des Saarreveirs', Bankhistorisches

Archiv, 11.

Thomes, P. (1988a), 'Sparkassen beiderseits der Grenze; die bayerische Pfalz und das preußische Saarrevier', *Zeitschrift für bayerische Sparkassengeschichte*, 2.

Thomes, P. (1988b), 'Sparkassen und Kreditgenossenschaften in der bayerischen Pfalz und im preußischen Regierungsbezirk Trier bis zum Ersten Weltkrieg', *Zeitschrift für bayerische Sparkassengeschichte*, 2.

Thomes, P. (1991), 'Zwischen Pump und Sparen – Unterschichtenhaushalte in der Industrialisierung', in T. Pierenkemper (ed.), *Zur Ökonomie des privaten Haushalts: Haushaltsrechnungen als Quellen historischer Wirtschafts- und Sozialforschung*, Frankfurt and New York, pp. 240–52.

Thomes, P. (1992), 'Die Diffusion der Sparkassen in Preußen', in M. Pix and H. Pohl (eds), *Invention – Innovation – Diffusion. Die Entwicklung des Spar- und Sparkassengedankens in Europa*, Frankfurt, pp. 187–205.

Trende, A. (1957), *Geschichte der deutschen Sparkassen*, Stuttgart.

Will, H. (1942), *Die deutschen Sparkassen*, Stuttgart.

Wysocki, J. (1980), *Untersuchungen zur Wirtschafts- und Sozialgeschichte der deutschen Sparkassen im 19. Jahrhundert*, Stuttgart.

Zweig, G. (1986), *Die deutsche Girozentrale – Deutsche Kommunalbank*, Stuttgart.

CHAPTER EIGHT

The National Savings Bank as an Instrument of Economic Policy: Portugal in the Interwar Period[1]

Jaime Reis

Portugal has a long history of savings institutions which goes back as far as the 15th century but modern savings banks emerged only in the middle of the 19th century. For the past 100 years, this sector has been dominated overwhelmingly by the state-owned and run Caixa Geral de Depositos (CGD). This was founded in 1876 in emulation of the French Caisse Generale des Depôts et Consignations 'which [has] contributed so much to the growth of credit and to the prosperity of France', as was admiringly claimed by the then Portuguese Finance Minister.[2] It was to receive both private savings and the compulsory deposits required by the authorities for judicial, fiscal or administrative purposes and was expected to apply these funds in a 'productive' manner.

The CGD had an early vigorous growth and soon occupied an unassailable leading position, not only within the savings sector but within the financial system as a whole. Already by the early 1890s it was the largest financial institution in terms of deposits and by the early 1920s not only did it continue to maintain this position but held 73 per cent of savings deposits and 28 per cent of all deposits in the country. This became even more pronounced in the course of the next two decades, with the result that on the eve of the Second World War, the CGD held 45 per cent of deposits.[3]

Until the late 1920s, the 'productive' application of this enormous mass of resources was interpreted as meaning some form of financial assistance to the Treasury. Indeed, in 1929, it was estimated that the State absorbed more than 90 per cent of the CGD's deposits. Ever since the reorganization of public finance in the middle of the 19th century, budget deficits had been the norm in Portugal. Not unexpectedly given their control over it, the CGD was used by successive governments throughout the first 50 years of its history as one more expedient to cover the shortfall in receipts, either by having it purchase Portuguese bonds, hold a current account for the Treasury or discount treasury notes of one kind or another. Apart from the justification of being in the national interest, this was the safest and best remunerated way of employing depositors' money and a practice generally followed abroad by savings banks (Institut International d'Épargne, 1935). Whether for this reason or because of the State's overall guarantee for its operations, there can be no doubt that the CGD was perceived as one of the safest places to leave one's savings, judging by the impressive long-run performance of its liabilities and considering that this was a country where the majority of the population entertained a strong suspicion of financial institutions until a late date.

In 1929, a series of reforms were enacted which profoundly transformed the economic role of the Portuguese national savings bank and ushered in a new phase in its history which has lasted, in fact, down to the present day. The main burden of these changes was to convert the CGD into a powerful but docile instrument for furthering the economic policies of the recently established nationalist-authoritarian regime headed by Dr Salazar.[4] There were two main strands to this. One was to scale down to a very low level the traditional financing of the deficit, which would no longer be needed given that balanced budgets were to become the rule and indeed the hallmark of the regime. The other was to use the considerable volume of resources thus released in order to foster the growth and modernization of the economy, particularly in those sectors considered most relevant to 'national' objectives, as well as to intervene in the most important product markets to ensure the stability of prices and production.

From a comparative point of view, there is nothing unusual for the interwar period in the use by the state of credit mechanisms in order to control the economy and achieve certain policy objectives. In most European countries, loan guarantees, interest subsidies and the underwriting of new share issues were commonly used either to stimulate or to salvage certain economic activities which were deemed important. Governments often stepped in directly to prevent the collapse of banks or of other firms which were considered too large to fail and became the owners and managers of substantial industrial, transport and other assets in the process, as happened for example in France or Austria. Most significantly of all, in several countries more or less official industrial and agricultural banks were established usually by the state or with the help of public money. The aim was to provide long-term capital for sectors which, it was thought, otherwise would either not survive or not develop given the high cost and difficulty for them of obtaining commercial loans. This was at least the case of Greece, with the Hellenic Corporation, the National Mortgage Bank and the Agricultural Bank of Greece; of Spain, with the Banco de Credito Industrial and others; of Ireland with the Industrial Credit Company; and of Britain, with the

Bankers Industrial Development Company.[5]

A number of reasons account for this shift in political attitudes regarding the proper role of the state in the economy in the aftermath of the First World War. In the first place, this was a time when it was felt that commercial banking was not able to satisfy all the credit needs of the economy and that vital sectors were suffering grievously as a result. In Britain, this became known as the 'MacMillan gap' but the idea circulated widely and insistently throughout Europe long before the 1931 Committee on Finance and Industry launched this concern into the wide public discussion which led to the coining of the expression. In peripheral countries where capital markets were less sophisticated, the propensity to save low and industry less advanced, this gap was perceived as being even wider and the logic for state promoted industrial banks all the more compelling. Exacerbated by nationalism and the post-war dislocation of economies, which could not easily supply themselves through imports because of balance of payments constraints, provided a second set of justifications for sectorial intervention through credit instruments. The goal in this case was to lessen external dependence through import substitution, industrialization and/or agricultural growth and diversification.[6]

The fear of social tensions and the connection between them and high unemployment levels were an additional reason for governments to try and prevent the closure of firms or the collapse of whole sectors by direct or indirect means. Where the national economy's dependence on agriculture was strong, the latter's persistent vulnerability to sharp swings in prices during this period became an additional reason for the urgency to diversify production. Lastly, it must be remembered that the intellectual climate of Europe was moving increasingly away from a liberal stance and more and more towards the virtues of state intervention in the economy. Habits and know-how for this had been built up during the war and the social and economic problems of the postwar and of the Depression were more than sufficient to warrant new measures and attitude. This inclination found even stronger support in societies, such as Salazarist Portugal or Fascist Italy where a deep ideological suspicion of market forces and a readiness to subordinate all other considerations to the 'superior interests of the Nation' were prevalent.

The case which this paper examines fits in well with this background but is interesting also because of the ways in which it departs from it. In Portugal, rather than create new financial institutions, an old established one was used. Instead of specialist banks, for industry, agriculture and so on, resort was had to a single 'development bank' encompassing all these sectors. Perhaps most remarkable of all was the fact that a national savings bank was employed for this purpose, in lieu of the more conventional banking solutions adopted elsewhere. Finally, it seems likely that state intervention in the Portuguese economy through credit facilities may have gone further and been more diversified than elsewhere in most of Europe. In the following pages, after describing the reforms of the CGD in 1929, I shall discuss why these particular institutional options were made and what mechanisms were devised in order to render viable such an unorthodox approach. The amount and nature of the credit provided will be considered and this will serve to discuss the nature and strategy behind the economic policies of the Salazar regime during the 1930s. An evaluation of these policies will also be attempted.

The creation of an investment bank

The reform of the Caixa Geral de Depositos in 1929 was based on a legislative package consisting of four decrees. The main provisions of the first three were the creation of two new bodies which would be placed under the aegis of the CGD but which, while sharing its staff and physical resources, would be autonomous from it. One was the Caixa Nacional de Crédito (CNC), which was charged with carrying out credit operations that would promote 'the activity and the wealth of the Nation', including the colonies, and such as no other financial bodies were normally prepared to undertake. The other was the Caixa Nacional de Previdência, an umbrella organization for the multitude of social security arrangements covering all the different categories of civil servants ranging from policemen to workers at the national Mint, and from central government clerical staff to employees of the nationalized railways. The fourth decree concerned the reorganization of the CGD staff itself. It stressed the merit system in promotions and allowed the closure of unprofitable branches and other such measures of economy and rationalization.

The financial means whereby the developmental side of this plan was to be implemented were to come from three sources. In the first place, the CGD was expected to continue to be a savings bank and the official receiver of all obligatory deposits. Second, thanks to the stabilization programme currently under way and to the novel achievement of balanced budgets, it would cease to have to furnish the Treasury with loans and instead would be reimbursed by the latter for all the government's outstanding debts to it. This was expected to generate a considerable volume of fresh money for lending. Third, the CNC was empowered to issue up to 300 000 *contos* (one *conto* was roughly equivalent to nine pounds sterling) of bonds of variable duration, which would enjoy the special guarantee of the state. These would either be offered for public subscription to raise cash for the CNC, or be used for lending directly to clients who would then place the bonds themselves in the market.[7]

According to the official justification for these reforms, all of this was only a part of the much broader programme adopted by the recently installed rulers of Portugal (1926) and which had as its aim, in the economic field, 'the financial regeneration and the agricultural, industrial and social transformation of the country' (Salazar, 1930: 239). The principal policy objectives, however, were strictly financial and monetary. They involved balanced budgets, strict limitations on further public loans and the complete funding of the floating debt, on the one hand; and, on the other, a stable exchange rate, possibly leading to the resumption of the gold standard, balanced external accounts and an end to the overissue of paper money by the Bank of Portugal, a tradition which had plagued the economy since 1914.

Although ranking only second to these objectives, the development aims of Salazarist economic policies were hardly of secondary importance, particularly as they tied in with the financial and monetary part of his programme in several ways. For one thing, balanced budgets and stabilization were indispensable to the success of the reform of credit in general and of the CGD in particular, since they would enable the release of the funds that the CNC was to loan. At the same time, Salazar believed that monetary instability could only be overcome in a lasting way 'by developing to the full all the elements of productivity and wealth which will render Portugal a net creditor abroad' (Salazar, 1916: 218).[8] Behind this was the notion that the dependence on 'essential' imports could be substantially lessened and that even the most scarce of raw materials could be substituted by domestic means. In order to render Portugal autarkic, however, it was obviously necessary to make much greater use of national resources and this entailed promoting hitherto neglected lines of agricultural and industrial production.

According to the regime's economic diagnosis, progress towards these targets depended on the removal of several obstacles. The appropriate measures to deal with this fell into three categories. One comprised the vast panoply of regulatory arrangements created during the 1930s to overcome what was termed the 'indiscipline' of factor and product markets, both in agriculture and in industry. They included administered prices, the control of wages, guaranteed purchase schemes and strict licensing for the establishment, expansion or even modernization of industrial plant.[9] A second strand in these policies was the provision of much needed infrastructure, particularly for transport, telecommunications, the supply of electricity, irrigation and public buildings, both in the metropolis and the colonies, following years of neglect by the previous liberal republican regime.[10] The last category but certainly not the least was the supply both of short- and long-term credit under favourable conditions, not only to make possible these public investment efforts but above all to encourage private enterprise to take the desired investment and production decisions.

As was claimed in the preamble to the 1929 CGD laws, 'nobody doubts that the country's reconstruction cannot be carried out without a strong credit structure that will satisfy the needs of the economy, in the metropolis and in the colonies' (Salazar, 1930: 242). High interest rates such as there had been during the 1920s were one of the problems. Another was the difficulty which businesses in certain sectors or of certain dimensions encountered when they sought the help of the commercial banks, either because they could not offer the requisite guarantees or because their credit requirements did not fit with the practices of these institutions. Farmers were especially penalized in this respect and were therefore often compelled to sell their produce too soon and too cheaply. Consequently, they were discouraged from increasing their output and improving their productive methods. Industrialists did not find things much easier, however, particularly when it came to long-term investments in the technological modernization which was so badly needed. Altogether, it was estimated that for this end alone more than 200 000 *contos* would be needed in the near future in order to achieve significant progress towards the aim of a 'Portuguese industrialization' based on national resources. For agriculture to escape the clutches of usury, increase food and raw material production and ensure a reasonable degree of autarky would take a further financial effort of more than 400 000 *contos*.

Another fact of Portuguese economic life which the 1929 CGD reform had to take into account was the state of the country's banking system.[11] Following a turbulent postwar decade and in spite of some useful shake-outs, it was still marked by a degree of fragility which prevented it from playing an adequate development-oriented role and even made it a potential factor of restriction for the productive sectors of the economy. The implication was that 'as long as the banking network and private initiative are so weak and deficient', the state would be the only entity strong enough to put together the credit package which the nation and the Salazarist programme needed (Salazar, 1930: 242). Indeed, from time to time the CNC would have to employ part of its funds in acquiring a substantial fraction of the banks' more illiquid loans, generally to industry. In this way it relieved them of undesirable assets, contributed to enhancing their solvency and placed them in a better position to help in the national economic effort.[12]

Accounting for the 1929 CGD reform

The institutional framework which the regime put in place in order to pursue its credit-based policies represented one among several possible options. For the time and in the broader context of Europe, some aspects of this choice were somewhat unusual and it is interesting to consider which circumstances dictated them. Before doing so, however, it should be pointed out that these reforms did not come out of thin air but were the result of past experience and discussions in Portugal for at least two decades.

Government sponsored agricultural credit, for example, had existed since 1911 and had been on the law books since 1867, although it had never reached significant amounts. It was distributed by local farmers' associations (*sindicatos agricolas*) on a mutual credit basis and was provided at a low fixed interest rate by the Bank of Portugal as one of its contractual obligations to the government. Demand for an official industrial bank, to save manufacturers from usurious money lenders went far back into the 19th century too but only began to be satisfied, again on a modest scale, in 1918, this time directly by the CGD in the form of warrants and mortgage loans on the surety of land and buildings.[13] In addition, during the 1920s the Treasury made occasional loans to individual firms, probably for political reasons, but hardly with the aim of fostering the economy's development in any coherent manner.

Besides these weak and dispersed official efforts in the field of credit to productive sectors of the economy, a variety of proposals were circulated from time to time in recognition of the problems that the Salazarist reforms finally attempted to solve in 1929. One example of this was the 1925 Bank Law which permitted the CGD for the first time to discount commercial paper and thereby opened the way for it to become a major player on the banking scene.[14] Another was the view espoused in 1924 by the committee appointed by the government to study ways of protecting Portuguese industry and which recognized that the principal and most urgent measure was credit assistance. Its proposal was for the Bank of Portugal to make loans for between 2 and 20 years, either to new industrial concerns or for the development of existing ones, provided that they belonged to any one of a list of 15 strategic branches of manufacturing. They would be made at the Bank's rate and the ceiling for the whole operation would be 250 000 *contos*.[15] Although formally somewhat different, this plan was the resurrection of earlier proposals made before the war by Tomas Cabreira, a leading banking expert who wanted the state to found an industrial bank, or even earlier, by industrialists in the 1880s and 1890s (Cabreira, 1916).[16]

The first point about the preference for the CGD/CNC tandem as a vehicle for a development-through-credit policy is to ask why one or more new banks were not created for this purpose instead. After all, this is what happened in Greece, Spain and Ireland, and given the special nature of the function involved, the question would seem to make good sense. Had the latter choice been made, there would have been two ways to go about this. One was to found state development banks for industry or for agriculture but there were two arguments against this. One was that this was unnecessarily costly as it would entail a wasteful duplication of personnel and installations, given that the CGD already had a branch network and an overstaffed administrative structure. For Salazar, with his concern for rationalizing bureaucracy, economizing resources, simplifying procedures, concentrating administrative functions and raising the efficiency of the civil service, this would have been anathema (Salazar, 1930: 22). The second objection was the additional expense for the state of having to provide at least some of the capital for the new institution or institutions, at a time when every effort was bent on reducing current and capital expenditure.

The alternative was for these costs to be borne by the private sector which would be called upon to establish the banks, perhaps with some official support. This had disadvantages too, however, one of which was perceptible across the border. During the 1920s the various Spanish public development banks failed to fulfil expectations and achieve their goals owing to the resistance of the very bankers who had created them but feared the harm that might thus be done to their own business (Aceña, 1991: 369).[17] The other was the regime's fear that this would breed collusion among banks and encourage concentration in this sector. Despite the fact that if anything banking was probably not concentrated enough in Portugal, strands of 'anti-plutocratic' feeling were still strong in the regime's ideology during the 1930s.

Once it was evident that credit policy would best be conducted through existing channels and that these would have to be a part of the machinery of the state, or at least very close to it, the alternatives boiled down to the CGD or the Bank of Portugal. The latter had in its favour the know-how acquired with the earlier agricultural credit schemes and thanks to its long discounting experience it knew well the markets in general. Although its involvement with agricultural credit had only had a limited success, this was not perhaps the most telling argument against it. A more serious problem was that in order to carry out new credit functions, it would have to be provided with fresh funds. These would probably come out of an increase in its issue of notes and this was an even greater anathema than the previously mentioned one for Salazar, who had partly staked his reputation on curbing the production of high-powered money. A third objection was that as part of the government's plan for monetary stabilization, the Bank of Portugal was expected to become a fully-fledged central bank, with exclusive responsibility for maintaining the stability of the escudo and for the control of the money supply, something which came indeed to pass in 1931. This was clearly incompatible with the functions of a national development bank. Finally, it seems likely that Salazar would have preferred a more docile institution, such as the CGD whose board was dependent on the government's pleasure and was politely described by one of its members, in 1938, as 'autonomous but dependent' (Correia, 1938: 373). The Bank, on the other hand, was still a joint-stock company whose shareholders elected its directors annually and neither were fully compliant with the government's wishes.[18] To a considerable extent its logic was still to make money for the shareholders and this made it unsuitable to become a major distributor of official credit. In the government's own words ,

> since its foundation the Bank of Portugal has been more a commercial bank for discount and deposits than a central bank and as such, the influences of the market on it are to be feared, as they may drive it to an excessive expansion of credit and to the creation of superabundant means of exchange.[19]

In contrast, the CGD had several features to recommend it. It had at least as much know-how in this kind of operation as a result of having handled industrial credit facilities since 1918. It had an already extensive and growing network of offices which covered the national territory, as well as the staff to go with it, both of which could be used without extra cost. In 1928, compared with the Bank of Portugal's 20 regional offices, the Caixa had 88 agencies in the provinces, a number which was to grow to over 400 by 1938. Above all, it had a large amount of financial resources which moreover could still be expected to grow, if the experience of the previous decade was anything to go by.

The decision to employ the CGD as the government's instrument for credit policy also helps to explain why Portugal did not follow the approach of countries like Spain and Ireland, where separate banks existed to administer credit to different sectors of the economy. Obviously, it made little sense to split up a 50-year-old institution for the sake of uncertain gains from such a division of labour, but other reasons for this option were made explicit at the time too. Besides the operating economies of scale which were expected to accrue from aggregating all these services into one institution, the feeling was that a single development bank would be stronger and more solid and therefore better capable of exerting influence over the economy. It would also be more efficient as a creator and distributor of credit because it would be able to keep relatively lower reserves. Lastly, in the eyes of the Estado Novo's policy framers there was no purpose in keeping separate the problems of agricultural, industry and colonial development when these were all part of the integrated 'national' whole which was the state's concern. In Salazar's words, 'there is no sense, when agricultural and industrial credit are really one single function, for the state to have them spread out among several ministries and the CGD and to use up many thousands of *contos* in this' (1930: 246).[20]

Probably the most innovative aspect of the 1929 reform was the way in which the credits supplied to the productive sectors of the economy through the CGD and the CNC were financed. Again, contrary to the Spanish experience where own capital and the issue of bonds were the two principal sources of funds, in Portugal most of these came from the savings accounts held at the national savings bank. By 1939 the CNC had issued a mere 30 000 *contos* of bonds but had incurred total liabilities of 600 000 *contos* in the shape of deposits which enabled it to make its loans to agriculture, industry, colonial development and exports. In addition, the CGD had separate credits outstanding worth 571 000 *contos* to various sectors of the economy and these too were entirely financed from its deposits.

The originality of the arrangement devised in Portugal lay in making it possible for long- and medium-term loans to be financed out of potentially volatile resources. Moreover, this was achieved without any need for a large and costly cushion of liquid reserves such as prudence and good banking sense would have required. Part of the solution was to interpose the state's guarantee between the short-term liabilities which were the Caixa's principal source of funds and the illiquid assets which came to constitute most of its portfolio. The other part was to make the CNC, which carried the slowly maturing loans, formally autonomous and separate from its parent, the CGD. Hence the repeated declarations to the effect that 'the deposits, the capital, the credits of the [CGD] can never be held liable for the obligations incurred by the other bodies which are attached to it [i.e. the CNC]' (Salazar, 1930: 241). Formally, the CNC obtained most of the money it leant out through a current account with the CGD, the safety of whose deposits was thus symbolically assured. At the same time, the operations of the CNC were secured, in the first place, by the assets of its debtors and, in the second place and more importantly, by the Treasury. In this way, the public could feel safe about its deposits, even though they were in fact being tied up in what otherwise would have been unsuitably illiquid applications. As Salazar reassuringly explained in a newspaper interview in 1929: 'as it is always remotely possible that there should be some losses in these operations of agricultural and industrial credit, the funds of the CGD . . . must be completely dissociated from any contingencies of the CNC'

(Salazar, 1930: 233). The great advantage in this for that 'poor capitalist', as he called the Portuguese state, was that in this way, it could carry out its credit reform without having to spend any more money. The best proof that the scheme was effective is that notwithstanding the large amount of long-term loans made during the 1930s, the public continued to flock fearlessly to the CGD which more than doubled its deposits in nominal terms between 1929 and 1939.

Finally attention should be drawn to another aspect of the CGD reform which at least for Portugal was new. This was the constant preoccupation to make the distribution of credit as simple, flexible and free of paper work as possible, so that those who really needed it managed to get it when it was necessary and not when it was too late. This spirit was evident from the beginning, as when the preamble to the CNC's by-laws stated that 'the amortization period for short-term loans may exceed the usual three months for commercial discounts because it must depend on harvests or on industrial production, the payment for which is known to suffer delays at times.'[21] It was also present in the decision to start lending to industry on a substantial scale without awaiting the results of a long promised industrial enquiry even though this was considered to be an essential tool for deciding how best to distribute credit to the manufacturing sector.[22]

Most important of all, however, was the nature of the collateral which borrowers had to provide. Mortgages, of course, were generally required for long-term loans but in the case of industry the great breakthrough by the CGD/CNC was that machinery, and not only land and buildings, now became acceptable too. In 1933, the government went even further, under decree n. 23 119, by allowing large loans to be made for starting up new large-scale ventures or for improving existing ones, even when the value of the plant was small by comparison with its turnover, providing the investment was proved to be in the 'national interest'. With the passage of time and in stark contrast with the stringent requirements imposed by the commercial banks, these requirements were relaxed even 'to the point where personal credit [by the CGD/CNC] has been allowed, despite the risks involved.'[23] In the case of short-term credits to farmers to help them finance the wheat crop and not have to market their produce prematurely for lack of money, the procedure was also exemplary in its simplicity. The one-year loans in question could be secured by real estate, farm equipment or just the crops themselves. Moreover, the crop could be sold freely before the reimbursement had to be made and the paperwork was kept to a minimum. Loans could be made out to individuals whose declarations concerning the amount of land farmed and the size of the expected crop only needed to be countersigned by two other farmers. Above all no trip to Lisbon was necessary because the request could be made locally at any counter of the CNC.[24]

Evaluating the CGD as a policy instrument

The first step towards evaluating the performance of the CGD and the CNC as tools of Salazarist economic policy during the 1930s is to consider how much and what kind of credit was given. Between the two institutions, the total credit provided to the productive sectors of the Portuguese economy grew strongly during the first ten years after the reform being considered here. Exact comparisons over time are difficult because accounting procedures used in compiling the published annual accounts and balance sheets changed during the period. Nevertheless, the very small initial participation of the CGD in this segment of the market before 1929 – outstanding industrial loans at the time of its reform totalled 20 000 *contos* – contrasted dramatically with the figure of 600 000 *contos* in long-term credits owed to the CNC alone by agriculture and industry one decade later. If we add to this the other credits to agriculture, housing and public infrastructure held also by the CGD, the figure rises to 1.5 million *contos*, that is, 75 times the amount of the base year. Comparison with the rest of the financial sector also yields results which are anything but modest. In 1939 not only was the CGD/CNC group larger than any commercial bank, either in terms of deposits or assets, but its aggregate loans to agriculture, industry, colonies and regional and local government authorities were greater than the discount portfolio of all commercial banks put together and were almost 70 per cent of the entire country's bank credit of every kind.

A second issue in this evaluation concerns one of the most important and enduring debates regarding Portuguese 20th century history and has to do with the distribution of power and influence within the Estado Novo during its early years. Was this an agrarian based political regime whose policies were designed to favour agricultural interests and ensure the stability of an essentially traditional rural society? Or was there a balance between this and the desire to promote industrialization, modernize the economy and stimulate its growth, even if sometimes at the expense of agriculture? (See Rosas, 1986; Amaral, 1992.) A look at the CNC published accounts for these years suggests that the second view may be closer to the mark since on average its credits were split roughly equally between agriculture and industry, with a smaller and diminishing share going to the colonies. Moreover, the trend indicates that industrial preoccupations were making themselves increasingly felt at least at this level. Although it has been claimed that industrial credit did not increase after the First Congress of Industry, in 1933, the reverse actually happened (Brito, 1989: 153). Agricultural credit was larger than its industrial counterpart until 1935 but steadily lost ground after this date and ended up being overtaken by the time of the war.

Industrial credit was divided into roughly two halves, with one going to short-term operations connected mainly with the purchase of raw materials and the payment of salaries. The other was used for investment in machinery, buildings and the purchase of land. Overall its distribution followed guidelines which point at an industrial policy with specific aims. According to the CGD board's report for 1934–35, industrial loans should serve to start new key manufactures, to renovate some old ones and also to reconstitute solid enterprises that were undergoing difficulties. Some of these firms could be very large but there should be and indeed was a 'social' concern also, to help the medium-sized and the small, as was indeed stressed in the legislation that regulated the concession of these credits.

Considerable archival research will be necessary in order to provide a detailed picture of the actual implementation of all this. A superficial examination of the records suggests, however, that at least these two criteria for distribution were observed. Loans were highly dispersed according to size and covered a range which went in any year from a few to a few thousands of *contos* each. The data below for the period 1934 to 1937 show that although the average loan was far from insignificant, their coefficient of variation was considerable.[25]

year	Average CNC industrial loan (*contos*)	coefficient of variation (*percentages*)
1934–35	503	187
1936	1258	718
1937	367	195

To a large extent industrial loans were made to export-oriented industries, which is hardly surprising given the policy concern at the time with the balance of payments. The fact that their sectorial allocation hardly coincided with the relative weight of the different branches of manufacturing in the economy also suggests that there really was an intention behind this of reshaping the country's industrial structure, as was recognized publicly by the CGD itself. The only quantification of this available so far was made in mid-1933. It shows that the four main recipients of CNC credits were flour milling, chemicals, textiles and the metallurgical industries.[26] Together they took up 63 per cent of the total, a distribution which indicates partly a concern with encouraging sectors which could be deemed basic to industrialization and in which the country was weak, namely chemicals and metals. The fact that emphasis was also placed on the other two traditional, light industries does not contradict the view that industrial credit was guided by a policy stance of modernization and development. It simply shows that the latter was tempered by the vision of influential people in the regime, like Araujo Correia, the strong man of the CGD, for whom although Portugal should not remain forever agricultural it should nevertheless base its industrial effort largely on the processing of its own raw materials, for example cork, fish, wood and foodstuffs. According to them, 'industrial countries are not only those which transform iron and coal into products for export or home consumption' (Correia, 1938, vol. 1: 381).[27]

The CNC was not, however, the only source of credit within this group. Just as much again or more originated in the CGD itself and when this is also taken into account and short-term credit in particular is included, then the interpretation of Portuguese political history of the 1930s suggested above must be revised. The reason is that the single largest sectorial block of credit did not arise with the CNC but with the CGD and was channelled into agriculture, making the latter the recipient of in fact two and a half times more than industry received during the same period. This would seem to provide fresh evidence in support of the view that 'there is some exaggeration in the opinion that the Estado Novo was unequivocally engaged in the country's industrialization and modernization during the 1930s' (Rosas, 1992a: 318).

Thus, under the initial designation of 'financial operations' and later as 'credit to corporative organizations', these were short-term credits to the producers of the country's most important crops, generally to help tide them over the period of the harvest and of the preparation of the following year's crop. They started in 1929 on an entirely *ad hoc* emergency basis, but became one of the most important instruments of Salazarist economic policy over the years. Through this, the government supplied the funds with which farm surpluses were bought and stockpiled and thus made it possible to keep agricultural prices steady while encouraging farmers to expand production. It was particularly significant in the context of the 1930s 'Campanha do Trigo', the agricultural stimulus programme whereby the Estado Novo sought to make Portugal self-sufficient in wheat.[28] By the time of the war, this account had risen to more than 400 000 *contos* outstanding and therefore twice as much as the amounts made available through the CNC to agriculture for long-term purposes.

Credit to 'corporative organizations' was not only a means for intervening in the conditions of agricultural supply. It soon became an important tool in the promotion of one of the Salazar regime's most cherished political objectives: the creation and consolidation of corporative institutions, particularly those whose membership was supposedly voluntary. For apparently pragmatic reasons, it was decided already in 1929 that the loans of both the CGD and the CNC should be channelled as much as possible through producer organizations, local credit cooperatives and the like, rather than handed out directly to clients. In the course of the 1930s, however, corporative unions of producers emerged and multiplied into all areas of economic activity and were given powers of regulation in their respective fields in conjunction with governmental bodies. At the same time, they became the principal recipients of these credits, something which enabled them not only to carry out their statutory attributions but also to enhance their capacity to attract adherents.[29] Not without reason was it stated that 'the corporative economy had [in the CGD] one of its strongest props.'[30]

The CGD was used to further another policy objective of the Estado Novo. Despite an allegedly ruralist inspiration and an ideological suspicion of large urban concentrations and their vices, from the start the regime attached considerable importance to the development of Lisbon, the nation's capital. This was done partly for symbolic reasons, partly as a means of absorbing unemployment and partly out of a spirit of centralization of power. Considerable public works were undertaken and received almost as much as all the funds made available to the CNC. The private building industry received substantial help too in the form of mortgage loans. These were no doubt instrumental in the construction of a large quantity of the residential building along Lisbon's so-called 'new avenues' and which arguably epitomized the characteristic architectural forms associated with the political system. Here too the CGD was generous, as by 1939 it had some 160 000 *contos* outstanding for this, almost as much as it had devoted to long-term agricultural lending.

Having given an idea of the amounts, types and policy motivations of the credit which the CGD/CNC mobilized during these years, we must finally turn to an attempt at gauging the impact of these institutions. Unfortunately, not enough data have been gathered yet to permit this to be done satisfactorily. From an international standpoint some rather incomplete comparisons can be made but they concern industrial finance only. One is with Greece where the Hellenic Corporation loaned a total of approximately 100 000 pounds sterling over a period when the CNC alone provided credits to industry worth ten times this amount. The second, at the other end of the Mediterranean, with Spain, is still favourable to Portugal though not as clearly. In 1935 the Spanish Banco de Credito Industrial had the equivalent of 324 000 *contos* owed to it by industrial ventures while in the same year, the CNC had 165 000. Spain's population was three and half times larger and its industrial output per capita was also probably larger than that of Portugal. The third case is Ireland where the Industrial Credit Corporation's aggregate industrial loans between 1933 and 1936 were substantially less than those made for the same purpose by the CNC in any single year of the same period.

It would be over ambitious to hope to pin down the exact contribution of the CGD to the evolution of the Portuguese economy after 1929 but a few points can be usefully made nevertheless. The first is that both its assets (including the CNC) and its loans even more so increased at a much faster rate than GNP, during this decade. The latter's growth rate was around 3.3 per cent per annum while CGD assets increased at 9.0 per cent and credit to agriculture and industry still a great deal more. This gains even more significance when we consider that commercial banking was meanwhile expanding at only 4 per cent per annum. By 1939, total credit outstanding to these sectors as well as to local government for infrastructure and to the housing industry by the CGD/CNC was equal to just over 6 per cent of GNP.

Some of the desired macroeconomic effects of this credit policy also seem to have been achieved. Falling interest rates in general, from 9 to 6 per cent, is one of them, although obviously this was the result of various other factors besides the intervention of the CGD. Stable agricultural prices is another. Here again other influences were just as important or even more so, including the political will and the institutional framework created to obtain this result. But there can be no doubt that the short-term finance of the CGD which made possible intervention in produce markets was crucial. The contrast with the behaviour of agricultural prices worldwide is quite noticeable and it should be pointed out that this happened while Portuguese agriculture was expanding at around 2.5 per cent a year and when there were several bumper crops which the marketing system was able to absorb without upset. Finally, the increased stability during the 1930s of the bank system, which was able to divest itself of much long-term lending and concentrate resources on short-term commercial operations instead, can also be ascribed in good measure, though not exclusively, to the new found role of the CGD and its vigorous move into the field of agricultural and industrial credit.

Conclusion

The 1930s comprised a period of intense institutional innovation in Portugal. To a large extent this was the result of the establishment of a new political regime, the Estado Novo, which aspired to a radical change not only of politics but of society and of the economy as well. Often it also came as a response of the moment to the unforeseen difficulties encountered so many times during these critical times.

The radical reform which the CGD underwent during these years is therefore more than just another chapter in contemporary financial history. It is a good illustration of this inventiveness in the face of a set of problems which were by no means peculiar to Portugal but were widely felt throughout Europe at this time. For this reason it provides a valuable basis for the comparative analysis of how countries devise different ways of satisfying similar needs, in this case in the financial field. It offers besides a useful test whereby one may assess the intentions of the early Salazar government with respect to the problems of economic development and industrialization and their social and political consequences. While not laying the matter to rest, the examination of the CGD's performance during the 1930s does indeed suggest that though significant concessions may have been made to industrial interests, it was still agriculture which was foremost in the concerns of the Estado Novo prior to the Second World War. Finally, being half blueprint and half *ad hoc* solution, the reform of the national savings bank of the prewar years constitutes a clear example of how institutional arrangements can be set up during turbulent times to deal with particular problems, only to gather their own momentum and consolidate an existence long past the circumstances which were responsible for their creation.

In spite of many changes in Portugal's society and economy, over the next half century the CGD remained the leading financial institution as well as its chief savings bank. It continued also to perform the role into which it was cast during the period we have studied here. Even after the Wheat Campaign had long become a thing of the past, industrial development had found new official institutions to assist it financially and even the CNC had eventually disappeared, the CGD continued to be a powerful lever for furthering economic policy by means of the allocation of credit to certain sectors or activities. Thus the 1929 reform which converted it from a traditional state savings bank into a development bank was significant not only for the innovative aspects it contained but also because it marked the start of an era in the field of official financial intervention in Portugal which may only now be drawing to a close, thanks to the liberalization and internationalization of this sector of its economy.

Notes

1. The author gratefully acknowledges the comments and suggestions of Gabriel Tortella, Cormac O'Grada, Manuel Braga da Cruz and Pedro Lains.
2. From the ministerial justification in Parliament of the law creating the CGD, in Oliveira (1991). There is no published history of this institution as yet but a research project is under way for this purpose.
3. *Annaes de Estatistica* (1894); *Situação Bancária* (1939).
4. Although they dealt with other problems as well – for example, rationalizing its bureaucratic structure and placing the Caixa in charge of social security arrangements for civil servants.
5. See, respectively, Dritsas (1992), Tortella and Jimenez (1986), Aceña (1991), Daly (1984) and Pollard (1969). On the Bank of England's efforts in this area, see Sayers (1976).
6. See Aldcroft (1978) for some of these manifestations and their economic consequences.
7. For the text of these laws, see *Colecção Oficial* (1929: 568–78).
8. This is the thesis he submitted to the University of Coimbra in order to become a junior lecturer in its prestigious Law Faculty where he would become the professor of Public Finance in 1918.
9. See Brito (1987) and Confraria (1990) on the industrial licensing system, Lucena (1976) for the institutional structure of the corporatist state in general and Rosas (1986) for economic policy during the 1930s.
10. See Nunes and Valério (1983) for a good analysis of the 1935 Law of Economic Reconstruction, a landmark in this respect.
11. For an overview of the banking system, see Reis (1994).
12. Relatório (1931–32): For the argument in Britain in defence of the Bank of England's intervention in industry in order to help the commercial banks, see Bowden and Collins (1992). Although it was not thought of as a bankers' bank, the CGD was called in occasionally after the crisis of 1931 to bail out commercial banks in distress, owing to its huge financial resources. Two instances are on record. In 1931, 75 000 *contos* were supplied to the Banco Nacional Ultramarino and in 1934 the Banco de Angola was helped also, to an unknown extent. See Comissão do Livro Negro (1987).
13. Not much is known about this first essay in industrial banking. Mendes (1984) has shown that between 1918 and 1928 altogether 229 loans were made for a total of 61 241 *contos*, most of them in Lisbon and Oporto. The average duration of these loans, in the case of Coimbra, the only town for which there are data, was 2.75 years.
14. See *Reforma Bancária (Decreto N.10.474)* (1925) for the terms of this legislation and for the views of its critics.
15. *Protecção às Industrias* (1924). The idea was taken up later by Armando Marques Guedes, a critic of the Salazar government, already when the CNC was in operation, and as an alternative to it. The new credit institution would be managed by representatives of the state and of industry. See Guedes (1933).
16. See the stress placed on these demands in a recent article on the obstacles to industrialization in Mendes (1990).
17. For the same problem in Ireland, see Daly (1992).

18. Xavier (1948) describes some of the friction between the Bank and Salazar during these years.
19. Surprisingly, this statement is in the preamble to the law which instituted the Bank as the central bank of Portugal. See Banco de Portugal (1946, vol.VI: 13).
20. It is interesting that in Ireland the government refused to countenance just such a solution, preferring to keep the Agricultural Credit Bank and the Industrial Credit Bank separate. See Daly (1992).
21. From decree n.17 215 in *Colecção Oficial (1933)*.
22. Relatório (1932–33), p. 25.
23. Speech by Antunes Guimarães, in *Diário das Sessões* (1935: 300).
24. These rules were laid out in decree n. 17 509, in *Colecção Oficial (1929)*.
25. Historical Archive of the CGD: Caixa Nacional de Credito, Credito Industrial/Mapas Relativos à sua Distribuição, 1918–1940.
26. *Relatório (1932–33)*, p. 24.
27. Rosas (1992b) traces the genealogy of this ideological current since the early 20th century. In Spain the food and textile sectors received only minor assistance from the industrial credit bank, the bulk of whose finance went to the more 'modern' metal-related industries, as well as to hydroelectric development.
28. For a detailed account of this Portuguese version of Mussolini's Battle of Grain, see Pais *et al.* (1976).
29. By 1936, there were national producers' organizations, ranging from insurers to wheat farmers, and from wine exporters to manufacturers of Madeira lace. See the full list in Lumbralles (1936). The best account of the structure of the corporative state is Lucena (1976).
30. Relatório (1934–35). It is interesting to note that there was a debate within the regime over whether these unions should be made to be self-financing or should be allowed to live thanks to the help of institutions such as the CGD.

References

Aceña, Pablo Martin (1991), 'Los Origenes de la Banca Publica' in Pablo Martin Aceña and Francisco Comin (eds), *Historia de la Empresa Publica en España*, Madrid.

Aldcroft, Derek (1978), *The European Economy 1914–1970*, London.

Amaral, Luciano (1992), 'O Plano Inclinado do Socialismo: Sobre o Intervencionismo Económico do Estado Novo' in José Luis Cardoso and Antonio Almodovar (eds), *Actas do Encontro Ibérico sobre História do Pensamento Económico*, Lisbon.

Annaes de Estatistica. Volume I. Serie I-Finanças.N.1 – Estatistica Bancária (1858–1892) (1894), Lisbon.

Banco de Portugal (1946), *Legislaçao Própria*, Lisbon.

Bowden, Sue and Collins, Michael (1992), 'The Bank of England, industrial regeneration, and hire purchase between the wars', *Economic History Review*, XLV(1).

Brito, José Maria Brandão de (1987) 'Concorrencia e Corporativismo' in António Costa Pinto *et al.* (eds), *O Estado Novo: Das Origens ao Fim da Autarcia, 1926–1959*, Lisbon.

Brito, José Maria Brandão de (1989), *A Industrialização Portuguesa no Pós-Guerra (1948–1965). O Condicionamento Industrial*, Lisbon.

Cabreira, Tomás (1916), *O Problema Bancário Português*, Lisbon.

Caixa Geral de Depositos, (several years) *Relatório e Contas*, Lisbon.

Colecção Oficial de Legislação Portuguesa Publicada no Ano de . . . (several years), Lisbon.

Comissão do Livro Negro sobre o Regime Fascista (1987), *Cartas e Relatórios de Quirino de Jesus a Oliveira Salazar*, Lisbon.

Confraria, João (1990), *Contribuição para o Estudo da Estrutura dos Mercados Industriais em Portugal. Uma Análise Económica do Condicionamento das Indústrias*, Lisbon.

Correia, José Dias Araujo (1938), *Portugal Económico e Financeiro*, Lisbon.

Daly, Mary E. (1984), 'Government finance for industry in the Irish Free State: The Trade Loans (Guarantee) Acts', *Irish Economic and Social History*, XI.

Daly, Mary E. (1992), *Industrial Development and Irish National Identity 1922–1939*, Syracuse.

Dritsas, Margarita (1992), 'Bank–Industry Relations in Inter-war Greece: The Case of the National Bank of Greece' in P. L. Cottrell *et al.* (eds), *European Industry and Banking between the Wars. A Review of Bank–Industry Relations*, Leicester.

Guedes, Armando Marques (1933), 'Crédito Industrial: Sua Organisação e Possibilidades de nele Inverter com Garantia os Capitais Portugueses Paralisados e Emigrados' in *Primeiro Congresso da Indústria Portuguesa*, Lisbon.

Lucena, Manuel (1976), *A Evolução do Sistema Corporativo Português. I O Salazarismo*, Lisbon.

Lumbralles, João Pinto da Costa Leite (1936), *A Doutrina Corporativa em Portugal*, Lisbon.

Mendes, José Maria Amado (1984), *A Area Económica de Coimbra. Estrutura e Desenvolvimento Industrial 1867–1927*, Coimbra.

Mendes, José Maria Amado (1990), 'Bloqueios à inovação no tecido empresarial português em finais do século XIX: Achegas para o seu estudo', *Revista de História*, X.

Nunes, Ana Bela and Valério, Nuno (1983), 'A Lei de Reconstituição Económica e a sua execução – Um exemplo dos projectos e realizações da política económica do Estado Novo', *Estudos de Economia*, III(3).

Oliveira, Mathieu de (1991), 'La Caixa Geral de Deposits: Origines, fondation et evolution', *Revue d'Economie Financiere*, numero speciale/La Caisse des Depots et Consignations 175 Ans.

Pais, José Machado *et al.* (1976), 'Elementos para a história do fascismo nos campos: A Campanha do Trigo, 1928–1938', *Análise Social*, 12.

Pollard, Sidney (1969), *The Development of the British Economy 1914-1967*, London.

Protecção às Indústrias. Relatório e Projecto de Estatuto de Protecção às Indústrias. Trabalho Elaborado pela Comissão Nomeada pela Portaria de 31 de Maio de 1924 (1924), Lisbon.

Reforma Bancária (Decreto N.10.474) Parecer da Comissão Nomeada em Assembleia Geral de Bancos e Casas Bancária de Lisboa e Porto, Reunida em 26 de Janeiro de 1925 (1925), Lisbon.

Reis, Jaime (1994) 'Portuguese Banking in the Inter-War Period' in Charles Feinstein (ed.), *Banking, Currency and Finance in Europe between the Wars*, Oxford.

Rosas, Fernando (1986), *O Estado Novo nos Anos Trinta, 1928–1938*, Lisbon.

Rosas, Fernando (ed.) (1992a), *Portugal e o Estado Novo (1930–1960)*, Lisbon.

Rosas, Fernando (1992b), 'O Pensamento Reformista Agrário no Século XX em Portugal: Elementos para o seu Estudo' in José Luis Cardoso and Antonio Almodovar (eds), *Actas do Encontro Ibérico sobre História do Pensamento Económico*, Lisbon.

Salazar, Antonio de Oliveira (1916), *O Ágio do Ouro. Sua Natureza e suas Causas (1891–1915)*, Coimbra.

Salazar, Antonio de Oliveira (1930), *A Reorganização Financeira. Dois Anos no Ministério das Finanças 1928–1930*, Coimbra.

Sayers, R. S. (1976), *The Bank of England 1891–1944*, Cambridge.

Situação Bancária nos Anos de . . . Bancos, Caixas e Companhias de Credito (several years), Lisbon.

Tortella, Gabriel and Jimenez, Juan Carlos (1986), *Historia del Banco de Credito Industrial*, Madrid.

PART TWO
Banks, Markets and Industry

Spoilt for Choice? Banking Concentration and the Structure of the Dutch Capital Market, 1900–40[1]

Joost Jonker

Banking concentration so typical of Western countries between approximately 1880 and 1930 is often associated with the capital demands of the large business concerns which characterized the so-called Second Industrial Revolution. Cameron even suggested dating the end of industrialization's early stages by the onset of banking concentration (Cameron, 1967: 310). The underlying idea would seem to stem from the example of the big German banks operating as market makers, creating facilities for business, and subsequently converting these into rights issues. This association is not universally borne out, however. The most obvious exception is the United Kingdom, if only because the centralization of credit limited the scope of regional finance, and no obvious connection can be established between industrial and banking concentration (Cottrell, 1980: 237; Capie and Rodrik-Bali, 1982). In Scandinavia, concentration seems to have been a consequence of the banking crisis during the 1920s (Larsson, 1991: 97–8).

Developments in Belgium did follow the German pattern however, as one would expect from a country with such a vigorous tradition of mixed banking. The evidence from the United States is not quite conclusive, but tentatively points the same way (White, 1985; Lamoreaux, 1991; Vanthemsche 1991: 105).[2] The interpretation of banking concentration in the Netherlands also leans heavily on the German example, all the more readily since most accounts go back to a classic book of the early 1920s eulogizing this as the modern way forward (Westerman, 1920; De Vries, 1989: 40–1; Vanthemsche, 1991: 106–7).[3] How the story unfolds is briefly outlined below.

Dutch industry expanded rapidly from 1895, but banking continued in an archaic state, fragmented, with hardly any deposits, concentrating on mercantile finance and refusing to consider commitments longer than the customary three month bills. Around 1910 things suddenly changed.

Rising profits finally won over investors and bankers who had, for a long time, been wary of industrial securities; since the stock exchange now eagerly took up new share issues, the banks started to forge closer ties with industry. From 1911 a wave of mergers heralded the advent of a new, heroic spirit, exemplified by one of the driving forces, the president of the Rotterdamsche Bank, W. Westerman, who acquired the nickname 'William the Conqueror'. The boom turned into a frenzy during the First World War, with new issues following each other in ever quicker succession as banks competed to meet growing demand, until the collapse in 1920. Shaken by a sharp crisis, the banking system prudently disengaged itself from the industry's dangerous embrace to consolidate its gains. Five big, modern banks now dominated the money market, fully equipped to serve modern business: the Amsterdamsche Bank, Rotterdamsche Bank,[4] Twentsche Bank, Nederlandsche Handel-Maatschappij and the Incassobank. Through a growing network of branches, they provided a complete range of services to clients, instead of just concentrating on mercantile finance, a switch evident in their being labelled *algemene banken* or general banks, rather than *handelsbanken* or commercial banks. While memories of the crisis lasted, the banks kept industry's rein short, gradually relaxing it towards the 1930s.

At first sight the data sustaining this story do indeed show an impressive growth in bank assets and liabilities, stock exchange activity, etc. On closer inspection, however, the figures tell a rather different tale in which the banks barely manage to keep pace with economic developments despite expansion and concentration. Moreover, both the suggested link with increasing business size, and the implied consequence of lasting structural changes on the capital market, are never more than tenuous. In this paper I want to argue that banking concentration in the Netherlands meant an expansion of the existing type of banking, rather than a qualitative change. The banks largely continued the passive intermediation typical of mercantile finance, without embracing the German model of dynamic financial management. My speculative attempts at analysis have been made possible by the Nederlandsche Bank's publication in 1987 of a very welcome volume summarizing the available bank balance sheets for benchmark years, supplemented by information culled from the records of the most important private firms (*Financiële instellingen*, 1987). While obviously not complete, this survey should be representative of trends in the banking system as a whole, as well as giving the best data we are ever likely to obtain.

The money supply

The money supply provides a good introduction to developments in the capital market. Figure 9.1 shows the value of M1 and the percentage of demand deposits in it from 1900 to 1940. Until 1914 the money supply rose by about 4.5 per cent a year to just over 500 million guilders, but demand deposits grew three times as fast, from under a fifth to over a third of the total. During the First World War and its aftermath M1 exploded reaching 2.5 billion guilders in 1920, with demand deposits now taking a 54 per cent share. A sharp decline in the income velocity of money V2 between 1911 and 1919 underlines the fact that a switch was taking place, from cash transactions to bank intermediation (Bordo and Jonung, 1987: 10). The postwar recession brought a sharp drop in volume to 1.7 billion guilders in 1927, demand deposits quickly falling by a third to under half of the total in 1924, before recovering to around 50 per cent, with M1 climbing back to just under 2 billion guilders by the early 1930s. The depression pushed the money supply and demand deposits down again until the devaluation of the guilder in 1936, after which both Government spending and a modest business recovery edged the money supply back up to a record 2.9 billion guilders in 1940.

What stands out most noticeably in this picture is the very low

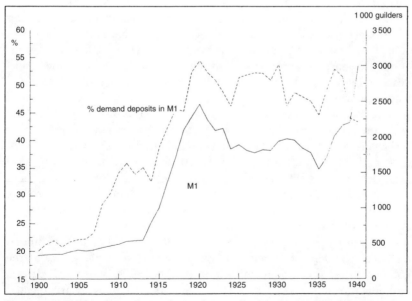

Figure 9.1   The money supply in the Netherlands, 1900–1940 (*Source:* Kuné and van Nieuwkerk 1974).

percentage of demand deposits in M1 until well into the 20th century, and the consequent very high volume of banknotes, which dropped below 60 per cent after 1915, continued at around 40-45 per cent during much of the interwar period, only to rise back to 61 per cent in 1939–40 (Nieuwkerk, 1974: 1–15). During the early 1920s deflation, the subsequent banking crisis, and the recycling of excess liquidity accumulated during the First World War, all contributed to M1 shrinking back to more normal proportions. Demand deposits stagnated, however, and the income velocity V2 rose sharply, indicating the commercial banks' return to the passive intermediation they practised before the war. As early as 1903 the prominent Dutch banker F.S. van Nierop described the uneven relation between demand deposits and banknotes as archaic (De Vries, 1989: 46, 59),[5] which indeed it was when compared with neighbouring countries. On the eve of the First World War, banknotes comprised only about 4 per cent of the circulation in the United Kingdom, 29 per cent in Belgium, and 43 per cent in France (Van der Wee and Tavernier, 1975: 385; Collins, 1988: 40–1). Banknotes continued to dominate because Dutch banking's deposit business hardly developed. Total deposits in the banking system stood at just over 40 per cent of liabilities before the First World War, rising to 60 per cent in 1918, before dropping back to around 50 per cent in the early 1920s to continue at that level until the late 1930s. Most of that amount went into current accounts; interest-bearing time deposits hovered around 15 per cent of liabilities throughout the period, to fall below 10 per cent after 1938. Cheques hardly figured at all. To all appearances then, the banks could not or would not attract deposits on a wide scale. As a result, efforts to start an inter-bank clearing or giro system remained half-hearted, foundering because the Nederlandsche Bank could not decide to lend support.

As for the supply side, a well-developed network of provincial bankers and stockbrokers provided easy access to the Amsterdam money market for savers and investors all over the Netherlands. The association of country bankers and brokers numbered about 450 members in 1930 (Van der Werff, 1988: 190–3). They supported the long-standing and widespread habit of sending spare cash to the stock market, either to buy shares, or to put it on *prolongatie*, that is, the lombard business on collateral of shares which formed the 'bread and butter' business of the Amsterdam stock exchange. The competition from this market limited the scope for deposit taking. The interest on *prolongatie* served as the going rate on the money market until the 1920s, when the private discount rate replaced it (Jongman, 1960: 167).[6] This very fragmented deposit-and-credit system amounted to about 400 million guilders at any given time just before the First World War, more than double the known fixed deposits of all banks taken together.[7] No adequate estimates exist for later years. During the early 1920s *prolongatie* seems to have continued at about the same level, gradually declining in relative importance until it disappeared around 1930 (Jongman, 1960: 166–75). This system explains the low level of demand deposits in M1, and suggests that measuring market share by demand deposits is not appropriate for Dutch banks (cf. Capie and Rodrik-Bali, 1982).

At first sight the long domination and sudden disappearance of the *prolongatie* system appears to be something of a puzzle. If savers preferred *prolongatie* to deposits for so long, why did the banks not outbid the stock exchange? The interest rate structure shown in Figure 9.2 holds the key.

We may safely leave speculation as to why interest rates moved the way they did to others (De Roos and Wieringa, 1953; Knoester and De Visser, 1991); suffice it to say here, that with short rates above the yield on Government bonds since the 1890s, banks could in no way have competed for deposits before the First World War. During the 1920s the *prolongatie* market retained much of its attraction, for the passive intermediation of finding takers for clients' money earned a steady commission of up to 2 per cent a year overall, at a time when interest rate fluctuations made the active intermediation of keeping deposits for ones own investments risky. If that suggests the banks were lacking in enterprise, circumstances clearly did not create enough pressure for change. With commission adding about 1 per cent a year on top of the

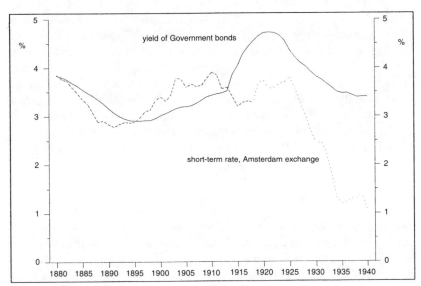

Figure 9.2   Dutch interest rates, 1880–1940.[8]

interest rate, *prolongatie* was an expensive form of credit for longer than a month. Perhaps finance was living off the rest of the economy, as suggested at the time; the latter did profit from supply and demand maintaining a steady balance (Eisfeld, 1916: 272–9).

The sometimes vociferous complaints about the banks' attitude to industry all concerned the availability and scope, not the cost, of credit (Jonker, 1991). Towards the end of the 1920s the interest gap widened, mainly because of a sharp fall in short rates, creating scope for building up deposits and ending the *prolongatie* system. The commercial banks were not the only institutions to profit; Figure 9.4 below shows a sharp increase in savings banks' assets from the late 1920s as well.

Bank assets

As indicated above, the data drawn from the summarized balance sheets have to be treated with some caution. Although they are comparatively full, they remain incomplete both in substance and in years covered.[9] Nevertheless, these data serve well enough to establish trends. Figure 9.3 shows bank assets as a percentage of net national income at market prices (NNImp) from 1900 to 1940 for all banks taken together, the commercial banks, as well as the Big Five: the Amsterdamsche Bank, Rotterdamsche Bank, Twentsche Bank, Incassobank, and the Nederlandsche Handel-Maatschappij.

The total assets/NNImp ratio broadly tallies with estimates of financial assets to GNP published by Goldsmith for the period up to 1929. After this they begin to diverge from these estimates because of Goldsmith's inclusion of insurance companies and pension funds (1969: 209, 529–30).[10] The figures tell a story similar to the development shown in Figure 9.1. From a fairly low level in 1900, when according to Goldsmith the assets/GNP ratio in the Netherlands was about half or less than half that of, for instance, Scandinavia, banking development quickened around 1905, to explode into activity during the First World War. The 1920s brought a setback, but by 1929 the gap with broadly similar countries had been closed.

An interesting difference lies in the steep peak during the First World War and the subsequent fall, plotting the banking crisis which hit the Netherlands in line with the other former neutrals (Jonker and Van Zanden, 1994). By taking 1913 and 1929 as benchmark years Goldsmith did not record this, perhaps deliberately ignoring what appears to be a temporary aberration from the overall upward trend. The assets/NNImp ratio for the Big Five printed in Figure 9.3 suggest it was just an aberration, a point underlined by Figure 9.4, which breaks down the

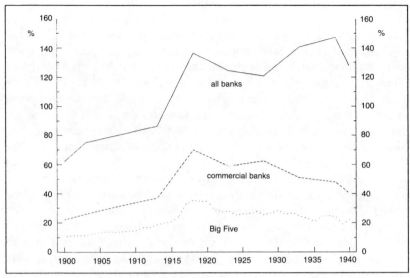

Figure 9.3   Bank assets as percentage of NNImp, 1900–40.[11]

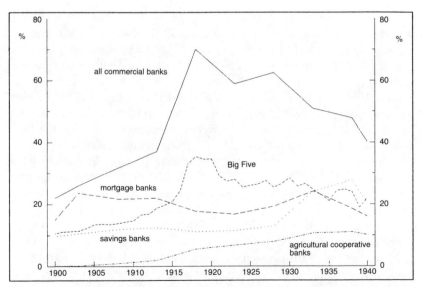

Figure 9.4   Assets/NNImp for five bank types, 1900–40 (*Source*: as Figure 9.3).[12]

data into different types of banks. Only the commercial banks show the pattern of rapid expansion followed by a setback; all other institutions developed gradually, without that particular peak and trough. The full analysis of changing relative positions between the groups need not detain us now, apart from one point that deserves attention. After 1920, commercial banking first stalled and then declined in relation to both the other institutions and NNImp. Though already noted by Goldsmith as an aspect of financial development in general (Goldsmith, 1969: 224–35, 261–73), some specific implications for the Netherlands bear comment. First, the flowering of commercial banking, in particular that of the Big Five, only lasted for a brief period of about ten years, and came about under exceptional economic circumstances. They occupied a commanding position on the financial scene from around 1910 to the early 1920s, thereafter remaining strong, but only just managing to keep pace with developments. Second, we need to see the concentration process which led to the emergence of the Big Five less as a sign of dynamic development in banking than as a defensive and ultimately unsuccessful effort to retain position. The first phase of concentration, traditionally dated from 1911 when the Rotterdamsche Bank took over the Deposito- en Administratiebank, coincided with a rapid rise in bank assets as a percentage of NNImp. However, subsequent mergers and takeovers during the 1920s and 1930s did not, for though total assets continued to rise, their ratio to NNImp tended to fall, and thus with the remaining commercial banks the gap increased.

Indeed, the scramble of 1910–20 left the Big Five stranded, as Figure 9.5 shows. At the turn of the century this group had an average capital/assets ratio of about 40 per cent. This had halved by 1920, but then it rose again to remain at 25–30 per cent until 1940. A comparison with other European countries shows the Dutch banks' capital/assets ratio to have been very high indeed. Around 1910 a figure of 20 per cent was common in Sweden, Belgium and Germany; in the UK and France it had even declined to 13 and 16 per cent respectively.[13] During the First World War the ratio sank to 15 per cent or below throughout Europe and stayed there throughout the 1920s and 1930s. One would have expected a difference between the Netherlands and countries ravaged by the war, but the Dutch ratio during the interwar period was double that of fellow neutrals such as Sweden and Switzerland.[14] Presumably the lack of a stable deposits base led the Dutch banks to maintain a high capital/assets ratio, and the crisis of the early 1920s increased their caution. But this feature also indicates a flagging drive on the part of the banks, weakening demand from customers, or both, after the brief heyday. A closer look at selected asset items should help to clarify this matter.

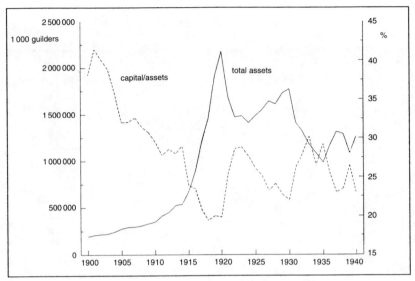

Figure 9.5   Total assets (left scale) and capital/assets ratio (right scale) of the Big Five, 1900–1940 (*Source*: as Figure 9.3).

Asset structure of the commercial banks

Two features stand out in the breakdown of selected asset items for the Big Five shown in Figure 9.6. First, the amount of shares, participations and consortia as a percentage of total assets dropped during the period under consideration. Part of that drop, of course, reflects the conversion of affiliated provincial banks into full-blown branches; on the other hand some long-term finance will have been camouflaged as bills and advances (Jonker, 1991: 122–3; Jonker, 1994). Yet the trend as a whole shows the banks less and less willing to undertake fixed commitments during the period under consideration. Second, the ratio fell sharply to its lowest level between 1910 and 1920, so even then the banks acted mostly as passive intermediaries between savers and investors, off-loading any commitments as quickly as they could. Between 1920 and 1925 the ratio recovered somewhat, but that was probably due only to the shifting of frozen advances during the crisis, as a similar hiccup during the 1930s indicates. The overall trend remained the same, even though the Big Five took over more and more business underwriting share issues from stockbrokers and private bankers. By 1939 the banks arranged nearly all intermediated flotations, perhaps half of the domestic total, with directly-placed Government loans making up most of the rest (Renooij,

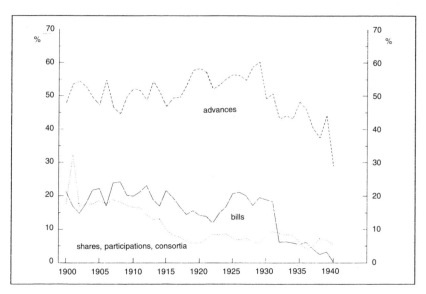

Figure 9.6   Selected asset items for the Big Five in percentage of total assets, 1900–40 (*Source:* as Figure 9.3).

1951: 194-205). Though clearly prepared to take a risk, the banks were still unwilling to hazard a stake. Combined with the high capital/assets ratio, the banks' asset structure thus underlines the stolidity of Dutch banking during the period under consideration.

The capital size of public limited companies, 1885–1940

On the other hand data on company finance suggest both a weakening demand from business and an absence of bottlenecks due to the banks' impassiveness during the 1920s and 1930s. There are three sets of figures available: net company investment in fixed assets from the National Accounts, rights issues on the Amsterdam stock exchange, and the number of *naamloze vennootschappen* (NVs) or public limited companies and their paid-up capital.

Figure 9.7 combines the data on net company investment in fixed assets and rights issues to show a lukewarm demand for finance from business during the interwar years. Net investment dropped from 1071 billion guilders in 1921 to 708 million guilders in 1925, recovered to

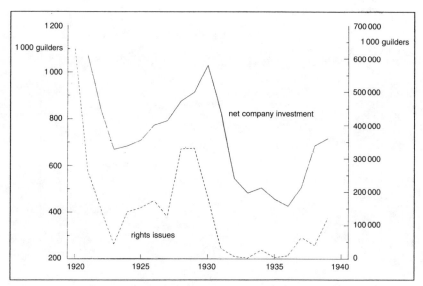

Figure 9.7 Net company investment in fixed assets (left scale) and stock market issues (right scale), 1920–1940.[15]

1 029 billion guilders in 1930 before another steep fall. There are as yet no data prior to 1921, but these figures suffice to show that company investment did not return to peak levels. Companies' rights issues during the interwar years equally remained well under the record levels achieved in 1919–20, and even then the relative peaks of 1924, 1926, 1929 and 1939 were largely due to share issues by the Royal Dutch/Shell group.

As for company growth, detailed data are hard to come by. However, from 1885 to 1918 and again from 1929 to 1939 the Dutch national statistical office CBS annually published the number of public limited companies or *naamloze vennootschappen* (NVs) plus their paid-up capital in the so-called *Jaarcijfers*. Derived from company tax registers these figures should be fairly reliable, though they have their limitations. First, paid-up capital reflects only part of a company's resources, varying in size and importance from one economic sector to another. Second, as the economic upswing after 1890 led to family firms going public, an increase in NVs and their capital does not automatically signify a rising demand for finance. As we shall see average company size declined, so as time went by people probably adopted the NV more to spread risk than to attract outside finance (Van Stuijvenberg, 1967: 212). For want of better, the data will do to indicate a trend, however.

Figure 9.8 broadly conforms to the pattern established so far. Until about 1912 both NV capital and bank assets as a percentage of NNImp

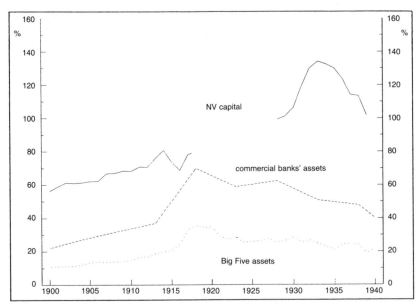

Figure 9.8   Paid-up capital of *naamloze vennootschappen* and banks assets as percentage of NNImp, 1900–40.[16]

rose in tandem, with bank assets lagging some way behind. Just to be perverse, we may note that it is highly probable for these positions to have been reversed at an earlier period. Goldsmith estimated bank assets to be 46 per cent of GNP in 1880, when the NV capital probably stood at something like 32 per cent (Goldsmith, 1969: 209).[17] In the absence of firm data for the 19th century, we will have to leave that for now as an intriguing pointer towards the shifting position of banks and industry after the 1880s.

Returning to the 20th century, we find that during the early years of the First World War the two sectors diverged, as bank assets grew faster than both NNImp and company capital. By 1918 they must have run parallel again. The data gap unfortunately prevents us following developments during a crucial part of the 1920s, but it seems quite likely that, at least initially, bank assets and NV capital went down together just as they had gone up before. However, at some point a new divergence set in; by 1929 the percentage of company capital had increased significantly, while bank assets continued their gentle downward trend. During the first half of the 1930s the distance grew as company capital rose steeply, only to drop back again towards 1940.

According to these data the commercial banks kept pace with business development as measured by company capital up to the 1920s, but somewhere during that decade they fell out of step. Some implications become clear if we look at average company size and average dividends in Figure 9.9. The number of NVs increased from 653 in 1885 to 8 722 in 1912, but average size fell from 545 744 guilders to 217 800 guilders, as sustained economic growth spawned numerous small firms and helped them to consolidate by going public. The hothouse conditions during the First World War partly reversed the trend, with companies growing more quickly in size than in number. In 1929, when we pick up the thread again, average NV size had grown by half to 328 740 guilders, mainly due to the emergence of big integrated industrial concerns like Royal Dutch/Shell, AKU, Philips and Unilever. Subsequently the crisis of the 1930s ended the trend towards expansion.

The banks thus followed NV development closest when the average size fell; the wave of concentration and capital increases started at the very moment when company growth hit bottom, and the retreat came when the large business concerns appeared. In the absence of quantitative concentration indices of Dutch industry, we must be content with this qualitative indication that in the Netherlands, industrial concentration followed banking concentration (cf. Capie and Rodrik-Bali, 1982: 291–2). Figure 9.9 also shows the incentive for the change in fashion. From about 1905, average NV profits as measured by dividends

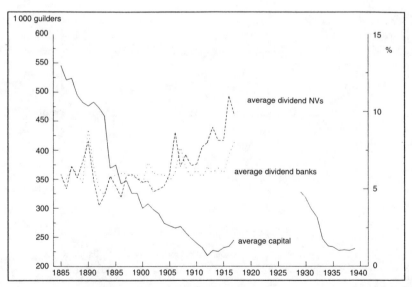

Figure 9.9   Average NV capital (left scale) and average dividends of NVs and banks (right scale), 1885–1940 (*Source:* as Figure 9.6).

rose steeply, outstripping the yield on Government bonds and then the banks' own dividends. However, with the threshold for a quotation at 500 000 guilders, more than double the average NV size, nursing companies towards a stock exchange flotation was no realistic goal for banking policies. The near perfect coincidence of advances and deposits at the Big Five in Figure 9.10 demonstrates that the steep rise in banking services from about 1910 consisted mainly of a swelling current account business, as the nearly congruent percentage of demand deposits plotted in Figure 9.1 and the simultaneous sharp drop in the income velocity of money V2 already indicated. The lines start to diverge with the boom turning into a frenzy at the end of the First World War, with the banks falling over themselves to grant and then extend facilities. As I have argued elsewhere, these advances were mostly disguised as finance bills or *kredietpapier*. These bills, with two instead of three signatures, were rolled over time and again, and were liquid in name only (cf. Jonker, 1991, 1994). Circumstances probably left no time to pioneer better ways to provide and monitor medium and long-term credits, but the use of this old mercantile form for purposes to which it was clearly unsuited also underlines the banks' half-hearted embrace of the investment role.

The subsequent steep drop in deposits, well below advances, graphically depicts the liquidity squeeze which brought one of the Big

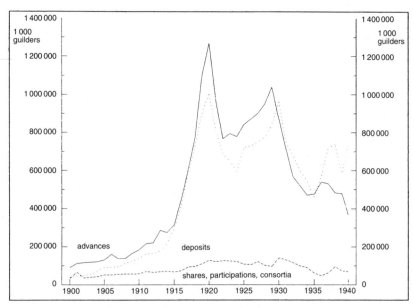

Figure 9.10 Advances, deposits, and shares, participations and consortia at the Big Five, 1900–40 (*Source:* as Figure 9.3).

Five, the Rotterdamsche Bank, to its knees in 1924. From then on both lines move up again, although at some distance from each other. Set against these spectacular ups and downs, shares, advances and consortia limped along the bottom. These items remained quite stable at the considerable amount of about 100 million guilders, but otherwise bore no relation at all to overall business, not even during the hectic decade of 1910–20, and they declined as a percentage of total assets, as Figure 9.6 showed.

The banks' half-hearted conversion makes their retreat from industrial commitments after the collapse in 1920 all the more easy to understand. First, losses were severe. According to one expert at the time, at least 200 million guilders, equivalent to just under 10 per cent of the total assets of the Big Five, was written off as bad debts during 1920–22.[18] A wave of bank failures swept the country, hitting the regions particularly hard (cf. De Vries, 1989: 227–57). Second, the crisis led to a general loss of business confidence and uneasiness about the future of Dutch industry in particular, which the prolonged erosion of dividends did nothing to alleviate. Prices at the stock exchange fell until 1924, industrial shares losing two-thirds of their 1920 value, banks half, and shipping three-quarters (Keesing, 1978: 31). According to a survey published in 1928, the average dividend of just over 100 companies fell from 13.2 per cent in 1919 to 3.6 per cent in 1923. During this period nine firms had gone bust, and 60 had paid no dividend at all until at least 1925 (Brandes de Roos, 1928, vol. 2: 15–21).[19] At between 4 and 5 per cent, Government bonds now gave a greater yield for no real risk.

The wealth of alternatives

If the banking boom and concentration remained limited to the expansion and extension of short-term facilities and did not make much difference to the availability of long-term finance, and if assets of the commercial banks as a whole and the Big Five in particular declined against NNImp while the capital of NVs continued to rise, do we have evidence of growing constraints on company finance? I have argued before that there were, but in the light of the data on company investment presented in Figure 9.7 the matter would seem to merit some further discussion.

A quick glance at the aggregate data on economic growth fails to reveal any bottlenecks. From the bottom of the cycle in 1923 to the peak in 1929, NNImp grew by 3.2 per cent a year. The capital paid up in NVs topped 6.6 billion guilders in 1930, an increase of 131 per cent over the next previous recorded level in 1917. Assuming half of that accumulation took place during the boom years up to 1920 still leaves an annual rise of 6.5 per cent during the decade. Both figures underline that company finance was no real problem. Indeed, during the 1920s advances and deposits of the Big Five ran at a greater distance to each other than before the First World War, as Figure 9.10 shows. So these banks at least went some way to meet demand, though the high capital/assets ratio testifies that they hardly stretched themselves.

Some important qualifications need to be made here, however. A sharp decline in the non-executive directorships held by bankers between 1923 and 1931 does indicate a contraction of facilities to business. Moreover, a breakdown of directorships by company seat shows regional interests in the Netherlands lost out to the centre, following the earlier example of the UK (Jonker, 1991: 127–8; cf. Cottrell, 1980: 237). Though less accurate because of the benchmark years, Figure 9.11 shows the advances and deposits of all commercial banks taken together more or less coinciding during the 1920s, so presumably the extension granted by the Big Five was cancelled out by other banks following more conservative policies.

Though understandable because of the banks' traumatic experiences during the early 1920s, this probable contraction must have grated with business concerns, particularly since it went hand in hand with an

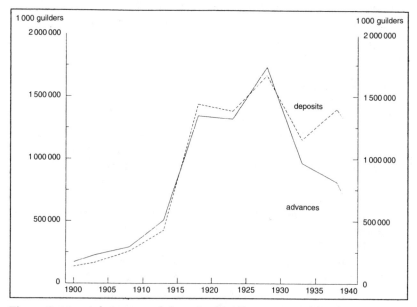

Figure 9.11 Advances and deposits for all commercial banks, 1900–40, benchmark years (*Source:* as Figure 9.3).

expansion of foreign credit. Keen to raise Amsterdam's stature as a financial centre, the Nederlandsche Bank sponsored the establishment of a foreign acceptance market, mainly dealing in German bills. From a modest beginning of 36.2 million guilders in 1922–23, this trade quickly rose to a peak of 799 million guilders in 1929–30, equal to 76 per cent of the total advances of the Big Five.[20] Moreover, between 1924 and 1929 1.4 billion guilders were raised on the Dutch capital market for foreign Governments and companies, against a domestic total of 1.9 billion guilders (Renooij, 1951: 107, 145).

The importance of foreign trade credit and capital export again serves to stress the lack of fundamental change in the Dutch capital market during the period under consideration. The banks behaved much as before, choosing between existing alternatives for the best balance between yield and risk, as any sensible investor would. One could criticize them for a lack of enterprise, failing to keep pace with industrial developments and not developing more sophisticated methods of credit assessment (Jonker, 1991: 124–6). But it is hard to fault them, hemmed in as they were as an investor among investors. The interest rate structure combined with easy access to the *prolongatie* market left little scope for expansion of liabilities. Continuing business traditions of thrift, self-finance, and preference for private investment must have offered a range of alternatives to companies unwilling to pay for the expensive Amsterdam-centred intermediation. After all, though business investment continued at lower levels than before, the data on economic growth and company development fail to show where the restrictions pinched, so we must assume that most companies succeeded in finding finance much as they had done before 1910. This tallies with both current opinion and recent research on the structure and development of Dutch business during the interwar years (Ruizendaal, 1967; Bloemen *et al.*, 1993; Sluyterman and Winkelman, 1993). After the belated spurt of 1890–1920, Dutch industry fanned out to advance over a wide front. Family-run companies continued to dominate well into the 1930s and, at the other end of the spectrum, large diversified concerns appeared. Both, by and large, provided their own finance from informal sources and retained earnings. Perhaps some enterprises failed through lack of resources, or because of unimaginative bankers. But then some always do. The aggregate growth rates fail to show up serious bottlenecks, and the industrial development corporations set up in the 1930s after a lengthy debate on the supposed problems business finance never really took off (De Hen, 1980; Jonker, 1991).

Thus, Dutch banking concentration and industrial growth ran parallel, but not in tandem. The mergers and capital increases during 1910 to 1919 were needed to finance the rising volume, not the changed character, of business, and to cover increased risks of bigger and more frequent company flotations. If the banks overall continued to prefer passive intermediation to active financial management, and thus cut short their heyday to a brief ten years, we must probably look for an explanation of their position on a market richly endowed with alternatives for both savers and investors.

Notes

1. I am indebted to Eugene V. White and Prof. M.M.G. Fase for their helpful comments on an earlier version of this paper, to Bouke Veldman, Nico van Horn and Co Seegers for their help and encouragement, and to Stella Piggot for her excellent editing.
2. Interestingly, White suggests a connection between the capital demands of growing business, whereas Lamoreaux stresses the coincidental factor of shares accumulating in a few hands being behind banking concentration in New England.
3. W. M. Westerman was a director of the Rotterdamsche Bank and a son of its president, W. Westerman, the driving force behind the expansion and concentration.
4. After merging with the Deposito-en Adminstratiebank in 1911 the Rotterdamdsche Bank called itself the Rotterdamsche Bankvereeniging or Robaver for short, only to revert to its previous name after the Second World War. To avoid confusion I have its original name throughout.
5. Van Nierop was chief executive of the Amsterdamsche Bank.
6. In 1924 the prominent businessman and shipper E. Heldring complained in his diary about the drain of the *prolongatie* market and the undesirable habit, in his eyes, of shipping lines putting their money on *prolongatie* instead of buying prime bills (De Vries, 1970: 539, 548).
7. Wolff (1913: 12, 23–4), estimating the 400 stockbrokers held posts of million guilders each. When the market collapsed on the eve of the First World War, an enquiry by the Nederlandsche Bank established a total of 325 million guilders (Jongman, 1960: 155–7).
8. The yield on Government debt and the short rate at the Amsterdam stock exchange up to 1914 are taken from De Jong (1967, vol. 3: 622–6), giving annual averages for both. The yield for 1914–40 and the short rate for 1918–40 come from *Zeventig jaren* (1970: 115). Homer and Sylla (1991: 485–87 give short rates for 1915–17. The break in the short-rate curve reflects the change from *prolongatie* to private discount as an indicator.
9. According to the editors of the *Financiële instellingen*, 13, the coverage should be about 27 per cent for the number of banks, but 73 per cent (1900) to 93 per cent (1918) for the balance sheet total.
10. Goldsmith gives a figure of 46 per cent for 1880 (no new data), 62 per cent in 1900 (new estimate 62.2 per cent), 83 per cent in 1913 (86.31 per cent), 110 per cent in 1929 (120.9 per cent in 1928).
11. The top line includes all banks and girosystems tabulated in the *Financiële instellingen*, Tables 1 to 7, for benchmark years 1900, 1903 and then every five years. The lower line of the Big Five banks represents Table 3c from

this book. NNImp calculated from *Zeventig jaar statistiek* 119.

12.   The total for commercial banks is that given by the *Financiële instellingen* 34–5, minus the overseas banks, the acceptance companies and the colonial banks, since these were of no consequence to the domestic banking scene. The acceptance companies, often set up by German banks, figured only during the 1920s as suppliers of trade credit to Germany. Except for the Big Five, data are for 1900 and 1903, and then at five year intervals.

13.   The figure of 23 per cent for Sweden in 1910 from Van de Wiel (1936: 181); 19.2 per cent for Belgium in 1913 from Van der Valk (1932: 56); from 20.5 for the big Berlin banks to 23.3 for other Kreditbanken, and 26.3 per cent for provincial banks in Germany in 1910 from *Deutsches Geld- und Bankwesen* 56–59; 16 per cent at the Crédit Lyonnais, the Société Générale, the Comptoir National d'Escompte and the Crédit Industriel et Commercial in France in 1911 from Treep (1934: 43). For the UK: Collins (1988: 102).

14.   A figure of 16.6 per cent in 1921 and 13.5 per cent in 1930 for eight big Swiss banks from Van Rhee (1934: 123–5).

15.   The data for rights issues from Renooij (1951: 116); net company investment from *Macroeconomische ontwikkelingen*.

16.   Sources: the company data are from the *Jaarcijfers*, for every year from 1885 to 1917 and from 1929 to 1939. The bank data are compiled as in Figure 9.4 from the *Financiële instellingen*. The NNImp calculated from *Zeventig jaren statistiek*, 119.

17.   The other figure obtained by dividing NV capital in 1885 by the latest guesstimates of NNImp for 1880, giving 32.4 per cent. I have taken NNImp for 1885 as the upper limit of 1.1 billion guilders from J. L. van Zanden's estimate for 1880 (1987: 53). A team under Van Zanden at Utrecht University is reconstructing the Dutch national accounts for the 19th century, but new data are as yet unavailable. The number of NVs is from the *Jaarcijfers* 1885–86.

18.   A survey of 20 banks quoted in Keesing (1978: 32–3). Keesing quotes another survey of 72 companies with a total capital paid up of 445 million guilders; by 1922, 24 of them had been reorganized for financial reasons, 19 were in the hands of receivers, 7 had gone bust, with just over 300 million guilders of capital being written off.

19.   The survey in the *Kroniek van Sternheim* 4 (1926) 60, gives a rather rosier picture of 64 companies with an average low of 8.24 per cent in 1922, pushed up by the inclusion of 20 colonial commodity traders with an average dividend of 12.3 per cent in 1922, 19.8 per cent in 1923 and 31.7 per cent in 1924.

20.   See Jonker (1991: 126, 131); details in De Vries (1989: 216–21), Houwink ten Cate (1989).

References

Bloemen, E.S.A., Kok, J. and van Zanden, J. L. (1993), *De top-100 van industriële bedrijven in Nederland 1913-1990*, The Hague.

Bordo, M. D. and Jonung, L. (1987), *The Long-run Behaviour of the*

Velocity of Circulation: The International Evidence, Cambridge.

Brandes de Roos, R. (1928), *Industrie, Kapitalmarkt und industrielle Effekten in den Niederlanden*, The Hague.

Cameron, R. E. (1967) 'Conclusion', in R. E. Cameron (ed.), *Banking in the Early Stages of Industrialization: A Study in Comparative Economic History*, Oxford.

Capie, F. H. and Rodrik-Bali, G. (1982), 'Concentration in British banking 1870-1920', *Business History*, 24.

Collins, M. (1988), *Money and Banking in the UK: A History*, London.

Cottrell, P. L. (1980), *Industrial Finance 1830–1914: The Finance and Organization of English Manufacturing Industry*, London.

Deutsches Geld- und Bankwesen in Zahlen 1876–1975 Frankfurt: Deutsche Bank.

Eisfeld, C. (1916), *Das niederländische Bankwesen*, The Hague.

Financiële instellingen (1987), *Financiële instellingen in Nederland 1900-1985, balansreeksen en naamlijst van handelsbanken*, Amsterdam: De Nederlandsche Bank.

Goldsmith, R. W. (1969), *Financial Structure and Development*, New Haven, CT.

Hen, P. E. de (1980), *Actieve en re-actieve industriepolitiek in Nederland, de overheid en de ontwikkeling van de Nederlandse industrie in de jaren dertig en tussen 1945 en 1950*, Amsterdam.

Homer, S. and Sylla, R. E. (1991), *A history of Interest Rates*, Brunswick, NJ.

Houwink ten Cate, J.Th.M. (1989), 'Amsterdam als Finanzplatz Deutschlands (1919–1932)', in G.D. Feldman *et al.* (eds), *Konsequenzen der Inflation*, Berlin.

Jaarcijfers voor het Koninkrijk der Nederlanden, The Hague: Centraal Bureau voor de Statistiek.

Jong, A. M. de (1967) *Geschiedenis van de Nederlandsche Bank*, 4 vols Haarlem: Enschede.

Jongman, C. D. (1960), *De Nederlandse geldmarkt*, Leiden.

Jonker, J. P. B. (1991), 'Sinecures or sinews of power? Interlocking directorships and bank/industry relations in the Netherlands, 1910–1940', *Economic and Social history in the Netherlands*, 3.

Jonker, J. P. B. (1994), 'Between private responsibility and public duty', forthcoming.

Jonker, J. P. B. and van Zanden, J. L. (1994), 'Method in the madness? Banking crises across Europe during the inter-war period', forthcoming.

Keesing, F. A. G. (1978), *De conjuncturele ontwikkeling van Nederland en de evolutie van de economische overheidspolitiek 1918–1939*, Nijmegen.

Knoester, A. and de Visser, H. (eds) (1991), *De hoge reële rente en de Nederlandse economie*, Leiden.

Kuné, J. B. and van Nieuwkerk, M. (1974), 'De ontwikkeling van de geldquote in Nederland, 1900-1970', *Maandschrift Economie*, 39.

Lamoreaux, N. M. (1991), 'Bank mergers in late 19th century New England, the contingent nature of structural change', *Journal of Economic History*, 51.

Larsson, M. (1991), 'State, banks and industry in Sweden, with some reference to the Scandinavian countries', in: H. James, H. Lindgren and A. Teichova (eds), *The Role of Banks in the Inter-war Economy*, Cambridge.

Macro-economische ontwikkelingen 1921–1939 en 1969–1985, een vergelijking op basis van herziene gegevens voor het Interbellum (1987), Voorburg: Centraal Bureau voor de Statistiek.

Nieuwkerk, M. van (1974), 'De geldhoeveelheid in Nederland 1900–1945', *Kwartaalbericht van de Nederlandsche Bank*, 3.

Renooij, D. C. (1951), *De Nederlandse emissiemarkt van 1904–1939*, Amsterdam.

Rhee, J. C. M. van (1934), *De betrekkingen tusschen banken en industrie in Zwitserland*, Haarlem.

Roos, F. de and Wieringa, W. J. (1953), *Een halve eeuw rente in Nederland*, Schiedam: NV Levensverzekering-Maatschappij HAV Bank.

Ruizendaal, N. L. (1967), 'De financiering bij Nederlandse ondernemingen sinds 1921', in R. Burgers *et al.* (eds), *Tot de orde geroepen, bundel ter gelegenheid van het veertigjarig bestaan der Vereniging van academisch gevormde accountants*, Deventer.

Sluyterman, K. E. and Winkelman, H. L. M. (1993), 'The Dutch family firm confronted with Chandler's dynamics of industrial capitalism', in *Business History*.

Stuijvenberg, J. H. van (1967) 'Economische groei van Nederland in de negentiende eeuw: een terreinverkenning', in W.J. Wieringa *et al.* (eds), *Bedrijf en samenleving, economisch-historische studies over Nederland in de negentiende en twintigste eeuw aangeboden aan prof.dr. I.J. Brugmans bij zijn aftreden als hoogleraar aan de Universiteit van Amsterdam*, Alphen a/d Rijn.

Treep, A. (1934), *De betrekkingen tusschen banken en industrie in Frankrijk*, Haarlem.

Valk, H. M. H. A. van der (1932), *De betrekkingen tusschen banken en industrie in België* Haarlem: Bohn.

Vanthemsche, G. (1991), 'State, banks and industry in Belgium and the Netherlands, 1919–1939', in: H. James, H. Lindgren and A. Teichova (eds), *The Role of Banks in the Inter-war Economy*, Cambridge.

Vries, Joh de, (ed.) (1970), *Herinneringen en dagboek van Ernst Heldring*, The Hague.

Vries, Joh de (1989), *Geschiedenis van de Nederlandsche Bank*, V, *Visserings tijdvak* 1914–1931, Amsterdam.

Wee, H. van der and Tavernier, K. (1975), *De Nationale Bank van België en het monetaire gebeuren tussen de twee wereldoorlogen*, Brussels: De Nationale Bank.

Werff, D. C. J. van der (1988), *De Bond, de banken en de beurzen*, Amsterdam.

Westerman, W.M. (1920), *De concentratie in het bankwezen, een bijdrage tot de kennis der economische ontwikkeling van onze tijd*, The Hague.

White, E. N. (1985), 'The merger movement in banking, 1919–1933', *Journal of Economic History*, 45.

Wiel, E. van de (1936), *De betrekkingen tusschen banken en industrie in Zweden*, Haarlem.

Wolff Ezn., J. E. (1913), *Over het afleveren van fondsen, het prolongatiesysteem ter beurze van Amsterdam en nog wat*, Amsterdam.

Zanden, J. L. van (1987), 'Economische groei in Nederland in de negentiende eeuw: enkele nieuwe resultaten', in *Economisch- en sociaalhistorisch jaarboek*, 50.

Zeventig jaren (1970), *Zeventig jaren statistiek in tijdreeksen 1899–1969*, The Hague: Centraal Bureau voor de Statistiek.

CHAPTER TEN

The New Issue Market as a Source of Finance for the UK Brewing and Iron and Steel Industries, 1870–1913

Katherine Watson

> When industry and finance become interwoven, it is not always easy to ascertain which dominates which. Sometimes the industrialist seems to be in control. . . . But as a rule the last word seems to be with the financier. . . . It seems probable that on the whole society may be at least as much enriched by his effective foresight as it is impoverished by his rapacity. (Robertson, 1923: 82)

Among the many economists and economic historians who have sought to understand the relationship between finance and industry, there has been a hesitance to accept Robertson's rather optimistic observation that financiers could not be held entirely responsible for the problems of industrialists. In particular, the exoneration of the late 19th and early 20th century domestic capital market from accusations of contributing to British economic decline remains incomplete.

The great expansion of capital exports from Britain prior to the First World War has naturally attracted the attention of economic historians who have tried both to explain the motivations for investment overseas and to identify the consequences of this expansion for the domestic economy. (See, for example, Hobson, 1914; Cairncross, 1953; Hall, 1968; Edelstein, 1982.) Edelstein's pioneering study of relative yields on portfolio investment in the UK and abroad revealed that yields tended to fluctuate procyclically with home and overseas investment – a discovery which makes it difficult to sustain the view that there was anything persistently irrational about the functioning of the British capital market at the end of the 19th century (Edelstein, 1982).

Yet while additional microeconomic evidence is being collected, a vigorous debate concerning the role of the financial market as a source of British economic decline continues. In defence of the capital market Michie has argued that the supply of capital was more than adequate to meet prevailing demand, but that demand was constrained by legislation at both national and local government level which impeded the pace of innovation (Michie, 1988: 493, 514–20). Michie also draws attention to the fact that industrialists were not solely dependent on public subscription of capital to meet their needs. As well as its formal institutions, the UK capital market provided an informal network for raising industrial finance (Michie, 1988: 501). Attention to these sources generates a more sympathetic appraisal of the UK capital market than is implied by an examination of the new issue market alone.

In contrast, Kennedy is among those convinced of capital market failure, arguing that market imperfections generated asymmetries in the information available to buyers and sellers of industrial securities. In order to compensate for the uncertainty which was associated with inadequate information, investors became excessively cautious in the allocation of their investment portfolios (Kennedy, 1987). In such a risk averse environment, entrepreneurs in new industries would find it especially difficult to raise finance, since they would have very limited evidence of previous success with which to support their claim. Furthermore, early company failures in new industries such as electrical engineering and motor vehicle manufacture transmitted negative signals of future profitability which jeopardized subsequent applications for capital (Kennedy, 1987: 125–30). Established industries could also face resistance against attempts to service investment required perhaps to develop new technology in response to the challenge of competition. Unless promises of future profits could be demonstrated confidently, investors would be unwilling to support such ventures. Kennedy argues that calcification of the UK capital market constrained industrial innovation, and hence impeded economic growth during the late 19th and early 20th centuries.

Byatt's study of the British electrical industry provides some interesting evidence which initially seems to offer support for Kennedy's thesis. While he argues that there is no real evidence to suggest that electrical supply companies had any difficulty financing their activities, since much of their funding came from local authorities, the fortunes of electrical manufacturers were less favourable. Byatt suggests that although electrical manufacturing was not especially capital intensive, it was handicapped by the long gestation period of its production process. Due to the maintenance of large inventories and work in progress, this resulted in costs being high relative to profits in the early stages of production (Byatt, 1979: 156–8). This long gestation period was particularly problematic given the tendency for the support of public investors to fluctuate cyclically with the fortunes of the industry (Byatt, 1979: 7–8).

Since electrical manufacturing would often have to be in business for some time before dividends could be declared, ordinary shares were less popular than fixed interest securities, unless business was booming. The use of equity capital by Byatt's 'early manufacturers' (Brush, Crompton and the Electrical Construction Corporation) declined from 43.44 per cent of total funds during the years 1880–96, to 27.17 per cent in 1896–1904, and by 1906–14, none of these companies relied on ordinary shares at all as a source of funds. New entrants to the industry (British-Westinghouse, Dick Kerr and British Thomson-Houston) were supported to a greater extent by finance in the form of debentures and preference shares. In 1896–1904 they obtained only 19.23 per cent of their total funding from equity, and again this diminished to nothing by 1906–14 (Byatt, 1979: 159, Table 35).[1]

Yet Byatt's observation that electrical manufacturers responded to cautious investors by offering safer forms of capital seems to run counter to the implications of Kennedy's argument. While asymmetric information cannot be ignored as an additional impediment which entrepreneurs seeking finance were forced to acknowledge, companies do seem to have adopted financial strategies which would reduce the impact of this problem. By selecting a capital structure that reflected the confidence of the Board of Directors, companies could signal to investors their expectations for future success. Like all principal-agent problems, there was a risk that 'false' signals would be generated by unscrupulous businesses. However, the debenture market provided its own 'enforcement contract' by means of the legal requirement for debenture interest to be paid annually if liquidation was to be averted. Thus issuing capital which implied that the company was safer than the directors really believed carried a heavy cost. Under these circumstances, it is by no means certain that if capital market imperfections did exist, they would induce the stultifying rigidities in industrial finance Kennedy describes.

Further evidence of the willingness of companies to alter their applications to the new issue market in order to secure funds is provided by Harrison's study of the cycle industry. Harrison analyses the distribution of public flotations made by cycle and motorcycle, cars, tyres and tube manufacturing companies between 1882 and 1914. He notes that although some applications were heavily oversubscribed (for example, the issues of 2 000 £5 shares by the Jointless Rim Company and the £5 million issue by Dunlop Pneumatic Tyres in 1896), others fared less well. Several courses of action were open to companies in this situation. The first was to abandon the issue altogether and try to obtain alternative private finance. A second scheme was to approach the market again, some companies being successful with later attempts. Another option was to proceed to allotment and try to operate within the constraints of the inadequate capital subscribed; but Harrison notes that the typical outcome for such enterprises was failure. The most common response was for vendors to adjust their specification of the way in which payment was to be made, and accept a larger proportion of the purchase price for the business in the form of securities rather than cash as originally intended, the capital subscribed providing the working capital for the new company (Harrison, 1981: 172–6). It is noticeable that the companies which proceeded in this way often attempted to supplement their capital at a later stage by additional issues of debentures and preference shares. This practice appears to have been a deliberate policy to reduce the risk associated with investment in the company concerned, and is indicative of the flexibility of corporate financial strategy in these trades (Harrison, 1981: 182–3).

Jefferys describes how corporate financial strategy evolved in response to changing market conditions, with more sophisticated portfolios being offered to the public in an attempt to capture a broader cross-section of investors' preferences. It was possible for firms to adapt their application for capital in order to secure the funds they required. During the 1880s the denomination of shares was reduced and the use of preference shares became more widespread (Jefferys, 1977: 156–292). Whereas in 1884 equity formed 74.4 per cent of the total share and loan capital securities raised by companies listed by *Burdett's Official Intelligence* in the groups commercial and industrial, shipping, iron, coal and steel, this had decreased to 47.6 per cent by 1914. In contrast, preference capital comprised only 8.8 per cent of the total in 1884, but almost 30 per cent by the First World War (Jefferys, 1977: 458, Appendix E).

Kennedy could respond to these arguments by suggesting that some industries simply could not afford to offer 'safe' securities with any confidence that their annual obligations could be met. A conflict of interests may emerge in the design of a company's financial structure: firms have to balance the need to secure adequate capital to pursue their intended projects, while simultaneously servicing those liabilities successfully so as not to jeopardize future applications for capital.[2] In investigating corporate financial structure it is valuable to consider whether companies were forced into suboptimal gearing ratios by the need to appeal to excessively risk averse investors, or whether industrialists were unimpeded in their design of capital structure. As the quote which opened this chapter suggested, it is important to establish whether financiers of industrialists dominate corporate financial decisions, and furthermore whether this relationship results in an efficient allocation of resources.

It is clearly imperative to be precise about what is meant by failure of the capital market. While the existence of capital market imperfections is not in dispute, the interesting question concerns the impact that this has on industrial finance. Was there any reason why investors should have supported industries that appeared to be destined for low profits? Did the capital market really fail if investors proved unwilling to assume such risks? The studies by Byatt and Harrison indicate that some industries did manage to alter their capital structure in order to secure finance. This implies that if investors were offered sufficiently attractive projects, they were amenable to supporting British industry. The onus may simply have been on companies to apply to the market for capital in a form which compensated for the risk associated with their business. If it transpires that some entrepreneurs found it easier than others to attract the capital they required, we may be pushed towards an explanation of British economic decline that does not rely so heavily on weaknesses of the capital market.

This chapter aims to contribute to this debate by extending the case-study evidence available to economic historians. The evidence presented here should be seen as complementary to the work of Kennedy and Michie which draws attention to the experience of 'new industries'. Two rather different industries have been selected deliberately to try to illuminate the variety of corporate financial strategy. The brewing industry offers insights into a sector producing a perishable consumer good, and one in which much of the investment undertaken by brewers was directed into property. It could also be argued that since the commercial environment in which brewers operated was heavily circumscribed by the proliferation of licensing legislation during the late 19th century, study of this sector should produce interesting parallels with Michie's work regarding legislative constraints on innovation. In contrast, examination of the iron and steel industry provides evidence for a staple producer trade in which a large share of investment was directed towards plant and equipment. In addition this industry is especially interesting because of the attention which its commercial and technological strategies have received from those seeking to explain British economic decline.

This chapter seeks to identify the scale and character of capital secured from the new issue market by these two sectors. In addition the motives behind the rather different capital structure adopted by these two industries is explored. It should be noted that in focusing on the new issue market alone, this chapter cannot hope to address in detail all the questions raised by the debate on capital market failure. Nevertheless, the conclusion to this chapter attempts to relate the evidence offered to this broader debate.

The brewing industry and the new issue market

As the 19th century drew to a close, British brewers entered one of the most turbulent periods in their history. During Victoria's reign, brewing had been transformed from a trade where approximately 40 per cent of beer produced in the UK was still brewed by publican brewers, to one in which a negligible proportion of beer consumed in licensed premises was brewed 'at home'. Perhaps even more significant was the concentration of production that occurred within the wholesale trade itself. In 1881 17 110 brewers were licensed to brew for sale. Of these, 200 firms accounted for 54.4 per cent of total output; the largest ten firms produced 20 per cent of domestic beer production. By 1913, the number of brewers licensed for sale had shrunk to 3 846; almost half the total output (48.8 per cent) of the industry was produced by just 50 firms and the ten largest firms accounted for 27.9 per cent of total output.[3]

Coinciding with this concentration of production, was a move towards a greater reliance on the public capital market as the principal source of industrial finance for brewers. While in 1880 scarcely any brewers were incorporated, two booms in public flotations in the late 1880s and again in the late 1890s ensured that by 1900 approximately 75 per cent of the capital invested in the industry had been raised by public subscription, or was held by the vendors of the original family firms.

During the late 19th century, competition in the brewing industry intensified. Brewers began to doubt that the expansion in beer consumption which had been maintained since the 1830s would continue. Initially they attempted to protect and defend their markets by offering discounts to regular customers. However, this practice soon accelerated out of control as brewers sought to undercut each other. It became clear that collusive agreements such as those monitored by the Brewers' Company in London were inadequate.

As competition intensified, the relatively harmonious relationship between brewer and publican also came under threat. Some publicans failed to abide by contracts established with their brewer and accepted ales from more than one supplier. Although brewers exercised little mercy in dealing with renegade publicans,[4] publicans persisted in trying to play one brewer off against another to obtain the best deals. In a climate where brewers were keen to secure retail outlets, publicans were also less fastidious about the quality of beer they sold. By diluting beer at the pump, a licensee could increase the earnings from a barrel of beer. Although brewers threatened to boycott publicans who were found to have cheated in this way, there was always likely to be some brewer who was willing to supply the publican concerned, and the practice became widespread. By the late 1880s most brewers realized that if they were to guarantee themselves a market, and ensure that their beer was sold in its original condition, they were going to have to formalize the relationship between brewers and publicans and purchase public houses.

In order to support their investment in property, brewers needed a large supply of capital. The scale of finance required was such that it was beyond the means of most private firms. The result was a rapid transition to the public capital market. The response of the public was encouraging: many of the issues were oversubscribed and the brewing 'mania' took off.

Initially some of the large breweries resisted the changes in the industry, believing that their reputations as brewers of quality ale would ensure their continued success. Their confidence was misplaced and brewers such as Tetley's and Allsopps were forced to enter the property boom late, when public houses were being auctioned at inflated prices. Tetley's centenary publication stresses that the firm only entered the property market as a defensive measure:

> The forming of breweries into public companies, with the attendant issue of ordinary and preference shares and debenture stock to the public, gave those Corporations almost unlimited capital with which to purchase licensed properties. The result was an active, if not riotous, competition for the public trade. . . . There was a veritable orgy of buying bricks and mortar to provide markets and outlets for the ale of this or that firm. House after house whose cellars hitherto Tetley's had supplied was sold to one or other of these wealthy companies and became 'tied'. In sheer self defence the firm had to adopt the policy of other breweries. (Tetley and Son, 1923: 28)

The flotation of brewing stocks and shares on the public capital market occurred in two main waves: in the late 1880s and then, to a greater extent, in the late 1890s. Table 10.1 illustrates the significance of these 'brewing booms', reporting the capital created and called (excluding vendors' shares) on applications by brewing companies to the new issues market between 1880 and 1913.[5] There is little in the evidence available from new issues prospectuses to suggest that brewers were at all constrained in their attempts to raise finance through the public capital market. The quality of information provided for potential investors in prospectuses was often poor. Clearly vendors and promoters were not going to print details that might damage the success of an issue; instead they made use of various devices: none of these were actually fraudulent, but, by the omission of certain details, some probably helped to mislead an optimistic public.

Assets were frequently described in the vaguest terms and valuations given as an aggregate figure, rather than identifying elements within this

Table 10.1 Brewing companies, percentage distribution of capital created and called, 1880–1913 (excluding vendors' shares)

Year	N	Debentures % of total	Preference % of total	Ordinary % of total	Total £
1880	2	–	–	100.00	125 250
1881	3	30.17	–	69.83	232 000
1882	1	–	62.50	37.50	80 000
1883	2	–	81.97	18.03	61 000
1884	0	–	–	–	–
1885	2	96.78	–	3.22	745 000
1886	9	22.68	33.20	44.12	3 307 169
1887	18	30.30	33.90	35.80	6 545 557
1888	33	57.19	22.21	20.60	7 783 292
1889	38	50.45	29.84	19.71	8 723 675
1890	36	27.01	60.23	12.76	6 008 423
1891	20	60.76	16.05	23.19	1 865 038
1892	10	64.89	4.60	30.52	511 200
1893	4	95.28	–	4.72	265 000
1894	22	74.85	19.80	5.34	2 859 500
1895	37	82.60	12.87	4.53	3 490 987
1896	87	65.61	29.65	4.74	11 091 826
1897	96	77.63	17.61	4.78	11 550 694
1898	68	50.65	21.92	27.93	9 536 985
1899	54	61.90	27.92	10.18	8 776 342
1900	23	88.17	6.62	5.21	3 109 544
1901	13	83.64	13.63	2.73	1 393 470
1902	7	84.30	10.06	5.63	709 884
1903	5	84.39	13.81	1.80	624 500
1904	7	83.49	12.26	4.25	1 060 000
1905	5	95.78	1.39	2.84	730 875
1906	0	–	–	–	–
1907	0	–	–	–	–
1908	1	–	–	100.00	7 250
1909	0	–	–	–	–
1910	2	59.26	18.52	22.22	675 000
1911	1	100.00	–	–	200 000
1912	3	95.38	4.62	–	432 800
1913	1	–	–	100.00	14 000

Source: derived from *Investor's Monthly Manual*, 1880–1914.
N = number of companies.

valuation. Sometimes an unspecified amount for goodwill would be included in the valuation, although during the second brewing boom this practice occurred less frequently. Information on a firm's profits was particularly easy to adapt: one useful technique was to avoid publishing full details of annual earnings, quoting instead averages for groups of years carefully selected to show an increase. The most common practice was to 'redefine' net profits: in prosperous years this would be quoted net of depreciation, interest and dividend charges as well as directors' fees, but profits could also be quoted having only deducted depreciation if this created a more favourable impression.

The quality of prospectuses issued obviously varied between companies, but, as the *Statist* frequently observed, the uncertainty surrounding these issues was rarely dispelled. It is the persistence of this uncertainty that is most telling about the attitude of investors; clearly if brewing issues continued to be oversubscribed throughout these two expansionary phases, despite the incomplete nature of the information offered to potential investors, the public was hardly reluctant to support this particular domestic industry. It seems that while public optimism was sustained, brewers had no incentive to break their 'code of silence' and risk deflating the boom.

There is no indication either that relatively small brewers were deterred from making applications to the public capital market throughout the period 1886–1900, although the smallest companies do appear to have been attracted at the peaks of the booms in public finance of brewing. In 1896 Haddington Brewery allotted ordinary shares to the value of £12 000 from an intended issue of 20 000 shares at £10 and called 10 per cent of the issue as a first payment. Pearson's Brewery issued shares and debentures worth £15 000 and there were three other flotations of less than £35 000 each in the same year.[6]

Further evidence of the positive public response which brewing flotations received is the frequency with which issues were successfully placed at a premium. Tables 10.2 and 10.3 draw on information available in new issues prospectuses to discover when premiums were charged.[7] Fewer issues were made at a premium during the first brewing boom than in the second, although the few premium issues that were made were concentrated, as expected, around the peak years of investment, 1888–90. Brewers seem to have exploited the enthusiasm of investors to a far greater extent in the late 1890s. Premium issues of preference and debenture capital dominated in 1896 and were significant during 1897–98.

Evidence from the new issues prospectuses suggests that the experience of large and small brewers may have differed slightly. Although we must beware of drawing firm inferences from such a limited study of small

Table 10.2 Issues of the 50 largest brewing companies at premium and at par

Year	N	Ordinary			Preference			Debentures		
		n	Pm.	Par	*n*	Pm.	Par	*n*	Pm.	Par
1885	1	–	–	–	–	–	–	1	1	–
1886	1	1	–	1	1	–	1	1	–	1
1887	4	4	–	4	3	–	3	2	–	2
1888	7	2	–	2	5	–	5	7	3	4
1889	7	2	–	2	5	3	2	7	3	4
1890	5	1	–	1	4	2	2	3	1	2
1891	4	1	–	1	1	–	1	4	–	4
1892	2	1	–	1	1	–	1	2	–	2
1893	2	–	–	–	–	–	–	–	–	–
1894	7	–	–	–	3	–	3	7	1	6
1895	4	1	–	1	2	1	1	3	1	2
1896	13	1	–	1	3	3	–	12	10	2
1897	14	–	–	–	6	4	2	12	5	7
1898	15	5	2	3	6	4	2	10	3	7
1899	8	–	–	–	3	2	1	6	3	3
1900	5	1	1	–	–	–	–	4*	1	2

Notes:

N	=	total number of companies.
n	=	number of companies making an issue in this form.
Pm.	=	issues made at premium.
Par	=	issues made at par.
*	=	One of these issues was offered by Allsopp at a price below par.
$\Sigma n > N$		since some companies issued more than one type of security.

issues, this does indicate a higher incidence of premium issues among the larger than among the smallest brewing companies. Furthermore, if the smallest companies made a premium issue it was typically offered on debentures. It is possible that this reflects a preference among small brewers for premia to be sought only on the least risky capital.

In some cases, the premium charges demanded by the large companies were quite large. In 1898 Parker's Burslem Brewery issued 2 500 ordinary shares with a nominal value of £10 at £20 per share and 2 500 preference shares of the same nominal value at £13 10s (*The Times*,

Table 10.3   Issues of the 50 smallest brewing companies at premium and at par

Year	N	Ordinary			Preference			Debentures		
		n	Pm.	Par	n	Pm.	Par	n	Pm.	Par
1889	3	3	–	3	3	–	3	3	–	3
1890	1	1	–	1	1	–	1	–	–	–
1895	3	1	–	1	2	–	2	2	1	1
1896	3	1	–	1	2	–	2	2	1	1
1897	7	2	–	2	2	1	1	5	2	3
1900	2	–	–	–	–	–	–	2	–	2
1901	1	–	–	–	–	–	–	1	1	–

Notes: See Table 10.2.

Issues, 16, 1898: 167). In 1896 Ind Coope issued £200 000 4 per cent 'B' Mortgage Debentures at 112 per cent (*The Times, Issues*, 11, 1896: 184). More frequently, however, the premium was £1 or £2 on a £10 share and 3–5 per cent on £100 debenture stock. The highest price charged by any of the small companies considered was £105 per cent on an issue of £80 000 in 4 per cent mortgage debenture stock by Albion Brewery of Leeds, at the peak of the brewing boom (*The Times, Issues*, 13, 1897: 191).

It was an attractive strategy for brewers to make premium issues. Public optimism presented the opportunity to raise capital surplus to current requirements, without incurring any additional liability for interest or dividend payments which were paid on the nominal value of the securities. Many companies announced that the sums collected from premium payments would be invested as reserves, thereby providing both a safety net if future trade should decline, and also a repository of capital which could be drawn on for further expansion without incurring the costs of making additional new issues.

The new issue prospectuses offer several examples of companies making large issues during this period who took the opportunities offered to raise more capital than was immediately necessary. In 1890, Sir A.B. Walker sold three businesses, Peter Walker and Son, Munro and Co. and A.B. Walker and Co., which combined to form the new company of Peter Walker and Co. The £3 million issued was divided equally between ordinary, preference and debenture capital, of which the vendor and his nominees retained all the ordinary shares and one-third of the remaining capital. The vendor's price was set at £2 850 000 plus the transfer of stocks and properties valued at £154 000. Contracts for advances on properties and improvements to the business had already been signed to the value of £160 000. This suggests that the new capital raised provided a surplus of approximately £144 000, which in itself was in excess of the total of many new flotations. The prospectus justifies this as providing, 'a considerable sum for working capital and to finance further improvements and purchases for the business' (*The Times*, 19 April 1890: 4). It seems likely that Walker was taking advantage of market optimism to create a capital reserve from which future expansion could be funded, thereby obviating the need to make additional applications.

A more extreme case was that of Barclay, Perkins and Co. who formed a joint-stock company in 1896. The capital consisted of £1 020 000 ordinary shares, all held by the vendor as payment of the total purchase price, £1 800 000 preference shares and £1 200 000 in 3.5 per cent mortgage debenture stock; a third of the non-equity capital was retained by the former partners, who were the vendors. The preference shares were issued at a premium of £1 at a price of £11 per share and the debentures were issued at 105 per cent, resulting in the proceeds of the public issue totalling £3 240 000. In addition to the vendors' price which was fully satisfied by the ordinary shares, the partners and their families were to be credited with £1 860 794 7s 7d which they were owed by the business. £250 000 was also to be invested in a special fund by the Trustees for the debenture stockholders in order to meet the payment of the mortgage on the brewery which was due to mature in 1898. These payments left a surplus of £1 129 205 12s 5d available for further working capital and general costs associated with the formation of the company (*The Times*, *Issues*, 11, 1896: 284–85).

It was also possible for small companies to raise 'surplus' capital, although clearly the sums involved were not as large as in the cases discussed above. In January 1897, Locke and Smith offered 4.5 per cent irredeemable debenture stock worth £60 000 at a premium of £2 10s per £100 of stock. The company was valued at just over £90 000, but the purchase price was set at £109 500 thereby allowing extra capital to be raised. The sale was to be settled partly by the issue of ordinary and preference shares worth £60 000 which were retained by the vendors, and partly by a cash payment which was to be financed by the debenture issue. Even once these liabilities had been met, the issue still raised a surplus of £12 000, which was to be used to purchase further properties and for the general development of the business (*The Times*, *Issues*, 13, 1897: 22).

If we accept the valuation of the business implicit in the purchase price set for Locke and Smith, the surplus capital raised in their conversion to form a public company amounted to almost 11 per cent of the company's value. In terms of the proportion of the company's valuation raised as a surplus, this is larger than that secured for Peter Walker and Co. It seems clear that even if premium issues were not made by all small companies, some succeeded in pursuing this strategy to great effect.

For any corporate industry, fluctuations in the quoted price of issued capital are an important indicator of the confidence of public investors. (See Appendix 10.1 for graphs of share prices.) The fact that public enthusiasm for brewing issues was not diminished by the growing tendency for new capital to be floated at a premium, suggests that during the 19th century public confidence in the continued prosperity of the brewing trade did not falter. Movements in share prices, however, did not only provide a historical reflection of the mood of the stock market, they also acted as a signal to potential investors; the promise of capital gains on brewing securities may have been an important factor encouraging public support of these companies.

During the peak investment periods, brewers making new applications for capital from the public were keen to advertise increasing prices of existing brewing shares in a deliberate attempt to attract investors to support their business. One example of many was the conversion of Parker's Burslem Brewery at the height of the first brewing boom in 1889. As well as supplying details of their commercial history, the recommendation in the prospectus that investment in their company would be a profitable venture was underlined by noting the general success of breweries:

> The success which has attended the conversion of private breweries into joint-stock companies is well known, and there is probably no class of investment which has become more popular. The daily quotations of the stocks and shares of brewery companies are sufficient evidence of this. (*The Times*, 4 April 1889: 14).

Brewers recognized that the public were attracted by the expectation of capital gains. New companies hoped that investors would associate what they perceived to be the positive attributes of increasing market values for existing public companies with their flotation, by virtue of the fact that they were a brewery. Clearly the aim was to encourage the view that investment in brewing could not fail, whatever the quality of the company on offer. Amid the general eagerness to 'get into brewing', the *Statist* offered a consistent, if somewhat weary, voice of caution: 'Of course while the mania is on it is something like preaching in the wilderness to even hint at danger, and the public, dazzled by premiums, must have its fling' (*The Statist*, 24, 1889: 656).

It is clear that investors were not necessarily as risk averse as historians have typically argued. Although the public were frequently advised to avoid industrial shares by articles in the financial press, it should not be assumed that this advice was heeded. Indeed the frequency with which both the *Statist* and the *Investor's Monthly Manual* criticized speculators and urged their readers to be cautious suggests that they felt compelled to repeat advice which had previously been ignored.

The fact that brewing issues continued to be offered – and, indeed, to be placed – suggests that cautious investors were not a dominant factor 'strangling' the capital market and forcing change.

The question to be addressed now is whether this enthusiasm for public issues was replicated for the iron and steel industry, or whether this impression of financial abundance was specific to brewers.

The iron and steel industry and the new issue market

One industry that has almost become synonymous with discussions of Britain's economic decline is that of iron and steel. In 1870 the UK produced more than half of the world's output of pig iron, but by 1890 the United States had exceeded the UK's output, and by 1904 Germany was also a larger producer of pig iron. Similarly the proportion of the world's output of steel produced by the UK fell from one-third in 1876–80 to less than one-seventh by 1904, being overtaken by the United States in 1886 and Germany in 1893. Far from continuing to dominate international trade in iron and steel, Britain found that she could not even meet her own demands adequately, and became a leading importer of steel by the First World War (Payne, 1968: 72–5).

Much of the traditional literature on the industry has emphasized weaknesses in entrepreneurial talent and inadequate technological progress as principal factors in the sector's decline relative to its international competitors (see for example, Burn, 1940; Burnham and Hoskins, 1943; McCloskey, 1973). Other explanations have stressed instead the disadvantage in world markets which the existence of tariffs represented for British producers. Temin, for example, argues that British producers found their products barred from exports to the growing markets for steel in Germany and the United States and were unable to extend their own home market any further in order to sustain significant rates of growth in the industry. Temin suggests that slower growth rates would have resulted in a slower replacement of existing capital equipment. This would have exacerbated the industry's problems by increasing the costs of production in the UK relative to her competitors, a problem that was already becoming evident as these countries exploited their abundant supply of natural resources suitable for the new techniques of production (Temin, 1966: 141–2). With 'all the odds' stacked against British suppliers, the incentive to update obsolete capital may have been diminished by the expectation that even investment in new equipment would not have been sufficient to overcome the barriers to profitable trade erected by foreign competitors.

Allen's work on the north-east coast pig iron industry has offered a more sophisticated characterization of the debate concerning 'entrepreneurial failure' in this industry. He argues that attempts to redeem the British entrepreneur on the basis of acting rationally in an adverse economic climate may not be adequate. Allen defines entrepreneurship as a dynamic concept, the progressive firms being those that move towards a new equilibrium most rapidly. In contrast, rationality and profit maximization are employed in a static analytical framework. The fact that a decision is rational (that is, currently profitable) given prevailing conditions may still be consistent with it being sub-optimal in terms of the long-run development of the industry (Allen, 1981).

One of the major problems with the debate on entrepreneurial failure is that it is difficult to define the problem in a form which can be tested empirically. One way of narrowing down the problem may be to consider whether there were any constraints which operated to a debilitating extent on adventurous entrepreneurs. For example, if the problems facing the industry were such that expectations of its future profitability were pessimistic, it may have proved too costly for entrepreneurs to raise the finance with which to implement the technical changes they perceived to be necessary. Thus if evidence can be found of iron and steel companies who applied for, but failed to secure, finance because investors remained sceptical of the industry's prospects, then the hypothesis of entrepreneurial failure may have been dented.

It seems clear that the process of identifying a 'culprit' for Britain's economic decline is complex. Even if we discover that iron and steel companies were constrained in their access to capital, we will not necessarily have proven the innocence of entrepreneurs and indicted the capital market. Given prevailing market conditions and expectations of future developments, it may have been rational for investors to withhold financial support. In short, the risk associated with investment in iron and steel companies may not have been adequately compensated by the returns which they could afford to promise. These returns may have been constrained by trade conditions facing the industry, which, in practical terms, could have been beyond their control.

If it were discovered that despite the problems facing this industry during the late 19th and early 20th century, even these companies *could* raise capital effectively, the argument for capital market failure would be seriously weakened. The way in which any finance secured was obtained may also give some indication what were the real constraints which hindered the industry's development, and thus indirectly shed light on the persistent criticisms of the sector's entrepreneurs.

In obtaining estimates of the role of the new issue market in the financing of iron and steel companies, it has been necessary to identify British iron and steel companies from lists of issues made by all trades operating both at home and abroad published in the *Investor's Monthly Manual*. In practice this task proved rather more challenging than was the case for the brewing industry where companies were more easily identified as brewing concerns. In this case cross-checking of companies and their principal commercial interests was required with trade directories.

The principal problem with any study of the iron and steel industry is how to define its constituent firms. In the early stages of the industry's development many of the iron producers were also involved in coal mining and/or iron ore mining; by the end of the 19th century several companies had extended their role as manufacturers of iron (and steel) products, or perhaps established businesses as engineers, and some of the largest companies had significant interests in the shipbuilding and armaments industries. Unfortunately, since it is difficult to be sure of the extent to which all the firms considered were committed to each of these related trades, any definition of the industry will almost inevitably be open to question. This problem is complicated further by the fact that the records for firms appearing in different trade directories are not always consistent.

The conditions for a company's inclusion in this study are that its major business was considered by contemporaries to be a contribution to the 'iron and steel industry'. This broad category has been refined to contain only those companies which were listed in at least two of the trade directories as being involved in the production and manufacture of pig iron, and/or the production and manufacture of steel. Where a firm's interests have grown by vertical integration, the definition becomes more complex. In these cases, the new issue is discarded from the series compiled below, if its purpose as revealed in the company prospectus was other than for the improvement of iron or steel production.[8] This definition cannot be regarded as comprehensive, but it should be sufficient to give a reasonable impression of the experiences of a significant sector of the companies operating in this industry in their attempts to raise finance.

Table 10.4 draws on summary reports of company balance sheets published in *Burdett's Official Intelligence* to estimate the total capital subscribed publicly (including vendors' shares) at five-yearly intervals for

Table 10.4   Total capital and the mean size of iron and steel companies

Year	No. of companies	Total capital £	Mean capital £
1881	46	23 494 912	510 759
1885	50	28 472 273	569 445
1890	56	32 015 976	571 714
1895	49	32 083 324	654 762
1900	69	47 124 212	682 960
1905	108	74 193 741	686 979
1910	106	86 465 325	815 711

Source: Burdett's Official Intelligence, 1882–1911.

the iron and steel industry between 1881 and 1910. The greatest period of expansion occurred at the end of the 19th century, with the new issue market assuming greater significance as a source of finance. The number of companies with a public quotation more than doubled between 1895 and 1910. In addition the mean size of iron and steel companies increased.

It is important to try and put the scale of corporate involvement in the industry into some perspective. It is impossible to estimate the total capital invested privately and publicly in any industry since the records for the unincorporated sector are at best sparse, and often non-existent. However, it is possible to provide some broad estimates of the physical capacity of an industry and estimate the percentage contribution to this total by public companies.

The companies listed in *Burdett's Official Intelligence* which are consistent with the definition of the industry applied in this study have been ranked by the total capital subscribed publicly. The number of blast furnaces have been identified for as many of these companies as possible. Of the 565 furnaces in blast in 1881, the companies included in this study represented 23.54 per cent (that is, 133 furnaces) (compiled from Hunt, 1882: 72–82). During 1900, the average number of furnaces in blast was 368 (The *Labour Gazette*, 10, 1902: 35) of which public companies constituted 64.95 per cent (that is, 239 furnaces) (compiled from *Ryland's Directory*, 1902). These figures suggest that the dominant businesses in the industry were incorporated by the turn of the century.[9]

Table 10.5 gives a clearer indication of the pattern of new issues created and called by iron and steel companies during the period 1870–1913. Table 10.5 can be compared with the results for the brewing

Table 10.5 Iron and steel companies, percentage distribution of capital created and called, 1870–1913 (excluding vendors' shares)

Year	N	Debentures % of total	Preference % of total	Ordinary % of total	Total £
1870	1	–	–	100.00	450 000
1871	4	–	75.32	24.68	753 500
1872	19	–	16.09	83.91	2 315 433
1873	18	13.53	0.37	86.10	2 262 093
1874	9	27.88	9.29	62.82	1 075 860
1875	7	–	29.28	70.72	341 496
1876	6	–	71.97	28.03	486 298
1877	4	–	36.69	63.31	340 700
1878	7	–	41.30	58.70	399 547
1879	5	31.58	46.05	22.37	380 000
1880	8	9.53	34.98	55.50	367 392
1881	9	13.33	18.76	67.91	562 480
1882	8	–	4.80	95.20	1 415 532
1883	9	–	22.67	77.33	2 226 436
1884	5	62.85	–	37.15	350 027
1885	3	–	–	100.00	274 340
1886	6	–	–	100.00	238 595
1887	2	–	–	100.00	61 800
1888	5	72.39	–	27.61	600 902
1889	5	17.17	32.70	50.14	407 800
1890	10	26.32	36.79	36.89	946 000
1891	8	10.11	62.15	27.74	889 850
1892	8	50.87	12.72	36.41	786 314
1893	5	–	57.87	42.13	336 086
1894	2	100.00	–	–	150 000
1895	4	73.33	21.33	5.33	375 004
1896	1	–	100.00	–	200 000
1897	5	–	66.12	33.88	78 648
1898	7	95.07	3.76	1.17	1 463 648
1899	11	18.24	23.95	57.81	2 618 307
1900	20	34.83	18.73	46.44	5 392 288
1901	11	24.51	37.66	37.83	1 956 681
1902	3	49.81	50.19	–	642 500
1903	5	69.99	–	30.01	940 900
1904	3	32.38	–	67.62	772 200
1905	2	100.00	–	–	750 400
1906	7	24.19	62.62	13.19	1 461 400

Table 10.5   Concluded

Year	N	Debentures % of total	Preference % of total	Ordinary % of total	Total £
1907	6	33.78	18.83	47.38	592 000
1908	8	89.27	5.45	5.28	2 688 494
1909	2	–	–	100.00	308 125
1910	3	90.38	2.11	–	664 990
1911	6	32.02	52.38	15.60	741 742
1912	7	22.91	60.00	17.09	1 287 500
1913	8	6.45	52.69	40.85	2 372 324

N = Number of companies making calls.

industry reported in Table 10.1.

The contrast between the experience of the iron and steel industry and that of brewers is clear. Whereas there were two clear waves of company conversions in the brewing industry during the late 1880s and mid- to late 1890s, and other years where no new issues were floated at all, iron and steel companies maintained a relatively steady, but largely 'unexciting' flow of applications to the market. Several 'minor peaks' in activity are noted: 1872–74, 1882–83, 1898–1901 plus some occasional years (due to individual large issues) in the first decade of the 20th century, but on aggregate they were certainly not of the scale of those in the brewing industry.

The impression gained from iron and steel company prospectuses also contrasts sharply with those of brewers in their apparent caution in approaching the new issue market. Unlike the almost euphoric promotion of brewing stocks, iron and steel companies were more circumspect in their predictions of future profits. A typical example of this reticence is the prospectus issued by Normanby Ironworks in 1900 to support their flotation of the company following the death of the last original partner Mr A. Pease. They were careful to stress the recent additions to the firm's equipment and report an increase in annual profits over the last three years, but the concluding paragraph reveals a slight wariness prevalent in the industry:

> The directors anticipate that the profits for the current year will be more than equal to the average of the three preceding years, and while they desire that the fluctuating character of the iron trade should not be lost sight of by intending subscribers, they feel justified at the same time in expressing their opinion that the condition of the works is now such that even in bad times they will

be in a position to compete with other furnaces in the Cleveland
District. (*The Times, Issues*, 20, 1900: 40.)

It is important to examine whether this apparent caution of iron and
steel companies was reflected in the form of their approach to the new
issue market, rather than just its style. Jefferys argues that the scale of
investment required by firms in this sector was significant. Although old
family firms were reluctant to relinquish control, as technology advanced
the scale of their enterprise proved to be beyond their financial capacity.
Jefferys notes that particularly with the dispersal of steelmaking, large
scale production was encouraged, and with it the spread of limited
liability. However, Jefferys argues that firms were still reluctant to adopt
the fully incorporated form of limited liability. He suggests that the
experience of these firms meant that they had private funds from which
they could draw, so that they would only be likely to seek a public
flotation when a substantial sum – he suggests in the order of a quarter
of a million pounds – was required (Jefferys, 1971: 72–9).[10]

One way of testing this hypothesis is to look at the fluctuations in the
scale of applications by iron and steel companies to the new issue market
over the period in which we are interested. In Table 10.6 the average
capital created by the companies seeking finance in each year is reported.
These estimates take applications by each company for capital in any
form that was to be quoted publicly and are derived from reports in the
Investor's Monthly Manual. The fact that the capital was created, does
not necessarily imply that it was allotted fully. However, the timing of
these applications to the market reveals something of the attitudes of the
companies concerned, and also presumably reflects their perception of
prevailing attitudes of potential investors. In order to give an indication
of the 'real' fluctuations in the industry, output figures for pig iron and
steel production are also reported in Table 10.6. It should be noted that
these figures are not always an accurate indicator of the trade's fortunes,
since we do not know what is happening to stocks. This evidence alone
is not sufficient to demonstrate that companies tried to issue more capital
when the industry was perceived to be in an expansionary phase.
However, there is some suggestion that the peak periods of applications
to the capital market did coincide with those years in which output
appeared to be in the 'upper half' of the cycle.

Some additional evidence to support this hypothesis is provided by the
new issue prospectuses. For example, the Earl of Dudley's Bound Oak
Iron and Steel Works chose April 1891 to launch an application for new
capital with which to finance the construction of a new steel plant. This
flotation came in a period when the stock prices for this industry were
relatively high and the general attitude was one of optimism. The
company estimated the cost of the new steel works at £50 000, but

Table 10.6 Iron and steel companies: mean capital issued publicly per company; GB output of pig iron and steel, 1870–1913

Year	N	Mean issue per company (£)	Pig iron output (million tons)	Steel output (million tons)
1870	1	600 000	5.96	0.22
1871	4	222 500	6.63	0.33
1872	13	277 211	6.74	0.41
1873	14	377 910	6.57	0.57
1874	4	152 445	5.99	0.63
1875	3	383 333	6.37	0.71
1876	0	–	6.56	0.83
1877	1	150 000	6.61	0.89
1878	0	–	6.38	0.98
1879	1	120 000	6.00	1.01
1880	3	81 743	7.75	1.29
1881	5	175 000	8.14	1.78
1882	4	606 750	8.59	2.11
1883	3	241 667	8.53	2.01
1884	1	220 000	7.81	1.77
1885	0	–	7.42	1.89
1886	1	100 000	7.01	2.26
1887	0	–	7.56	3.04
1888	1	160 000	8.00	3.30
1889	4	334 750	8.32	3.57
1890	3	243 333	7.90	3.58
1891	4	184 600	7.41	3.16
1892	2	262 500	6.71	2.92
1893	1	94 500	6.98	2.95
1894	1	75 000	7.43	3.11
1895	4	112 501	7.70	3.26
1896	1	200 000	8.66	4.13
1897	4	47 500	8.80	4.49
1898	5	380 000	8.61	4.57
1899	7	364 453	9.42	4.86
1900	20	384 081	8.96	4.90
1901	6	329 390	7.93	4.90
1902	1	340 000	8.68	4.91
1903	5	386 620	8.94	5.03
1904	2	187 500	8.69	5.03
1905	2	375 200	9.61	5.81
1906	6	233 125	10.18	6.46

Table 10.6   concluded

Year	N	Mean issue per company (£)	Pig iron output (million tons)	Steel output (million tons)
1907	5	391 800	10.11	6.52
1908	4	311 875	9.06	5.30
1909	2	154 063	9.53	5.88
1910	2	95 000	10.01	6.37
1911	4	196 875	9.53	6.46
1912	6	199 083	8.75	6.80
1913	6	435 935	10.26	7.66

Source: for output figures, Burnham and Hoskins (1943: 272–4).
N = Number of companies creating capital in this year.

issued capital totalling £160 000. The prospectus does not make clear how this additional capital was to be employed (*The Times, Issues*, 1, 1891: 59–60). One suggestion arising from Jefferys' work is that the Earl of Dudley's company was seeking to raise 'extra' finance to try and ensure the minimum of £50 000 was actually secured, and also perhaps to take advantage of the comparative rarity of a buoyant market.

A further contrast in the presentation of prospectuses by brewers and by iron and steel companies is in their use of the share price performance of their competitors as a signal of the expected capital gain on their own capital. While this was a practice widely employed by brewers, in the prospectuses considered for the iron and steel industry, it was only employed once. Not surprisingly that one company, Kayser Ellison, adopted this tactic late in 1895, when iron and steel share prices were enjoying a revival (*The Times, Issues*, 10, 1895: 198). Interestingly this revival coincided with the 'home investment boom', which suggests that iron and steel companies may not have been completely neglected in the 'rush' for domestic industrials.

Iron and steel companies also displayed their cautious approach to the new issue market in their reluctance to issue any shares at a premium. All the issues covered by the 38 prospectuses considered in this study were made at par value. Once again this is in sharp contrast to the brewing industry where as already noted premium issues were common during the boom periods of the late 1880s and 1890s. The key difference seems to have been that optimism in the capital market regarding the future performance of iron and steel companies was not as persistent as it was during the 'brewing booms'.

The confidence of public investors would be likely to be reflected in iron and steel equity prices. If it is true that the mood of the capital market was more volatile with respect to iron and steel than to brewing, we would expect this to be reflected in share price profiles which fluctuated more for the former than the latter industry. (See Appendix 10.2 for iron and steel equity prices.)

The contrast between equity price index for iron and steel and for brewing is clear. Whereas brewing prices increased in two stages corresponding to the two great expansionary phases in the industry and were then followed by a sharp decline after 1900, iron and steel equity prices are more reminiscent of the trade cycle. If industrialists in this sector could not rely on stock prices remaining buoyant, and therefore the new issue market represented a more risky arena in which to raise funds it seems likely that this risk would be reflected in the capital structure of the industry. This is a question which is examined in the next section of this chapter.

The fact the finance of the iron and steel industry seems to have been allied closely to the trade cycle is not to admit that these firms found it particularly difficult to obtain capital. Jefferys's observation noted above that iron and steel companies relied on private finances and banks, as well as the new issue market to support their enterprise suggests that further work covering a broader range of financial sources is necessary before the investment strategy of iron and steel companies can be comprehended fully.

Despite this apparently pessimistic interpretation of the relationship between the iron and steel industry and the new issue market, some companies were able to raise significant sums of capital from this source, and clearly were not deterred from making applications.[11] As already noted, the fact that by 1900 the dominant firms in the industry were incorporated as public companies suggests that there was an important role for the new issue market in facilitating the implementation of new technology by at least part of the trade. Although the relationship between iron and steel companies and the new issue market was perhaps not as 'easy' during the late 19th century as it was for brewers, it is also true that they did not have to endure the financial crises which plagued brewers during the first decade of the 20th century.[12]

Several of the witnesses to the Tariff Commission of the iron and steel trades commented on the financial support for their business. In general they raised no complaints about the nature of this provision. What they did mention was the (reasonable) difficulty of raising capital in a period of depressed or insecure trade (Report of the Tariff Commission, 1904). While this evidence may have been influenced by the context of the questions witnesses faced – namely whether or not the existence of foreign tariffs was causing damage to the trade – the impression given lends support to the general thesis of this chapter that finance essentially followed rather than led the fortunes of industry.

This point was also made by the Departmental Committee on the Iron and Steel Trades which reported in 1918 and commented that there was a need for greater investment in the industry. Yet they also noted that:

> this capital can only be obtained by some guarantee of a reasonable return upon it. It is a matter of sad experience that no investment in an iron and steel undertaking in Great Britain could really be regarded as reasonably safe. Unless confidence is created in the financial world as to the stability and future prosperity of the iron and steel industries, it would be futile to expect the investing public to subscribe so large an amount as is necessary for the equipment of an iron and steel plant. (Report of the Departmental Committee on the Iron and Steel Trades, 1918: 20)

This question as to whether the iron and steel industry found it especially difficult to raise capital by means of the new issue market can be explored in more detail by comparing the capital structure of the two industries under consideration.

Corporate financial structure

From the pattern of new issues created and called by the two industries (Tables 10.1 and 10.5 above) it is clear that the two sectors approached the new issue market in very different ways. In the case of brewing issues, debenture capital was clearly very popular. By contrast, the pattern of issues by iron and steel companies was far more erratic, with no individual form of capital dominating public issues persistently.

This apparent difference in the gearing of the two industries becomes more apparent if we look at the capital structure inclusive of vendors' shares revealed by the summaries of balance sheets reported in *Burdett's Official Intelligence*. In order to compile these estimates the percentage distribution of capital was calculated for each company. For each class of capital the proportion it constituted in the average company was estimated by calculating the mean percentage for each stock over the whole industry. These estimates are reported in Tables 10.7 and 10.8 below. Standard deviations for each estimate are also reported to give some indication how representative these averages are.

Comparison of Tables 10.7 and 10.8 reveals the extent of the difference in capital structure of the two industries. Brewing companies became increasingly highly geared as the expansion of public limited liability proceeded. However, what is particularly interesting is the

Table 10.7   The percentage distribution of publicly traded securities in the brewing industry

| Year | N | % of total securities subscribed | | | | | |
| | | Ordinary | | Preference | | Debenture | |
		mean	st.dev.	mean	st.dev.	mean	st.dev.
1885	17	77.55	27.47	13.89	22.62	8.55	15.76
1890	111	39.68	17.74	27.07	14.61	33.25	16.14
1895	143	34.32	13.98	27.50	13.48	38.44	15.44
1900	314	30.89	14.21	26.78	12.92	42.50	16.19
1905	316	30.20	14.21	26.89	13.45	42.86	16.98
1910	310	30.09	14.39	26.86	13.74	43.05	17.33

Source: estimated from *Burdett's Official Intelligence.*

Table 10.8   The percentage distribution of publicly traded securities in the iron and steel industry

| Year | N | % of total securities subscribed | | | | | |
| | | Ordinary | | Preference | | Debenture | |
		mean	st.dev.	mean	st.dev.	mean	st.dev.
1881	46	80.40	19.07	5.78	11.90	13.82	14.75
1885	50	81.01	17.51	5.94	11.08	13.05	13.87
1890	56	76.80	20.32	8.14	13.57	15.06	15.53
1895	49	70.50	23.30	14.49	17.08	15.01	15.57
1900	69	59.54	25.80	23.61	20.31	16.85	16.86
1905	108	57.24	22.90	24.90	20.78	17.86	17.27
1910	106	55.36	23.21	25.81	20.79	18.83	17.51

Source: estimated from *Burdett's Official Intelligence.*

difference in the apparent gearing suggested by the new issue market (that is, excluding vendors' shares in Table 10.1) and that of the industry including vendors' shares (that is, Table 10.7). The fact that for brewers debentures are more dominant in the capital profile of new issues rather than in the total stock of capital, suggests that of the equity capital issued, by far the greatest proportion was retained by the vendors. In the case of iron and steel, the new issue market presented a more balanced impression of the industry's financial gearing (see Table 10.5), whereas the total picture provided by *Burdett's Official Intelligence* is one in which equity capital clearly dominated (Table 10.8).

This difference provides yet more evidence of the diversity of approaches which could be adopted by industrialists trying to secure finance from the public capital market. The interesting question is to try and discover why these industries differed so markedly in their gearing.

One hypothesis might be that the brewing industry found it difficult to raise capital in the new issue market, and was forced to offer the safest form of capital in order to encourage subscriptions. However, given the scale of support apparent for brewers seeking incorporation, and the frequent description of the market for brewers' capital approaching a mania, this hypothesis does not seem to reflect accurately the mood of investors. Although debenture capital was the safest form of capital that could be publicly subscribed, the desire to respond to risk averse investors was clearly not the primary motivation for brewing companies to issue such stocks.

An important characteristic of debenture capital is that holders had no voting stake in the company, although they did enjoy powerful protection in that payment of interest on the debt was the primary commitment of the business. If these obligations were not met by the company, the debenture holders could press for its liquidation and they would be the first to have their capital repaid from the assets of the company's receiver.

Similarly, those investing in preference shares had no voting power in the company either. In practice, the only investors who ostensibly exercised any voting influence were those holding equity capital. Thus, one way in which vendors of an old family firm could maintain control of the new company after incorporation was to issue only non-voting stocks and retain the equity capital among members of the family and friends, who frequently became the new directors. These 'vendors' shares' effectively denied, or at least limited, the influence of shareholders not originally associated with the business. By examining the use of vendors' shares we can discover much about the way in which entrepreneurs intended to use the facilities of the Stock Exchange and also about the implied flexibility of a company's liabilities.

The rules of the Stock Exchange required that the original partners could not hold more than a third of any capital publicly quoted. This suggests that the 'cost' of issuing ordinary shares included a loss of two-thirds of the nominal voting stake in the company. For a family firm wanting the advantages in terms of a broader capital base available as a joint-stock company, but desiring to retain ultimate command of the business, this cost may have been unacceptable. In consequence, wherever possible debenture capital was issued by brewers.

A further advantage of debenture issues was that the cost of servicing the debt was relatively cheap when the industry was buoyant. If companies expected to be able to maintain relatively high profits and had sufficient property with which to secure the loan, debentures could be a cheap source of finance. Whereas the dividend on ordinary capital varied with the profits of the company, the interest payable on debentures was determined when the loan was established and remained constant until the debt was redeemed. Of course, if trade deteriorated the risk associated with high gearing was significant, since the commitment to continue paying interest did not diminish with profits as could the dividends on equity. The brewing industry was particularly well placed to employ this financial strategy. The chief reason why they needed finance was to purchase property in the form of public houses with which to secure their licensed trade. These investments made excellent security for mortgage debenture issues.

If this characterization is correct, as it seems to be for the brewing industry, a logical hypothesis would be that given a buoyant industry (and expectation that this would continue), receptive investors and established firms with family interests, companies would generally prefer to issue more debt than equity. This hypothesis would also suggest that those businesses issuing ordinary capital were either those where perhaps due to death or retirement, the interests of the old partners were being reduced, or those where a public flotation was motivated by the inadequacy of existing private finance. In the latter case, the vendors may not have had sufficient private funds or reserves from retained profits both to retain control of equity capital and raise the capital required. Many of the brewing companies that did issue ordinary shares ensured that the directors and their families owned the maximum proportion of the issue allowed by the Stock Exchange. This suggests that there was a reluctance to relinquish voting power on the part of the former partners, perhaps through fear that their sovereignty as directors might be infringed.[13]

In contrasting the financial histories of the brewing and the iron and steel industries, it is interesting to note that both had long histories as family businesses before incorporation. Thus, if family loyalty was the sole factor promoting debenture issues by brewing companies, similar gearing ratios might reasonably be expected among iron and steel companies. Of course, there are crucial differences between the two sectors which make such similarities unlikely.

First, it is important to note that iron and steel companies seem to have been almost as keen as brewers to retain control of a large proportion of the equity capital in their business. This study of 38 iron and steel company prospectuses covering issues between 1891 and 1913 indicates that 17 flotations included the issue of equity capital; a further 19 issued no equity at all; the remaining two issued equity, but did not identify sufficiently clearly the proportion taken by the vendors. Of the 17 prospectuses in which equity was issued, in 11 cases it was all retained by the vendors; the stock exchange maximum of one-third was retained by a further five companies. Only one company did not 'protect the family interests' by withholding the ordinary shares from the public. Family loyalty appears to have been as strong an influence on the financial decisions of iron and steel companies as was the case for brewers.

The alternative hypotheses offered below to explain the low gearing ratio of iron and steel companies relative to brewers, focus on the suggestion that there may have been practical reasons associated with the unpredictability of the metals trade that contributed to a reluctance to overcapitalize these firms.

The assets of iron and steel companies may have been less appropriate than those of brewers to support debenture issues. An initial comparison of the structure of the assets of brewing and of iron and steel companies suggests that in 1900 property constituted 80–90 per cent of brewers' total assets, whereas for iron and steel companies the proportion was 55–75 per cent.[14] Furthermore the character of this property was clearly somewhat different for the two sectors. Whereas a large proportion of brewers' assets consisted of public houses – the main purpose for raising the capital in the first place – iron and steel companies rarely held such a marketable or prized asset.

Iron and steel companies were also likely to be less willing than brewers to accept the risk associated with high capital gearing. Whereas brewers may have believed that debenture capital offered them the cheapest way of raising the capital they needed to support their purchases of licensed property, and also believed that such investments would secure their trade so that servicing these debts would not prove onerous, iron and steel firms were probably less confident that new investment would be sufficient to guarantee the future prosperity of their business. The industry was widely known to be vulnerable to trade fluctuations, so that entrepreneurs would probably have been conscious of the risks associated with heavy reliance on debt.

To some extent, the security of the industry was jeopardized by its reliance on coal as a major raw material. Whenever there was a dispute in the mines, production within the metals industry was threatened. One example of the problems transmitted from the pits to the furnaces was the Durham coal strike of 1892. It lasted for three months, restricting the supply of coal and raising its price, with damaging consequences for the iron and steel trades (*The Economist*, 51, 1893: 25). The prospectus supporting an issue of 2 000 6 per cent cumulative preference shares by the Lowther Hematite Iron and Steel Company in 1897, illustrates the impact of this strike. They reported that their blast furnaces were damped for almost four months. At the end of 1892 one furnace was extinguished and the remaining three ceased production in 1893. The application for capital was partly intended to try and bring these works back into full operation (*The Times*, *Issues*, 13, 1897: 144).

To emphasize this point, the relative security of brewing debentures is revealed in Table 10.9 below.[15]

For the period of the 'brewing boom' brewing debentures offered an attractive investment in terms of its safety, especially relative to other industrials. In 1896 the *Statist* conducted a similar exercise, for a much smaller sample of companies and concluded that the average yield for brewing debentures was 3.32 per cent, which they noted was unusually low (The *Statist*, 37, 1896: 145). In July of the same year they drew attention to the fact that yields had fallen to the level of that offered on consols 20 years previously (The *Statist*, 38, 1897: 143–4). They declared that this declining yield reflected (unwarranted) speculative

Table 10.9 Weighted average of debenture yields

	1890	1896	1897	1900	1905	1910	1913
Brewers	4.06	3.66	3.72	3.93	4.47	5.71	5.47
Iron, coal and steel	–	5.13	5.06	4.50	4.63	4.50	4.36
Consols	2.75	2.30	2.30	2.62	2.78	3.10	3.37
ConsolsG	2.67	2.06	1.96	2.53	2.78	3.09	3.40
3% Local loans	2.91	2.13	2.13	2.13	2.90	3.03	3.54
GB railways	3.14	2.55	2.64	2.91	3.18	3.63	3.63
Insurance	4.65	4.15	4.01	4.31	4.44	4.68	4.35
Elec., light and power	–	3.85	3.89	4.04	4.54	5.22	5.31
Gas	3.45	3.31	2.85	3.16	3.72	3.73	4.09
Shipping	–	–	3.34	3.97	4.15	4.24	4.50

Source: The Investor's Monthly Manual, 1890–1913.
ConsolsG: Harley, 1977.

pressure boosting demand for brewing stocks; clearly such optimism did not prevail with respect to iron and steel issues. It was not until the collapse of confidence in the brewing industry after 1900 that yields on iron and steel suggested that public perception regarded these stocks as being safer than those offered by brewers.

Conclusion

What must be emphasized in this chapter is that iron and steel companies did not complain of a scarcity of capital. By adopting a capital structure that was appropriate for the industry they could raise the funding that they perceived to be required by their business. In contrast a different financial structure appeared to be efficient for brewers during the same period.

Given that there seems to be little evidence of rejected applications to the new issue market, it seems unwise to argue that the capital market 'failed' these industries by denying them funds. On the contrary, the fact that there was this diversity of approaches to the new issue market suggests that there was at least some adaptability evident in the matching of the demand and supply of industrial finance. To return to Robertson's quote on page 209, it is not clear that the relationship depicted here between these industries and the new issue market was one which was dominated exclusively by financiers either to the enrichment or the impoverishment of industrialists and society.

Appendices

Appendices follow on next six pages.

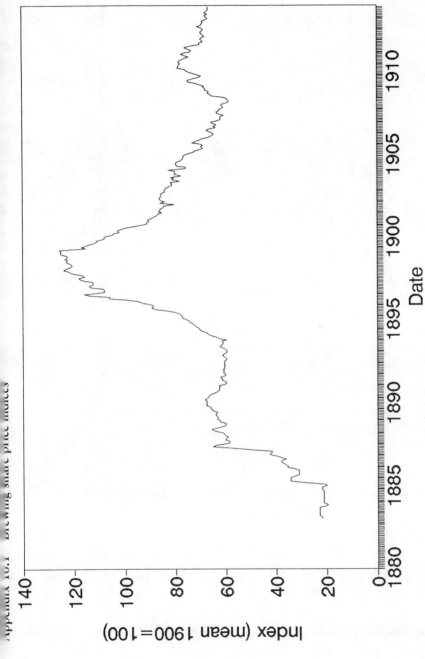

Figure 10.1 Equity share price index: brewing, monthly data, 1883–1913.

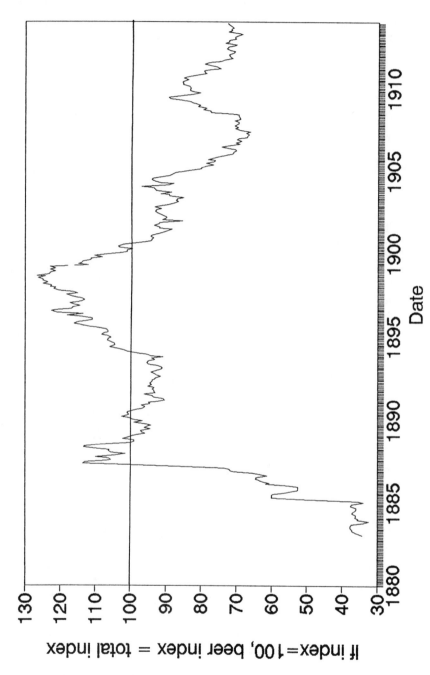

Figure 10.2   Equity price index: brewing, relative to total equity, 1883–1913.

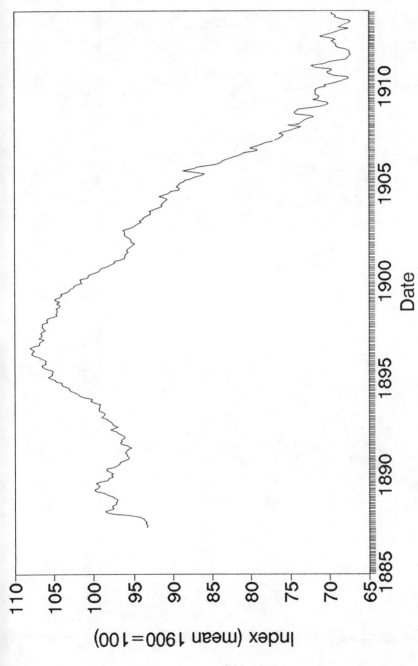

Figure 10.3 Debenture price index: brewing, monthly data, 1887–1913.

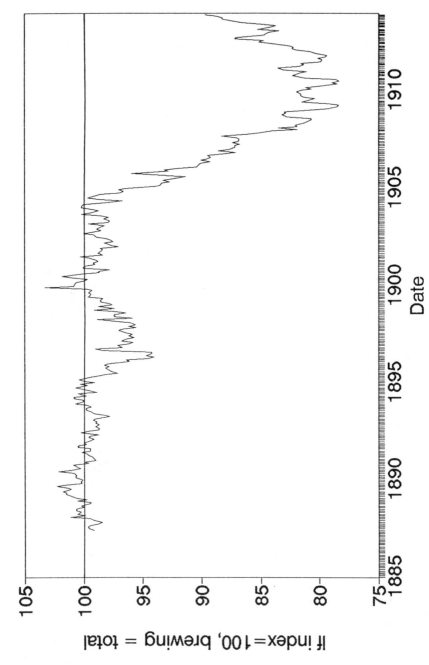

Figure 10.4   Debenture price index: brewing, relative to total debentures, 1887–1913.

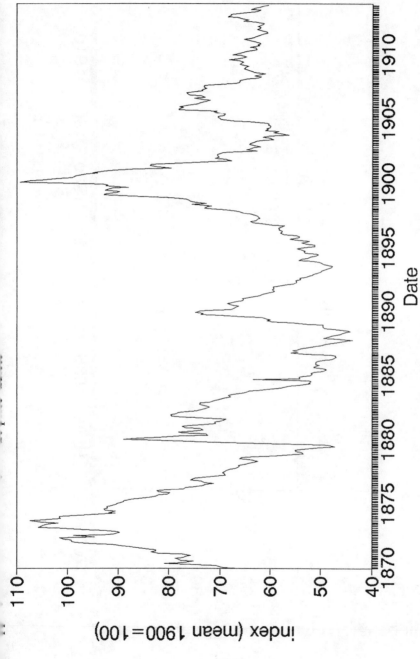

Figure 10.5 Equity share price index: iron and steel industry, monthly data, 1870–1913.

243

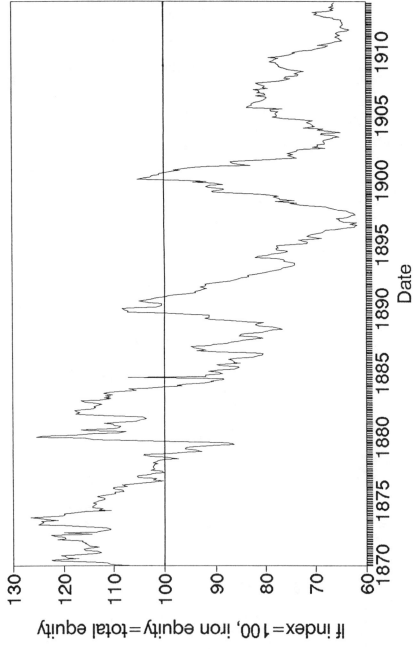

Figure 10.6   Equity price index: iron and steel industry, relative to total equity, 1870–1913.

244

Notes

1. Byatt's figures are drawn from company balance sheets. Total funds therefore include loans and an estimate of retained profits as well as capital subscribed publicly (Byatt, 1979: 158).
2. There is a large economics literature concerning the theoretical aspects of this question. See, for example, Modigliani and Millier (1958), Jensen and Meckling (1976), Myers and Majluf (1984) and Myers (1984).
3. These estimates are based on parliamentary reports of licensing returns for the brewing industry (1880–1914) and are compiled by converting a distribution of duty paid into their output equivalent. For further details, see Watson (1990 Ch. 3).
4. For example, in 1888 Mr H. Andrew came before Southampton County Court charged with breaking a trading contract with Victoria Brewery by buying goods worth £281 from other suppliers (*Brewers' Journal* 22, 15 April 1886: 137).
5. This series is constructed from monthly reports of capital called and created appearing in the *Investor's Monthly Manual*. For each company, each call made for an issue has been traced. Where intermediate calls have been omitted from the journal in error, these have been imputed.
6. These estimates are derived from reports in the *Investor's Monthly Manual*.
7. The sample is drawn from the ranking of capital subscribed, compiled from summaries in *Burdett's Official Intelligence* for 1900. Attempts have then been made to trace the new issues prospectuses that accompanied all the issues made by the 50 smallest and 50 largest companies.
8. One example of an issue to be excluded would be the Cammell Laird issue of £750 000 in 5 per cent mortgage debenture stock on 25 June 1906, which was to be used largely to erect a new armour plate mill and accessories, and also to establish a new shell manufacturing department (*The Times*, Issues, 3, 1906: 234–5).
9. Similar estimates for the brewing industry based on duty statistics suggest that the incorporated sector of the brewing industry contributed less than 20 per cent of total output in 1881, approximately 50 per cent of total output in 1890 and more than 75 per cent of total beer production by 1900. See Watson (1990: 80–99).
10. Jefferys also suggests that iron and steel firms were unusual in their ability to raise long-term capital from the banks, and therefore their need for public capital was reduced. This hypothesis is being pursued elsewhere using bank and company archives.
11. See, for example, the issue of £150 000 5 per cent first mortgage debenture stock by Partington Steel and Iron Company in 1913. This issue was to continue with the construction of a completely modern steel works to supply the needs of local Yorkshire and Lancashire manufacturers. Since the works were not yet in operation, no profits could be quoted; the company was reliant on the guarantee it had secured from Pearson and Knowles, its 'parent company'. The fact that this issue was a success, despite presenting limited evidence of its value, suggests that investors were willing to support the industry. (See, *The Times, Prospectuses of Public Companies*, 45, 1913: 222–3.)
12. The financial problems experienced by brewers were largely a result of

falling profits during the early 20th century which proved especially problematic for companies which had become highly geared. As a result, several companies were forced to 'write down' their capital.

13. This hypothesis is explored more fully using the evidence of brewing company prospectuses in Watson (1990: 129–38).

14. These approximations are based on a comparison of balance sheets for companies with total assets of a similar scale in both industries.

15. These estimates of debenture yields are based on a sample of British companies in various sectors of the domestic economy. The samples were drawn from the 1900 issue of the *Investor's Monthly Manual*. In each case the calculated yield represents the weighted average of quarterly yields (for March, June, September and December), the weights being the value of the capital issued by each company in June of the year considered. Yields for 1896 and 1897, rather than 1895 are reported to allow comparison of yields at the peak of the home investment boom and at the peak of the boom in brewing issues. Two estimates for consols are reported. The first is constructed using exactly the same method as for all other sectors. The yields for 1890, 1896, 1897 and 1900 refer to 2.75 per cent consols; thereafter the yield on 2.5 per cent consols is used. However, this takes no account of the possible disruption of yields due to the replacement of 2.75 per cent consols with 2.5 per cent stock in 1903; Harley's series does take account of this change.

References

Primary sources

Brewers' Journal
Bristol Mercury
Burdett's Official Intelligence
The Economist
Investor's Monthly Manual
Kelly's Directory of the Engineering, and Iron and Metal Trades
Labour Gazette
Liverpool Daily Post
Report of the Departmental Committee on the Iron and Steel Trades (1918), London: HMSO Cd. 9071.
Report of the Tariff Commission (1904), Vol. 1, *The Iron & Steel Trades*, London.
Ryland's Iron, Steel and Allied Trades' Directory
Scotsman
Statist
The Times
The Times, Issues
The Times, Prospectuses of Public Companies.

Secondary sources

Allen, R. C. (1981), 'Entrepreneurship and Technical Progress in the Northeast Coast Pig Iron Industry: 1850–1913', *Research in Economic History*, 6.

Burn, D. L. (1940), *The Economic History of Steelmaking, 1867–1939: A Study in Competition*, Cambridge.

Burnham, T. H. and Hoskins, G. O. (1943), *Iron and Steel in Britain, 1870–1930*, London.

Byatt, I. C. R. (1979), *The British Electrical Industry, 1875–1914, The Economic Returns of a New Technology*, Oxford.

Cairncross, A. K. (1953), *Home and Foreign Investment, 1870–1913*, Cambridge.

Edelstein, M. (1982), *Overseas Investment in the Age of High Imperialism. The UK, 1850–1965*, London: Methuen.

Hall, A. R. (ed.) (1968), *The Export of Capital from Britain, 1870–1914*, London.

Harley, C. K. (1977), 'The Interest Rate and Prices in Britain, 1873–1913: A Study of the Gibson Paradox', *Explorations in Economic History*, 14(1), January.

Harrison, A. E. (1981), 'Joint-Stock Company Flotation in the Cycle, Motor-Vehicle and Related Industries, 1882–1914', *Business History* 23(2), July.

Hobson, C. K. (1914), *The Export of Capital*, London.

Hunt, R. (ed.) (1882), *Mineral Statistics of United Kingdom of Great Britain and Ireland, 1881*, London.

Jefferys, J. B. (1971), *Business Organisation in Great Britain Since 1856*, New York.

Jensen, M. and Meckling, W. (1976), 'Theory of the Firm: Managerial Behaviour, Agency Costs and Ownership Structure', *Journal of Financial Economics*, 3(4).

Kennedy, W. P. (1987), *Industrial Structure, Capital Markets and the Origins of Economic Decline*, Cambridge.

McCloskey, D. N. (1973), *Economic Maturity and Entrepreneurial Decline, British Iron and Steel 1870–1913*, Cambridge, Mass.

Michie, R. C. (1988), 'The Finance of Innovation in Late Victorian and Edwardian Britain: Possibilities and Constraints', *Journal of European Economic History*, 17(3), Winter.

Modigliani, F. and Miller, M. H. (1958), 'The Cost of Capital, Corporation Finance and the Theory of Investment', *American Economic Review*, 48(3), June.

Myers, S. C. (1984), 'The Capital Structure Puzzle', *Journal of Finance*,

39(3), July.

Myers, S. C. and Majluf, N. S. (1984), 'Corporate Financing and Investment Decisions when Firms Have Information that Investors do Not Have', *Journal of Financial Economics*, 13(2).

Payne, P. L. (1968), 'Iron and Steel Manufacturers' in Aldcroft (ed.), *The Development of British Industry and Foreign Competition, 1875–1914*, London: Allen and Unwin.

Robertson, D. H. (1923), *The Control of Industry*, Cambridge.

Smith, K. C. and Horne, G. F. (1934), 'An Index Number of Securities, 1867–1914', *Cambridge Economic Service, Special Memorandum*, 37, June.

Temin, P. (1966), 'The Relative Decline of the British Steel Industry, 1880-1913', in H. Rosovsky (ed.), *Industrialisation in Two Systems*, New York.

Joshua Tetley and Son, Ltd. (1923), *A Hundredth Birthday, Reviewing A Century of Progress, 1823–1923*, privately printed.

Watson, K. (1990), *Industrial Finance in the UK: the Brewing Experience, 1880-1913*, unpublished D.Phil thesis, Oxford University.

CHAPTER ELEVEN

Bankenmacht: Universal Banking and German Industry in Historical Perspective

Harald Wixforth and Dieter Ziegler

Bankenmacht: a German peculiarity?

In Germany discussions about an alleged bank dominance over industry regularly come up when spectacular business transactions intermediated by major banks are performed. Additionally, sensational press reports distribute this news even more widely than those of any other economic events. While some authors demonize the influence of particularly the great banks on the rest of the economy and demand the nationalization of these banks, others stress the necessity of an efficient and competitive banking system. The issue, which is frequently debated in a very polemic way, often suffers from a weak theoretical and empirical basis.[1] Criticism of alleged bank dominance is at times countered by the presumption of conspiracy against the highly efficient German banking system, while the critics interpret such counterattack as a red herring aiming at trivializing the real power of the banks. While starting out from the empirically unfounded assertion that the modern industrial society tends to create dominant positions for those who command its savings, they look at the bankers as the personification of the banks' claim of power, and bankers even become the wire-pullers behind the scenes.[2]

Since the German banks from the very beginning of the industrialization process, have been more heavily engaged in industrial finance than most other banks in Europe[3] and the US, the problem seems to be a German – and possibly Austrian[4] – peculiarity so that the debate is also centred in the German speaking world.[5] In this paper we discuss the dimensions of *Bankenmacht* on the basis of the specific development and organization of the German banking system, since all participants in the discussion about *Bankenmacht* agree that the problem is founded in the specificly German – or central European – variety of banking – the mixed or universal banking system. First we try to define the dimensions of *Bankenmacht* in the abstract and second to examine the applicability of our definitions to the historical reality.

'Es riecht nach Konspiration und Komplott': *Bankenmacht* and the public opinion

The universal banking system, with its close contact to industry and commerce, and its principle of offering almost all banking transactions and services 'under one roof' has especially been the target of criticism. Further criticism is aimed at the decision-making power of the banks in the granting of credits, the participation of banks in non-bank corporations and the right to vote in stockholder meetings of non-bank corporations on behalf of those who have deposited their securities with the banks (proxy voting rights, 'Depotstimmrecht'). The fact that bank representatives can obtain seats on supervisory boards of joint-stock companies in industry and commerce is also a target of numerous attacks. In bundling various functions under the roof of a bank it follows, according to the critics, that the banks have far-reaching influence and potential for abuse of their power.[6]

The critics of the universal banking system, however, belong to two different camps with conflicting ideological backgrounds. The first (or socialist) group of critics which was very active during the 1970s and early 1980s argues in the tradition of Rudolf Hilferding's book *Das Finanzkapital* of 1910. While attempting to apply Hilferding's analysis to the present situation in the Federal Republic, many authors conclude that the Big Three universal banks are to be seen as a cartelized power bloc dominating the rest of the economy. The great banks are described as the commanding heights of the German economy, controlling not only individual industrial companies, but also whole sectors of the economy. In line with Hilferding these critics call for the nationalization of the Big Three as a means to establish an efficient public control over the whole economy. The state, they argue, has only to utilize the mechanism which the privately owned banking power bloc had already developed in the past.[7]

The other (or liberal) group of critics fears that the power and influence of the great banks may impair two important conditions for the functioning of a market economy, that is, free enterprise and free competition. They point out that by agreements about business strategies between the great banks and by pegging out spheres of interest, competition is not only restricted in the banking sector but also in the economy at large. The increasing dominance of the great banks results in a decreasing efficiency of the services of the banking sector and, by a conservative and risk-averse lending policy and lack of competitive pressure, to a misallocation of monetary capital. According to these critics a fundamental reorganization of the universal banking system is needed. They call for the breaking down of mixed banking practices and the establishment of financial intermediaries specialized in particular banking functions. In order to prevent the reestablishment of both universal banking practices and distortions of competition, they also demand efficient public control of the banking sector, including certain guarantees for smaller and highly specialized businesses.[8] Despite the different ideological background of these criticisms, both camps agree on certain fundamental points: in particular the great banks are credited with the capability of strategic control of whole sectors of the economy by subordinating the business policy of a large number of individual non-bank enterprises. It is asserted that the banks, after having achieved control of a certain customer by the supply of credits,[9] will be able to quickly extend this control by institutional factors such as ownership of stock, board representation and proxy voting rights (Hein and Flöter, 1975: 342; Büschgen and Steinbrink, 1977: 142–3).

Although assertions such as distortions of competition in the banking sector and restrictions of managerial freedom of action in non-bank corporations are as yet not empirically verified at all, it is largely taken for granted that *Bankenmacht* is responsible for many evils of the German economy, while, as Richard Tilly has recently noted in astonishment (Tilly, 1992: 147), in modern historiography banks are almost always overlooked as a determining factor of the *Wirtschaftswunder*.

Although the harshness of the criticism today is hardly comprehensible, the situation with the post-1931 criticism is different. The dramatic events of that year, the traumatic experience of the crash of two great banks and a large number of smaller provincial banks which resulted in a far-reaching destruction of the whole monetary sector were largely attributed to the structural weaknesses of the universal banking system. Many critics then demanded a radical conversion of the whole of this system.[10] The *great* Berlin banks in particular were accused of a flawed lending strategy biased towards big industry and disregarding the provinces, of a bureaucratic and inefficient administration and of a dramatic misjudgement of the risks involved in international capital flows. The majority of contemporary observers agreed that the universal banking system as such was a misplaced experiment which had to be replaced by an English-style, market-oriented financial system, characterized by highly specialized financial institutions.[11] After the breakdown of the Third Reich, when the Allies took charge of the German banking sector, the US administration was extremely hostile to the universal banking system in general and to the great banks in particular since they were seen to have had closely collaborated with the Nazi administration.[12] In order to break up this concentration of power the three great banks were split up into ten regional banks each. Yet, the allied deconcentration efforts did not effectively exterminate universal banking practices and as early as the Deutschland-Vertrag of 1952 the reestablishment of the great banks was permitted to take place three years hence (Pohl, 1975: 31). Only a few years later in 1959, however, the Bundestag discussed the unhealthy interconnection of great banks and big industry and possible consequences of an abuse of *Bankenmacht*. Since then this issue has taken hold not only in the Bundestag, but on various official and semi-official commissions yet, however, no major legal reform has been enacted.

Bankenmacht: concept and dimensions

Our survey of the major trends in the criticism of the particular relationship between banking and industry in the universal banking system clearly proves the lack of conceptional clarity. Since the different dimensions of this relationship are mixed up, resulting in an arbitrariness of its analytical contents, general propositions are at times opposed by reference to deviations in certain individual cases. A particular problem in this respect is the assertion, supported by the majority of the critics, that banks exert power on non-bank corporations. Some authors, like Hilferding, regard the banks' dominance as an inevitable condition of capitalist development as such, while others, like Gerschenkron, stress its transitory character. Most economists and political scientists, however, take *Bankenmacht* simply as an integral part of modern industrial societies without regard to its historical determinedness.

According to Hilferding *Bankenmacht* is established, if, first, banks were put in a position to reap an increasing portion of the profits of a non-bank corporation; second, if they absorb, in the case of the issue of stock, the lion's share of the *Gründergewinn*, that is, the premium between the par value and the price of the stock issued; third, if they have the potential to dictate the business policy of the non-bank corporation (Hilferding, 1968: 117–20, 252–3). In this respect it is important to note that German corporation law prescribes the separation of supervisory and executive boards and permits banks to obtain seats in supervisory boards of non-bank corporations. This legal framework enables representatives of both banks and non-bank corporations to create a network of personal linkages between several big industrial concerns and between banks and industry by accumulating seats in the administrative and particularly in the supervisory boards of these companies ('big linkers').

Contrary to Hilferding, Gerschenkron stresses bank financing as a necessary condition of a successful industrialization of 'latecomer' economies of the first generation (like Germany). Only in this particular historical situation does their centrality in the whole process allow for the dominant position of banks over industry whereby they possess the potential to influence the business policy of non-bank enterprises by personal and business penetration. The economic foundation of such penetration, however, disappears in the course of industrialization when self-financing becomes more important so that non-bank enterprises could gradually emancipate themselves from the banking sphere (Gerschenkron, 1966). Thus the logic of the Gerschenkronian evolutionary theory of bank–industry relationships leads to the opposite result to that of the Hilferding theory. While the former expects two relatively independent sectors in a mature capitalist (that is, competitive market) economy, the latter forecasts a transformation of interconnectedness of the two spheres into a merger, the so-called finance capital. In this model the capitalist economy of free competition is superseded by a general cartel enabling finance capital to exert substantial regulatory power.[13]

The historical evidence during the period of Hilferding's study, however, was hardly in line with the alleged tendency of a finance capital-like merger of banks and industry.[14] Furthermore, during the Weimar Republic the strength of the banks was seriously shattered.[15] Yet, neither is Gerschenkron completely supported by the historical evidence, since the evidence collected by the Monopoly Commission shows – by Gerschenkronian criteria of penetration – that the banks were in a very strong position in the 1960s and 1970s.[16]

The lack of a general (only cyclically interrupted) underlying tendency of bank dominance seems to disprove any evolutionary theory of the bank–industry relationship at all. On the other hand, modern political scientists who are often not interested in long-run developments are busy creating indicators to measure *Bankenmacht* which, after having counted the numbers, will conclude whether *Bankenmacht* threatens the competitive market economy (or not) and praise (or condemn) the regulatory potential of the banks in the economy.[17] The mechanics by which the underlying forces and counterforces work, however, are not detected. How does the granting of *de facto* long-term credits create a regulatory capacity? Which criteria are essential in the chain of factors in creating *Bankenmacht* and in what position in the chain? True, on the micro-level we cannot expect reliable empirical information from the persons involved, and the background of more recent spectacular business transactions will remain in the dark, providing only enough material for sensational press reports. But we can analyse the mechanics of *Bankenmacht* in the past when the provision of reliable sources is (at least) possible (though in Germany still difficult), with the proviso that we have set up the criteria necessary to differentiate between the peculiarities of the particular historical situation and the basic mechanics at work in the process. The aim is to understand when certain indicators of *Bankenmacht* such as equity ownership or board representation are an expression of *Bankenmacht* or a precondition of *Bankenmacht* exerted by other means or, possibly, the result of a weakness.

Firstly, we must differentiate between two cases. Some authors do not explicitly state whether they understand *Bankenmacht* to mean the power of the banking system over the industrial system or to mean the power of individual banks over individual non-bank corporations which is manifested as a mass phenomenon in the dominance of banks. In the following we distinguish two different dimensions of *Bankenmacht*:

- the power of the individual bank, and
- the power of the banking system.

Both dimensions can furthermore be distinguished by their respective economic dimension, that is

- the power of the individual bank over its customers (microeconomic dimension of economic power), and
- the potential of the banking system to act as a regulatory authority in and between markets (macroeconomic dimension of economic power),

and their respective political and social dimensions, that is

- the potential of representatives of the banking system to influence (or even dictate) Governmental or Parliamentary decisions (macro-political dimension of social and political power), and
- the potential of the individual bank to influence the social status of their individual customers (microsocial dimension of social and political power).

These distinctions are possibly not complete, but they shall help us to avoid the mixing up of the different levels of *Bankenmacht* even if these levels are closely interwoven with each other in reality. In this paper, however, we shall confine ourselves to the economic dimensions. As yet the extent of the political power of even outstanding bank representatives such as Gerson von Bleichröder, Karl Helfferich, Hermann Josef Abs or Robert Pferdmenges is impossible to assess. Despite an extensive literature about the political power of banks and their representatives respectively we are not able at present to decide on fact and fiction.

Microeconomic dimension of economic power

Taking the well-known definition of 'power' by Max Weber as a basis, that is, that power is 'the probability that one actor within a social relationship will be in a position to carry out his own will despite resistance, regardless of the basis on which this probability rests' (Weber, 1976: 28)[18] a 'powerful' bank or group of banks ought to be in the position of pushing through their own interests in a non-bank corporation, if necessary even against the resistance of the latter's executive board or other interests represented in the supervisory board. In theory a prerequisite for such far-reaching determination of the non-bank's business policy is the establishment of a long-lived dominance by 'institutionalized bridgeheads' such as equity ownership and board representation. Once these bridgeheads are established and the more the bank can influence the decision-making process, the weaker the autonomy of the executive board becomes. In practice, the crucial question is, how are banks put in a position to build up such bridgeheads and how and when are these bridgeheads established. In order to properly analyse the role and function of the bridgeheads we distinguish between different components:

- the demand for external finance by the non-bank corporation,
- the growth rate and the size of the non-bank corporation (in relation to the size of the bank), and
- the degree of bank competition and bank cooperation respectively and degree of internationalization of capital markets.

In general, even in Germany, big industry is on average only marginally dependent on external finance (Rettig, 1978; Esser, 1992: 112). Yet, for an investigation of the microeconomic dimension qualifications concerning macroeconomic averages are irrelevant. Almost all industrial enterprises might some time in their history experience a situation when the ploughing back of profits was not sufficient to finance certain urgently needed investments. The reasons for (additional) external finance may be manifold, but it is likely to be pressing, if reconstruction or rationalization schemes require a substantial injection of finance without delay. Second, a trough in business activity may erode reserves which have been kept for capital deepening, without any prospect of replenishment in the medium-term. The gestation period of a certain investment may last longer than the shareholders are prepared to tolerate. In capital intensive industries, when the expected profitability of a new investment is only attained if the investment in production facilities is large enough to exploit a technology's potential of economies of scale, the provision of external finance may become a matter of survival.

In the following we try to exemplify the basic mechanism of both the establishment and instrumentalization of *Bankenmacht* and the reestablishment (or maintenance) of entrepreneurial autonomy on the part of the bank's (or banks') customer by several instances taken from different phases of German capitalist development. Although the selection of these examples implies a certain degree of chance, we believe they also have a certain degree of representativeness.

The first case we examine is that of a successful attempt by a banker to push through his own interests in a central institution of a non-bank corporation, and dates from the very beginning of the industrialization process. It is a well-known fact that industrialization in Germany was largely sustained by the so-called 'heavy industrial leading sector complex'. Yet, the establishment of the most prominent sector of this complex, the railways, was largely due to either the banks or the state. In the case of Prussia, particularly in the beginning of railway development, bank financing was of almost indispensible importance. In the Rhineland bankers were among the most prominent railway promoters, and the first railway companies, from their incorporation on, often had at least one banker either in the supervisory board or in the *Direktion*. In the first supervisory board of the Rhenish Railway Co. there were as many as four representatives of Cologne private banking houses: I.H. Stein, A. Schaaffhausen, I.D. Herstatt and Sal. Oppenheim jun. & Co. The latter alone held 25 per cent of the nominal capital of two million Talers.[19]

Despite a very promising beginning in 1835 the company faced enormous difficulties before the track between Cologne and Aachen was finally opened in 1841. When the cost estimate proved to be insufficient, from the outset unfavourable circumstances in the late 1830s (including a seemingly hostile legislation) made every effort to raise additional finance through the market a lost case. Since the Prussian state was also very reluctant to support the company, it relied heavily on its bankers. In 1838 a consortium consisting of Oppenheim, Stein and Herstatt agreed to pay for the whole of a new stock issue of 1.5 million Talers. Yet, downward price movements of stock very soon rendered the shares held by the banks unsaleable, and the 'lock up' of the bankers' resources posed a serious threat to the latters' solvency. By the end of 1838 the bankers urged the directorate to repurchase a substantial part of the company's stock in order to stabilize the price. At first the directors were reluctant, hiding behind the argument that the company statutes did not allow such manipulation. Finally, however, when the bankers threatened to unload their holdings of stock completely and without regard to the losses involved, the directors agreed to take back the whole issue of 1.5 million Talers. This operation was not only kept secret, but even the supervisory board was not informed.

Despite this seemingly very unfavourable result, the outcome did not signify an abuse of *Bankenmacht*. On the contrary, the bankers had to pay a very high price for the concession by the company. It was stipulated that the bankers lost the whole amount of calls already paid (20 per cent), if the shares were kept in the hands of the company until mid-1839 – later prolonged to the end of that year. The stipulations of this contract clearly prove that both sides had tried to find a compromise which enabled both to survive. They knew that because of the interlacing of capital interests the breakdown of the one partner would definitely follow the breakdown of the other.

In 1843, however, the balance of power had shifted. The repurchase manipulation had ended favourably for the bankers, as the Belgian Government had agreed to pay for the stock before the bankers had to write off their calls. Abraham Oppenheim in particular had made the most of his interlocking position as director of the company and its banker and was accused by his co-directors of only having an eye to his own interests.[20] The smouldering conflict escalated when the majority of the directors decided to follow the practice of other railway companies and abandon the payment of a fixed interest of 5 per cent on the paid up capital as laid down by the statutes. This emergency measure was backdated to 1 January 1843. This decision infuriated Oppenheim and he even refused the compromise proposed by the directorate to pay an ordinary dividend out of current profits instead of the fixed interest. Since the supervisory board finally decided against the majority of the directors and suspended the payments of the fixed interest only temporarily (subject to backpayment in due course), with the exception of the two bankers (Oppenheim and Schnitzler) all directors and deputy directors resigned from the board at the next shareholders meeting.

Although seemingly a prototype of bank dominance generated by typical universal banking practices, this example represents an extreme exception rather than the rule. Despite the fact that the general components of *Bankenmacht* as described above were strongly in favour of the bank (a chronically strong demand for external finance and no competition between the banks operating in a still highly segmented market), the extent of the institutional bridgehead was untypical for the German bank–industry relationship. The Rhenish Railway Co. was by the mid-1830s one of only a few joint-stock companies in the Rhineland. As the moneyed classes were as yet unaccustomed to investing in shares of railway companies or other corporations, a banker having realized the potential of this new venture did not only have to invest an extremely high portion of his own resources, by later standards, but had to become involved in the management of that company himself.

There are similarities between the Cameronian banker-entrepreneur (Cameron, 1967: 318–20) and the banker-(non-bank corporation) director. Just as the banker-entrepreneur was a peculiarity of the early stages of industrialization, the omnipotent banker-director became more or less a nonentity, when industrial capitalism had reached a stage of maturity – even in Germany. When investment opportunities for enterprising bankers such as Oppenheim became more widespread, they could not only diversify risks enabling them to restrict their activities to a supervisory role, but they were not in a position to spend as much time as demanded by an executive directorship any longer.[21] After having diversified their business activities they also diversified board representation, that is, some of them collected supervisory board seats and became 'big linkers'. Additionally, non-bank enterprises were equally also interested in having an outsider among the executive directors. A banker-director was much too powerful simply by the combination of these two functions, and as competition among banks increased (by the breaking up of regionally segmented finance markets or otherwise, see below), they were less frequently compelled to elect a banker onto their executive board.

A more representative case of *Bankenmacht* on the micro-level is the often discussed interrelation between the Deutsche Bank and Mannesmannröhren–Werke AG. Soon after the company was set up technical problems in the production process of 'Mannesmann' tubes resulted in severe financial problems which persisted, until a reconstruction scheme was laid down. Apart from several loans already granted in advance, the Deutsche Bank got some 10 million Marks of the 35 million Mark total stock issued (Wessel, 1990: 124–25; Wessel, 1991: 56; Wellhöner, 1989: 126). Its position as major shareholder was manifested by a massive representation of the Bank on the Mannesmann supervisory board. Apart from up to four Deutsche Bank representatives other bankers on the supervisory board were seen as 'friends', which in this case meant, subordinated to the Deutsche Bank. This massive involvement of the Deutsche Bank resulted, on the one hand, in a strong financial backing which enabled Mannesmann to finally overcome its financial problems. On the other hand, the Deutsche Bank, by building up a very strong institutional bridgehead, did not have to reckon with any competition from a rival bank even when Mannesmann's earning capacity had substantially improved after the turn of the century (Wellhöner, 1989: 134–7; Wixforth, 1990: 22).

The *de facto* monopoly of the Deutsche Bank in Mannesmann's banking transactions, which lasted until the 1920s, was not the result of an ever-increasing demand for external financing but simply of the Bank's position as major shareholder. These traces of *Bankenmacht* manifest themselves not only by a strong supervisory board representation, but also by a considerable degree of influence on the business strategies of the concern, exerted by the supervisory board chairman and Deutsche Bank representative Max Steinthal. Yet, even such a seemingly concrete bridgehead was not immune from crumbling. The internationalization of the capital markets in the 1920s considerably enhanced the managerial autonomy of the concern and weakened the old-established dominance of the bank (Wixforth, 1991: 184–5).

In this respect Mannesmann was certainly no exception. During the Weimar Republic both industry and banking underwent a hitherto unknown process of concentration. As the banks were substantially weakened by War and inflation, the largest industrial combines found themselves in a position to substantially increase the scope of their business relations with banks from both home and abroad. The iron and steel concern Phoenix raised the number of its banking relations to 48, the Gutehoffnungshütte to 43 and the Deutsch-Luxemburgische Bergwerks- und Hütten AG even to 55. The largest and most important company of the German heavy industry in the Weimar Republic, the Vereinigte Stahlwerke – a trust established in 1926 by the merger of six combines – maintained business relations with 56 banks.[22] Although we lack comparable data, the same happened with the large companies of the electrical and the chemical industry. Notably, the two large combines of the electrical industry, the Siemens combine and the AEG, and the giant of the chemical industry, the I.G. Farbenindustrie, maintained business relations with a multitude of banks from home and abroad (Feldenkirchen, 1990: 42–7; Plumpe, 1990: 123).

In addition, during the inflation some of the combines set up their own investment companies or 'house banks'. For example, in 1923 Krupp established the AG für Unternehmungen der Eisen- und Stahlindustrie. By purchasing shares of the various enterprises of the Krupp combine its house bank provided the combine with investment capital. A similar function was carried out by the Oberhausener Kohle- und Eisenhandelsgesellschaft for the Gutehoffnungshütte, the Montana AG – a Swiss investment company – for the Eisen- und Stahlwerk Hoesch, Thyssen & Co. and the Bank voor Handel en Scheepvaart in Rotterdam for the Thyssen combine, and the Phoenix-Trust-Maatschappij – a Dutch holding company established by German shareholders of the Phoenix, Dutch banks and the Dutch iron- and steelworks Hoogovens – for the Phoenix. The Sichel combine – a 'mixed' combine which arose rapidly in the inflation period – acquired the Westbank AG and reorganized it as its house bank. BASF bought the majority of stock of the Deutsche Länderbank and re-established it as a house bank, which even became house bank of the I.G. Farben when BASF had joined the IG.[23]

The relative strength of the large industrial combines vis-à-vis even the great banks in the early phase of the Weimar Republic is best exemplified by the fact that at the end of the inflation period some industrial combines even tried to take over well-known universal banks. The Stinnes combine, for example – a gigantic trust, built up during the inflation by the German industrialist Hugo Stinnes – tried to acquire the majority of stock of the Berliner Handelsgesellschaft, one of the oldest and most famous German universal banks. In October 1923 the Cologne industrialist Otto Wolff attempted to acquire the majority of stock of the Schaaffhausen'sche Bankverein, an old-established and most important provincial bank.[24]

Although both attempts failed, the fact that these industrialists felt strong enough to dominate a certain bank clearly indicates a weakening of *Bankenmacht* during the inflation. The increasing number of banking relations as well as the setting up of house banks and investment companies tended to loosen the formerly close credit relations between the Berlin universal banks and their large industrial customers. This development was reinforced by an extreme liquidity, caused by abundant central bank credit. After the inflation German industry suffered from a general shortage of capital and credit. Despite a hazardous credit policy the German banks did not have enough funds to adequately feed their large industrial customers' hunger for capital. The larger companies, however, overcame this situation by borrowing from abroad. Many American and British banks had enough money to lend to foreign industrial companies on easy terms (Gehr, 1960: 86–7; Hardach, 1984: 217). Moreover, these banks wanted to strengthen their ties to German industrial companies in order to get new customers. In this situation, the German banks were unable to keep their foreign rivals out of the market. The increasing number of business relations and increased competition among the banks resulting from the internationalization of the capital market tended to loosen the German banks' former influence in the larger industrial companies.

Yet, in a recent article we were able to show that the weakening of the *Bankenmacht* did not result in a decline of the banks' bridgeheads. The number of supervisory board seats in a sample of 40 industrial concerns (most of them big heavy industrial firms from the Ruhr area) held by banks did not significantly decrease during the phase of weakness. In fact, the number of seats increased from 95 (1913–14) to 155 (1923–24) (Wixforth and Ziegler, 1994 forthcoming: Table 4). Another substantial difference to the prewar period was representation by foreign bankers in non-bank supervisory boards which had been concentrated on a handful of multinationals before the War and which rose to 13 per cent of all bankers in 1923–24.

This seemingly contradictory development resulted from the successful attempt by the industrial concerns to intensify competition between banks by giving them the same degree of inside information in order to reduce risks resulting from information asymmetry between the rivals. This means, that the same instrument functioning as a bridgehead in order to control the business policy of a customer turned out to become an important tool to (re-)establish entrepreneurial independence – possibly even despite a strong demand for external financing.

The results of our empirical investigation of the microeconomic dimension of the bank–industry relationship in Germany before 1933 reveal that the hypothesis of a general supremacy of the banks over their industrial clientele (or even such a tendency in the long-term) has to be rejected. In contrast to Hilferding's theory of a subordination of industry in a bank-dominated 'finance capital' we stress the particular macroeconomic framework and the microeconomic conditions under which banks and industry act. They may, at times, result in a subordination and loss of entrepreneurial independence on the part of the industrial customer. But the balance of power may also change resulting in a complete destruction of the alleged *Bankenmacht*.

The macroeconomic dimension

The power of the universal banking system as such is at least as difficult to analyse as the *Bankenmacht* on the micro-level. Financial institutions are multifariously connected with the economic, political and social systems in modern societies. Since we are concentrating in this section on the macroeconomic dimension of *Bankenmacht* as a correlate to the microeconomic dimension discussed above, we have to ask whether the banking system has, by a particular functional interrelation with the rest of the economy, a dominant position over other sectors.

In a very broadly defined system theoretical approach the industrial and the banking systems are to be seen as subsystems of the economic system of a certain state. The economic system is also subordinated to a greater system, that is, to the whole society. Between the subsystems of banks and industry exist many different relations. These relations are a subset of all relations between the different subsystems, and the total of all subsystems and relations among themselves form the structure of the economic system. The subsystems of a certain system, in this case the banking system and industrial system, are only functionally interrelated.

Dominance of one subsystem over the other is excluded by definition (Baecker, 1991: 40).

Because of its harmonizing character, system theory is at times called in to support the arguments of those who maintain that banks and industry were equivalent elements of the economic system, the relations of which could not, because of their solely functional character, create a hierarchical order.[25] Contrary to the protagonists of system theory, empirical research clearly shows, however, that banks as a systemic or coherent unit have the capacity to dominate decisions both in the sphere of the economic system and of the political system. The hierarchical nature of the relationship between banks and industry is formed by the privileged position of the banking system in the information flows of the whole economic system. To analyse empirically the mechanism which creates the structural dominance of the banking system (on the macro-level), we have to turn again to microeconomic theory. Anglo-American financial economists emphasized at first the particular shortcomings of their respective (market-oriented) financial systems by asserting that the financing of industry provided by functionally separated financial intermediaries was inadequate, because informational imperfections and the lack of efficient capital control resulted at times in credit rationing. If these arguments are applied to the alternative system, the bank-oriented financial system, *Bankenmacht* has to be seen in a different light. In contrast to the liberal critics of the 1970s and early 1980s the hierarchical interrelation between the banking system and industry becomes a determining factor for the relative success of the German economy both before the First World War and after the Second World War (Tilly, 1986; Kennedy, 1988; Ziegler, 1994 forthcoming). The reason for the stability of the hierarchical interrelation between the financial institutions and industry is not a structural superiority of the one fraction of capital over the other, but the mutual advantage deriving from, on average, the regulatory potential of the German universal banks in the face of the high degree of uncertainty under which both industry and investors act on auction markets.

The basis of this analysis is the theory of informational imperfections in the capital market. According to Stiglitz and others it is not primarily the interest rate that is used to explain investment behaviour of firms but rather the availability of credit. Auction markets tend to increase credit rationing in recession periods even without any necessary concurrent change in interest rates because of greater uncertainty of the prospects of firms. It is assumed that the interest rate charged by the bank may itself affect the riskiness of the loan. Good borrowers may withdraw, while those who are willing to pay high interest rates, on average, not only constitute greater risks, but raising interest rates may even lead borrowers to take actions which are contrary to the interests of the lender by, for example, taking higher risks in business transactions. In any case, even if the increasing of interest rates does not result in an excess of supply over demand for credits, by the lack of perfect and costless information higher interest rates do not necessarily optimize the return for the bank, and the latter will at times resort to credit rationing instead of interest rates. Consequently, by imperfect (or asymmetric) information credit rationing will not only affect bad borrowers but all borrowers.

In this situation of credit rationing by financial institutions any attempt to sell equity may convey a strong negative signal about a firm's quality and reduces its market value accordingly. The cost of issuing stock may become so high as to be prohibitive so that credit rationing by financial institutions is supplemented rather than obviated by the capital market (Stiglitz and Weiss, 1981; Greenwald et al., 1984).

The temporary impossibility of raising external finance certainly affects not only the efficiency of an individual firm, but also of the system as a whole. Consequently, the key factor for the allocative efficiency of the capital and credit markets is the way information is distributed among agents (Cable, 1985: 118; Kennedy, 1988: 115; Kennedy, 1991), and as the market cannot provide a satisfactory distribution of information both for the borrower and the lender (investor), banks are seen as the only institutions that can distribute information more evenly. True, this model also implies the possibility of abuse, but historical evidence shows that banks rarely slaughtered the cows that were to be milked.

The advantage of the regulatory capacity of the bank-oriented system over the market-oriented system can be explained by the example of electrification and the setting up of an electrical industry in Germany and Britain respectively. In his masterly account of the introduction of Edison's electric lighting system in Britain and Germany, Thomas Hughes makes this point very clear. The fact that Hughes confirms the conventional wisdom that 'the most penetrating explanation for the failure in London and the success in Berlin is neither technological nor economic: it is political' (Hughes, 1983: 77) (that is, a hostile and short-sighted legislation) only explains that he is interested in the electrical system and not in the banking system. A more systematic account of the working of the respective financial system clearly proves that it was not the legislation as such, but how legislation was perceived by those who decided on the flow of capital and credit, that made the difference. When in 1882 the English Electric Light Co. was set up, a major London banker, Sir John Lubbock, was among its board members. But unlike German bankers who collaborated with Emil Rathenau and his Deutsche

Edison Gesellschaft, Lubbock was not in a position to supply the capital which was necessary to exploit the technology's potential of economies of scale. Instead the English Electric Light Co. (and the other companies engaged in the generation of electricity and the manufacture of electrical equipment) relied on the (formal or informal) capital markets.

Yet, auction capital markets in a situation of an untried innovation react in a unpredictable way. Individual investors with no inside information irrationally act on 'noise'[26] as if it were information that would give them an edge. In the case of the electrical industry, the wild fluctuations in profit expectations, fuelled at first by the fascinating quality of the innovation and later by a seemingly hostile legislation, rather than inside information, determined its fate in Britain. In an early stage a speculative boom in electricity supply companies stimulated by astute company promoters created enormous profit expectations which were hardly realistic, at least in the short-term. When these exaggerations of profit expectations became obvious, share prices fell and the industry was starved of funds for many years. The slackening in the development of electricity supply companies during the 1880s was directly transferred to the equipment makers who now faced an uncertain level of demand for their new products.[27]

In contrast, the control of capital and credits exerted by the banks in Germany enabled the latter to fund their customers during periods of unfavourable capital market conditions both by granting current account credit and by keeping undistributed stock in their respective portfolios. Only when the general conditions in the capital markets had improved and when profit expectations had become favourable and companies had begun to successfully exploit the technology's potential for economies of scale, did banks find themselves in a position to successfully unload their portfolios and to turn current account credits into stock ready to be digested by the (formal) capital market.

Conclusion

In this paper we have tried to show that *Bankenmacht* has very different dimensions and it seems that the fruitlessness of the discussions so far is at least partly due to the fact that both sides – the critics and the advocates of a close relationship between banks and industry – are fixing their gaze on different dimensions of *Bankenmacht*. While the critics stress the microeconomic dominance of banks, the advocates counter with its much more harmonic macroeconomic dimension. A discussion in the sense of an exchange of different views cannot be entered into while the dimensions of *Bankenmacht* are not clarified. Up to now the confusion about the topic under discussion has created a polemic tone which, in turn, makes an exchange of views even more difficult.

Second, financial economists at times propose the universal banking system as remedy for the (alleged or real) shortcomings of Anglo-American finance markets which are characterized by a high degree of division of labour and consequently by a comparatively loose relationship between banks and industry. Yet, the microeconomic dimension of a German-type banking system is rarely taken into account by these reformers.[28] It is certainly not sufficient to industrialize the English banks, as the Austrian C.W. von Wieser had demanded before the First World War (Wieser, 1919); and John Cable was certainly right with his notion that 'the relationship between industrial banking and firm performance has more to it than the provision of credit alone; it is bank control as well as bank lending which raises profitability (Cable, 1985: 130). But bank control is – as the German experience has shown – not as harmonious as macroeconomic considerations may suggest. Additionally, historical experience shows that an artificial importation of business practices is doomed to failure. The different institutional framework (and possibly even a different business culture)[29] often prevents a successful application of new business practices.

In the case of bank control an important precondition is the specific German legal division between the executive board of directors constituted exclusively of full-time corporate officers and the supervisory board made up solely by 'outsiders'. In the case of companies with only one board of directors combining supervision with certain executive duties it is impossible to create a German-Austrian type of a 'big linker'.[30] The duties associated with a seat in such a board prevent the collection of more than a handful of seats by one person. This means that a bank may, by the election of a bank's nominee onto the board of directors enforced by its position as major creditor, achieve a dominant position in the company. This dominance, however, is not based on those particular services which the reformers have in mind, that is, the removal of information asymmetries, provision of financial expertise, or regulating market integration by, for example, facilitating cartel or other inter-firm arrangements, but rather on the capacity of the bank to subordinate the business strategies of the customer to its own objectives. In short, a bridgehead such as a seat in an executive board of directors enables the bank to perform the most extreme form of microeconomic bank dominance which, as historical evidence proves, was an exception rather than the rule in the universal banking system. Such institutional arrangement does not enable the bank to gather the information needed to minimize the risks involved in the industrialization of the banks' lending practices in a relatively costless way, and was not only a serious threat to the non-bank's management autonomy – as demanded by Stiglitz – but also to the interests of other groups affected (shareholders, workers, other creditors). The bank will only find itself in such a position, if the balance between lender and borrower has already become extremely lopsided. A regular and harmonic penetration of boards of industrial companies by representatives of different banks as a supporting measure of an industrialization of the banks' lending practices (problem of the control of capital and credits) is impossible to achieve without an adequate and historically grown institutional framework, or, more concretely, it is unlikely 'that German lending conventions would be sustainable . . . outside the German structural context (Cable, 1985: 130; see also Tilly, 1992: 153).

Third, in Germany any legislative attempt to avoid abuse of microeconomic bank dominance, particularly as regards the voting power of banks in non-bank corporations by proxy voting rights, has to take its macroeconomic consequences into account. Outside Germany the macroeconomic consequences of *Bankenmacht*, that is, the provision of substantial long-term finance accompanied by an efficient control of capital and credits through equity ownership (supplemented by proxy voting rights) and supervisory board representation, are largely considered as an important factor in the favourable overall performance of German industry after the Second World War.[31] In modern Germany bank lending to industry is conditional on control, and measures effectively to reduce that control could also reduce the availability of bank finance. Legislation has to be careful not to throw out the baby with the bathwater.

Notes

1. Recently the 'serious' studies about the role and function of banks in post-Second World War Germany have clearly shown that after having discharged the ideological ballast our knowledge about the bank-industry relationship in the Federal Republic is very poor indeed. See Esser (1992) and Tilly (1993).
2. See for example the polemics of Pritzkoleit (1961) and Czichon (1979).
3. When the Monopoly Commission was set up by the Federal Government, of all countries in the EEC it was only in the Federal Republic and in Luxembourg that banks were subject to no restrictions at all in their ability to participate in non-bank corporations. See Eckstein (1980: 466).
4. Before the First World War and even before such tendencies were to be seen in Germany. Rudolf Hilferding characterized the role of banks in his homeland as follows: 'Austria . . . provides the clearest example of a direct and deliberate influence of bank capital upon cartelization'. Hilferding (1968: 291).

5. This is particularly true for Britain, where criticism of the efficiency of the finance markets' role in industrial finance is aiming at completely different aspects, particularly the relatively loose connection between banks and industry. See for the historical origins of the modern bank-industry relationship in Britain: Cottrell (1979); Kennedy (1987); Ziegler (1994 forthcoming); although less critical see also Thomas (1978); Ross (1990); Collins (1991).

6. Even politicians of the christian-liberal coalition are critical of the power of the great banks. See most recently 'Bonner Koalition streitet über die Macht der Banken', in: *Frankfurter Rundschau* vom 26.7.1989 and Otto Graf Lambsdorff, 'Die Macht der Banken – eine Herausforderung für die Ordnungspolitik', in: *FAZ 22. 8. 1989.*

7. 'Taking possession of the . . . great banks would mean taking possession of the most important spheres of big industry, and would . . . greatly facilitate the initial phases of socialist policy'. Hilferding (1968: 504). In the 1970s these arguments were supported even by a strong minority in the SPD, see 'Gegen die Macht der Banken – für Demokratisierung', *Materialien der Jungsozialisten in der SPD*, Nr. 17/1974; see also Usoskin (1975: 9); ' Gerhards (1982); Gossweiler (1988); Hummel (1972). A general account of the discussion on nationalization is given in Büschgen (1978) and Büschgen and Steinbrink (1977).

8. A liberal critique is the basic trend of the different Reports of the Monopoly Commission. See Monopolkommission, Hauptgutachten 1973/75: Mehr Wettbewerb ist möglich, Baden Baden: Nomos 1976; Monopolkommission, Hauptgutachten 1976/77: Fortschreitende Konzentration bei Großunternehmen, Baden Baden: Nomos 1978; see also Eckstein (1988: 465–82; Arndt (1980: 15); Moesch and Simmert (1976: 74); Geiger (1975: 79).

9. A lender can exert control through both the formal terms of the loan contract and the refusal to renew the loan.

10. For the banking crisis of 1931 see Born (1967); Irmler (1976); James (1984); Balderston (1991).

11. See the critical reports in: *Untersuchungen des deutschen Bankwesens*, 1933, Berlin: Hobbing 1933, part 1, edited by the official Untersuchungsausschuß für das deutsche Bankwesen; for contemporary criticism and proposed remedies see also Bankensystem Umbau. Beiträge zur Bankenenquete, Frankfurt 1933; Verlag 'Die Wirtschaft' (ed.), *Europäische Banken 1932 – eine kritische Darstellung*, Prag 1932.

12. See Office of Military Government for Germany, United States (OMGUS) 1986, *Ermittlungen gegen die Dresdner Bank* (German edition prepared by Hamburger Stiftung für Sozialgeschichte des 20. Jahrhunderts) Nördlingen: Die andere Bibliothek; OMGUS (1985), *Ermittlungen gegen die Deutsche Bank*, Nördlingen: Die andere Bibliothek; see also Horstmann (1991).

13. See Hilferding (1968: 243, 321); a neo-Marxist critique of these forecasts most recently in Jürgens and Lindner (1974) and Wellhöner (1989).

14. At about the same time when Hilferding began writing his *Finance Capital* the leading German industrialist, Emil Kirdorf, qualified the recent development of the bank–industry relationship as follows: 'It is sometimes asserted . . . that great banks, big finance dominate industry completely. I reject this notion firmly "auf das entschiedenste". The influence of the

great banks on big industry in the Rhineland and in Westphalia has never been as weak as today' (Speech by Emil Kirdorf, 1906: 285).

15. Recent research tentatively rejects the Hilferdingian description of the relationship between great banks and big industry both during the Kaiserreich (see Wellhöner, 1989) and in the Weimar Republic (see Wixforth, 1991; Balderston, 1991: 588–96).

16. See Eckstein (1980: 465–82); and particularly stressing the importance of interlocking directorates Ziegler (1984); Pappi *et al.* (1987).

17. This is particularly true for the Report of the Monopoly Commission and many of the liberal critics taking up the data compiled by the Commission; although arguing from a different point of view, see also Shonfield (1965); Fennema (1982).

18. See also the definition by Schuster (1977: 98).

19. On the Rhenish Railway 'case' see Kumpmann (1910); Stürmer, *et al.* (1989: 84–5).

20. The Vice President of the company, David Hansemann, agreed with his colleagues in private that 'at times they doubted whether Herr Abraham Oppenheim speaks as a banker or as a director' (cited in Kumpmann, 1910: 425).

21. While, for example, the directorate of the Rhenish Railway Co. met at least once a weak, the supervisory board met only once per half year (in practice during the construction period, however, once per month). See Statutes of the Company, reprinted in Kumpmann (1910: 447–66).

22. See Archive of the Mannesmann AG (MA), P 1 25.26.2, P 1 25.29; Haniel-Archive (HA), 300/71/52-53; Archive of the Thyssen AG (TA), FWH 126/53, 126/54; 527/03; TA, A 768/3, A 815/1, A 771/1; TA VSt 955, VSt 4141.

23. See HAK, 41/2-198; HA, 300/193/000; Hoesch-Archive, A 3 b 24; TA, A 522/2; MA, P 1 25.38. See also Ufermann (1925: 62); Hagemann (1930: 21); Wittkowski (1937: 17).

24. Die deutschen Banken im September/Oktober 1922, in: *Die Bank*, Jg. 1922, p. 817, p. 979; Die deutschen Banken im Oktober 1923, in: *Die Bank*, Jg. 1923, p. 746. Wittkowski (1937: 15); Fürstenberg (1965: 145–6); Gossweiler (1971: 125).

25. This argument is held up particularly by the bankers themselves. See, for example, Alfred Herrhausen (former chairman of the Deutsche Bank executive board), 'Es riecht nach Komplott und Konspiration', in *Die Welt*, Nr. 251 (27 October 1989); see also Baecker (1991: 23).

26. 'Noise is the arbitrary element in expectations . . . Noise makes financial markets possible, but also makes them imperfect'. Black (1986: 529–30); see also De Long, J. Bradford *et. al.* (1990).

27. We owe this information to Bill Kennedy who has computed the formal capital market's financial inflows into both electricity supply and equipment making companies.

28. This is particularly true for Joseph E. Stiglitz who ends up his proposals for an institutional reform aiming at a more efficient control of capital with the assertion that equity ownership may induce the banks to extend their present concern for the 'lower tail of the distribution [of profits] towards the mean' (Stiglitz, 1985: 148). The means by which the banks could exercise their control, however, are only barely touched upon.

29. For this particular aspect see Berghahn (1985: 180–3).

30. It has to be noted, however, that at least US legislature has explicitly been intending to prevent interlocking directorates when in Germany such networks were built up.
31. In Britain the discussion about an applicability of German-style lending practices as remedy for industrial decline is as vulgarized as the discussion about *Bankenmacht* in Germany. See 'Why Germany Beats Britain', in *Sunday Times* 2 November 1980 and 'How to Bank on Britain', in *Sunday Times* 9 November 1980.

References

Arndt, Helmut (1980), *Wirtschaftliche Mach*, Munich.

Baecker, Dirk (1991), *Womit handeln Banken*, Frankfurt.

Balderston, Theo (1991), 'German Banking between the Wars: The Crisis of the Credit Banks', in *BHR*, 65: 581–5.

Berghahn, Volker (1985), *Unternehmer und Politik in der Bundesrepublik*, Frankfurt.

Black, Fisher (1986), 'Noise', *Journal of Finance*, 41: 529–30.

Born, Karl Erich (1967), *Die deutsche Bankenkrise von 1931*, Munich.

Büschgen, Hans E. (1978), 'Die Frage der Macht der Banken im Spiegel wirtschafts- und gesellschaftspolitischer Ideologien', *Bankhistorisches Archiv*, Beiheft Nr. 2, pp. 21–9.

Büschgen, Hans E. and Steinbrink, Klaus (1977), *Verstaatlichung der Banken? Forderungen und Argumente*, Cologne.

Cable, John (1985), 'Capital Market Information and Industrial Performance: The Role of West German Banks', *EJ*, 95: 118.

Cameron, Rondo (1967), 'Conclusion', in *Banking in the Early Stages of Industrialization*, Oxford.

Collins, Michael (1991), *Banks and Industrial Finance in Britain, 1800–1939*, London.

Cottrell, Philip L. (1979), *Industrial Finance 1830–1914*, London.

Czichon, Eberhart (1979), *Der Bankier und die Macht*, Cologne.

De Long, J. Bradford *et al.* (1990), 'Noise Trader Risk in Financial Markets', *JPE*, 98: 703–38.

Eckstein, Wolfram (1980), 'The Role of Banks in Corporate Concentration in West Germany', *Zs. für die gesamte Staatswissenschaft*, 136.

Esser, Josef (1992), 'Banken und Industrie in der Bundesrepublik Deutschland', in Karl Rohe, Gustav Schmidt and Hartmut Pogge von Strandmann (eds), *Deutschland – Großbritannien – Europa*, Bochum, pp. 105–24.

Feldenkirchen, Wilfried (1990), 'Unternehmensfinanzierung in der deutschen Elektroindustrie der Zwischenkriegszeit', in Dietmar

Petzina (ed.) *Zur Geschichte der Unternehmensfinanzierung*, Berlin, pp. 42–7.

Fennema, M. (1982), *International Networks of Banks and Industry*, The Hague/Boston.

Fürstenberg, Hans (1965), *Erinnerungen*, Wiesbaden.

Gehr, Martin (1960), *Das Verhältnis der Banken zur Industrie in Deutschland 1850–1931*, PhD, University of Tübingen.

Geiger, Helmut (1975), *Bankpolitik*, Stuttgart.

Gerhards, Michael (1982), *Die Industriebeziehungen der westdeutschen Banken*, Frankfurt.

Gerschenkron, Alexander (1966), *Economic Backwardness in Historical Perspective*, Cambridge, MA.

Gossweiler, Kurt (1971), *Großbanken-Industriemonopole-Staat*, Berlin.

Gossweiler, Kurt (1988), 'Die Rolle der Großbanken im Imperialismus', in idem, *Aufsätze zum Faschismus*, Cologne.

Greenwald, Bruce, Stiglitz, Joseph E. and Weiss, Andrew (1984), 'Informational Imperfections in the Capital Market and Macroeconomic Fluctuations', in *AER, Papers and Proceedings*, 74: 194–200.

Hagemann, Wilhelm (1930), *Das Verhältnis der deutschen Großbanken zur Industrie*, Berlin.

Hardach, Gerd (1984), 'Banking and Industry in Germany in the Interwar Period 1919–1939', *Journal of European Economic History*, 13 (2).

Hein, Manfred and Flöter, Helmut (1975), 'Macht der Banken – Folgerungen aus der bisherigen Diskussion', *WSI-Mitteilungen*, 28 (7).

Hilferding, Rudolf (1968), *Das Finanzkapital*, Frankfurt.

Horstmann, Theo (1991), *Die Alliierten und die deutschen Großbanken*, Bonn.

Hummel, G. (1972), 'Zur Rolle der Banken im Imperialismus', *Wirtschaftswissenschaften*, 20.

Hughes, Thomas (1983), *Networks of Power*, Baltimore, MD.

Irmler, Hans (1976), 'Bankenkrise und Vollbeschäftigungspolitik (1931–1936)', in Deutsche Bundesbank (ed.), *Währung und Wirtschaft in Deutschland 1876–1975*, Frankfurt, pp. 284–90.

James, Harold (1984), 'The Causes of the German Banking Crisis of 1931', *EcHR*, 37: 68–87.

Jürgens, Ulrich and Lindner, Gisela (1974), 'Zur Funktion und Macht der Banken', *Kursbuch*, 36: 121–60.

Kennedy, William P. (1987), *Industrial Structure, Capital Markets and the Origins of British Economic Decline*, Cambridge.

Kennedy, William P. (1988) 'Capital Markets and Economic

Development in Germany and Great Britain in the Late Nineteenth Century. Lessons for Today?', in Adolf M. Birke and Lothar Kettenacker (eds), *Wettlauf in die Moderne*, Munich.

Kennedy, William, P. (1991), 'Portfolio Behavior and Economic Development in Late Nineteenth Century Great Britain and Germany: Hypothesis and Conjectures', *REH Suppl.* 6: 93–130.

Kirdorf, Emil (1906) Speech in *Vereins für Socialpolitik, Verhandlungen der Generalversammlung in Mannheim 1905*, Leipzig.

Kumpmann, Karl (1910), *Die Entstehung der Rheinischen Eisenbahngesellschaft 1830–1844*, Essen.

Moesch, Irene and Simmert, Diethart (1976), *Banken: Strukturen, Macht, Reformen*, Cologne.

Pappi, Franz Urban, Kappelhoff, Peter and Melbeck, Christian (1987), 'Die Struktur der Unternehmensverflechtung in der Bundesrepublik', *KZSS (Kölner Zeitschrift fur Soziologie und Socialpsychologie)*, 39: 693–717.

Plumpe, Gottfried (1990), *Die I. G. Farbenindustrie*, Berlin.

Pohl, Manfred (1975), 'Zerschlagung und Wiederaufbau der deutschen Großbanken, 1945–1957', *Beiträge zu Wirtschafts- und Währungsfragen und zur Bankgeschicte*, 13: 31.

Pritzkoleit, Kurt (1961), *Auf einer Woge von Gold*, Vienna.

Rettig, Rudi (1978), *Das Investitions- und Finanzierungsverhalten deutscher Großunternehmen, 1880–1911*, PhD., University of Münster.

Ross, Duncan (1990), 'The Clearing Banks and Industry: New Perspectives on the Interwar Years', in Youssef Cassis and J. J. van Helten (eds), *Capitalism in a Mature Economy*, Aldershot.

Schuster, Leo (1977), *Macht und Moral der Banken*, Bern.

Shonfield, Andrew (1965), *Modern Capitalism*, Oxford.

Stiglitz, Joseph E. (1985), 'Credit Markets and the Control of Capital', *Journal of Money, Credit and Banking*, 17.

Stiglitz, Joseph E. and Weiss, Andrew (1981), 'Credit Rationing in Markets with Imperfect Information', *AER*, 71: 393–410.

Thomas, William A. (1978), *The Finance of British Industry 1918–1976*, London.

Tilly, Richard (1986), 'Financing Industrial Enterprise in Great Britain and Germany in the Nineteenth Century: Testing Grounds for Marxist and Schumpeterian Theories?', in J. W. Drukker and H. J. Wagener (eds.), *The Economic Law of Motion in Modern Society*, Cambridge.

Tilly, Richard (1992), 'Zur Entwicklung der deutschen Universalbanken im 19. und 20. Jahrhundert: Wachstumsmotor oder Machtkartell?', in Sidney Pollard and Dieter Ziegler (eds), *Markt, Staat, Planung*, St

Katharinen.

Tilly, Richard (1993), 'Geschaftsbanken und Wirtschaft in Westdeutschland seit dem Zweiten Weltkrieg', in Eckart Schremmer (ed.), *Geld und Währung vom 16. Jahrhundert bis zur Gegenwart*, Stuttgart, pp. 315–43.

Uferman, Paul (1925), *Könige der Inflation*, Berlin.

Usoskin, Vladimir (1975), 'Finanzkapital und Finanzoligarchie im heutigen Kapitalismus', in *IPW-Berichte*, 10.

Weber, Max (1976), *Wirtschaft und Gessellschaft*, Tübingen.

Wellhöner, Volker (1989), *Großbanken und Großindustrie im Kaiserreich*, Göttingen.

Wessel, Horst, A. (1990), 'Finanzierungsprobleme in der Gründungs- und Ausbauphase der Deutsch-Österreichischen Mannesmannröhren-Werke AG, 1890–1907', in Dietmar Petzina (ed.), *Zur Geschichte der Unternehmensfinanzierung*, Berlin.

Wessel, Horst A. (1991), *Kontinuität in Wandel. 100 Jahre Mannesmann*, Düsseldorf.

Wieser, Carl Wolfgang von (1919), *Der finanzielle Aufbau der englischen Industrie*, Jena, pp. 460–74.

Wittkowski, Margaret (1937), *Großbanken und Industrie in Deutschland 1924–31*, Tampere.

Wixforth, Harald (1990), 'Unternehmensfinanzierung dursch Banken – ein Hebel zur Etablierung der Bankenherrschaft?', in Dietmar Petzina (ed.), *Zur Geschichte der Unternehmensfinanzierung*, Berlin.

Wixforth, Harald (1991), *Banken und Schwerindustrie in der Weimarer Republik*, unpublished PhD. thesis, University of Bielefeld.

Wixforth, Harald and Ziegler, Dieter (1994 forthcoming), 'The Niche in the Universal Banking System: The Role and Significance of Private Bankers in German Industry 1900–1933', *Financial History Review*.

Ziegler, Rolf (1984), 'Das Netz der Personen- und Kapitalverflechtungen deutscher und österreichischer Wirtschaftsunternehmen', *Kölner Zeitschrift für Soziologie und Sozialpsychologie*, 36: 585–615.

Ziegler, Dieter (1994 forthcoming), 'The Origins of the Macmillan Gap: Comparing Britain and Germany in the Early Twentieth Century', in Philip L. Cottrell, Alice Teichova and T. Yuzawa (eds), *Finance and Industry in the Age of the Corporate Economy: Britain and Japan*, Leicester.

CHAPTER TWELVE

Information, Collateral and British Bank Lending in the 1930s[1]

Duncan M. Ross

The British economy in the 1930s is – despite the upturn of 1933–37 – usually represented as having performed poorly in an international context. This poor performance can be seen particularly in the framework of structural change and the very slow, delayed and reluctant emergence of a corporate economy centred on the industries of the 'second industrial revolution' such as had emerged in the United States in the period between the 1890s and 1920s (Chandler, 1977,1990; Gourvish, 1987). The 'new industries for old' debate on Britain in the interwar years has long been settled in favour of the continued dominance of the old, staple and long-established industries in the period before rearmament began to provide its usual shot in the arm for technologies and management structures which were essentially obsolete (Alford, 1981).

The charge of slow change is a powerful one, too, when applied to those industries which continued to dominate the manufactured export earnings, employment levels and psyche of the British economy. The saga of rationalization and its failures is well-known, as are the largely unsuccessful attempts of Montagu Norman at the Bank of England to promote restructuring in the steel, cotton and other industries (Sayers, 1976; Bowden and Collins, 1992).

The search for an explanation of these phenomena – which are assumed to be closely linked since the fragmented and atrophied structure of the staple industries acted as a significant barrier to the release of potentially productive resources for investment elsewhere in the economy – has focused on a number of possibilities. The institutional sclerosis arguments of Elbaum and Lazonick have, for example, recently gained considerable currency (Elbaum and Lazonick, 1986; Kirby, 1992). Perhaps the most enduring of these criticisms has been the perceived failure of the financial system in Britain to provide either the capital or the leadership required to effect fundamental change in the economy (Best and Humphries, 1986; Cain and Hopkins, 1993).

This argument has generally taken one of two forms, and occasionally both. In the first place, the historic preference of the British banking system for short-term overdrafts, repayable on demand, is seen as both depriving British industry of a source of long-term capital analogous to that provided by the Universal Banks of the Continent, and at the same time introducing a considerable degree of uncertainty (and therefore short-termism) to the investment process itself. The second focus of this argument has been the role of banks as major creditors of British industry in the interwar years. High levels of customer indebtedness put the banks in a unique and powerful position to enforce rationalization or industry-wide restructuring in individual borrowers or sectorally-concentrated groups of firms. That the banks failed to use their position and take such initiatives has been cited as an example of organizational conservatism and entrepreneurial failure in the financial sector (Tolliday, 1987; Bamberg, 1988). After citing a number of occasions on which the banks became involved in rescue operations, or pursued liberal lending policies of support for their beleaguered industrial customers, Michael Collins concluded that these were exceptions and that the banks, when dealing with industrial lending, 'continued to emphasize liquidity, remained at the short end of the money market' and charged high rates of interest for their loans. The support granted in these exceptional cases 'entailed acquiring a more detailed knowledge of their client's [sic] businesses than was normal for English banks' (Collins, 1988: 258–9).

The nature and operation of the European banking and financial sector before 1939 has recently been subject to a great deal of comment and analysis (James et al., 1991; Cottrell et al., 1992). This work has produced two major conclusions; in the first place the British capital markets in the late 19th and early 20th centuries were significantly different from those to be found elsewhere in Europe. Second, the individual institutions in these markets were reasonably efficient.[2] In short; British banks were not like German banks, but they were good at what they did. The specialization which was such a feature of the London capital markets meant that the British banks offered a much narrower range of services to their customers than their counterparts in Europe. The issuing and underwriting of stock, provision of long-term finance, and other services which were standard aspects of Universal banks' business, were each performed by separate, highly specialized institutions in the London market (Grant, 1967; Michie, 1988). The niche which belonged to the clearing banks was that dictated by custom, practice and their role as deposit-collectors; short-term provision of liquidity on a non-interference, non-responsibility basis.

The traditional approach to the relationship between the banks and their customers has concentrated on the mechanism for the supply of funds. This is despite the well-documented features of the typical British industrial unit – small, single-site, relying on internal finance for investment with the prospects for expansion constrained by the limited imagination of owner-managers unwilling to dilute shareholding, which meant that there was little demand for reform or extension of banking products into the corporate finance area. The narrow range of services and limited points of contact are held to illustrate the banks' disdain for industrial lending in general and their industrial customers in particular. It is in this presumed disdain, and their consequent unwillingness or inability to take the leading role in encouraging restructuring and rationalization that the banks are said to have failed British industry in the interwar years (Best and Humphries, 1986; Newton and Porter, 1988). This raises a number of interesting questions, such as the point at which the costs of internalization and complexity exceed economies of scale and scope in an industry such as banking and the institutional environment which might define that point. It is the bank–customer relationship and the implied levels of separation which will, however, be focused on here. In particular, this paper will explore the extent to which the bank–customer relationship can be characterized as one in which the former had little information on and knowledge of, the latter.

A model of bank lending with information asymmetry

The literature on the economics of banking has recently made significant advances in developing an understanding of the nature of the intermediation process, and of the role of banks in transferring funds from savers to borrowers. There has not been, however, a concomitant reappraisal of the historical role of banks in the financing of industrial activity. In particular, there is a paradox in that as theoretical and financial literature has identified the ability of banks to exploit economies of information as delegated monitors as a key explanation for their existence, the historical literature has continued to stress the separation between British banks and their industrial customers and to use this separation as an explanation for poor economic performance.

The fundamental role of financial intermediaries is to minimize the transactions costs associated with the transfer of financial resources from individual borrowers to individual lenders. They do this by offering a range of liabilities designed to attract funds which can then be offered to borrowers on terms which they (the borrowers) find attractive. In order to ensure a steady stream of income to meet their liabilities, intermediaries manage their assets in such a way as to minimize the variance of returns from their investments. Financial intermediation according to this simple view, therefore, becomes a process of risk diversification and portfolio management (Goodhart, 1989: Ch. 5).

This view was first augmented by the work of Leland and Pyle (1977), who showed that informational asymmetries between borrowers and lenders are of crucial importance in any analysis of the role of financial intermediaries. In an environment characterized by incomplete contracts, the borrower knows more about the likelihood of default than the lender and there therefore exists uncertainty about the outcome of investments. The specific role of financial intermediaries in conditions of uncertainty has been redefined as the reduction of these asymmetries by developing expertise in information gathering and analysis. Individuals delegate the tasks of appraisal, investigation and monitoring of a loan project, as well as verifying the outcome, to financial institutions, which are able to combine their expertise with economies of scale and reduce the costs associated with this process (Diamond, 1984; Williamson, 1986; Hillier and Ibrahimo, 1993). The extent to which information asymmetries can be reduced, however, is clearly limited. The costs of reducing them – and therefore the risk of insolvency – to zero would greatly exceed the marginal benefits of doing so.

The particular nature of banks' loan portfolios exposes them to the risk of not only insolvency, but also illiquidity. Banks specialize in non-marketable loans which have a very high degree of information asymmetry and they therefore develop considerable expertise in assessing applications for credit and in monitoring the performance of a loan throughout its life. One of the characteristics of the relationship between banker and customer, however, is privacy – which is necessary to protect customer confidentiality and possible competitive advantages – and so the information gathered during the monitoring process remains the private knowledge of the banker. Bank creditors (depositors), in contrast to those of financial institutions specializing in marketable security investment (such as investment or unit trusts and insurance companies) have no way of monitoring the performance of a bank's loan portfolio.[3] They will therefore not accept returns to their deposits which are contingent on this performance. A fixed-interest debt contract, then, becomes the optimal form of bank deposit. The repayable on demand nature of this debt is a crucial incentive to the banks to perform their tasks of delegated monitoring and risk minimization effectively (Calomiris and Khan, 1991). As noted above, however, there are constraints on how far this process can be pursued and the risk of loss is always present. This risk of loss, in a fractional reserve banking system, implies that, faced with a run on their deposits, banks may very quickly find themselves unable to meet the demand for repayment.

Banks can protect themselves from this risk of loss in a number of ways. The most obvious response to the asymmetries in the lending market would be to charge very high interest rates on loans, in an attempt to discourage all but the most sure of success from borrowing. There are, however, considerable problems attached to such an approach. The literature on credit rationing has shown that in a market with asymmetric information there is an interest rate above which it would be uneconomic for a bank to enter into any loan contracts, even if there were potential borrowers willing to pay higher rates (Stiglitz and Weiss, 1981; Stiglitz, 1987). There are two factors which explain this phenomenon. On the one hand, creditworthy borrowers would be able to obtain funds at a lower rate elsewhere and would therefore drop out of the market (the adverse selection effect) and, on the other hand, the high interest rate would attract high-risk projects (the adverse incentive effect). The average risk profile of the bank's loan portfolio would therefore rise significantly, and the bank's expected return would fall. The optimal response of a bank faced with a demand for loans schedule which could place them in a potentially illiquid situation, therefore, is not to raise the interest rate but to ration credit.

The crucial question in this case becomes how, in conditions of information asymmetry, do banks set about rationing credit? One answer given has been that any firm unable to provide collateral security to the bank, which the bank could use to offset any losses from the loan, will not receive finance. The shortcomings of the literature on collateral are well known, however. In much of this work borrowers have unlimited access to collateral which is used either to overcome asymmetric project valuations of borrower and lender or to increase the funding available (Chan and Kanatas, 1985; Chan and Thakor, 1987). In this view loans serve only to overcome temporary liquidity problems rather then add to the real resources at the firm's disposal. The peculiarity of this is that it is possible to find banks lending on projects which they expect not to succeed, because they are able to get unlimited collateral from the borrower (De Meza and Webb, 1987). Where collateral constraints are imposed, borrowers signal the risk associated with the project by a combination of collateral provision and interest rate, where these are inversely related (Besanko and Thakor, 1987). The very wide spectrum of possible interest rates and combinations of price and security which would result from such an approach appears to be unworkable. It is also, of course, unlikely that bankers would see collateral as a substitute for a safe return on the loan. The liquidation and disposal costs act as an incentive for the bank to reject loan proposals, the merits of which they are not convinced of, even if adequate collateral is available.

The third important way in which banks might be able to reduce the possible exposure to loss on their lending portfolio is by a reduction in the information asymmetries in the loan contract itself. This is derived from the importance of banks' role as delegated monitors and the powerful incentive structure designed to encourage effectiveness in that function. Here, collateral has a much more sophisticated and important role to play.

Calomiris and Hubbard (1991) note that characteristics of different firms vary. For some firms – those with very high levels of internal net worth and/or very sound public reputations – the transactions costs involved in the bank formally taking collateral may be higher than the perceived benefits (that is, the risk of loss on the loan). In these cases, collateral will not be required by the banks. For other firms – those having high levels of information intensity – there will be little information on which to base the lending decision (that is, there are large information asymmetries between prospective borrowers and lenders) and the role of collateral as a device to aid the bank in its role as a delegated monitor becomes of crucial importance.

There are, in this view, a differentiated range of borrowers and conditions. In the first case, that of extreme information intensity, the bank may be unable to make a decision on the firm's likelihood of default on the loan. It is also difficult to identify the means by which the bank can undertake effectively the process of monitoring, which is crucial to protection of its depositors. In an attempt to solve this problem, two fundamental principles of information intensive loan contracts have been developed.[4] The first is that the banks should only lend up to a maximum proportion of the entire funding needed, the remainder to be found by the company. The proportion provided by the company must be sufficient to cover any loss incurred in the project – which will therefore be borne by the company and not the bank. This is so for two reasons. First, an inability to provide working capital in itself provides a number of signals about the liquidity and possible insolvency of the firm. Second, moral hazard becomes increasingly important since the temptation for default will increase at the same rate as the firm's contribution to the project declines. For these reasons, the bank will demand that the firm provide a minimum amount of working capital to the project and without this minimum – which will reflect the bank's perception of the risk involved in the project – no loan will be made.

The second principle is that loans should be self-liquidating. Lending on the security of stock purchased or bills for goods ordered greatly reduces the banks' risk of loss. In an industrial environment, this has been interpreted as meaning that bank loans may be made for the purposes of current expenditure, but not for capital investment. The rationale for this is linked to the repayable-on-demand nature of bank liabilities; it is important for them to avoid long-term commitment of funds which they may be required to repay (Dacey, 1958: 91; Thomas,

1978). Information-asymmetric lending, then, should be focused on working capital and should be self-liquidating. Collateral accepted by the bank as security for the loan should then be associated with the particular project for which the loan is made. This is justified by the consideration that if collateral is directly related to the project, it provides information on the inputs and outputs, suppliers and customers of the project as well as its progress, since funds will only be made available to the borrower once they have actually entered into the production process. The bank therefore also has a means of assessing the productivity of the firm's spending, and ensuring that the funds supplied are in fact being used for the purposes agreed. Collateral used in this way helps the bank overcome the asymmetries associated with the information intensity of some firms and is integral to the process of monitoring the loan. There is a further justification for this. In information asymmetric conditions, the bank knows nothing about the outcome of previous projects or the company's financial position or prospects. Tying the loan to the current project makes sense, since that is the only aspect of the company's business that the bank has any knowledge of. If the bank has made a (however incompletely informed) commercial judgement that the project is likely to be successful, it may feel that its depositors' money is fairly safe.

In cases where the information intensity is less complete, the bank is able, using either public reputation, internal net worth grounds, or, in the multi-period case, the outcomes of previous projects (Diamond, 1989) to make a judgement on the likelihood of loss on the loan, and it will accept as security additional, unrelated assets. What is in effect happening here is that the bank is substituting additional lending secured on additional information for some of the working capital provision of the firm (with the constraint noted above that the bank should never provide all the funds required for any one project). The minimum working capital contribution of the firm should decline at approximately the same rate as the information asymmetry. The latter, of course, will never actually reach zero, but there will be a point at which symmetric-information conditions are approximated. The firms at this point are those which Calomiris and Hubbard characterize as having extremely sound public reputations and/or very high levels of internal net worth. It is here that the transactions costs associated with the formal process of collateral appraisal and acceptance will be higher than the benefits – that is, the bank's perception of the risk of loss on the loan. It is clear from this discussion that the higher the level of information asymmetry, the higher the bank will perceive the potential for risk of loss to be.

The structure of British bank lending in the 1930s

The framework developed in the previous section can be used to reach a better understanding of the British banks' behaviour in the interwar years. In particular, the levels of information asymmetry which prevailed in their relationships with industrial customers can be explored.

Institutional factors are often important in relating the observed behaviour of organizations to the theoretical constructs designed to illuminate that behaviour. This is so for the British banks in two important ways. The first is that opportunities for adverse selection in what appears to be essentially a monopolistic cartel are necessarily limited. The small number of large banks which dominated the system, organized through the 'magic circle' of the Committee of London Clearing Bankers, had considerable market power and were able, to some extent, to select their chosen customers. The absence of vigorous competition in the banking market meant that there were few alternatives for those who might have been able to gain access to cheaper funds elsewhere (Griffiths, 1973). A very powerful market position would allow the banks to set a horizontal supply curve above the market rate. The information characteristics of those demanding credit would become irrelevant.

The force of this observation is somewhat reduced, however, by two considerations. The first is that it is by no means clear that price was the sole determinant of the demand for credit in this period. Other factors, such as availability of funds or the firm's perception of the need for, or possible profit from, the investment may have been equally important (Ross, 1992). Despite this, the banks themselves perceived adverse selection as having a serious impact on their lending business in the 1930s (Midland Bank, 1936). This may or may not have been the case, but it reveals the second consideration; a monopolistic cartel may have existed in the banking sector, but this did not provide a monopoly over the entire range of credit provision. Alternative sources of finance were available in this period, either through trade credit or other informal avenues, borrowing from insurance companies or by raising capital on the new issue market. In addition, many industrial companies were highly liquid in this period. The banks were not monopolistic price setters.

The second important observation which should be made about the institutional structure of the British credit market relates to the form which bank provision of finance generally took. In the theoretical literature discussed above, loans are assumed to be made on a 'one loan per project' basis, where each project operates, and is assessed, independently. In the general case, the bank has no knowledge of previous projects or their outcome. In those models which include previous performance, the individual project remains the focus of the bank's lending decision. The bank credit market in Britain, where loans were seldom made on an individual project, but on an overdraft system, does not conform to these views. Generally, an agreed credit limit would be established between bank and firm and the firm could borrow funds up to that limit whenever they needed it, for whatever purpose. The entire amount of the overdraft could be used at any one time, or a small proportion. These overdrafts were repayable on demand, with the facility being reviewed each six months or so. In fact this was a purely nominal condition; it is well established that overdrafts were routinely renewed, the relationship often lasting for decades (Munn, 1988). A more formal review would usually be required, however, if the borrower requested an increase in the available funds.

This form of lending has the important characteristic of providing the bank with information on its customers. The long-term relationship between the bank and its customer clearly reduces the level of information asymmetry present at any review of the facility. A check on how long the overdraft has been available to the borrower, the extent to which it has been used and any violations of the agreed ceiling – as well as the bank's knowledge of the macroeconomic conditions affecting the particular industry in which the customer was engaged – could provide important clues to the bank on the likelihood of loss in the future. The potential levels of information asymmetry were, therefore, significantly reduced by the form which bank lending typically took in Britain.

Applying the model to the British case

When banks provide finance on a long-term overdraft system, the borrower will tend to absorb the agreed amount of credit into their expectations of available funds. Overdraft limits often became, not the maximum which the bank felt could be safely lent, but the minimum level of credit which the company needed to operate. Any increase in the necessary level of working capital (for example in response to a new order for the company's product), would then be passed directly on to the bank in the form of a request for an increased overdraft limit (Macmillan, 1930). One of the characteristics of the bank–customer relationship in interwar Britain was that by supplying long-term funding, without which it is clear that many firms could not have survived (or which would have had to be replaced from alternative sources) the banks encouraged their customers to view overdrafts as an integral component of their balance sheet (Collins, 1991: 76–9).

This situation has some interesting implications for the monitoring process and the role of collateral in the loan contract. The loans were, as noted above, being made in an environment of less than complete information intensity and, since the overdrafts were absorbed into the company's financial position, it is difficult to identify individual project outcomes on which they could be secured.

The amount and nature of collateral security which the banks insisted upon for their loans reveals much of their attitude towards industrial lending. Table 12.1 shows the results of a survey of 75 firms which banked with the Midland and Lloyds in the 1930s.[5] They were of various sizes, were taken from a number of different regions and engaged in a disparate range of activities. They should not be considered as a representative sample of either the banks' lending portfolio or the industrial structure of Britain.

The types of security reveal a flexible approach by the banks, as well as the impact that the structure of lending had on the loan contract. In the long-term lending situation, credit was being extended to the company or the entrepreneur rather than to a single project which could be considered on its individual merits. The absence of the minimum working capital contribution of the firm to individual projects meant that the moral hazard problem was potentially acute, and the penalties for default were therefore designed to have an impact which would reach beyond the consequences of a loss on any individual loan and affect the company's ability to engage in future projects in a way that simple failure of one project would not. The nature of the collateral, moreover, indicates that the loans were not information intensive.

The most common form of security for a loan was the guarantee – either in the form of a personal guarantee of an entrepreneur, the joint

Table 12.1   Forms of collateral used as security

guarantee	21
mortgage	17
debenture	14
shares	8
government paper	5
promissory notes	2
property	2
ships	2
charge on assets	1

Source: see text.

and several guarantee of the directors of the borrowing company, or, in some cases, the corporate guarantee of a large customer or parent company. The next most common form of security was a mortgage over the assets of the company, closely followed by debentures. These two were similar, in that in most cases the debentures were secured on the physical assets of the company. Following debentures, shares were also used as security, as were government paper and gilt-edged securities, promissory notes, property, ships and a charge on assets, which appears separately from the mortgages and debentures.

The role of mortgages and debentures as security is interesting, since they were to some extent a formalization of the debt which the borrower had contracted. They also gave the bank considerable control over the borrower, since the banks were usually careful to ensure that they had first charge over the company's assets. Here, it is clear that the banks were structuring the contract in such a way as to ensure that the penalties for default on the loan were very serious for the operation of the company. It was not unknown, for example, for debentures to be issued to the bank for a short period in which the company's overdraft might exceed their customary limit. These would be surrendered when 'normal' operation of the account resumed. In the case of debentures, the existence of a secondary market also made them an attractive form of security since they could be sold. They were, in this sense, more liquid than the non-marketable debt contract which an overdraft represented but this also had negative aspects, in that any attempt to sell debentures might provide negative market signals and reduce their ultimate value. Further, realization of these assets in the event of default on the loan could involve considerable costs and delays for the bank. Their role as a prime form of collateral for a bank overdraft was therefore severely constrained.

There was also a range of attractiveness for the bank in accepting shares as security. Clearly, an equity holding in the indebted company itself was not an attractive option for the bank, since in many cases this exposed the bank to a double risk. If the firm were to default on a loan, the value of the shares would obviously fall considerably. This type of security was, accordingly, only accepted by the bank where other forms were unavailable – a situation which in turn provided important information on the general state of the company. Of more use to the bank would be shares in a profitable or well-known parent, or a portfolio of shares unrelated to the borrower in any way. These cases were both observed in the sample. The availability of a ready market for such security made it more attractive to the bank.

The next category of security – government paper – refers to holdings of such things as War Loans, Victory Bonds and gilt-edged securities.

These were clearly a satisfactory form of collateral from the bank's point of view, since they could be easily sold and were therefore significantly more liquid than many of the other types of collateral. Holdings of property as security is clearly similar to mortgages. This, again, has the advantage of giving the bank a powerful position in negotiations and ensuring that default has very serious consequences for the firm. It also, however, has significant disadvantages inherent in the nature of property ownership – the land or buildings may have very little value other than that associated with the company, and the banks' ability to sell it or obtain rent from any alternative use may be seriously restricted.

One of the key aspects of the less liquid forms of collateral, with the partial exception of ship mortgages, is that they do not represent currently-generated security, but rather additional assets of the firm. The requirement established above for this type of lending was that the bank should have additional information available on which it can make a commercial decision on the likelihood of repayment. The long-term relationships which were typical of bank lending in this system would provide this information when a formal review of the overdraft facility was carried out. Regular, in-depth interviews with managers and partners, detailed analysis of balance sheets and trading results, intimate knowledge of the state of a firm's relations with customers, suppliers, etc. and cognizance of the independent wealth of those signing guarantees were typical and crucial features of these relationships.

Further evidence that it was these sources of information on which the banks relied to reduce the levels of information asymmetry in their lending business can be found in consideration of the extent to which the banks were secured, as shown in Table 12.2.

Table 12.2 was derived by comparing the overdraft limit with the value of all the security held by the bank. It was fairly common practice

Table 12.2   Percentage of overdraft secured by collateral

% secured	no. of firms	% of firms in sample
0	22	29.3
1–20	5	6.7
21–40	4	5.3
41–60	5	6.7
61–80	5	6.7
81–99	4	5.3
100 and above	30	40.0

Source: see text.

for the firms to offer more than one form of collateral, and the bank would often note what they valued the cover to be. Where the bank had provided a valuation of the security, this was the one used; otherwise, the face-value figure was accepted. Since the bank's valuation was usually considerably lower than that of the borrower, Table 12.2 will probably be biased towards the upper ranges to the extent that face-value information was more often available than bank valuations. The costs of liquidation and the nature of the collateral itself add to this impression, since a personal guarantee may be almost valueless in the event of a bankruptcy. Despite the underestimation of the banks' exposure to risk contained in the table, it remains the case that 60 per cent of the overdrafts in the sample were less than fully covered by collateral.

There are two possible explanations for this behaviour. The first is that many of these firms were of such internal net worth that the transactions costs of taking collateral outweighed the benefits of doing so. If there is an inverse relationship between the net worth of the company and the percentage of the overdraft secured, it would appear that the available financial information was sufficient to enable the banks to tailor their collateral demands appropriately. Figures 12.1 and 12.2 are a first attempt to explore this. They plot the asset values of those firms for which this could be obtained (in some cases provided by the bank, in others taken from the company's balance sheet) against the extent to which their overdraft was secured by collateral. Figure 12.1 includes all firms in the sample; Figure 12.2 excludes the distorting effects of those firms with asset values in excess of £1 million.

Given the quality of the data and the limited sample on which these graphs are constructed, care is needed in interpreting the results. What can be said, however, is that they show no discernible relationship between the two variables. It is difficult to argue, therefore, that, based on this evidence, the banks were modifying their collateral requirements in line with available information on the internal net worth of their customers.

The second possible explanation for the banks' behaviour in this period might lie in the liquidity position of the banks themselves. Throughout the 1930s, they operated at very low advances to total assets ratios. While in the years 1924 to 1929, this had fluctuated between 41 and 48 per cent, between 1933 and 1937 the range had fallen to 34–6 per cent. Far from being exposed to illiquidity through the reckless nature of their loans, the banks could be held to be in an overly safe – and therefore unprofitable – position. The Midland Bank in 1936, clearly worried about this situation, instituted a major enquiry into the causes of the decline of its industrial advances business (Midland Bank, 1936), while in the same year the National Provincial stressed to its

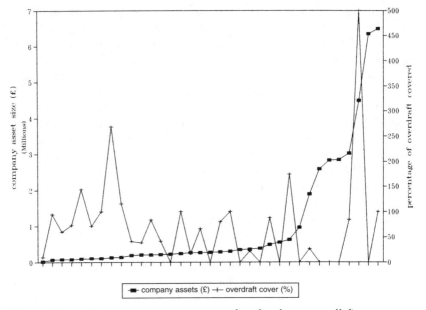

Figure 12.1   Company assets compared to bank cover: all firms.

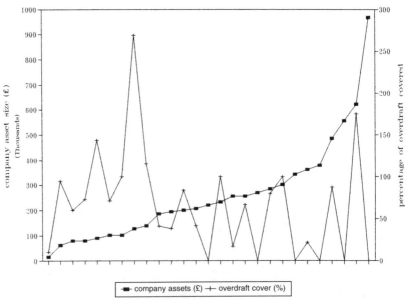

Figure 12.2   Company assets compared to bank cover: asset size <£1m.

branch managers the need to expand their lending and attract new business. The extent of their willingness to accept less than full security on their loans may simply have reflected the banks' attempts to expand their business by sanctioning loan applications which in less liquid periods they would have rejected.

Some support for this position can be found in the protestations of bankers such as Beaumont-Pease who maintained that levels of credit-worthiness were being relaxed in the 1930s in an attempt to entice borrowers (Lloyds Bank, 1936). There are clear limits to such behaviour, however. The example of the post-First World War boom, when profligate lending resulted in heavy losses in a number of sectors, served as a cautionary reminder to bank managers of the perils of too much relaxation. High levels of provision for bad and doubtful debts continued to provide some cause for concern in the 1930s (Holmes and Green, 1986: 189–90). Profits in British banking were the worst performing of all sectors in the economy after 1933 (Capie and Webber, 1985: 62). It is unlikely that the banks would have responded to these conditions by significantly reducing the quality or quantity of collateral acceptable for any loans. High levels of liquidity certainly encouraged increased lending, but in order to increase profitability, this lending had the condition that it should be of better quality than that which had prevailed in the previous period. The historian of Lloyds Bank has noted that under Pease the bank's lending policies were actually characterized more by caution than by adventure (Winton, 1982: 64).

Information asymmetry has emerged in this discussion as the key problem for banks operating in a credit market. In order to perform effectively the particular type of financial intermediation in which they specialize, they need to develop ways of protecting themselves from the possibility of loss inherent in the incomplete and information-asymmetric nature of the loan contract. They can do this either by ensuring that their estimate of the risk of loss on each loan is covered by collateral or by structuring each loan in such a way as to reduce the asymmetry. The British banks clearly adopted the latter. The overdraft form of lending, because it was often absorbed into the borrower's expectations of available funding, gave rise to considerable security, moral hazard and monitoring problems for the bank. The primary advantage which it entailed, however, was the provision to the bank of a steady stream of information on the company which could at any time be augmented by a formal review of the facility. Had the latter aspect not outweighed the former, the illiquid, partly-secured loans which were typical of much banking business would have posed a much greater threat to the banks' liquidity and profitability than could have been safely maintained. Neither could they be interpreted as a form of loss leader in banking, since the profit position in the 1930s as well as recent experience militated strongly against such an approach. It is hard to escape the conclusion that the banks performed their allotted tasks of information gathering and delegated monitoring effectively.

Bank lending in a market-oriented financial system

Detailed and intimate knowledge of their customers, effective information gathering and reduction of information asymmetry through long-term overdrafts do not, however, completely exonerate the banks of the charges which have been laid against them. It would be possible to argue that, precisely because the banks had good information on their customers and the state of their business, the imperative to take a leading role in reorganization and restructuring was correspondingly strengthened. Further, the importance of long-term relationships and the banks' ability to make informed judgements on the credit-worthiness of a borrower seeking new or increased funds raises crucial questions about the financing of new companies in this period, on which any structural shift in the economy would rest.

That, in some cases, banks in this period had considerable influence over their heavily-indebted customers, is not in doubt. Equally, it is clear that this influence was often used to encourage some reorganization of ownership or management. Lloyds were instrumental in the removal of William Lever from overall control of Lever Brothers in 1920 (Wilson, 1954: 259–60). The Midland Bank, as a prominent member of the creditors' committee of the Austin Motor Company in the 1920s, installed Carl Engelbach 'in sole charge of production, the works drawing office . . . the plant and all works staff' (Church, 1979: 64–5). Tolliday has shown how the strength of the bankers, conferred by the company's indebtedness, was used to push through a merger of Bolckow Vaughan with Dorman Long in the Tyneside steel industry in the 1920s (Tolliday, 1987: 67–9).

The failure of the banks to use this influence more generally and in a wider range of industries is the crux of the rationalizers' argument. But this is to confuse the properties of debt with those of an equity stake in a company. British banks, unlike their Universal counterparts on the Continent, did not take equity stakes in their customers and consequently had no ownership obligations. An efficient and potentially very powerful mechanism for industrial reorganization existed in the British capital market and it is clear that only where the banks considered their depositors' funds to be at risk, were they willing to bring their influence to bear and become involved in restructuring. This approach to rationalization is consistent with the categorization of the British financial system as being market-oriented (Rybczynski, 1984, 1988). One of the features of this type of financial system is that, in normal times, corporations find external finance – whether for expansion or reorganization – by recourse to the capital market. Those providing the finance in exchange for equity or other instrument gain control rights over the company. Only in times of severe financial distress might residual control rights be transferred to institutions holding debt (Berglof, 1990). In a bank-oriented financial system, characterized by large banks with both debt and equity shareholdings, control rights rest in those banks. This was not the case in Britain, and involvement in, and financing of, full-scale rationalization of British industry would have been expensive and fraught with risk for institutions defined by the short-term liability structure of the clearing banks.

One important aspect remains to be considered; the role of banks in financing new firms, or firms in new industries, since it is in this area that structural shift in an economy must take place. Raising capital for a new or small company can be very difficult or prohibitively expensive. In the 1930s it was estimated that the minimum amount that could be raised on the financial market was in the order of £200 000 (Chapman, 1984: 100). This is the root of the Macmillan Committee's famous gap in the provision of finance over the medium term for small and medium-sized companies (Macmillan, 1930: para. 404). Further, it is also well-understood that small companies can experience considerable difficulty when trying to raise loan finance (Binks *et al.*, 1992).

Information once again has a crucial role to play in explaining this difficulty. The absence of a track record or long-term relationship between the borrower and the lender means that high levels of information asymmetry prevail in these contracts. The bank is unable to make an informed judgement on the likely outcome of the loan and will be correspondingly more cautious. Even if collateral is available – which of course is more difficult for a small or new company to provide – it will usually be in the form of additional assets or wealth of the leading individuals associated with the company. A public reputation for credit-worthiness may in this case mitigate the information problems, as will the incentive structure of securing the loan on a house or other personal asset. This latter aspect will be countered by the reduction in limited liability which it entails, however. In addition, moral hazard remains – unscrupulous borrowers may not value their reputation; fraudulent borrowers may have no intention of providing bona fide collateral. The more cautious approach of banks to lending to small or new companies should be understood as sensible protection of their customers' interests (Hutchison and McKillop, 1992).

Conclusion

It is the case that the clearing banks in Britain in the interwar years failed to take the leading role in encouraging rationalization and restructuring in industry. It is also the case that the slow pace of restructuring probably contributed to the poor performance of British industry in the 1930s and perhaps beyond. Any attempt to link these two statements and conclude that the banks were in some way responsible for the poor performance of British industry is mistaken, however, since it rests on two fundamental misunderstandings. The first of these relates to the relationship between banks and their industrial customers; the second to the role of banks in the British financial and credit system.

The case for high levels of information asymmetry in the bank–customer nexus in Britain has often been made. The implications of this case are that the banks took little to do with their industrial customers and lacked the knowledge, information and expertise to encourage rationalization. This view of banks is difficult to reconcile with the position that, in order to perform effectively the particular form of intermediation in which they specialize, they must work to reduce the levels of information asymmetry in the loan contract. It has been shown in this paper that the British banks structured their loans in such a way as to provide themselves with as much information on their customers as they could gather. This information enabled them to operate in a way that, had they been unable to make informed judgements on the credit-worthiness of borrowers, would have resulted in significant losses in the banking sector.

The implications of this position are important, since it clearly removes one possible explanation for the banks' failure to encourage rationalization. To argue that British banks should have used their position as well-informed creditors in the interwar years to enforce changes in industrial operation or structure is to confuse creditor status with ownership obligations. The market-oriented financial system in which the banks operated contained a specialist mechanism for transfer of ownership of industry. Control rights were invested in marketable instruments, and could therefore be traded. The short-term and liquid nature of their liabilities precluded the banks from taking an active role in this function, unless, *in extremis*, they perceived their depositors' funds to be at risk.

Finally, information asymmetries have been shown to provide one explanation for the difficulties which small or new firms might experience when trying to raise equity or loan capital. The absence of a track record of success and/or inability to provide sufficient collateral means that any prudent bank would treat an application from such borrowers with considerable caution. Criticism of banks can take many forms, but prudence should always be one of their characteristics.

Notes

1. This paper was prepared for the Colloquium of the European Association for Banking History, May 1993. I would like to thank the participants, especially Richard Tilly, for their comments. Earlier versions were presented at the Business History Unit, LSE, the Monetary History Group and the economic history seminar at Victoria University of Wellington. Gordon Boyce, Forrest Capie, Leslie Hannah, Leslie Pressnell and Neil Quigley provided helpful comments, criticisms and advice. Lloyds and Midland Banks and their respective archivists, John Booker and Edwin Green, were extremely helpful.
2. An obvious exception to this is Kennedy (1987).
3. Partial monitoring can of course take place through watching a bank's liquidity or reserve ratios, or levels of bad and doubtful debts, but this information is necessarily limited.
4. This approach was originally developed in Quigley (1987).
5. The sources used to construct the sample were: Midland Bank Archives, Management Committee Minutes, volumes 7–26, 1930–39; Lloyds Bank Archives, Board Minute Book, volumes 34–9, 1930–40; Newcastle Area Board Minute Book, branch personal memoranda books, 16,19 (King St Manchester), 2335 (Stirchley), 3276–7 (Aston Road, Birmingham), 3527 (Smethwick), 3846 (Moseley), 3985 (Summerfield), 4012 (Longton), 4015 (Fenton), 4033 (Hanley) and 4035 (Burslem).

References

Alford, B. (1981) 'New industries for old? British industry between the wars', in R.Floud, and D. McCloskey (eds), *The Economic History of Britain Since 1700, volume 2, 1860 to the 1970s*, Cambridge.

Bamberg, J. (1988), 'The rationalization of the British cotton industry in the inter-war years', *Textile History*, 19(1).

Berglof, E. (1990), 'Capital structure as a mechanism of control: a comparison of financial systems', in M. Aoki, B. Gustaffson and O. Williamson (eds), *The Firm as a Nexus of Treaties*, London: Sage.

Besanko, D. and Thakor, A. (1987), 'Collateral and rationing: sorting equilibria in monopolistic and competitive credit markets', *International Economic Review*, 28(3).

Best, M. and Humphries, J. (1986), 'The City and Industrial Decline' in B. Elbaum, and W. Lazonick (eds), *The Decline of the British Economy*, Oxford.

Binks, M., Ennew, C. and Reed, G. (1992), 'Information asymmetries and the provision of finance to small firms', *International Small Business Journal*, 11(1).

Bowden, S. and Collins, M. (1992), 'The Bank of England, industrial regeneration and hire purchase between the wars', *Economic History Review*, 45(1).

Cain, P. and Hopkins, A. (1993), *British Imperialism: Crisis and Deconstruction 1914–1990*, London.

Calomiris, C. and Hubbard, R. (1991), 'Firm heterogeneity, internal finance and credit rationing', *Economic Journal*, 100(1).

Calomiris, C. and Kahn, C. (1991), 'The role of demandable debt in structuring optimal banking arrangements', *American Economic Review*, 81(3).

Capie, F. and Webber, A. (1985), 'Profits and profitability in British banking, 1870–1939'. City University Monetary History Discussion Paper, no.18.

Chan, Y. and Kanatas, G. (1985), 'Asymmetric valuations and the role of collateral in loan agreements', *Journal of Money, Credit and Banking*, 27(1).

Chan, Y. and Thakor, A. (1987), 'Collateral and competitive equilibria with moral hazard and private information', *Journal of Finance*, 42(2).

Chandler, A. (1977), *The Visible Hand: The Managerial Revolution in American Business*, Cambridge, MA.

Chandler, A. (1990), *Scale and Scope: The Dynamics of Industrial Capitalism*, Cambridge, MA.

Chapman, S. (1984), *The Rise of Merchant Banking*, London.

Church, R. (1979), *Herbert Austin: the British Motor Car Industry to 1941*, London.

Collins, M. (1988), *Money and Banking in the UK: A History*, London.

Collins, M. (1991), *Banks and Industrial Finance in Britain 1800–1939*, Basingstoke.

Cottrell, P., Lindgren, H. and Teichova, A. (eds) (1992) *European Industry and Banking Between the Wars*, Leicester.

Dacey, W. (1958) *The British Banking Mechanism*, London.

De Meza, D. and Webb, D. (1987) 'Too much investment: a problem of asymmetric information', *Quarterly Journal of Economics*, 102(3).

Diamond, D. (1984), 'Financial intermediation and delegated monitoring', *Review of Economic Studies*, 51(3).

Diamond, D. (1989), 'Reputation acquisition in debt markets', *Journal of Political Economy*, 97(4).

Elbaum, B. and Lazonick, W. (eds) (1986), *The Decline of the British Economy*, Oxford.

Goodhart, C. (1989), *Money, Information and Uncertainty* (2nd edn),

Basingstoke.

Gourvish, T. (1987), 'British business and the transition to a corporate economy; entrepreneurship and management structures', *Business History*, (19).

Grant, A. (1967), *A Study of the Capital Market in Britain From 1919–1936*, London.

Griffiths, B. (1973), 'The development of restrictive practices in the UK monetary system', *Manchester School*, 61(1).

Hillier, B. and Ibrahimo, M. (1993), 'Asymmetric information and models of credit rationing', *Bulletin of Economic Research*, 45(4).

Holmes, A. and Green, E. (1986), *Midland: 150 Years of Banking Business*, London.

Hutchison, R. and McKillop, D. (1992) 'Banks and small to medium sized businesses in the UK: some general issues', *National Westminster Bank Quarterly Review*, February.

James, H., Lindgren, H. and Teichova, A. (eds) (1991), *The Role of Banks in the Interwar Economy*, Cambridge.

Kennedy, W. (1987), *Industrial Structure, Capital Markets and the Origins of British Economic Decline*, Cambridge.

Kirby, M. (1992), 'Institutional rigidities and economic decline: reflections on the British experience', *Economic History Review*, 55(4).

Leland, H. and Pyle, D. (1977), 'Information asymmetries, financial structure and financial intermediation', *Journal of Finance*, 32(2).

Lloyds Bank (1936), Chairman's annual address to shareholders.

Macmillan (1930), Evidence to the Macmillan Committee of F.Hyde, 9 January, Q981.

Macmillan (1931), *Report of the Committee on Finance and Industry*, Command 3897; London.

Midland Bank (1936), Inquiry into the decline of advances 1931–36, 11 December 1936; Intelligence Department Files, 11/12/1936, Midland Bank Archives.

Michie, R. (1988), 'Different in name only? The London stock exchange and foreign bourses c1850–1914', *Business History*, 30(1).

Munn, C. (1988), *Clydesdale Bank: The First Hundred & Fifty Years*, Glasgow.

Newton, S. and Porter, D. (1988), *Modernization Frustrated: The Politics of Industrial Decline in Britain*, London.

Quigley, N. (1987), 'Credit rationing and collateral', paper presented to the New Zealand Association of Economists' Conference, Christchurch.

Ross, D. (1990) 'The clearing banks and industry – new perspectives on the inter-war years', in J. van Helten and Y. Cassis (eds), *Capitalism in a Mature Economy: Financial Institutions, Capital Exports and British Industry, 1870–1939*, Aldershot.

Ross, D. (1992) 'Bank advances and industrial production in the UK: a red herring', in P. Cottrell, H. Lindgren and A. Teichova (eds), *European Banking and Industry Between the Wars*, Leicester.

Rybczynski, T. (1984), 'Industrial finance system in Europe, U.S. and Japan', *Journal of Economic Behaviour and Organization*, 5(2).

Rybczynski, T. (1988), 'Financial systems and industrial restructuring', *National Westminster Bank Quarterly Review*, November.

Sayers, R. (1976), *The Bank of England 1891–1944*, Cambridge.

Stiglitz. J. (1987), 'The causes and consequences of the dependence of quality on price', *Journal of Economic Literature*, 25(1).

Stiglitz, J. and Weiss, A. (1981), 'Credit rationing in markets with asymmetric information', *American Economic Review*, 71(3).

Thomas, W. (1978), *The Finance of British Industry 1918–1976*, London.

Tolliday, S. (1987), *Business, Banking and Politics: The case of British Steel 1918–1939*, Cambridge, MA.

Williamson, S. (1986), 'Costly monitoring, financial intermediation and equilibrium credit rationing', *Journal of Monetary Economics*, 18(2).

Wilson, C. (1954), *The History of Unilever*, London.

Winton, J. (1982), *Lloyds Bank 1918–1969*, Oxford.

CHAPTER THIRTEEN

Finance in the Regions: The Case of England after 1945[1]

Francesca Carnevali

Introduction

The aim of this chapter is to provide a different perspective from which to approach the much debated question of the relationship between English banks and industry. The question of whether British banks have failed industry has been debated at length by many distinguished scholars. Industry, though, has often been treated as a single, abstract, entity, without specific consideration of the size of the firms within it or of their spatial location. A consequence of this has been to see the relationship between the banks and the firms from an angle that does not take into consideration the effect on this relationship of the problems of location and distance.

What is being argued is that the parallel processes of concentration and (inter-)nationalization of the industrial and banking structure (Hannah and Kay, 1977), which were well under way in England before the Second World War, reduced the direct involvement of the banks in regional-local economies. As the financial intermediaries became more London-centred, the local firms lost much of their importance as customers to the banks. Those local firms for whom the contact with local sources of finance was most crucial were small businesses.[2] As a consequence of this loss of relevance, banks reduced the loan capital available to small firms. The impact of this reduction on the firms' capacity to innovate and remain competitive is dicussed elsewhere.

This chapter looks at the structure and lending activity of three national English banks – Barclays, Midland and Lloyds – and at the lending of one provincial bank, Martins. The object is to identify if the banks' lending activity and choice of customers was influenced by the distance between the periphery (the firms and the branches) and the centre (head offices) and how the exchange of information between these two poles was organized.

The evidence found suggests that Barclays, the bank with the most decentralized (in terms of organization and existence of autonomous peripheral centres) structure and Martins, the provincial bank, restricted credit to smaller local customers to a lesser extent than the other two centralized London banks, Midland and Lloyds. Two explanations for this behaviour have been found. The first one is that a provincial bank, like Martins and autonomous local head offices (such as those of Barclays) would have a strong, direct interest in supporting, to a certain extent, the economy of the region, since their profits depended on the local business activity; the smallness of their market would also not allow them to discriminate against customers. The second explanation is more general and concerns the advantage local decision centres had in terms of lower transaction costs, compared with the centralized London banks, when dealing with local businesses.

Local managers could make decisions on the basis of information, derived from direct and protracted contact with local firms and local economies which would have been too time consuming, that is expensive, to formalize and transmit to London head offices.

This advantage implied a higher propensity to enter transactions with relatively low profit (in absolute terms) customers such as small firms. The reduced transaction costs meant that for local banks or local head offices, small firms were low cost-low profit customers, whereas for the London banks these same customers were classifiable as high cost-low profit ones.

The origins of the detachment of the banks from small firms and regional economies go further back in time than the postwar period. However, this chapter is concerned with the study of a precise historical period, that marked by the credit restrictions imposed on the banks and on industry by the government, under various forms, from the end of the Second World War well into the 1960s. The external impositions on the lending activity of the banks provide a good test to verify if the banks' choice of customers diverged from one bank to another and advance explanations about the link between organizational structures and lending patterns.

To make the argument presented in the paper less abstract, one particular area of England was chosen to see how the banks defined the periphery and how information flows between the periphery and the centre were organized. The area chosen is the Midlands.

This chapter will first define the different boundaries of the 'Midland Region' in terms of the administrative unit considered by the banks. Then the internal structure of the banks will be presented considering how the communication from the periphery (the branches) to the centre (head office) was organized concerning, in specific terms, advances, and, in more general ones, the information about the economy of the region. Subsequently, on the basis of the archival evidence, the impact of these structures on the loan activity of the banks will be analysed verifying also the claim made that the credit restrictions had a negative effect on the availability of finance for small firms.

The Midland district

The maps in Figure 13.1 show the boundaries of the Midlands in 1950 as conceived by the three banks. The banks defined this region differently, both in extent and name. It was called 'Midland Division' at Midland Bank, and 'Birmingham District' both by Barclays and Lloyds. In 1950 Midland had 163 branches in this division,[3] Lloyds 114 (figure for 1948),[4] and Barclays 91.[5] In 1968 the boundaries had not changed greatly but the number of branches had increased. Midland's had grown to 209, Lloyds' to 174[6] and Barclays' to 151 (Tuke and Gillman, 1972).[7]

The difference between the three banks' 'Midlands' does not rest only in the number of branches held in this district/division but also, if not especially, in its geographical boundaries.

The maps show how Barclays and Lloyds adhered most closely to the 'normal' regional boundaries in the definition of the district. Midland Bank instead had a more amorphous, in geographical terms, region, including areas not belonging to the traditional Midland industrial district, like Oxford and Windsor. This meant that Midland Bank did not conceive its districts on the basis of a more or less conscious perception of the existence of a local identity that had to be preserved and reflected by the structure (as Barclays and Lloyds seem to have done), but instead merely as an administrative collection of branches. Lloyds and Barclays also segmented the country more intensively, since, by 1950, Lloyds had formed 10 districts (which had become 16 in 1968) and by 1947 Barclays had 32 (31 in 1968) whereas Midland maintained throughout this period just five broad divisions.

This difference in the banks' concept of 'region' may be due to a precise strategy or simply to the historical development of their structures. To resolve this point the following pages will show how the structure of these banks evolved through time.

The structure of the banks

By the beginning of the 20th century all three banks were firmly established as London banks. Nevertheless they were organized with different degrees of centralization.

The more centralized the structure, the higher the number of applications for advances that had to be processed by the centre would

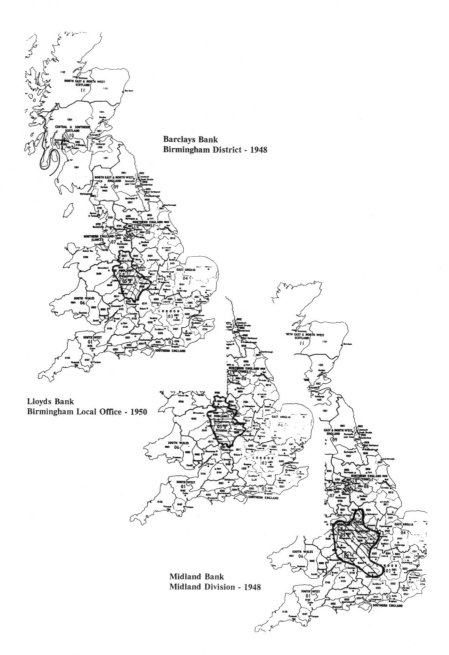

Figure 13.1 Boundaries of the Midlands in 1950 as defined by Barclays, Midland and Lloyds.

be. To contain costs, information had to be formalized in standardized and manageable formats. It is argued here that this effect of centralization had a negative effect on small firms as the personal knowledge of local managers was nullified as the decision by head office to grant an advance had to be based on standardized requirements, out of context from the regional economy. By denying small firms their context it would have been much more difficult for the banks to assess the firms' ability and competitiveness. The transaction costs of assessing this would have been too high compared with the returns brought by loans to this type of customer. Therefore, the small firm would have been considered by the bank solely within the limits of the standardization imposed by cost containment.

In the following pages it will be shown how, by chance and/or strategy, the three banks expanded creating organizations that even though they might look similar were, in fact, quite different, because of the differences in how information flowed and in the location of decision making points.

Midland Bank

The expansion of Midland Bank followed the same pattern as that of its competitors. The bank increased its size and the area over which it operated through subsequent amalgamations with other banks. Following an amalgamation, Midland would select individual directors from the taken over bank and recruit them to the main Board in London. This structure was thought to be the one that would eliminate all differences between the various amalgamated banks and quickly create a homogeneous 'Midland Bank'.

At the beginning of the century Midland was well established as a London bank and, apart from the board of directors, the directing core of the bank was constituted by one managing director and three Joint General Managers. The branches were grouped in divisions each one allocated to a Joint General Manager.[8] The Joint General Managers were assisted by branch superintendents and inspectors.

Apart from the local branch managers all other managerial functions were based in London. Information therefore had to move through communication channels directly from the individual branches to London. This structure did not change in its basic conception of strong centralization until the end of the 1950s.

Information about the economic conditions of the regions flowed from the branch managers in the form of reports to the Intelligence Department in London and from this department to the Management Committee. These reports were used to comment on the changes in deposits and advances occurring in each Division. Nevertheless the top management thought that information was held by the centre and dispensed from the centre to the periphery as the: 'Joint General Managers and their Assistants [visited] their branches from time to time and [attended] meetings of branch managers, at which policy [could] be explained, while branch managers [went] to Head Office to discuss their individual problems and to obtain guidance from senior officials' (Holmes and Green, 1986: 108). Thus, though the information concerning the economic conditions of the places from which the business of the bank was generated came from the periphery, all policy decisions emanated from the centre.

Decisions about the business of the bank were also centralized. Each application for a loan or overdraft was examined by the manager of the branch and then sent to London to the branch superintendent for the area in which the branch was located. If the amount of the advance was above the superintendent's limit then the advance would be passed on to the General Manager's Assistant or further up depending on the amount, to the Assistant General Managers or the Joint General Manager in charge of the section from which the application had come.[9] Because of the centralization of control, the bank had the policy of promoting successful branch managers to London, therefore assuring that the General Managers and their Assistants had 'first-hand experience of the work they controlled' (Rouse, 1950: 194).

In 1959 Midland Bank lost its position of pre-eminence among the London clearing banks as Barclays Bank overtook it in terms of advances.[10] Among the senior management it was recognized that one of the reasons behind the loss of pre-eminence lay in the distance between the branches and head office. The success of Barclays Bank was being attributed also to its strong semi-autonomous regional boards and their capacity for attracting local businesses. Therefore, in 1957, a number of area managers were appointed to act as personal representatives of the General Managers in their divisions. These representatives had no executive powers but formed a new link in the communication chain between the branches and London, allowing information about customers to be less formalized. Ten years later the bank decided to acquire a regional structure by giving the regional managers authority over the branches they controlled in matters of lending, staff and marketing of services and by creating regional offices. By 1970 there were 21 regional offices in operation (Holmes and Green, 1986: 223, 246–7).

The change in the size and focus of the bank, from the Midlands (the place were the bank had started its activity) to a more national and even international perspective over a number of years, induced variations in the treatment of different types and sizes of business accounts. Large businesses, themselves with a broader national outlook, won a 'small but discernible advantage' (Holmes and Green, 1986: 113) over the local industrial customers which had been so important in the early years of the bank's history. The main advantage for the new large company customers lay in the possibility of negotiating overdrafts and loans directly with the centre of the bank, bypassing any form of localism. The smaller firms suffered the disadvantage of having to deal with a more distant, and complex, bureaucracy. According to Holmes and Green the disadvantage was not so much that of an increased 'bureaucratic' element in the lending decisions, which meant that applications needing local knowledge were sent to London bankers with no knowledge of regional economies, but instead it lay in the enormous number of accounts handled by the bank, implying thus that, as the bank grew, accounts were not judged on the basis of their security and track record but lumped together for the purpose of controlling lending by sectors (and presumably by type of customer) (Holmes and Green, 1986: 113–15).

Knowledge of individual customers, or even of the sector and environment they operated in, rested with whatever local experience the General Managers and their Assistants had accumulated during their careers. A study of these people's careers[11] shows that in more than one case these managers' connection with the Midlands had been very tenuous.

Lloyds Bank

Whereas Midland Bank applied a policy of centralization, Lloyds Bank pursued, through the merger period, the formation of local committees made up of the directors or partners of the amalgamated bank. This policy seems to have had more the intent of smoothing over the period of transition, 'preserving interest and goodwill and placating local opinion',[12] than of creating an integral and necessary part of the administration and direction of the bank.[13] The local committees were chaired by a full Director of the bank based in London, who would know the particular trades of the district and could advise on them. The other members of the committee, apart from the district manager, would be three or four directors of local businesses, 'men of local position, influence and knowledge, who would each contribute something towards fostering interest in the bank and bring new business to it'.

Apart from the local committees, local district offices were also set up. These, in contrast with the local district committees, had a more precise role in the organization of functions inside the structure of the bank.

District managers were responsible for the district office and acted as a link between head office and the local branch managers and, by residing in the area, used their knowledge of the local environment to procure new business and to report to London any important changes and developments taking place in the district.

However, neither the district committees, nor the district offices, had any executive powers. Even though the advances generated from the district were discussed in meetings neither had any sanctioning powers. In fact, the role of the committees was essentially social. The objects these committees were supposed to achieve were:

> To provide a wider channel of communication both ways between Head Office and the branches. To create a stronger feeling amongst the managers and staff that they [were] not being overlooked and that every endeavour [was] being made to search out and reward merit. To acquire a larger share of new business for the bank. To make greater use of local knowledge by focusing it together, discussing it and applying it for the bank's benefit. To provide a few more posts which [would] serve as training grounds and stepping stones to higher executive officers.[14]

Notwithstanding the number of managerial positions created to increase the flow of knowledge from the regions to head office, the communication of information about a customer was quite formalized. All the advances sanctioned by the branch managers had to be authorized also by controllers in the Advances Department in London.

How managers in the periphery and controllers in London should communicate was often a source of disagreement. The controllers required, in order to grant an advance, a careful listing of the client's securities and, in the case of an overdraft or loan for a company, a three-year analysis of the company's balance sheet with a breakdown of each individual liability and asset. The controllers also required a trading account together with the balance sheet. The branch manager often did not include all of this information with the application because the manager's recommendation of the client was based mainly on personal knowledge of the person involved, the client's business and on local knowledge of the economy. On the other hand, the Advances Controller in London received 40–50 applications a day, often from branches in very different areas, therefore communication had to be formalized before an advance could be considered.[15] The Advances Controller was also responsible for any bad debt, together with the Branch manager. But whereas the Branch manager might know that the debt would be honoured from knowledge of the person and the circumstances, this was the type of information that could not be standardized in a form to the Advances Controller.

Barclays Bank

Barclays' policy towards the amalgamated banks was different both from that of Midland and that of Lloyds. After an acquisition Barclays would appoint the former owners of the local bank as directors of a local board in order not to destroy the: 'essentially local character of the new acquisition' (Tuke and Gillman, 1972: 78). There was no particular strategic design behind this decision in the sense that no evidence has been found that the Directors at Barclays thought that the independence of the local boards would increase the bank's market share. This policy resulted simply from the desire not to risk a change in existing market shares. The local boards were seen more as excellent training grounds for future head office directors than anything else.[16]

Archival evidence from Barclays Bank provides some information on the work of the local boards. In particular there is relatively rich documentation on Birmingham local head office. In 1950 the business of this district amounted to between 5 per cent and 6 per cent of the whole deposits of the bank (this made Birmingham the most important district, together with Manchester).[17] The Birmingham Local Board consisted of three prominent local businessmen[18] in addition to the Chairman (a professional banker). In 1950 the inspection done by London of this district reveals that the business of the district was run with such competence and that its record was so good, that 'the Local Board should be granted as much autonomy as possible and that they should be encouraged and given every opportunity of conducting their businesses as is reasonably possible with the minimum amount of reference to Head Office for all those matters concerning advances, premises and staff'.[19]

At the end of the 1960s A. W. Tuke, in his recollections of the bank, wrote about the local boards in similar terms:

> Policy in such fields as lending, staff salary scales, and the opening and closing of branches is a matter for Head Office and very large lendings and senior managerial appointments require Head Office approval. Within that framework it is for local directors to manage their District in the light of their knowledge of local conditions. (Tuke and Gillman, 1972: 78–9).

This evidence suggests the degree of decentralization of Barclays Bank structure and the importance and independence of the local boards.

The local boards had the power to authorize all advances up to £30 000 (1945–53) but these also had to be registered and confirmed by the Assistant General Manager and also sanctioned by the General Manager. All advances above the local board's limit had to be submitted to the board of London head office.[20] None the less the local boards discussed and took an active part in the affairs of their customers. The limits discussed during local board meetings generally far exceeded the limit allowed[21] and the minutes of the Birmingham board meetings make it clear that head office considered the board's opinion on the firms to be final and gave its assent as a matter of course. In fact there were cases when the local board overruled the instructions from head office when it felt that head office did not have a clear enough knowledge of the local situation.

The description of the internal structure of the banks shows how communication between the centre (head office) and the periphery (the branches) was organized. On the basis of the structure of the three banks studied, the one to rely the most on local knowledge and to leave most scope for informal circulation of information seems to have been Barclays, whereas the most formalized was Midland. Lloyds, while not allowing the periphery much autonomy, had more transmitters of information. If the hypothesis this research wants to test is true, then Barclays' structure, in theory, made it easier for a small, local firm to gain access to finance. Such a firm would have less to show for itself in terms of documentation, suitable for transmission to head office. Under the Barclays system, it could instead rely on the local manager's knowledge and on the authority of the local board.[22]

The distance between the centre and the periphery can be 'measured' by the number of stops the application for an advance had to undergo from the moment the application was filled in at the branch until it was granted. The stops are represented by the discretionary limits granted to each managerial level. The further an application for an advance had to travel, the more standardized the information had to be thus forcing the quality of a business, or the potential for development, to be quantified, reducing the relevance of local knowledge held by the local managers.

The shaded area of Figure 13.2 shows those elements of the structure that operated at a local level. All the others were based in London.

Although in theory all Barclays advances had to be sanctioned by various managers in London, the evidence presented in the preceding pages shows that the autonomy of the local boards often even exceeded its formal discretionary powers. In practice in 1953 Barclays local boards had as much authority as Lloyds board of directors and as much as Midland's chief general managers.

By the mid-1960s, Barclays local boards still had as much power as Lloyds' Assistant Joint General Managers and Midland's Assistant General Managers. Therefore Barclays, by allowing its regional offices to have autonomous decisional powers was, of the three banks, the one to most reduce the distance between the bank and its customers.

The description of the structure of the banks and of the various levels

Barclays Bank Branch: < 3 000	Midland Bank Branch: (n.a.)	Lloyds Bank Branch: < 5 000
Local board < 30 000 (50 000 in 1953 and valid until 1975)	Branch superintendent: 1–3 000	Advances dept.: < 15 000
Assistant GM: < 25 000	GM assistant: 3 000–7 000	Joint GM: 15 000–25 000 (50 000 in 1957)
General manager: < 30 000	Assistant GM: 7 001–15 000	Board of directors: >50 000
Advances committee: > 30 000	Joint GM: 15 001–25 000	
Board of directors: > 50 000	Chief GM: 25 001–50 000	
	Management committee > 50 000[24]	

Figure 13.2   Discretionary limits.[23]

of autonomy existing inside these structures, provides some insight on how the banks perceived their relation with the periphery. The effect of this perception on the availability of credit to smaller firms is not easily quantifiable. But by looking more closely at the behaviour of the individual banks during the long period of credit restrictions, it might be possible to identify differences that could be explained by the banks' varying involvement with the regional economies.

Credit restrictions and the banks

Table 13.1 shows the percentage annual change in total national advances in real terms (in 1963 prices) for the London Clearing Banks, Barclays Bank, Midland Bank, Lloyds Bank and Martins Bank (this bank has been introduced to study the effect of the restrictions on a smaller, provincial bank). With different lags and to a different extent the credit restrictions affected the advances of all the four banks. The degree of reduction, though, was different and it seems to follow a pattern.

Table 13.1 shows that the first time the credit restrictions affected advances in a significant way was in 1952, following the election of the Conservative Party (November 1951), the increase of the Bank Rate from 2 per cent to 4 per cent and the Treasury's appeals to the banks for further restriction of advances to contain inflation. The concurrence of these events makes it difficult to determine if the reduction of advances was due more to the steep increase of the interest rates or to the Treasury's directives, that is to a demand or a supply problem.

Appeals for credit restrictions had been going on since 1946 with the Borrowing (Control & Guarantees) Act and the Bank of England Act. Following these Acts, directives were issued to the banks in December 1947, after the convertibility crisis and also after the outbreak of the Korean War. Nevertheless Table 13.1 shows that advances did not decrease until 1952. Therefore, the decrease which occurred in that year may perhaps be attributed more to the effect which rising interest rates

Table 13.1 Advances in constant terms (1963), Barclays, Midland, Lloyds, Martins and London clearing banks, yearly percentage increases, from 1945

Year	Barclays	Midland	Lloyds	Martins	LCB
1946	13.36	20.44	17.04	31.70	15.09
1947	15.09	15.80	27.36	18.85	16.13
1948	11.83	9.05	11.47	7.89	6.45
1949	0.48	3.32	15.86	1.96	7.38
1950	5.71	0.72	3.02	5.37	4.02
1951	2.20	4.12	7.73	7.83	7.14
1952	−14.88	−15.04	−16.80	−20.10	−16.87
1953	1.75	−8.13	−9.20	5.05	−5.01
1954	8.59	14.39	2.86	13.08	9.73
1955	−12.40	−7.98	−2.82	−11.53	−7.30
1956	−1.75	−1.56	4.26	−7.71	−1.51
1957	−1.40	−3.43	−6.21	2.73	−5.02
1958	17.66	15.38	16.40	14.09	17.12
1959	41.22	30.63	30.02	33.70	28.49
1960	17.00	20.76	12.30	14.95	8.93
1961	−1.46	−3.88	−2.88	−4.66	−3.89
1962	4.14	0.37	0.74	1.16	9.96
1963	17.91	14.13	10.96	9.11	5.63
1964	−2.13	8.26	14.02	14.74	11.01
1965	−2.48	−0.87	−4.58	−3.69	−3.88
1966	−1.63	20.95	−4.84	−5.82	−5.45
1967	2.87	6.89	35.57	15.80	5.61
1968	3.18	−5.02	0.40	−2.40	−1.00

Source: Annual Reports for the banks and Abstract of Statistics for LCB.

had on the demand for credit than to the effectiveness of the appeals of the Treasury. The following year, the advances of Barclays and Martins were already increasing whereas those of Midland and Lloyds were not.

Martins Bank was a regional bank and Barclays had, as shown above, autonomous local head offices which were, more often than not, nothing else but the original local bank. The autonomy of the local head offices allowed Barclays' local directors to make decisions based on first-hand knowledge of the regional economy and on personal relationships with their clients built through the years. This knowledge was of little use to the managers, say of Midland and Lloyds, as the local centres had no, or little, decisional autonomy, as far as advances were concerned.

The existence of personal relationships between managers with strong powers of decision and local clients meant that these managers could have tried to reduce the effect of the increase in the Bank Rate in the period we are observing. Thus, after the initial shock of the rise of the Bank Rate had worn off, customers would go back to the bank confident that a suitable rate could be arranged. Furthermore, both Martins and Barclays local boards were directly dependent for their profits on the economies of their district and thus prone to protect their rather small and not very segmented markets. This interpretation would also explain why, after three years of decreasing advances, Martins managed to increase its advances in 1957, and the decrease for Barclays was much lower than that of Midland's and Lloyds', when interest rates had risen from 3 per cent (1954) to 7 per cent (1957) and after the Treasury had, in 1955, intensified the credit restrictions, imposing a 10 per cent reduction in advances.

To consider Barclays as a bank with a more intense involvement with local businesses is also consistent with the greater, compared with Midland and Lloyds, increase of its advances after the credit restrictions were lifted in 1958 and interest rates decreased from 6 per cent to 4 per cent. The lifting of the restrictions meant that Barclays could go back to lending in full to all those customers who for years had been penalized by the restrictions, namely the smaller ones. This is also the year when Barclays became the first lender within the country, having overtaken Midland.

No evidence has been found to suggest that Barclays recognized its structure as being a competitive advantage. In fact, in 1955 Barclays head office started issuing circulars to the local boards asking them to restrict their advances by reducing overdraft limits and scanning new applications more carefully. These appeals continued all through the 1950s, with reminders to the local boards that the bank was incurring increasing difficulties in maintaining the 30 per cent liquidity ratio imposed by the government and that this ratio was being kept only by continuous selling of investments which was possible only at progressively lower prices, sometimes involving capital losses. Even after the credit restrictions were lifted, the bank encouraged the local offices to restrict advances to reach a 35 per cent liquidity ratio. These appeals seem to have fallen on rather deaf ears since in August 1960 head office wrote to the local head offices:

> This analysis [of the Classified Return of Advances] is now before us, and compared with mid-May there has been an increase of £20.6 millions. But over 50% of our advances come under the headings of 'Personal and Professional', 'Other Financial', 'Hire Purchase', 'Builders and Contractors' and 'Retail Trade'. With the exception of 'Hire Purchase' which is almost unchanged, all these categories show increase, and *frankly we find this disappointing because it was in these categories in particular that we were hoping for reductions.*[25]

These categories listed by head office were, except for 'Other Financial' those where small customers were predominant. Thus these instructions reveal how the autonomy of the local boards allowed them to be more involved with local customers than with head office instructions and Treasury policies. These instructions also show the difference in focus between London head office and the local head offices as one asked for the reduction of advances to small customers while the other maintained its role of local lender.

The propensity of the Barclays local boards not to limit credit to the same extent as head office is confirmed, in the case of Barclays Birmingham District, by Table 13.2 where all advances granted in the district up to £30 000 (and £50 000 in 1968) are shown. This table shows how advances in this district did decrease between 1951 and 1952, possibly because of the effect of the rise of interest rates, but nevertheless at a smaller percentage rate than at the national level. The introduction of the quantitative restrictions in 1955 did not have any effect on advances.[26]

Some qualitative evidence

The banks seem to have been well aware of the effect of the credit restrictions on small firms but not to have been unduly concerned. The chairman of Lloyds, in a speech delivered in 1960 on the subject of advances, among other things commented on some findings by the Radcliffe Committee which revealed that 98 per cent of the Bank's borrowing customers borrowed less than £10 000 but accounted for only one-third of the money lent. The remaining two-thirds of the money lent went to the 2 per cent of larger borrowers. Three borrowers out of

Table 13.2   Barclays Bank, Birmingham local head office, advances ('000), constant values (1963)

1947	25 401
1948	23 730
1949	22 856
1950	23 416
1951	25 295
1952	21 264
1953	22 396
1954	22 420
1955	25 699
1956	28 252
1968	100 158

Sources: 1947-56: Birmingham local board, Minutes of Meetings
1968: Birmingham local head office, Return of Advances, 1968.

four were holders of personal accounts (classified under Personal and Professional in the classification of advances). Of the remaining quarter approximately one-third were farmers and one-third retailers. These three categories accounted for about 40 per cent of the total lent. In other words this means that a very small percentage of the banks customers borrowed most of the money. Sir Oliver Franks argued that in the light of these facts if 2 per cent of larger customers accounted for two-thirds of the money lent, in theory then any restriction of credit could be concentrated upon them and the remaining 98 per cent could be left alone. This presented a dilemma for the authorities and the banks. The banks recognized that small concerns, and many personal borrowers too, stood in special need of bank credit but at the same time had to remember that the sectors of the economy given preference by the Treasury were those where larger firms predominated, such as chemicals, iron and steel and engineering. The larger concerns made an exceptionally important contribution to exports. The chairman pointed out that as much as 30 per cent of exports were produced by the 40 largest companies alone. At the other end of the scale, only one quarter of exports came from smaller firms, even though these employed more than half of the total labour force in manufacturing.[27]

A report by the General Manager for Research and Statistics at Midland Bank in March 1956 reveals how the response of many businessmen to the restriction of bank advances seems to have been to seek finance elsewhere rather than curtail operations. Smaller firms though were finding it more difficult than larger firms to tap alternative sources of finance and were increasing their applications for advances. The report does not say whether these applications were being accepted by the bank but it reveals that the credit restrictions were starting to affect capital expenditure: 'in Birmingham plans for factory building are stated to have been slowed down and in some case suspended' and 'some companies in the Midlands were stated to be re-examining commitments for capital expenditure'.[28] Another report, this time from the Intelligence Department, written a few months later, reveals how branch managers were starting to describe the credit squeeze as having a 'considerable impact' on business expectations and plans, especially for those firms which had no alternative sources of finance. Moreover the report reveals another effect of the restricted lending as 'the loss of flexibility in bank borrowing . . . strained the debtor–creditor position in industry'. Many large firms were taking extended credit and as a result of this 'small firms [were] being hard pressed to make ends meet'.[29]

Confidential reports from a branch of Lloyds Bank in Birmingham provide a different angle from which to view the effect of credit restrictions on small firms. These reports were written on an annual basis by all the branch managers and sent to head office. Few have survived and the report from the Bristol Street branch is the only one left for the Midland district. This branch was situated in the inner city, in an area of small working class properties and small factories. The reports reveal that the customers of the branch were mostly small businesses in the light engineering, brasswork and metal smallwares, platers and polishers, leather goods and dial makers sectors (the businesses which made up the traditional Birmingham industrial district). This branch's advances had grown steadily from the end of the war until 1951 when they started decreasing as credit and raw material restrictions started affecting the local businesses. The reports clearly state that the decrease in advances was a supply side problem, due to the shortage of metals affecting the small manufacturers of the area (1950) and to the 'credit squeeze' (1952–55).[30]

No archival evidence states clearly the bank's position towards small firms, except for general lamentations about the effects of the restrictions on them. The fact remains though that the banks were in the difficult position of having to decide which customers to displease, either large firms with large accounts or smaller businesses who carried much less weight. Indirect (and probably biased) evidence of the impact of the bank's policy on the small firms, at least in the Midland area, has been found in the Parliamentary Debates papers. In July 1955 the MP for Wednesbury (a Black Country constituency) lamented the effect the credit restrictions were going to have on the small firms in the constituency. The Black Country was defined as the 'stronghold of family business'. Within ten miles of Wednesbury town hall there were no fewer than 10 000 small manufacturing concerns, each employing less than fifty people. Most of these firms worked as subcontractors for the car industry and the MP feared that since these firms were not directly involved in exports they would suffer badly from the restrictions. A reduction in credit would affect the small manufacturers very seriously since 'the people running these small family concerns have always been taught to look to the banks for money with which to modernize and expand their businesses. They [knew] nothing of the money market'. The MP addressed Parliament to ask the Government to impose on the banks some sort of regulation which would prevent them from reducing advances at the expense of smaller customers. He was answered by the Economic Secretary to the Treasury, Sir Edward Boyle, in terms that leave little doubt that the fate of small firms was not one of the major concerns of the Treasury in formulating policies to curtail demand and maintain low inflation. The Treasury's main concern was to 'encourage firms to postpone their marginal investment plans and, whenever possible, to postpone replacing their fixed assets'. Credit restrictions were to accomplish this and the Government '[were] right to attempt to reduce internal pressure by asking the banks themselves to take what steps they regard[ed] as necessary to reduce the volume of credit'. The smaller businesses were not to be protected from the 'full rigours' of the Government's policy.[31]

Conclusion

This chapter has attempted to assess the impact of the existence of a London-centric banking system combined with credit restrictions on the availability of finance for small firms in the post-1945 period. The extent of this impact cannot be measured but it would seem that those banks which had a centralized structure operated on a wide, national and cartelized market and therefore had little reason not to restrict advances to less remunerative customers such as small firms. The bank with a decentralized structure was less able to do this since its local autonomous centres had a direct interest in protecting their own local small market from the credit restrictions. This cushioned to some extent the smaller firms from the effect of higher interest rates and the credit squeeze.

Notes

1. This chapter is part of the author's doctoral dissertation on 'Regional Economies: Do Banks make a difference? The Case of England and Italy after 1945'. Much gratitude and many thanks are due to Forrest Capie, Leslie Hannah, Mary Morgan and Adam Tooze who commented on earlier drafts.
2. It is a recognized fact that large firms have a relatively smaller need for bank financing, especially for fixed capital investments, since they have the ability to operate on wider financial markets. On the other hand, small and medium-sized firms, either self-finance their needs or have to have recourse to bank loans both for working capital and for fixed capital investments.
3. Midland Bank Archive (from now on MBA), Booklet for internal use with list of branches divided by division.
4. Lloyds Bank Archive (from now on LBA), Regional Offices, Birmingham, Record sheets submitted by the branches to Birmingham District Office, 1946–49.
5. Barclays Bank Archive (from now on BBA), Inspection of Birmingham District Advances, 1950.
6. LBA, Regional Offices, Birmingham, Record Sheets submitted by the branches to Birmingham District Office, 1968.
7. Nationally the figure had increased: from 2044 to 2712 for Midland; from 1798 to 2260 for Lloyds; and from 2009 to 2610 for Barclays.
8. At the time the districts were: London, Lancashire, Midlands, Southern and Yorkshire.
9. In 1950 England and Wales were divided in five sections (also known as divisions), each under the control of a joint general manager. These divisions were: City of London and Overseas Branch; rest of London and suburbs; northern counties; Midlands and eastern counties, southern counties and Wales (see Rouse, 1950: 182).
10. In 1959, Barclays Annual Report shows for the first time that the bank had higher advances than Midland bank. This advantage lasted until 1964. The dates for profits and deposits are slightly different.
11. These careers have been reconstructed through the bank's internal magazine, the *Midland Chronicle*.
12. LBA, R. A. Wilson, S. Parkes, Chief General Managers, paper on Decentralization submitted to the Board Of Directors, 22 July 1943, Winton File.
13. Before the beginning of the war there were six Local Committees of Directors – Liverpool, Salisbury, London, Halifax, Birmingham and Newcastle.
14. LBA, R. A. Wilson, S. Parkes, Chief General Managers, paper on Decentralization submitted to the Board Of Directors, 22 July 1943, Winton File.
15. LBA, Managers Meetings Minutes, Nottingham Group, 25 May 1933.
16. In 1929 Barclays had 1 270 branches and these were divided into 37 districts, with 37 corresponding local head offices. In 1968, just before the incorporation of Martins Bank, the local head offices had been reduced to 31 but the number of branches had increased to 1 906 (without including the sub-branches and the DCO branches).
17. BBA, Inspection of Birmingham Advances, 1950. These inspections

supplemented the role of the Inspections Departments (found in Midland and Lloyds) and were a feature of the rather decentralized structure of the bank.

18. The practice of having local businessmen managing the local boards is not peculiar to the Birmingham district. The inspection of a much smaller district, that of Peterborough, which relied for most of its business on farming, reveals that the managers in charge all had a close knowledge of the agriculture of the district and of the problems connected to it thanks to them all being gentlemen farmers (BBA, Inspection of Peterborough Advances, 1948).

19. BBA, Inspection of Birmingham Advances, 1950.

20. BBA, London Head Office, Minutes of Directors Meetings, 13 March 1947.

21. In one case the limit of the overdraft granted was higher than £1 million (BBA, Birmingham Local Board, Minutes of the Meetings, 6 October 1941), and in the case of a very important tea merchant the limit was as high as £2 250 000 (BBA, Birmingham Local Board, Register of Advances, 1954).

22. Barclays Bank: BBA, Inspection of Birmingham Advances, 1950; Head Office Instructions and Information, section on Advances, 1928 (used until 1952) and 1953 (used until 1975); London Head Office, Minutes of Directors Meetings, 13 March 1947.
Midland Bank: MBA, Applications and Renewals, 1947.
Lloyds Bank: LBA, Memo to the Board, 1950, Winton File on Discretionary Limits; Board Minutes, 15 February 1957, Winton File on Advances.

23. The transaction costs for Barclays would have been lower since the trustworthiness of a firm could be more easily judged by local managers than by London offices.

24. In 1964 the limits, starting from the lower level were: £10 000 for the Superintendent of Branches, £25 000 for the General Manager's Assistants, £50 000 for the Assistant General Managers, £100 000 for the Joint General Managers and £200 000 for the Chief General Manager. Advances above this limit had to be authorized by the Board. (MBA, Board Minutes, 31 January 1964, courtesy of the Group Archivist.)

25. BBA, Instructions to Local Head Offices, 1955–60. The emphasis is not in the original.

26. The decrease in advances between 1947–49 can be attributed to the fact that after the war the firms in the manufacturing sector were very liquid, especially those who had been directly involved in wartime productions like many firms in the Midlands.

27. LBA, Sir Oliver Franks, 'Bank Advances as an Object of Policy', pp. 5–6, 1960, Winton File.

28. MBA, Management Committee File.

29. MBA, Intelligence Department, July 1956, Management Committee File.

30. LLB, Confidential Reports to Head Office, Smallbrook Branch (formerly Bristol Street).

31. Hansard, vol. 554: 1413–25, 28 July 1955.

References

Hannah, L. and Kay, J. (1977), *Concentration in Modern Industry: Theory, Measurements and the UK Experience*, London.

Holmes, A. and Green, E. (1986), *Midland: 150 Years of Banking Business*, London.

Rouse, H. (1950), 'Midland Bank Limited', in G. E. Milward, *Large Scale Organisations*, London.

Tuke, A. and Gillman, R. (1972), *Barclays Bank Ltd 1926–1969*, Oxford.

CHAPTER FOURTEEN

Banks and Small Enterprises in France

Michel Lescure

In the first half of the 20th century, small and medium-sized firms in France were short of banking capital. Statistics reconstituted in an attempt to assess the extent of the deficiency bear out the idea that there was a real financial gap. In 1929, for instance, of the 188 industrial firms seeking loans from the Crédit National, aid from financial intermediaries represented 27.4 per cent (average weighted rate) of the total indebtedness of firms with 100 or fewer employees, as against 37.1 per cent of that of larger ones. The difference can essentially be attributed to medium- and long-term indebtedness (respectively 15 per cent and 46.7 per cent) (Lescure, 1992a). When the very great precariousness that was such a major feature of the financial organization of small and medium-sized industrial firms at the time is taken into consideration (Lescure, 1992b), the traditional way of explaining it in terms of the existence of specific means of financing, such as partners' current accounts and family loans, which were better adapted to the strategical considerations supposedly shaping the management mode of such undertakings, namely a desire for autonomy and security (Landes, 1951), seems inadequate.

As complaints from the period in question suggest,[1] the problem was in the first place that of the part played by financial intermediaries. Many studies have stressed that the French banking system of the time was deeply averse to risk. Without at all wishing to predetermine the outcome of this discussion, it seems appropriate to point out that what I shall seek to assess with regard to credit for small and medium-sized firms is precisely this notion of risk. The starting-point of this approach is the new formulation of the banking profession in a great number of recent works (Goodhart, 1975; Leland and Pyle, 1977; Stiglitz and Weiss, 1981; Diamond, 1984; Lewis, 1992).

In such studies, the role of the banker is to reduce the asymmetry of information between lenders and borrowers (the latter always being seen as better informed about the risks in the operations to be financed than the latter). In taking the place of isolated individuals, banks base their usefulness on their particular expertise in amassing and handling information and their experience in monitoring loan operations. Such expertise is part of a wider ability expected of banks, namely that of reducing the costs of transactions connected with transferring capital from individual lenders to individual borrowers. In that model, the level of securities required from borrowers depends on the extent to which the asymmetry of information is reduced.

Analyses of this type seem to be able to account for the difficulties in obtaining finance encountered by small- and medium-sized firms. Both their small size, their low level of administrative structures and an often very closed legal and social organization were factors tending to create a high degree of asymmetry and consequently a very cautious approach on the part of banks.

If we study the discussions in this area, however, it is clear that such problems do not seem to have been so difficult in every case.[2] This leads us to raise the problem of the possible contribution of historical factors in weakening the banks' efficiency and thus slowing down the growth of small and medium-sized firms at the beginning of the second period of industrialization in France (1900–40).

In order to highlight factors of this kind, we shall examine in turn the two ways of reducing disparities of information used during the period in question. The first was based on proximity, the second on institutional procedures with regard to information gathering and loans monitoring.

The proximity factor

This was the most usual mode of operation, adopted by local and regional banks, and its importance during the first three decades of the 20th century can be seen from the financial structure of firms in the late 1920s. Despite its limits and drawbacks, the source used here[3] indicates quite clearly a phenomenon of polarization in financing circuits at the level of commercial banks (columns 1 to 4 of Table 14.1).

In the 1920s, local and regional banks were still the main financial support for small and medium-sized firms. At the average rate, credits from regional banks accounted for 46.4 per cent of the banking indebtedness of firms with a hundred or fewer employees. Although certain large firms were just as heavily in debt to regional banks (as shown by the percentages expressed in average of rates and median rates), they seemed much less dependent on the whole of this type of intermediary. A much greater proportion of the finance they needed came from large credit establishments and business banks.

The dependence of small and medium-sized firms on regional banks should probably not be allowed to induce us to neglect the part played by banks with a national network, particularly the major credit

Table 14.1 Share of various types of banks in total indebtedness to banks of Crédit National firms in 1929 (%)

Emps	Major estabs	Medium-term estabs	Business banks	Regional banks	Mutual banks estabs	Para-public banks	Foreign banks
Average weighted rate							
20 and under	23.0	0.0	0.0	52.8	1.6	22.6	0.0
21 to 100	20.1	10.8	3.2	45.7	0.0	19.0	1.1
101 to 500	31.1	2.0	27.2	37.0	0.0	2.7	0.0
500+	45.6	1.2	0.0	35.5	0.0	13.0	4.7
Total	36.4	2.5	13.9	37.4	0.8	7.0	2.1
Average of rates							
20 and under	21.8	0.0	0.0	57.6	3.3	17.3	0.0
21 to 100	32.9	2.6	5.6	42.5	0.0	13.7	2.8
101 to 500	35.7	2.5	15.3	42.2	0.1	4.2	0.0
500+	12.5	2.1	0.0	53.4	0.0	19.5	13.0
Total	28.1	1.7	7.9	46.4	3.3	9.6	3.0
Median rate							
20 and under	0	0	0	70.1	0	0	0
21 to 100	0	0	0	3.8	0	0	0
101 to 500	3.5	0	0	13.8	0	0	0
500+	0	0	0	63.5	0	0	0
Total	0	0	0	27.8	0	0	0

Source: see note 3.

establishments (Crédit Lyonnais, Société Générale, CNEP and CIC). Quite naturally, small and medium-sized firms made up the main part of the clientele of such banks (Bonin, 1992), and the very active role played by some of them in the affairs of medium-sized firms which were leaders in their sphere shows a readiness to commit themselves quite at odds with the classical image of the deposit bank (Lescure, 1992b). Moreover, their role over the whole range of sizes would be much more important if discount credits (which do not appear among the firms' liabilities) were taken into account. It should be borne in mind that immediately before the First World War the value of commercial bills in circulation reached 13.2 billion francs, double the total amount of advances granted by banks publishing their balance sheets, of which around 60 per cent were held by banks (Teneul, 1960, Lévy-Leboyer and Bourguignon, 1985; Plessis, 1991). The evidence is that discounts accounted for a far bigger share of the large deposit banks' operations than for those of the other banks. Between 1900 and 1910 the advances/commercial portfolio ratio was 0.8 per cent in the case of the four big deposit banks, but 1.5 per cent for the other banks publishing their balance sheets. In the provinces, it ranged from 1 per cent (Crédit du Nord) to 7.2 per cent (Société Nancéienne de Crédit).

But it was precisely the distinction between the various types of credit that made the regional banks so useful for small and medium-sized firms. Unlike discount operations, advances, even if they were disguised as short-term credits, were often medium-term ones aimed at increasing firms' working capital. Thus their relative importance in the assets of regional banks reflects the latters' support for small and medium-sized firms, either for buying intermediate products or acquiring new equipment, and in a great number of cases the advance was associated with a subsequent share issue. However real it might have been, the risk of illiquidity banks ran should not be exaggerated. The resources structure of regional banks was much more favourable to stable capital than that of the major establishments.[4] In addition, regional banks were in a position to have short-term but regularly-renewed bills representing such credits discounted by the Bank of France. Indeed, at the local level certain branches of the latter, particularly in eastern France, were all the more inclined to discount such documents as the major establishments made less use of its rediscounting facilities.

This strategy of the regional banks, which was dictated by the competition of the major credit establishments in the discount field, was based on ways and means of obtaining information and security that were largely available only to them. In contrast to the hierarchical procedures operated by the big establishments, where the top management guided banking practices through rule books (Bouvier,

1961), it involved the play of what we might call the effects of proximity, in particular the intimate knowledge local bankers had of business circles in their geographical area. In such circumstances, acquiring information was a result of long-standing and ongoing relationships between banks and industry. The fact that many advances were made in the form of overdrafts rather than as loans was a further source of information, since it enabled bankers to keep a daily record of the situation of those in debt to them

As well as such external information, there was the internal information provided by the close interpenetration of the banking and industrial worlds at the local level. In 1909, the 35 administrators of the four chief banks in Nancy in Lorraine held 234 seats on the boards of 143 regional firms. Such interpenetration occurred in two types of situation. The first was when banks had been led to act as sleeping partners in industry. Except where there was a local shortage of capital (as in Marseilles) this strategy was not the one chosen by regional banks, but was however very widespread, it would appear, at the level of small local ones, for which shareholding in industry was the only way of ensuring adequate returns on the deposits they could not afford to lose (Collot, 1973). More often, however, at least among the upper echelons of regional banks, interpenetration was the result of the part played by local industry in setting up a regional banking system. Sixty per cent of the bank administrators in Nancy were also leading industrialists and traders (Jacquemard, 1911). Seventy-one per cent of members of the board of the Crédit du Nord came from a background in textiles (Pouchain, 1986). The concern of creditors to reduce risks arising from a lack of information was a further factor encouraging banks to maintain a presence on the boards of firms. This to some extent explains the part played by banks in converting firms into joint-stock companies (either limited partnerships or limited companies) with their own supervisory or decision making bodies.

The effect of reducing risk by better information was the high level of non-secured advances. In addition to secured long-term advances, many banks, particularly in the north and east of France 'boldly took the path of personal credit' (Jacquemard, 1911). In the Société Nancéienne de Crédit, for example, 'uncovered' credits amounted to 52 per cent of total advances in 1909. Given the level of information available to banks, the transaction costs for setting up guarantees might seem unrelated to the profits to be expected. If Marseilles was one of the few areas where personal credit did not develop, it was probably because the unspecialized nature of industrial activities and the speculative nature of the market there prevented banks from reducing asymmetrical information and thus made it impossible to assess rigorously the risks creditors were incurring.

Despite its importance, the role of local and regional banks with regard to small and medium-sized businesses tended to diminish in the period under consideration. The first factor playing a part in loosening the ties between banks and firms was the gradual disappearance of small local banks from the turn of the century onwards (Plessis, 1985). They had already had to face up to competition from savings banks since 1875–81, from the big establishments from 1894, and finally from the Bank of France, which had been seeking direct customers, since 1897. Reduced to the level of risky shareholdings in local industrial companies, many of them collapsed in the very early years of the new century, the victims of their own fixed assets and competition from regional banks.

The growth of regional banks between 1900 and 1930 was the second factor. Reacting to the extension of the network of branches of the major establishments from 1894 onwards, they tried to set up or develop their own from 1900 onwards. From 1900 to 1923, the number of outlets available to the eight main regional banks in the north increased from 24 to 364. As had already happened with the major establishments, however, the greater geographical spread brought with it a weakening of the benefits of proximity and the desire for higher levels of security and liquidity. As hierarchical regional networks emerged, real credit tended to replace personal credit and discounting to take the place of medium-term operations. In the Crédit du Nord, for example, the advances/commercial portfolio ratio fell from 1 to 0.3 between the 1890s and the 1920s. On average, however, the level of commitment of regional banks remained higher than that of the major credit establishments, which explains why they collapsed during the slump of the 1930s. Of the 670 banks that failed between 1929 and 1937, the great majority were of the regional type. These three patterns of events put an end to the twofold structure of the banking system that had gone hand in hand with the process of industrial development until the beginning of the 20th century.

The institutional factor

In compensation, however, the interwar years saw a new financial sector, under state patronage in a number of ways, growing up in France. Even before the First World War, the extra-parliamentary commission set up in 1911 by J. Caillaux had sketched in the outline of the organization that was to fill the gap left by the deficiencies of local banks. The cooperative sector was to be responsible for filling in the gaps in the provision of short-term personal credit for small commercial and industrial firms, and a new body connected with the financial market was to be given the task of providing medium-term credit for small and medium-sized industries. The reorganization of the people's banks (1917) and the creation of the Crédit National (1919) were in line with these objectives.

If we first base our analysis on the Crédit National, whose role was most akin to that of regional banks with regard to small and medium-sized industrial firms, we can detect three new features with regard to the previous system of allocation, information and securities. Given the new geographical separation of borrowers and lenders, loan contracts now took the place of overdrafts on current accounts. Each request for credit entailed an expert opinion which, although it did not match the formal statistical analysis American lenders commonly required, was nevertheless subject to a set of highly graduated rules. The loan inspector's report, which was drawn up on the basis of an on-site visit and documentary evidence, was not restricted to the project or situation justifying an application for a loan. It also included a report on the recent background of the firm, a very detailed analysis of its technical and economic future, a financial study collating accounting data with information received *in situ* (such as the credit the firm was receiving and the value of stocks) and an analysis of its programme (including financial arrangements). It was highly structured and used a large set of ratios, aimed in particular at assessing the firm's profitability and liquidity, but also allowed a very wide scope for human factors, such as the quality and origins of the directors, particularly where individual and family undertakings were concerned. The sheer scale of its means of investigation and analysis enabled the Crédit National to reduce the risk of inadequate information, but not to eliminate completely any asymmetry or the risks linked to the management of a long-term loan. This meant that advances had to be protected by either a high-level mortgage, securities acceptable to the Crédit National, or a third-party guarantee.

People's banks, which specialized in short-term credit, were not automatically compelled to accept such obligations. Since they were local institutions, they were thought to benefit to some extent from the effect of proximity. The latter was different from that enjoyed by regional banks, since on the one hand it was introduced by an outside body (mutual guarantee companies), and on the other it was more closely applicable to guaranteeing loans than to acquiring information. The reciprocal surveillance its members engaged in was supposed to allow a mutual guarantee company to guarantee and endorse bills issued by firms. But the system of people's banks worked very differently from what had been expected. If we examine opinions on this point in the interwar years, we see that they constantly favour real as distinct from personal credit

(Chamley, 1938; Gueslin, 1982): 'Personal factor are not the exclusive or major basis for credit, but further conditions to be met in addition to current criteria for granting commercial credit' (Chamley, 1938).

In the case of both long- and short-term credit, the arrival of new ways of acquiring information thus entailed a higher threshold for securities stipulated by intermediaries. How significant a factor was this in the growth of credit for small and medium-sized firms?

From a purely quantitative point of view, the importance of the new financial intermediaries increased only to a limited extent. In 1930, the total current credit granted by the Crédit National and the people's banks did not exceed 1.3 billion francs, or 8 per cent of that granted by the six main deposit banks.[5] This is largely explained by the difficulties of financing and the management constraints experienced by the new establishments. So as to avoid being seen as competitors of the commercial banks, the new intermediaries eschewed certain operations (managing private portfolios in the case of the people's banks and taking deposits in that of the Crédit National), thus reducing their ability to widen their field of action. In addition, new bodies came into being in the 1920s which, following the banks' lead, attempted to capture the demand of small and medium-sized businesses for medium-term credit (see Table 14.1, column 2). Given the banks' influence within the Crédit National (they held 61 per cent of its capital in 1920), it was logical that they should not encourage an establishment competing with their subsidiaries to develop too quickly.[6]

An examination of the clientele of the parapublic intermediaries also leads, however, to a reflection on the ability of the new mode of information and securities set up between 1917 and 1919 to satisfy demand from small and medium-sized firms. As Plessis's study of the example of the Banque populaire de Montrouge shows, it seems to have been the top section of the SMis that made up the major part of the customers of the people's banks. Between 1926 and 1939 the very smallest firms accounted for a mere 22 per cent of total customers and their authorized discounts never went beyond 7 per cent of total authorizations (Plessis, 1956). Although some people's banks may have been tempted to seek 'a certain proportion of very high-quality risks' (Chamley, 1938) in order to improve their position, it is unlikely that large firms represented a significant level of business (1.5 per cent of holders and 5 per cent of discount authorizations). Indeed, such customers had already been more or less monopolized by the major credit establishments, and it was thus 'medium-sized "personal" firms that made up the clientele of the people's banks' (Plessis, 1956), providing three quarters of account holders and receiving 88 per cent of discount authorizations (Plessis, 1956). Even if this trend did not represent a deviation from the social aims of the people's banks, it was nevertheless a narrowing of the objectives of the 1917 legislation.

The same could be said of the customers of the Crédit National. In the 1920s, firms employing fewer than 100 people received credits amounting in value to only 29.5 per cent of those granted by the Crédit National. The very smallest, those with 20 or fewer employees, received only 2.4 per cent. This low figure is partly explained by the nature of the demand from small and medium-sized firms. The average amount of credit requested was 29 400 francs for firms of 20 employees and under and 2 630 000 francs for those with over 500. Another explanatory factor is that the statutes of the Crédit National limited the maximum total credit that could be granted to a firm to 30 per cent of its net assets. Nevertheless, if we look at the ratio of credits requested to those granted in each classification of size, it is legitimate to wonder whether there were perhaps other reasons for the low level of credit obtained by small and medium-sized firms. In terms of both number and value, there was a regular increase in the percentage granted as the size of the firm increased, at least until we begin to reach the largest ones (see Table 14.2).

The percentage of firms obtaining the credit they requested rises from 36.7 in the case of the smallest firms to over 60 in that of the largest. This means that firms with under 100 employees – almost two-thirds of those applying to the Crédit National – accounted for only just over half of its eventual customers. A selective top-slicing of that kind is explicable in terms of the effects of the guarantees and level of security the institution required for each type of loan.

Taking all the various sizes of firms together, insufficient guarantees account for 72.7 per cent of refusals of requests for credit. The high rate can be accounted for by the strict rules for assessing securities,

Table 14.2 Loans granted by the Crédit National by size of firm (combining 1927 and 1930 statistical groups)

Emps	Loans granted as % of loans requested		Final distribution of loans
	by number	by value	
20 and under	36.7	22.8	2.4
21–100	46.4	51.6	27.1
101–500	69.9	68.2	60.4
500+	61.5	41.5	10.1
Total	52.9	57.1	100

particularly when the guarantee was in the form of a mortgage on the firm's industrial assets. In terms of its assessment by loan inspectors, the liquidation value of such assets (land, buildings and equipment), was in fact only very distantly related to the current actual cost of setting up plant. Reductions in the estimated value of goods were always very considerable, with the liquidation value set on average at between 33 per cent and 40 per cent of the current value. As the upper limit for loans was fixed at 60 per cent of the value of the guarantee, it would appear that even in the most generous assessment, loans amounted to 25 per cent of the current value of industrial assets. Such guarantees were hence often judged to be 'insufficient for a useful loan'. In the face of such very strict rules for assessing the value of industrial securities, the best-placed firms for obtaining loans from the Crédit National were those in a position to offer additional guarantees unrelated to working assets. The figures for agreed loans ranged from 40.6 per cent for firms offering only industrial securities to 70.8 per cent for those for which such securities amounted to between 51 per cent and 99 per cent of the total and 86.8 per cent when the securities offered were totally unrelated to working assets.

From this point of view, of course, large firms were in a much more favourable position than small or medium-sized ones (see Table 14.3). The proportion of industrial assets in the range of securities offered to the Crédit National falls regularly as the size of firms increases. In the case of large ones, the security provided by administrators, banks or other group companies, a mortgage on real estate unconnected with working assets or pledges often formed a useful complement to industrial securities, and sometimes made it unnecesary to mortgage the latter.

Small and medium-sized firms enjoyed no such advantages, and two-thirds of them could offer no securities other than their industrial assets. The most heavily penalized were recently-established businesses in which all available finance had been used to set up the concern. Along with the

Table 14.3   Industrial assets as a percentage of total securities offered to the Crédit National

Employees	100%	51–99%	50% and under	Total
20 and under	64.6	20.8	14.6	100
21–100	63.0	17.6	19.4	100
101–500	50.7	11.3	38.0	100
500+	53.8	7.7	38.5	100
Total	56.7	17.0	26.3	100

risk to the lender specifically arising from new firms (and particularly from the absence of adequate information), this factor probably accounts for the high level of refusal in the case of recently-established concerns. The rate of credit acceptance drops from 68.2 per cent in number (and 63 per cent in value) in the case of the longest-established firms (over 50 years) to 37.5 per cent (and 41.8 per cent) in that of the most recently-established ones (5 years and under). In the situation of extreme 'entrepreneurial turbulence' that typified the 1920s, the Crédit National was unable to act as a stabilizing factor for the newest undertakings.

What has been said so far indicates the need to stress the difficulties of a period of transition rather than a questioning of the banking system as a whole. At a time when traditional modes of financing such as private capital, current accounts and individual loans and local and regional bank credits were no longer sufficient to ensure the financial equilibrium of small and medium-sized businesses, the intermediate institutions in the parapublic sector were slow to take over that role. Without underestimating the importance of other factors (and particularly financial ones), it is clear that the problems of such a period can partly be explained in terms of the incomplete nature of the reforms implemented at the beginning of the century. Whatever the causes (the urgency felt at the time, the rejection of state interference, or the excessive trust in the spirit of mutual support) the legislators of 1917 and 1919 did not fully appreciate the problem of securities. The failure of mutual guarantee companies – the function of which had been seen as guaranteeing advances by people's banks – and the abandonment of auxiliary shareholding banks – originally intended to facilitate guaranteeing Crédit National loans – deprived the new intermediaries of stages likely to maintain the effects of proximity. In such circumstances, the expertise acquired by the latter in information gathering and analysis was insufficient to reduce the risks of lenders. In the troubled atmosphere of the interwar years, that could not but reinforce the role of guarantees, the main factor excluding small and medium-sized firms from access to credit.

Notes

1. See for example the debates preceding the voting of the law of 13 March 1917 on people's banks. The commentaries accompanying the voting are analysed in Plessis (1956).
2. For a study of the conditions of financing small and medium-sized firms in the 1960s, see Courbot (1973). The views expressed in the Courbot report suggesting that small and medium-sized firms did not seem to lack finance have been confirmed by Evraert (1978).

3. The statistical and documentary basis for this research is chiefly the loans files of the Crédit National. It is not without some risks and limitations, but for the period in question it is the only one allowing a quantitative study of business financing following the methods of the Centrales de bilans. The statistical group includes all industrial firms seeking credit in 1927 (148 cases) and 1930 (188 firms). It comprises (17.3 per cent) small firms with 20 or fewer employees, (47.5 per cent) medium-sized (21–100), (29.9 per cent) large (101–500) and (5.3 per cent) very large (500+) undertakings. These are broken down as follows: agricultural and food industries (11 per cent); intermediate industries (30 per cent); consumer industries (39 per cent); equipment industries (15.2 per cent); building and public works (4.8 per cent). Forty per cent of the firms were located in the Paris area, 24 per cent in the north and east of the country. For a fuller description of the source, see the author's state doctoral thesis (Lescure, 1992b).

4. From 1900 to 1909, private capital accounted for 16.6 per cent of the resources of the four big deposit banks and 24.3 per cent of those of the other banks publishing their balance sheets. The corresponding figure for the Société Nancéienne de CIC and the Société Marseillaise de Crédit was between 20 per cent and 30.5 per cent. See Lescure (1985a) and Lévy-Leboyer and Lescure (1991).

5. To these advances there should be added, in the case of people's banks, discount of commercial bills operations rising to 5.9 billion francs for the whole of 1930.

6. The banks were much more concerned by the other tasks the state had given the Crédit National, particularly that of financing postwar reconstruction. See Lescure (1985).

References

Bonin, H. (1992), 'Une grande entreprise bancaire: Le Comptoir national d'escompte de Paris dans l'entre-deux-guerres', Comité pour l'Histoire Economique et Financière, *Etudes et Documents*, IV.

Bouvier, J. (1961), *Le Crédit Lyonnais de 1863 à 1882: Les années de formation d'une banque de dépôts,* Paris.

Chamley, P. (1938), *Les banques populaires françaises*, Paris.

Collot, C. (1973), 'Les banques meusiennes de 1871 á 1914', *Revue d'histoire économique et sociale*, 4.

Courbot, H. (1973), 'Conseil Economique et Social: Le financement des entreprises petites et moyennes', *JO*, 17 April.

Diamond, D. W. (1984), 'Financial Intermediation and Delegated Monitoring', *Review of Economic Studies*, 51.

Evraert, S. (1978), 'Croissance, efficacité et rentabilité des petites et moyennes entreprises', unpublished doctoral thesis in management sciences, University of Toulouse.

Goodhart, C. A. E. (1975), *Money, Information and Uncertainty,*

Cambridge, MA.

Gueslin, A. (1982), *Le Crédit mutuel: De la caisse rurale á la banque sociale*, Strasburg.

Jacquemard, P. (1911), *Les Banques Lorraines*, Paris.

Landes, D. (1951), 'French Business and the Businessman: a Social and Cultural Analysis', in *Modern France: Problems of the Third and Fourth Republics*, Princeton, NJ.

Leland, L. E. and Pyle, D. H. (1977), 'Informational Assymmetries, Financial Structure and Financial Intermediation', *Journal of Finance*, 32.

Lescure, M. (1985a), *Banque et investissements en Méditerranée à l'époque contemporaine*, Marseilles.

Lescure, M. (1985b), 'La concurrence des secteurs bancaires public et privé dans la France de l'entre-deux-guerres: l'example du Crédit National', in J. Bouvier and J. C. Perrot (eds), *Etats, Fiscalités, Economies*, Paris.

Lescure, M. (1992a), 'Les banques et le financement des PME en France pendant les années 1920', *Entreprises et Histoire*, 2.

Lescure, M. (1992b), 'Les petites et moyennes entreprises industrielles dans la France des années 1920', unpublished state doctoral thesis, University of Paris X-Nanterre.

Lévy-Leboyer, M. and Bourguignon, F. (1985), *L'economie française au XIXe siécle: analyse macroéconomique*, Paris.

Lévy-Leboyer, M. and Lescure, M. (1991), 'France', in R. Sylla and Toniolo, G. (eds), *Patterns of European Industrialization, the Nineteenth Century*, London and New York.

Lewis, M. K. (1992), 'Modern Banking in Theory and Practice', *Revue Economique*, 43.

Plessis, A. (1956), *La clientèle des banques populaires de 1917 à 1939*, DES, University of Paris, unpublished.

Plessis, A. (1985), 'Les concours de la Banque de France à l'economie (1842–1914)', in J. Bouvier and J. C. Perrot (eds), *Etats, Fiscalités, Economies*, Paris.

Plessis, A. (1991), 'Les banques et l'économie', in M. Lévy-Leboyer and J. C. Casanova (eds), *Entre l'Etat et le Marché: L'économie française des années 1880 à nos jours*, Paris.

Pouchain, P. (1986), 'Banque et crédit à Lille de 1800 à 1939', *Revue du Nord*, 270.

Stiglitz, J. E. and Weiss, A. (1981), 'Credit Rationing in Markets with Imperfect Information', *American Economic Review*, 71.

Teneul, G. F. (1960), *Contribution a l'histoire du financement des entreprises en France depuis la fin du XIXe siècle*, Paris.

Index